PERSPECTIVES ON PLAYS

PERSPECTIVES ON PLAYS

A READER EDITED BY JANE LYMAN
AT THE OPEN UNIVERSITY

ROUTLEDGE & KEGAN PAUL
London and Henley

First published in 1976
by Routledge & Kegan Paul Ltd
39 Store Street,
London WC1E 7DD and
Broadway House,
Newtown Road,
Henley-on-Thames, Oxon RG9 1EN
Reprinted in 1979
Printed in Great Britain
by Redwood Burn Limited
Trowbridge and Esher
Selection and editorial material
© The Open University 1976

ISBN   0 7100 8419 6

CONTENTS

ACKNOWLEDGMENTS

The Open University and the publishers would like to thank the following for permission to reproduce copyright material:
1.1: Copyright (c) 1969 by Thomas Y. Crowell Company, Inc.; first published in Great Britain 1970 by Methuen & Co. Ltd. 1.2: George Allen & Unwin Ltd. 1.3: Copyright 1949 by Princeton University Press. 1.4: Methuen & Co. Ltd. 1.5: The editor, 'Drama'. 2.1: Oxford University Press. 2.2: The editor, 'Phoenix'. 2.3: Text copyright (c) 1970, 1971, 1972, 1973 by Jan Kott; translation copyright (c) 1973 by Random House, Inc.; first published in Great Britain 1974 by Eyre Methuen Ltd. 2.4: Robert Graves. 2.5: (c) University of Toronto Press 1967. 2.6: Wole Soyinka. 3.1: Edward Arnold Ltd. 3.2: copyright (c) 1959 by Princeton University Press. 3.3: The Folio Society Ltd. 3.4: The Governors of the Royal Shakespeare Theatre. 3.6: Faber and Faber Ltd. 3.7: The Estate of W.H. Auden. 3.8: Copyright (c) 1964 by Panstwowe Wydawnictwo Naukowe; translation copyright (c) Boleslaw Taborski; first published in Great Britain 1965 by Methuen & Co. Ltd. 3.9: Columbia University Press. 3.10: Cambridge University Press. 3.11: Edward Arnold Ltd. 3.12: Originally published by the Oxford University Press 1947; first published by Eyre Methuen & Co. Ltd 1948. 4.1: Translation (c) The Open University 1976. 4.2: Translation (c) The Open University 1976; notes copyright (c) 1969 by Thomas Y. Crowell Company Inc.; first published in Great Britain 1970 by Methuen & Co. Ltd. 4.3: Copyright 1953 by Princeton University Press. 4.5: Oxford University Press. 5.1: Macmillan London and Basingstoke. 5.3: Oxford University Press. 5.4: The author's literary estate and The Hogarth Press. 5.5: (c) 1959 by the President and Fellows of Harvard College. 6.1: Avon Books. 6.2: Chatto & Windus. 6.3: Calder & Boyars Limited. 7.1: Oxford University Press. 7.2: The Society of Authors on behalf of the Bernard Shaw Estate. 7.3: Faber and Faber Ltd. 7.4: Copyright (c) 1964 by Rolf Fjelde. 7.5: Copyright (c) 1956 by Mary McCarthy. 7.7: Cambridge University Press. 7.8: Oxford University Press. 7.9: Sigmund Freud Copyrights Ltd, The Institute of Psycho-Analysis and The Hogarth Press Ltd. 7.10: The British Library Board. 7.11: Maurice Valency. 7.12: (c) 1955-56 by 'The Drama Review'. 8.1: Peter Owen, London. 8.2: Copyright (c) 1962, 1963, 1964 by Robert Brustein. 8.3: Routledge & Kegan Paul Ltd. 8.4: The

National Theatre. 8.5: The editor, 'Modern Drama'. 8.6: TQ Publications Ltd and Egil Törnqvist. 9.1: (c) Oxford University Press 1964. 9.2: (c) 1964-65 by 'The Drama Review'. 9.3: Copyright (c) 1962, 1963, 1964 by Robert Brustein. 9.4: (c) Oxford University Press 1964. 9.5: Methuen & Co. Ltd. 9.6: Copyright 1949 by Princeton University Press. 9.7: Chatto & Windus. 10.1, 10.2, 10.3, 10.4: The Society of Authors on behalf of the Bernard Shaw Estate.   10.5: Copyright 1949 by Princeton University Press. 10.6: Macmillan Publishing Co. Inc. 10.7: Methuen & Co. Ltd. 10.8: (c) 1952 by Alan Dent. 10.9: The Society of Authors on behalf of the Bernard Shaw Estate. 10.10: (c) 1924 by the New York Times Company.   10.11: The Society of Authors on behalf of the Bernard Shaw Estate. 10.12: Methuen & Co. Ltd. 11.1: Copyright 1922, 1952 by E.P. Dutton & Co., Inc., renewal, 1950, in the names of Stafano, Fausto and Lietta Pirandello. 11.2: Copyright (c) 1962, 1963, 1964 by Robert Brustein. 12.1, 12.2: Original Poems copyright 1955 by Suhrkamp Verlag, Berlin; copyright in the translations (c) 1976 by Eyre Methuen Ltd. 12.3: Translations copyright Eric Bentley and Hugo Schmidt. 12.4: Eyre Methuen Ltd, and the Viking Press, Inc.; copyright (c) 1965 by Eric Bentley. 12.5: Copyright (c) 1957, 1963, 1964 by Suhrkamp Verlag, Frankfurt am Main; translation copyright (c) 1964 by John Willett. 12.6: (c) 1968 by 'The Drama Review'. 12.7: Chatto & Windus. 13.1: TQ Publications Ltd. 13.3: Eyre & Spottiswoode Ltd; Faber and Faber Ltd, Grove Press, Inc. 13.4: Les Éditions de Minuit. 14.1, 14.3: 'The Times'. 14.4, 14.5: 'The Observer'. 14.6: David Higham Associates Ltd on behalf on Herbert Farjeon. 14.7: Martin Esslin. 14.8: The Estate of James Agate. 14.9: Michael Billington. 14.11: The editor, 'The New Statesman'. 14.12, 14.13: The literary executors of Desmond MacCarthy. 14.15, 14.17: Curtis Brown Ltd on behalf of Kenneth Tynan. 14.16: Methuen & Co. Ltd; Atheneum Publishers; copyright (c) 1957 by Eric Bentley.

INTRODUCTION

'Perspectives on Plays' has been prepared as a companion Reader
for the third-level course, 'Drama', presented by the Faculty of
Arts at The Open University. The course, which is primarily
play-centred, offers detailed study of selected dramatic masterpieces of the past and focuses on the most important modern playwrights from Ibsen to Brecht. The plays themselves have been
chosen for several reasons, some because they illustrate particular types of theatre, some for thematic relevance to other works
in the course and some because they stretch the possibilities of
dramatic form. 'Drama' has been designed with two related and
hoped-for results in mind: to help students learn how to read
plays as literature and to understand and respond to plays in
performance.

Drama is a performing art with a mainly literary starting-
point. The playwright (like the novelist and often the poet as
well) uses words to communicate thought and feeling, to create
character and action. Proper response to any type of literature
depends on an understanding of the author's words in context.
Then, too, it is characteristic of an intelligent, informed response to literature to look at other elements of the text and to
raise pertinent questions. For example, what styles and devices
advance the ideas? How does this specific situation fit into the
complete action? Why does this character elicit a certain response? Because most great art is complex, because many parts con-
tribute to whole effects, a play text should be studied like the
text of a novel or the score of a symphony. For critical awareness of all various elements can not always be achieved the first
time one reads or hears a composition.

But, if drama has a literary basis, it also has a distinctive
form and special features of its own. It is, after all, literature planned for the theatre where the action and dialogue is
performed, not narrated, and where actors impersonate characters.
It may be helpful to read a poem aloud to appreciate its metre or
rhythm but a poem on the page is not incomplete in the sense that
a play is before it has been set and seen on the stage. This further dimension distinguishes drama from other types of literature,
for mediating between the author of a play and the audience are

all the elements that make up a production - the presence of the actors, setting, properties, costumes, lighting, all shaped by the shared creative acts of the director and company; and, of course, the architecture of the theatre itself.

Then, unlike the novelist, the playwright and his interpreters conceive an intense and continuous action. The playgoer, unlike the reader, cannot pause for reflection or re-reading. The impact and meaning must be communicated by whatever is happening on the stage at any particular moment. We must believe in Oedipus's agony, Millamant's spirit or Undershaft's ideas as they are expressed in action in front of us. The relationship between playwright and performers, the performers themselves and the performers and audience thus makes for a greater immediacy and complexity than is found in other forms of literature.

It cannot be repeated often enough that a play in performance, the making of a theatrical experience from a text, is the collaborative act of many people and a combination of many arts. So it is not surprising that we can regard plays from different points of view. As readers, we might refer to Shakespeare's 'Macbeth' or Strindberg's 'Miss Julie'. As playgoers, we often speak of Edith Evans's Lady Bracknell or Peter Brook's 'A Midsummer Night's Dream'.

In selecting the material for this collection of writings on drama, I have tried to follow the two-fold aims of the course. Because drama is a type of literature, essays are included on formal elements such as action, structure, language and character. Because drama must then be considered in a theatrical context, I have shown a preference for discussions of potential or actual productions. Therefore, playwrights' prefaces and letters are included to indicate the authors' intentions. Actors and directors, who read with the stage in mind, are also represented in this anthology, as are dramatic critics who often provide the only written record of past interpretations.

The material has been gathered from a variety of sources - books, specialist periodicals, newspapers, correspondence, programme notes and interviews. I have chosen contemporary criticism not always available in other drama anthologies and criticism that is controversial or original. For instance, Wole Soyinka sees too much of the class struggle in 'The Bacchae', while Freud sees too simple an explanation for Rebecca West's behaviour in 'Rosmersholm'. But I am assuming that the readers have passed the plays through their minds and imaginations so that they are able to appreciate and evaluate perhaps only one of many possible critical approaches.

For co-operation in the preparation of this book, I am grateful to the following: Brian Stone and members of the 'Drama' Course Team at The Open University, Routledge & Kegan Paul and the staffs of the Theatre Museum at the Victoria and Albert Museum, the Reading Room of the British Library, and the British Theatre Association.

The Open University, 1976   Jane Lyman

SOPHOCLES:
THE OEDIPUS TRAGEDIES

1. 1 FRIEDRICH NIETZSCHE

The Birth of Tragedy (1872), trans. W. Haussman,
'Reader's Encyclopedia of World Drama', ed.
J. Gassner and E. Quinn, Methuen, 1970, pp. 1001-2

The most sorrowful figure of the Greek stage, the hapless Oedipus,
was understood by Sophocles as the noble man, who in spite of his
wisdom was destined to error and misery, but nevertheless through
his extraordinary sufferings ultimately exerted a magical, wholesome
influence on all around him, which continues effective even after
his death. The noble man does not sin; this is what the thoughtful
poet wishes to tell us: all laws, all natural order, yea, the moral
world itself, may be destroyed through his action, but through this
very action a higher magic circle of influences is brought into play,
which establish a new world on the ruins of the old that has been
overthrown. This is what the poet, in so far as he is at the same
time a religious thinker, wishes to tell us: as poet, he shows us
first of all a wonderfully complicated legal mystery, which the judge
slowly unravels, link by link, to his own destruction. The truly
Hellenic delight at this dialectical loosening is so great, that a
touch of surpassing cheerfulness is thereby communicated to the entire
play, which everywhere blunts the edge of the horrible presuppositions of the procedure. In the 'Oedipus at Colonus' we find the
same cheerfulness, elevated, however, to an infinite transfiguration:
in contrast to the aged king, subjected to an excess of misery, and
exposed solely as a *sufferer* to all that befalls him, we have here a
supermundane cheerfulness, which descends from a divine sphere and
intimates to us that in his purely passive attitude the hero attains
his highest activity, the influence of which extends far beyond his
life, while his earlier conscious musing and striving led him only
to passivity. Thus, then, the legal knot of the fable of Oedipus
which to mortal eyes appears indissolubly entangled, is slowly
unravelled - and the profoundest human joy comes upon us in the
presence of this divine counterpart of dialectics. If this explanation does justice to the poet, it may still be asked whether the

substance of the myth is thereby exhausted; and here it turns out
that the entire conception of the poet is nothing but the light
picture which healing nature holds up to us after a glance into the
abyss. Oedipus, the murderer of his father, the husband of his
mother, Oedipus, the interpreter of the riddle of the Sphinx!
What does the mysterious triad of these deeds of destiny tell us?
There is a primitive popular belief, especially in Persia, that a
wise Magian can be born only of incest: which we have forthwith
to interpret to ourselves with reference to the riddle-solving and
mother-marrying Oedipus, to the effect that when the boundary of
the present and future, the rigid law of individuation and, in
general, the intrinsic spell of nature, are broken by prophetic and
magical powers, an extraordinary counter-naturalness - as, in this
case, incest - must have preceded as a cause; for how else could
one force nature to surrender her secrets but by victoriously
opposing her, i.e., by means of the Unnatural? It is this intuition
which I see imprinted in the awful triad of the destiny of Oedipus:
the very man who solves the riddle of nature - that double-
constituted Sphinx - must also, as the murderer of his father and
husband of his mother, break the holiest laws of nature. Indeed,
it seems as if the myth sought to whisper into our ears that wisdom,
especially Dionysian wisdom, is an unnatural abomination, and that
whoever, through his knowledge, plunges nature into an abyss of
annihilation, must also experience the dissolution of nature in
himself. 'The sharpness of wisdom turns round upon the sage:
wisdom is a crime against nature': such terrible expressions does
the myth call out to us: but the Hellenic poet touches like a sun-
beam the sublime and formidable Memnonian statue (*) of the myth,
so that it suddenly begins to sound - in Sophoclean melodies.

NOTE

* This refers to the 'singing statue' of Memnon in Egypt. A hollow,
  seated, stone figure with an orifice at the back of the mouth,
  the statue produced a sound at dawn when the sun's rays forced
  hot air through the open mouth.

1. 2 SIGMUND FREUD

       The Interpretation of Dreams (1900), 'Standard
       Edition of the Complete Psychological Works of
       Sigmund Freud', vol. 4, trans. J. Strachey,
       Hogarth Press, 1953, pp. 262-4

In my experience, which is already extensive, the chief part in the
mental lives of all children who later become psychoneurotics is
played by their parents. Being in love with the one parent and
hating the other are among the essential constituents of the stock
of psychical impulses which is formed at that time and which is of
such importance in determining the symptoms of the later neurosis.

It is not my belief, however, that psychoneurotics differ sharply
in this respect from other human beings who remain normal - that
they are able, that is, to create something absolutely new and
peculiar to themselves. It is far more probable - and this is
confirmed by occasional observations on normal children - that
they are only distinguished by exhibiting on a magnified scale
feelings of love and hatred to their parents which occur less
obviously and less intensely in the minds of most children.

This discovery is confirmed by a legend that has come down to
us from classical antiquity: a legend whose profound and universal power to move can only be understood if the hypothesis I have
put forward in regard to the psychology of children has an equally
universal validity. What I have in mind is the legend of King
Oedipus and Sophocles' drama which bears his name.[...]

'Oedipus Rex' is what is known as a tragedy of destiny. Its
tragic effect is said to lie in the contrast between the supreme
will of the gods and the vain attempts of mankind to escape the
evil that threatens them. The lesson which, it is said, the deeply
moved spectator should learn from the tragedy is submission to the
divine will and realization of his own impotence. Modern dramatists have accordingly tried to achieve a similar tragic effect by
weaving the same contrast into a plot invented by themselves.
But the spectators have looked on unmoved while a curse or an
oracle was fulfilled in spite of all the efforts of some innocent
man: later tragedies of destiny have failed in their effect.

If 'Oedipus Rex' moves a modern audience no less than it did the
contemporary Greek one, the explanation can only be that its effect
does not lie in the contrast between destiny and human will, but is
to be looked for in the particular nature of the material on which
that contrast is exemplified. There must be something which makes
a voice within us ready to recognize the compelling force of
destiny in the 'Oedipus', while we can dismiss as merely arbitrary
such dispositions as are laid down in [Grillparzer's] 'Die
Ahnfrau' or other modern tragedies of destiny. And a factor of
this kind is in fact involved in the story of King Oedipus. His
destiny moves us only because it might have been ours - because
the oracle laid the same curse upon us before our birth as upon
him. It is the fate of all of us, perhaps, to direct our first
sexual impulse towards our mother and our first hatred and our
first murderous wish against our father. Our dreams convince us
that this is so. King Oedipus, who slew his father Laius and
married his mother Jocasta, merely shows us the fulfilment of our
own childhood wishes. But, more fortunate than he, we have meanwhile succeeded, in so far as we have not become psychoneurotics,
in detaching our sexual impulses from our mothers and in forgetting
our jealousy of our fathers. Here is one in whom these primaeval
wishes of our childhood have been fulfilled, and we shrink back
from him with the whole force of the repression by which those
wishes have since that time been held down within us. While the
poet, as he unravels the past, brings to light the guilt of
Oedipus, he is at the same time compelling us to recognize our own
inner minds, in which those same impulses, though suppressed, are
still to be found. The contrast with which the closing Chorus
leaves us confronted -

> ... Fix on Oedipus your eyes,
> Who resolved the dark enigma, noblest champion and most wise.
> Like a star his envied fortune mounted beaming far and wide:
> Now he sinks in seas of anguish, whelmed beneath a raging tide
>
> > ...

- strikes as a warning at ourselves and our pride, at us who since
our childhood have grown so wise and so mighty in our own eyes.
Like Oedipus, we live in ignorance of these wishes, repugnant to
morality, which have been forced upon us by Nature, and after
their revelation we may all of us well seek to close our eyes to
the scenes of our childhood.

There is an unmistakable indication in the text of Sophocles'
tragedy itself that the legend of Oedipus sprang from some
primaeval dream-material which had as its content the distressing
disturbance of a child's relation to his parents owing to the
first stirrings of sexuality. At a point when Oedipus, though
he is not yet enlightened, has begun to feel troubled by his
recollection of the oracle, Jocasta consoles him by referring to
a dream which many people dream, though, as she thinks, it has
no meaning:

> Many a man ere now in dreams hath lain
> With her who bare him. He hath least annoy
> Who with such omens troubleth not his mind.

To-day, just as then, many men dream of having sexual relations
with their mothers, and speak of the fact with indignation and
astonishment. It is clearly the key to the tragedy and the complement to the dream of the dreamer's father being dead. The
story of Oedipus is the reaction of the imagination to these
two typical dreams. And just as these dreams, when dreamt by
adults, are accompanied by feelings of repulsion, so too the
legend must include horror and self-punishment. Its further
modification originates once again in a misconceived secondary
revision of the material, which has sought to exploit it for
theological purposes. [...] The attempt to harmonize divine
omnipotence with human responsibility must naturally fail in
connection with this subject-matter just as with any other.

1. 3   FRANCIS FERGUSSON

> 'Oedipus': the Imitation of an Action, 'The Idea
> of a Theater', Princeton University Press,
> Princeton, N.J., 1949, pp. 35-9

The general notion we used to compare the forms and spiritual
content of tragedy and of ancient ritual was the 'imitation of
action.' Ritual imitates action in one way, tragedy in another;
and Sophocles' use of ritual forms indicates that he sensed the
tragic rhythm common to both.

But the language, plot, characters of the play may also be

understood in more detail and in relation to each other as
imitations, in their various media, of the one action. I have
already quoted Coleridge on the unity of action: 'not properly a
rule,' he calls it, 'but in itself the great end, not only of the
drama, but of the epic, lyric, even to the candle-flame cone of an
epigram - not only of poetry, but of poesy in general, as the
proper generic term inclusive of all the fine arts, as its
species.' [The essay on Othello.] Probably the influence of
Coleridge partly accounts for the revival of this notion of action
which underlies the recent studies of poetry which I have mentioned.
Mr. Burke's phrase, 'language as symbolic action,' expresses the
idea, and so does his dictum: 'The poet spontaneously knows that
"beauty *is* as beauty *does*" (that the "state" must be embodied in an
"actualization").' ('Four Tropes.')

     This idea of action, and of the play as the imitation of an
action, is ultimately derived from the 'Poetics.' [...] At this point
I wish to show how the complex form of 'Oedipus' - its plot,
characters, and discourse - may be understood as the imitation of a
certain action.

     The action of the play is the quest for Laius' slayer. That is
the over-all aim which informs it - 'to find the culprit in order
to purify human life,' as it may be put. Sophocles must have seen
this seeking action as the real life of the Oedipus myth, discerning it through the personages and events as one discerns 'life
in a plant through the green leaves.' Moreoever, he must have seen
this particular action as a type, or crucial instance, of human
life in general; and hence he was able to present it in the form of
the ancient ritual which also presents and celebrates the perennial
mystery of human life and action. Thus by 'action' I do not mean
the events of the story but the focus or aim of psychic life from
which the events, in that situation, result.

     If Sophocles was imitating action in this sense, one may schema-
tically imagine his work of composition in three stages, three
mimetic acts: 1. He makes the plot: i.e., arranges the events of
the story in such a way as to reveal the seeking action from which
they come. 2. He develops the characters of the story as indivi-
dualized forms of 'quest.' 3. He expresses or realizes their
actions by means of the words they utter in the various situations
of the plot. This scheme, of course, has nothing to do with the
temporal order which the poet may really have followed in elabora-
ting his composition, nor to the order we follow in becoming
acquainted with it; we start with the words, the 'green leaves.'
The scheme refers to the 'hierarchy of actualizations' which we
may eventually learn to see in the completed work.

     1. The first act of imitation consists in making the plot or
arrangement of incidents. Aristotle says that the tragic poet is
primarily a maker of plots, for the plot is the 'soul of a
tragedy,' its formal cause. The arrangement which Sophocles made
of the events of the story - starting near the end, and rehearsing the past in relation to what is happening now - already to
some degree actualizes the tragic quest he wishes to show, even
before we sense the characters as individuals or hear them speak
and sing.

     (The reader must be warned that this conception of the plot is

rather unfamiliar to us. Usually we do not distinguish between the
plot as the form of the play and the plot as producing a certain
effect upon the audience - excitement, 'interest,' suspense, and
the like. Aristotle also uses 'plot' in this second sense. The
mimicry of art has a further purpose, or final - as distinguished
from its formal - cause, i.e., to reach the audience. Thinking
of the Athenian theater, he describes the plot as intended to show
the 'universal,' or to rouse and purge the emotions of pity and
terror. [...] At this point I am using the word *plot* in the first
sense: as the form, the first actualization, of the tragic
action.)

   2. The characters, or agents, are the second actualization of
the action. According to Aristotle, 'the agents are imitated
mainly with a view to the action' - i.e., the soul of the tragedy
is there already in the order of events, the tragic rhythm of the
life of Oedipus and Thebes; but this action may be more sharply
realized and more elaborately shown forth by developing individual variations upon it. It was with this principle in mind that
Ibsen wrote to his publisher, after two years' of work on 'The
Wild Duck,' that the play was nearly complete, and he could now
proceed to 'the more energetic individuation of the characters.'

   If one considers the Oedipus-Tiresias scene which I have
quoted, one can see how the characters serve to realize the action
of the whole. They reveal, at any moment, a 'spectrum of action'
like that which the tragic rhythm spread before us in temporal
succession, at the same time offering concrete instances of almost
photographic sharpness. Thus Tiresias 'suffers' in the darkness
of his blindness while Oedipus pursues his reasoned 'purpose';
and then Tiresias effectuates his 'purpose' of serving his mantic
vision of the truth, while Oedipus 'suffers' a blinding passion of
fear and anger. The agents also serve to move the action ahead,
develop it in time, through their conflicts. The chorus meanwhile,
in some respects between, in others deeper, than the antagonists,
represents the interests of that resolution, that final chord of
feeling, in which the end of the action, seen ironically and
sympathetically as one, will be realized.

   3. The third actualization is in the words of the play. The
seeking action which is the substance of the play is imitated
first in the plot, second in the characters, and third in the
words, concepts, and forms of discourse wherein the characters
'actualize' their psychic life in its shifting forms, in response
to the everchanging situations of the play. If one thinks of
plotting, characterization, and poetry as successive 'acts of
imitation' by the author, one may also say that they constitute,
in the completed work, a hierarchy of forms; and that the words of
the play are its 'highest individuation.' They are the 'green
leaves' which we actually perceive; the product and the sign of
the one 'life of the plant' which, by an imaginative effort, one
may divine behind them all.

   At this point one encounters again Mr. Burke's theory of
'language as symbolic action,' and the many contemporary studies
of the arts of poetry which have been made from this point of
view. It would be appropriate to offer a detailed study of
Sophocles' language, using the modern tools of analysis, to

substantiate my main point. But this would require the kind of
knowledge of Greek which a Jebb spent his life to acquire; and I
must be content to try to show, in very general terms, that the
varied forms of the poetry of 'Oedipus' can only be understood on
a histrionic basis: i.e., as coming out of a direct sense of the
tragic rhythm of *action*.

In the Oedipus-Tiresias scene, there is a 'spectrum of the
forms of discourse' corresponding to the 'spectrum of action' which
I have described. It extends from Oedipus' opening speech - a
reasoned exposition not, of course, without feeling but based
essentially upon clear ideas and a logical order - to the choral
chant, based upon sensuous imagery and the 'logic of feeling.'
Thus it employs, in the beginning, the principle of composition
which Mr. Burke calls 'syllogistic progression,' and, at the other
end of the spectrum, Mr. Burke's 'progression by association and
contrast.' When the Neoclassic and rationalistic critics of the
seventeenth century read 'Oedipus', they saw only the order of
reason; they did not know what to make of the chorus. Hence
Racine's drama of 'Action as Rational': a drama of static
situations, of clear concepts and merely illustrative images.
Nietzsche, on the other hand, saw only the passion of the chorus;
for his insight was based on 'Tristan,' which is composed essentially in sensuous images, and moves by association and contrast
according to the logic of feeling: the drama which takes 'action
as passion.' Neither point of view enables one to see how the
scene, as a whole, hangs together.

If the speeches of the characters and the songs of the chorus
are only the foliage of the plant, this is as much as to say that
the life and meaning of the whole is never literally and completely present in any one formulation. It takes *all* of the
elements - the shifting situation, the changing and developing
characters, and their reasoned or lyric utterances, to indicate,
in the round, the action Sophocles wishes to convey. Because
this action takes the form of reason as well as passion, and of
contemplation by way of symbols; because it is essntially moving
(in the tragic rhythm); and because it is shared in different ways
by all the characters, the play has neither literal unity nor the
rational unity of the truly abstract idea, or 'univocal concept.'
Its parts and its moments are one only 'by analogy'; and just as
the Saints warn us that we must believe in order to understand, so
we must 'make believe,' by a sympathetic and imitative act of the
histrionic sensibility, in order to get what Sophocles intended by
his play.

It is the histrionic basis of Sophocles' art which makes it
mysterious to us, with our demands for conceptual clarity, or for
the luxury of yielding to a stream of feeling and subjective
imagery. But it is this also which makes it so crucial an instance
of the art of the theater in its completeness, as though the
author understood 'song, spectacle, thought, and diction' in their
primitive and subtle roots. And it is the histrionic basis of
drama which 'undercuts theology and science.'

1. 4 H.D.F. KITTO

The 'Oedipus Coloneus', 'Greek Tragedy', Methuen,
1939, pp. 385-9,393-5

The 'Coloneus', like other late works of genius, is more imaginative than the earlier works of that same genius. The late quar-
tets of Beethoven - and if this particular parallel means nothing
to the reader he will be able to find his own illustration in
Rembrandt or some other artist - are less definite in statement,
more fluid in form, deeper and more remote in feeling, than the
great works of his middle period. The difference between the
'Coloneus' and the 'Tyrannus' is similar. [...]As Beethoven needed
a much more fluid form for his last utterances than that which he
had forged for the dramatic and intense utterances of his middle
period, so Sophocles now transcends the bounds of his own
Aristotelian perfection. This most poetic of plays convinces us
of its unity, but as to where that unity lies, there is room for
difference of opinion.[...]
     A plain presentation of the story was not Sophocles' idea - and
we need not be sorry for it. In the separate themes of the play -
the local interest, the innocence of Oedipus, the working-out of
the legend, the character of Oedipus - we shall find only variety,
not unity; but if we stand back and look at the play from a distance, we see that there exists in the whole piece a certain
governing movement or rhythm. We can see that Oedipus enters the
play a disregarded outcast and leaves it - followed by the King of
Attica - to keep a strange appointment with Heaven. This rhythm
controls the play, and will explain it.
     It is complex. We may notice, from our present point of van-
tage, that Oedipus enters as one who has learned resignation from
suffering. Perhaps he has; but gradually, through successive
references to his sons, then through his resistance to Creon,
finally in the tremendous scene with Polyneices, he passes from
resignation to the full height of the wrath that is in him. We may
notice that in the opening scene Oedipus is at everyone's mercy,
a blind old man, dependent on the decency of a casual passer-by;
at the end he towers above everybody.
     This complex rhythm pervades everything in the play. There is
no sudden revelation of a new Oedipus; Sophocles leads us step by
step, almost insensibly, with the same skill that made the
'Electra'. The important difference is that it is rhythm which
cannot incorporate itself in one sweeping, heroic action, but
must be created from the outside, out of separate actions or
interests on which it draws as need arises. We may trace this
rhythm in some of its aspects. Let us take our sense of
Oedipus' power, not the power of his personality, which culminates in the scene with Polyneices, but that mysterious reflection of this, the power which is entrusted to him by the gods -
or found in him by the gods, as there is no suggestion that a
special gift or honour has been accorded him.
     We must begin with the impression which the blind old man
makes when first we see him. To the Stranger he is 'noble

except in fortune'; the Chorus on the other hand, seeing him rise
within the sacred grove, is terrified at the mere sight of him and
the sound of his voice. Such is the figure whom we see, led in by
his daughter. We hear that rest has been promised him at the
grove which he has now reached, but of his strange power, that of
benefiting Athens, we have only two bare hints.

The revulsion which the chorus feels towards Oedipus brings
this rhythm, if we can yet call it begun, back to its starting-
point. Oedipus has to fight to maintain his position, but it is
maintained. [...] Then Ismene comes, with new oracles. We feel
perhaps a little hazy about them all, what exactly is the difference between these new ones and those that Oedipus had received
before? As the earlier ones are not quoted we cannot possibly
say. But why was the Ismene-scene wanted? Why cannot Oedipus
have all the oracles at the beginning? Because our sense of his
new power must be made to grow. As far as the action of the
play is concerned Ismene's part could be considerably reduced;
she might well, as we suggested above, enter after Theseus, and
announce nothing but the coming of Creon. The rhythm of the play
however needs the reinforcement that her fresh oracles give, and
to emphasize the reinforcement Oedipus is twice made to refer to
his present lowly position, both times before the oracles are
declared. Afterwards Oedipus speaks with a new confidence, as
one whom Athens may be glad to welcome and Thebes may vainly hope
to capture.

The next stage is the Theseus-scene. What Oedipus can do for
Athens is fully set forth; it is such as to outweigh even the
chance of embroilment with Thebes. The stature to which Oedipus
has now attained can be seen in the speech from which we have
already quoted, 'Dear son of Aegeus'. This is a very different
Oedipus from the one who had to ask favours of the Stranger and
of the old men of Colonus. Next, Creon and the violence which he
is prepared to use emphasize Oedipus' importance even more;
finally in the two scenes which concern Polyneices he is presented as the arbiter of destiny. [...]

In this complex but always mounting rhythm one thing remains
stationary, Oedipus' insistence that what he did was no sin. It
remains stationary because it was no part of Sophocles' plan to
develop it; it is an axiom, implicit in the assurance with which
he first addressed the Eumenides. To the horrified chorus he
develops his argument at length; later this chorus is made to
drag the most repulsive details from him in order that his
innocence may be set in the strongest possible light. Yet, we
must observe, there is neither discussion nor judgement. The
chorus professes neither belief nor disbelief. Theseus comes,
and before him no claim to purity is necessary; his large humanity
can accept Oedipus as he is. When next the chorus speaks, in the
Colonus-ode, there is no reference to this question; Oedipus is
simply accepted.

Nevertheless we have one last passionate assertion before
Creon - and how dramatically it is managed. Again, men and not
arguments are at grips, for the speech is as much an onslaught on
Creon as it is Oedipus' own apologia. In the mechanics of the
play the apologia is nothing, for Theseus does not need it nor

Creon merit it, and the substance has been given before. The
argument is repeated because it has become part of Oedipus' very
soul, and because it is the very core of Sophocles' philosophy,
that virtue alone cannot assure happiness nor wickedness alone
explain disaster. [...]

In the 'Coloneus' we have the same Oedipus, but now he can look
back on his ruined life. He has nothing with which he can
reproach himself; repentance is not in the picture at all: 'Pure
before the law unwitting I have come to this'. He thinks of some
wrath of Heaven, but this is his explanation, not Sophocles'. To
say that he could not have escaped is indeed neither true nor
tragic; he could have escaped, but only if his towering intelligence had towered as high as the peculiarly malignant circumstances arrayed against him. It did not; if it had he would have
been more than a man, he would have been a god. There was no
sin, only the necessary frailty of being human.

Such was Oedipus, such he remains, and we may doubt if it was
ever in Sophocles' mind to leave him crushed, hidden from sight
in the Theban palace. Pessimist Sophocles may have been, with
little faith in future bliss, with no confidence in present prosperity, but no Greek believed more firmly in the dignity of being
a man, and it was because of this belief that he had to write the
'Coloneus' before he died. Oedipus could not be left there. So,
with even more sufferings and indignities heaped upon him, with
his one fault, hastiness, defiantly unmodified, he is driven
forth. To the gods he has made no concessions; just before his
last summons he is at his most violent. But this play, though it
presents the same Oedipus, reverses the movement of the
'Tyrannus', for Oedipus goes not from greatness to misery but from
misery to greatness; and it reverses it in a higher plane, in the
dark, not in the light. The kingly power that shines from him in
the 'Tyrannus' is still in him, but now, on the edge of death, it
is transmuted into a superhuman power, and we see it growing. It
is not a recompense given him by the gods; why should it be?
Apollo in the 'Tyrannus' was no enemy of Oedipus'; he merely saw
what was coming and answered questions. So now, Apollo is no
friend and champion of his; he sees the greatness that is in him
and states facts. In taking Oedipus to themselves as a Hero the
gods are but recognizing facts. By his stature as a man Oedipus
imposes himself on the gods; it is not forgiveness, for there was
no sin. The 'Coloneus' is Sophocles' answer to the tragedy of
life. He knows that he cannot justify God to man, but he can
justify man to man.

1. 5 HOVHANNESS I. PILIKIAN (*)

The Swollen-Footed Tyrant, 'Drama: The Quarterly
Theatre Review', no. 113, summer 1974, pp. 31-2,
34-5

Oedipus killed Laius and his men on their way to Delphi, at a
cross-road. Two powerful deities, Hermes, the god of Travellers,

and Hecate, a goddess of the Underworld, had their 'images' posted
at cross-roads.   A road-side image implied an improvised altar.
[...] That Oedipus should kill in broad daylight, with full awareness, at the very altar of not one, but even two major gods, presents an inexplicable case of irrational behaviour.

[...] Moreover, he kills viciously, violently, gratuitously.
There is absolutely no textual evidence that Oedipus' feud at the
cross-roads with the old man could not be resolved peacefully,
without resorting to violence. [...] There is no version of the
myth before Sophocles' play which contains the poet's variant,
that Laius with his retinue *was on his way to the Delphic oracle*
(coming *from* Thebes) when Oedipus meets them on his way to Thebes.
Delphi was the Vatican of the ancient Greek world.   As pilgrims,
Laius and his men would travel under the protection of Apollo.
Therefore their madly violent and perverse extermination at the
hands of Oedipus is *triply* blasphemous.

External evidence of vital importance has been totally neglec-
ted by the interpreters of the play throughout its stage-
history; the city-state of Thebes remained pro-Persian during what
the Athenians considered their greatest national war-effort, which
led to their victory against the Persian empire.   And Sophocles'
Oedipus here is the Tyrant of Thebes.

It is impossible that Sophocles, as the most respected Athenian
citizen, could ever do otherwise than shed a 'negative' light on
the character of Oedipus. [...] Sophocles could not, would not,
forgive the Thebans for being pro-Persian during the wars.
Aristotelian notions of a Grand, noble, demi-god hero, cannot be
textually substantiated.   Oedipus is a mad man in the grip of
forces he cannot control.   He is the great villain of a political
tragedy. [...]

Tiresias is not a saintly figure.   He is a nasty old man, with
a personal grudge against Oedipus, who outdid his bid for power by
finding the right answer to the Sphinx's riddle. [...] There is
much hatred between the two.   Very early in the play, Tiresias
enters to reveal all about Oedipus, and in front of the whole
city.   The moment comes right after Oedipus' 'Television' speech to
the people.   Everybody including Oedipus hears Tiresias' call for
'impeachment'. [...]

'Oidipous' means 'swollen-foot', but the Greek word for foot
also means leg.   What happened to him as a baby has been invariably
misunderstood since the play was written.   Translators render
Jocasta's testimony on the question as the ankles of the feet
being pierced and pinned together, while the Greek means, '*and he*
(Laius) *yoked* (like one would yoke the oxen for the plough) *its*
(baby's) *feet through the joints*'.

[...] Sophocles' Laius seems to have *held* the infant *by the*
ankles (as Jocasta's line suggests) and stuck a skewer through the
knee-joints.   That is the *only* thing Sophocles' line can mean,
especially if one takes into account the tradition from classical
midwifery of holding a baby upside down by the ankles, which would
make it totally impossible to stick a skewer through the ankles,
as it would only pass through the fingers holding the ankles. [...]

The question is, what would be the physical effects on the
adult, of the baby who was so terrifyingly mis-treated?   The answer

is - maybe nothing.[...] However, the play's textual given is that
in the case of Laius' child, the damage was permanent. Oedipus
is named after his physical deformity: he has a swollen leg. The
mention of Oedipus' name in the play, for its original audience,
could signify nothing else but that. [...]

The regúlar repetition of Oedipus' name throughout the play is
like the beat of a pendulum. 'It represents a most significant
element hitherto ignored. Adult Oedipus is bruised not only
psychologically but also deformed physically. Everytime therefore his name is pronounced in the play, it spotlights the
character's physical deformity and tells the cruel tale of his
birth.

The evidence of the name [...] coupled with the Tiresias-
scenes leave no doubt that Sophocles intends his play to be understood as Tyrant Oedipus' attempt to cover-up his murderous past.
Oedipus is not the admirable man, the physically and spiritually
perfect hero dedicated to truth but a murderer, a rogue, and a
grotesque-looking thief-of-the-(cross)-roads, who rises to political
power (just like Brecht's Arturo Ui) and whose successful cover-up
at last cracks down and destroys him (like Spiro Agnew).

The theme of the 'bloody foreigner' is a fundamental predicament in Greek Drama mostly ignored by classical scholarship.[...]

Politically, the most astounding dimension of Sophocles' play
lies precisely in this: it explores the predicament of a big-
power nation (Sophocles is really writing a play about Athens),
being governed by a dark-skinned foreigner, a common criminal,
which Oedipus was before usurping the tyranny in Thebes. [...]

NOTE

* Hovhanness I. Pilikian directed 'Oidipus Tyrannus' at the
  Chichester Festival Theatre in 1974 with Keith Michell as
  Oidipus and Diana Dors as Iocasta.

EURIPIDES:
'ALCESTIS' AND 'THE BACCHAE'

'ALCESTIS'

2. 1 A.M. DALE

    The Characters and the Action, Introduction to
    Euripides' 'Alcestis', Oxford University Press,
    1954, pp. xxii-xxix

The play is called 'Alcestis' because the conspicuous glory is
hers [...] But the central theme of the tragedy - that in virtue
of which it *is* a tragedy in the Greek sense of the word - is
exemplified in the experience of Admetus. It might be summed up
in his words 'now - now when it is too late - I understand.'
The same words are spoken in a flash of awful realization at the
end of the 'Bacchae', and they might be made the burden of many
tragedies, ancient and modern [...] What Admetus realizes too
late is that this life of which he has cheated Destiny is a useless possession; the loss of Alcestis and of his own fair fame
has made it a desert for its owner. The 'dark' scenes of the
drama have been remorselessly leading to this climax, but in and
out among them the beneficence of Apollo, working through Heracles,
has been preparing a way towards the light, which dawns upon an
incredulous Admetus and Chorus in the last scene.
    The progress towards this insight into the real nature of 'what
has been done' - is a better clue to the understanding of each
scene than the search for psychological complexities. To that
school of thought which sees in the creation of character, the
chief and most original contribution of Euripides to the drama,
scanning every turn of incident, every line of dialogue, for
little touches to fill in some complex portrait, the chief
interest of this play lies in an elaborately unflattering
'character-study' of Admetus, who is seen to be vain, shallow,
egotistical, bad-tempered, lying, hysterical, and insincere; some
would have him despicable, or at best ridiculous, to the very end,
others reform him slightly in time for the happy ending. Now, some

of this indictment has arisen from demonstrable misunderstandings
of dramatic technique and of Greek usage [...] and in particular
we ought to be suspicious of any such synthetic portrait as turns
out to be at variance with considered, and unrepented, judgements
expressed by one of the characters upon another in the course of
the play. [...] The explanation is simply that our portrait-
painters have failed to understand the tone and level of these
remarks. Heracles enters with the veiled woman, and begins:
'Admetus, to a friend one should speak candidly and not suppress
one's grievances in the silence of the breast. Coming so close
to your troubles I should expect to have been given the chance to
prove my friendship; yet you did not reveal the presence of your
wife's body laid out for burial, but entertained me as a guest in
your house, ... and I garlanded my head and poured libations to
the gods under your afflicted roof. *I do protest* at being treated
so; however, the last thing I want is to distress you in your
grief.' [...] Which of us, on discovering that a friend had put us
under a heavy obligation of which he had intended us to remain
ignorant, so that we appear to have acted unfittingly, would not
react with just this mixture of feelings? Commentators are often
finding touches of Thessalian 'local colour' in this play; what is
much more remarkable is its echoes from the civilized courtesies
of contemporary social life in Athens; in this respect the 'Alcestis',
more perhaps than any other play, shows Euripides the forerunner
of Menander.

    But the real gravamen of the indictment built up against
Admetus lies in the earlier scenes, in his attitude to Alcestis'
sacrifice and death. In the first place, it is said, he ought
never to have accepted it; in the second, his expression of grief
at the death he has caused is too extravagant to be sincere (that
image-business!), and shows the same lack of balance as his later
outburst against Pheres. Most of the psychologists, however,
relent towards the later Admetus; Pheres' home truths have punc-
tured his self-esteem, and when he returns from the funeral his
grief and contrition have somehow become genuine. Admetus in fact
is seen as a clever, though unpleasant, 'character study'.
Alcestis, considered from the same point of view, is a more awkward problem; the psychologists content themselves with labelling
her an 'elusive' or 'complex' character, and it is usually left to
young readers to voice a more open disappointment. She should not
sing her own praises so loudly, they feel, and they remain uncon-
vinced even when told that this was not considered such bad form
in ancient Greece. And her severity towards Admetus, the lack of
any word of love or affection for him in all her death-scene, are
chilling to the romantic feelings. Hence Wilamowitz's belief that
if we read with the proper insight we shall see that Euripides is
subtly conveying the disillusionment of her marriage which makes
her now regret that impulsive promise given on her bridal night.

    The root of the trouble is, I think, our inveterate modern habit
of regarding a drama almost exclusively in terms of its characters.
The modern conception of the actor's function, with each actor
concentrating on the 'interpretation' of his single part, strongly
reinforces this habit. It works quite well with modern drama,
which is largely composed from the same point of view. It can be

made to work with Shakespeare. But it will not work satisfactorily
with Greek tragedy. Of course the Greek, like every serious drama,
involves 'characters', whose part in the action, and therefore
whose words, to some extent reflect their several natures. But in
Greek tragedy their speeches, and the interplay of their dialogue,
can rarely be interpreted as *primarily* or *consistently* expressive
of their natures, and whenever we find ourselves trying to build
up some elaborate or many-sided personality by *adding up* small
touches gleaned from all parts of the play we can be pretty sure
of being on the wrong lines. It usually means that we are not
allowing enough for two considerations always very important to
Greek dramatists, the trend of the action and the rhetoric of the
situation.

Of the trend of the action in the 'Alcestis' something has
already been said. The bitter lesson Admetus learns is not 'I see
now that I ought never to have accepted this sacrifice', but 'I
see now that Alcestis in dying is better off than I in living,
since I have lost my happiness and my reputation'. The gifts of
the gods may by a kind of paradox prove ambiguous and self-
defeating. So far as there is any 'ought to have' in the story it
is Pheres or the mother who ought to have died instead; both
Alcestis and the Chorus make that quite clear. But in a brilliant
and shameless speech Pheres manages to stand that argument on its
head and make it show Admetus to be a coward and a murderer.
Paradox again. It is not Admetus' *conscience* that is eventually
stricken by this; Pheres is hardly the mouthpiece of truth. What
Admetus comes to realize is the handle he has given to malice
[...] 'my enemies will say...' That is Pheres' contribution towards the opening of his eyes. Alcestis did the rest, Alcestis
who loved him and died for him. The strangest paradox of all.
The whole play, or at least the whole dark side of it, is permeated
by a sort of grave irony of plot, the irony of human intentions
measured against their outcome. To safeguard her children's
future, Alcestis exacts his promise never to marry again, and for
the sake of the plot we must indeed be left quite certain that
Admetus will know no more domestic felicity. If we do not realize
the absolute sincerity of his response, by which he pledges himself
to turn his life into a desert, we miss half the point of the plot.
We are not at liberty to argue that, because Alcestis makes no comment on his intentions except for what concerns the children, she
is rebuking him for extravagance or expressing scepticism by her
silent contempt. The *argumentum ex silentio* is never weaker than
when it tries to make psychological deductions from what Euripidean
speeches leave unsaid. The action requires that Admetus shall not
be consoled and fortified in this scene by words of love and sympathy from Alcestis; and by making her concentrate upon leaving the
children rather than leaving Admetus Euripides avoids the slightly
ridiculous trap into which more than one of his successors has
fallen, of showing Alcestis so devoted to her husband that she is
only too happy and eager to die for his sake, thus deflecting our
sympathies to the harder lot of the survivor.

Yet Euripides cares very much that we should know his conception
of the character of Alcestis. The description by the Maidservant
of her last hours in the house, the words of the Manservant about

the mistress they are all heartbroken at losing, give us Alcestis as
we know she must have been - brave, gentle, full of loving-kindness.
And of course she loves Admetus - what else made her die for him?
Our speech, songs, and literature are so saturated with the expression of this theme that we are apt to forget how unaccustomed Greek
eyes and ears would be to the spectacle of a high-born young wife
expatiating in public to her husband upon such a subject. [...]
But with beautiful reticence the strength of this feeling is conveyed in the Maidservant's description of her mistress's address to
her marriage-bed, at sight of which her calm for the first time
breaks down and she weeps and kisses it and suffers at the thought
of a successor in her place. It is strange that so many commentators should deny that this means love and jealousy.

Of the characters in this play, Alcestis, Heracles, and Pheres
stand out in much more definite outline than Admetus. Their part in
the action is limited, and in itself goes a long way to character-
ize them, while for Alcestis we also have the benefit of description. Selfish father, unselfish wife, gluttonous and heroic son of
Zeus: they have to be the sort of people they are or the action
would not work. But for Admetus this applies only to his regal
hospitality, which affects only a small area of his part in the
action. For the rest, Admetus as a person is blown hither and
thither by every wind of incident; he is a person to whom things
happen, it is his experience that matters, his reactions to what
people do or say to him. So far from considering the 'Alcestis'
a full-length study of naiveté, weakness, hysteria, egotism,
character-development, and so forth. I do not believe that
Euripides had any particular interest in the sort of person Admetus
was. The situations in which the plot involves him are too diverse
for much personality to appear, or to be intended. For in a well-
constructed Euripidean tragedy what controls a succession of situations is not a firmly conceived unity of character but the shape of
the whole action, and what determines the development and finesse
of each situation is not a desire to paint in the details of a
portrait-study but the rhetoric of the situation. Rhetoric is a
concept which we tend to hold in some suspicion, as if in its
nature there must be something slightly bogus; but we shall never
properly understand Greek tragedy unless we realize how closely
related were the rhetoric of Athenian life, in the assembly and
law-courts and on other public occasions, and the rhetoric of the
speeches in drama. Nourished on the psychological novel, we tend
to assume that the poet had brooded on the story until the characters took shape in his mind, as if he had asked himself: What
would X, being such a man, be likely to say in such a situation?
whereas we might sometimes get nearer to the meaning by imagining
the question: Suppose a man involved in such a situation, how
should he best acquit himself? How gain his point? Move his
hearers? Prove his thesis? Convey information lucidly and
vividly? The aim of rhetoric is Persuasion, and the poet promises
to do his best for each of his clients in turn as the situations
change and succeed one another. This does not by any means exclude
an interest in character [...] But the dominating consideration is:
What *points* could be made here? The points may be developed in a
set speech or made and countered in stichomythia. Fertility in

arguments, a delight in logical analysis - these are the essen-
tials, though they may be skilfully made to produce an effect of
spontaneity. Alcestis has to win her husband's promise never to
marry again; her strongest arguments are the magnitude of her own
sacrifice and the emotion aroused at the thought of the mother-
less children and her own death. So like a skilful pleader she
makes the most of these things, and sometimes the skill of the
pleading obscures the woman Alcestis, as when she emphasizes her
own virtue in contrast to the conduct of the parents, or when at
the end of the speech she says: 'And you, my husband, can boast
that you had the noblest of women to wife, and you, my children,
that you were born of the noblest of mothers.' It is a pleader's
peroration, not the spontaneous cry of a noble heart. A modern
actress, intent on 'being' Alcestis, might well find these lines
embarrassing; not so the Greek actor, trained not in 'interpretation' but in rhetorical performance, before an audience that
expected nothing less. And the dramatist as well as the actor
has a technique to which we are unaccustomed. In an earlier scene
he has conveyed to us, among other qualities, Alcestis' love for
Admetus, which in any case is implicit in the story. But in this
scene the action does not require it (it might indeed be a disturbing element), so he omits its expression and leaves only its
effect, in her sacrifice; and all the emphasis goes into her
anguish for the children. Our presuppositions about dramatic
character lead us to expect that such a love will inform her
whole utterance everywhere, and so we feel rebuffed. But if we
start projecting these feelings into a Euripidean 'Portrait of
Alcestis', we shall end up with the Alcestis of that delightful
modern comedy 'The Thracian Horses' who was furious with Heracles
for stealing her limelight and chiefly concerned lest she should
become famous hereafter as the subject of his Labour number 8(a).
It was great fun, but of course it was not Euripides.

2. 2 WESLEY D. SMITH

      The Ironic Structure in 'Alcestis', 'Phoenix',
      14, 1960, pp. 134-40

Through recurrent themes the Greek dramatist makes clear his reason
for being attracted to the traditional material he has chosen for
his play, and for shaping it in the way that he has. Justice in
the 'Oresteia,' sight and knowledge in 'Oedipus Tyrannus,' friendship and chance in 'Heracles' are examples of themes which point in
the direction of the dramatist's purpose in those plays, and
through which one must seek the meaning the poet draws from the
myth he has chosen. Euripides has made three themes particularly
prominent in Alcestis: good breeding, death and its meaning, and
the house and family. [...]
    As the chorus says in the third stasimon, commenting on
Admetus' action in bringing Heracles into the house under false
pretenses: 'Good breeding makes a man virtuous, and leads him
instinctively, in spite of himself, to do the right thing.' The

chorus has proof of its conclusions: Admetus treated Apollo well
and acted as the perfect host even when he need not have, and as
a result he was rewarded with prosperity and continued life by
Apollo. Perhaps, hopes the chorus, his entertainment of Heracles
will have similarly good results. The chorus was shocked at first
but cannot imagine that Admetus' good breeding would play him
false. Surely good will come from the apparent breach of manners.
Of course the chorus is correct.
    Heracles, too, is conscious of the obligations of a gentleman,
and when he discovers that Admetus has lied to him he is not such
a boor as to interpret Admetus' behaviour unfairly, but echoing
the chorus' sentiments he says:

> He concealed his trouble, since he is well bred, out of
> respect for me. What Thessalian loves guests more, what
> Greek? He will never say that he did a good turn to a
> base man, nobleman that he is.

Heracles, in his own mind, is put to it to prove that he too has
manners, and is not low born. As a result he rescues Alcestis,
and so can speak freely, or as a free man, as Admetus' social and
moral equal, after having done so. In this way the ideal of good
breeding serves as the motive force in the action of the melodramatic plot. Its use in the ironic structure is more complicated.
    Concern for social status is general among the male characters,
but is especially associated with Admetus. He assures Alcestis
that he will not marry again, because there will not be a girl
from a good enough family. His memories of their wedding are
memories of the guests' congratulations on how well born both the
bridal pair were: both eupatrids, both from the aristocracy.
The battle between Admetus and Pheres, which is introduced by the
choral ode on good breeding, hinges on the standards of a gentleman, to which each finds the other inferior. [...]
    Admetus is a gentleman, and the audience is assured that his
manners are perfect as they apply to strangers and guests. He is
a lover of guests. But during the play he renounces kinship with
his parents first implicitly and then explicitly, and when he is
asked whether the 'dead woman' is a member of his family he
answers that she is a foreigner who came to live with him when her
father died. She was simply a homeless person, not even a guest.
[Homeless person] in tragedy is used only in this play. Euripides
uses and emphasizes the prose word in order to draw attention to
Admetus' strange assertions as to who is dear or belonging to him.
The act is ambiguous. Admetus later offers the defence that his
sudden tergiversation was required by noble motives of hospitality.
It is noteworthy, however, that his view of the host's office
requires denying the status of guest to the woman who was more
than life to him shortly before. The problem will recur in the
final scene.
    In his nobility Admetus is like his father in all respects, not
least in calculating the value of a wife in terms of profit and
loss. Admetus says to the dying Alcestis that he hopes he can
get some profit from the children, since Alcestis herself is

bringing him not profit but grief, a calculation repeated by
Eumelus and by Pheres in slightly different ways. Indeed the
family of Pheres keeps a strict balance sheet of obligations
within the family, and both Admetus and Pheres use it as a text in
their argument.

In this way the theme of good breeding, combined with the dear
or belonging *vs*. not-belonging theme and the theme of profit and
loss, is used ironically to draw a contrast between the values
invoked by Admetus and his family and the qualities that they
exhibit. The contrast is between external and internal, public
and private. The chorus and Heracles appreciate the external
nobility of Admetus, while the audience, through Admetus' mirror-
image Pheres and through the ironic treatment of Admetus and his
claims, is led to appreciate also the private character of the
man, and to judge it in Admetus' own terms of nobility.

A related theme, that of house and family, emphasizes the same
contrast between internal and external, public and private.
Admetus is conscious of his house as an institution, as an aristocratic dynasty. But contrasted with his concern for the house
as institution is the feeling of the rest of its inhabitants for
the house as home, as a quality of life. When the child says
'With your death, mother, the house is dead,' he speaks not of the
royal line but of the home. There is no technical vocabulary
developed for the contrast [...] Rather the contrast is built on
a series of associations which reveal what the house means to the
people who live in it.

Alcestis dies for her home, as she makes clear in her death
scene as well as in what the maidservant reports of her. To the
goddess of the hearth she gives her farewell prayer, addressing
her as mistress and entrusting the children to her. After putting
suppliant boughs at the other altars she addresses her bed, the
symbol of her marriage and home, which she would not betray by
taking another husband. She bids goodbye to all the household
individually, stretching out her hand to each. 'And there was none
so low-born that she did not address him and receive his address
in return.' Not the personal relationship with her husband or distinctions of breeding, but her relationship with the home which
includes her husband is what we are told moves Alcestis, and is
what she talks about. There is no indication in the play that
Alcestic is disappointed in her husband in her final moments.
Alcestis is not cold. All we see and hear of her shows her single-
minded and passionate about the house and family of which Admetus
is the head. Admetus characteristically mistakes the intention of
her request that he not marry again, and assures her that he cannot
find as noble or pretty a girl as she, and does not want any more
children, and therefore will find his vow easy to keep. Alcestis
perhaps has reason to be disappointed, but the text gives no
indication that Euripides intended her to show it. [...]

The house is prominent from the first word of the play to the
final exit of Admetus and Alcestis into the house. The house is
the stage setting, of course, and Apollo's opening speech is an
address to the house.   Death enters there before the servant girl
and later Alcestis and Admetus come out. Heracles is entertained
in one part of the house while preparations for the funeral are

going on in another. The complementary views of the house as home
and as institution are elaborated separately, the former through
Alcestis herself and the household's memories of her, the latter
through Admetus' defence of himself and his use of the house as
proper for a gentleman and dynast. [...] The ironic use is first
made explicit in Admetus' statement to Heracles that the dead
woman was not a member of the family, but was nevertheless essential to the house. Finally the contrast in attitudes, once established, is put to dramatic use in Admetus' return from the funeral.
There Admetus studies the house very carefully, and concerns himself with domestic problems (note the dirty floor), realizing now
that he is father and mother. And he addresses the house in new
terms along with the old ones, as part of the suggestion in that
scene that he may be seeing things in a new light. But interspersed is the ironic commentary which suggests rightly that
Admetus' change and development are likely to come to nothing.
[...]
    The third theme, death and its meaning, also develops on a
series of contrasts. Each character's response to the fact of
death serves as a focus for the playwright's interpretation of his
other characteristics. The attitude of the myth itself is explored
through imagery and through the character Thanatos, an attitude
which is amended and corrected by the ironic view.
    The drunken Heracles delivers a speech on life's meaning for the
benefit of the outraged servant: 'Do you know the nature of mortal
affairs? I think not. Where would you learn? Well hear me.
Every man must die. No mortal knows whether he will be alive
tomorrow.' Heracles, in his cups, speaks like a drinking song:
eat, drink, love, for tomorrow we may be dead. That every man must
die, and can never know how or when, is a commonplace often
repeated, since we never cease to be surprised that it is so.
Here, however, the commonplace has extraordinary piquancy because
'Alcestis' deals with a man who was an exception to that common
lot. Heracles argues that, since death is inevitable, the very
uncertainty of the time when it will come forces us to pay attention to life, an argument that allows many interpretations, from
those of Sarpedon and Achilles in the 'Iliad' to that of Trimalchio.
Heracles' hedonism here has as its immediate conclusion 'come have
a drink with me,' and Euripides uses the fact of his drunkenness
throughout the scene (note his confidence that he will find Thanatos
drinking beside the grave). But in Heracles' second speech Euripides also manages to suggest that other side of hedonism, the
heroic view of death celebrated in the 'Iliad.'
    Alcestis is brave but passive. She sees death as an alternative
which circumstances may make desirable, although 'nothing is more
valuable than life.' Her death scene is presented twice, first by
the maidservant who acts as a messenger, later by dramatic representation. The reason why the normal order is reversed and the report
of the death scene precedes its dramatization is shown by the differences between the two versions. The first introduces Alcestis
and her emotions to the audience, though the audience does not see
her. The second introduces her husband and gives the audience a
close look at him in the light of what they already know about
Alcestis.

Though Alcestis has a clear vision of Death, Admetus never sees
anything clearly, particularly necessities. He blames the gods for
her undeserved death, begs Alcestis not to betray him by dying, and
dramatizes himself and his grief with such inappropriate statements as 'stand up,' and 'your death is worse than death to me.'
It is not Admetus who says that nothing is more valuable than life,
but Admetus cannot conceive of actually facing death. Admetus
seems unaware of the situation that is clear to everyone else. His
own death is never real to him, his wife's death barely. Shortly
after her death Admetus describes for Heracles the condition of
Alcestis: 'Dead and not dead. She troubles me.' But six lines
later she troubles him no longer: 'One who is going to die is
already dead, and the dead is non-existent,' a mocking echo of
Alcestis' prediction a few moments earlier that she would be forgotten, since the dead are nothing. 'To be and not to be are considered two different things,' says Heracles, anticipating his
later speeches.

Besides being presented as an idea in the minds of the characters, which can vary widely, Death is a character in his own
right: a nervous bully who is afraid of a fight, a grotesque bogey
out of a fairy tale. Through the body of the play death is treated
more seriously, but the fairy-tale character from the prologue is
recalled for the final scene as the victim of a wrestling match.
[...]

In the final stasimon the chorus recapitulates the imagery of
the play, and resolves the tension by rejecting finally any hope
for resurrection. Says the chorus: neither religion, in the form
of Orphism, nor philosophy, nor poetry, nor the art of the Ascle-
piadai and Apollo can offer a comforting solution to the problem of
death. Necessity keeps no altars and listens to no prayers. It is
the will of Zeus and nature. But still there is some comfort: the
necessity of death is balanced by the possibility of making life
meaningful. The chorus suggests that Admetus take comfort in the
fact that though Alcestis is dead and will never return, still she
has a hero's grave, and her nobility will bring her honour like
that of the gods. Travellers by her tomb will invoke her as a
blessed daimon.

2. 3 JAN KOTT

The Veiled Alcestis, 'The Eating of the Gods',
trans. B. Taborski and E.J. Czerwinski,
Eyre Methuen, 1974, pp. 105-8

[...] In the prologue to Plautus' 'Amphitryon,' Mercury addresses
the audience:

What? Frowning because I said it's tragedy! I'm a god.
I'll change it for you: transform this selfsame play from
tragedy to comedy and never blot a line. ... We'll have a
mixture: tragicomedy.

In this, the earliest known use of the term 'tragicomedy,'
there are two different definitions. The first is that tragedy
can be turned into comedy without one word being changed. Mercury
was a god, the god of industry to boot, so he, of course, knew
structural operations; it was enough to change the code to attribute a different 'signified' to the 'significant' (icon). In the
second definition, *Faciam ut conmista sit tragicomoedia,'* what is
essential is the mixing and joining of gods, royalty and slaves in
one story.

Perhaps we should follow Mercury and his amazing first definition and attempt a final reading of 'Alcestis' seeing it first
as a tragedy and then as a comedy. Apart from 'The Bacchae' (and
there is a marked, though not easily pinpointed kinship between
Euripides' first and last masterpieces), 'Alcestis' is the only
Greek drama in which one can find the structure of ritual which,
according to the Cambridge school of anthropology (Jane Harrison
and Gilbert Murray), is also the 'deep form' of tragedy. (1) The
six agones [encounters] of 'Alcestis' correspond almost exactly
to the six successive elements of this 'metaform': first, a
contest between a god and his adversary - Apollo and Death in the
prologue; second, *pathos,* or suffering - Alcestis' farewell to her
marriage bed, children and Admetus, and her terror when she hears
Hades calling her; third, a *messenger* announcing death - the old
servant, who gives the sad tidings to Heracles; fourth, *threnos* -
Admetus' lament on his return from the burial; fifth, *anagnorisis,*
or reversal - the recognition of Alcestis in the strange woman;
and sixth, the final *theophany* - the return of the resurrected
wife to the house. This is how T.S. Eliot, influenced perhaps by
the Cambridge anthropologists, interpreted 'Alcestis' in 'The
Cocktail Party':

It is a serious matter
To bring someone from the dead ...
Ah, but we die to each other daily.

But in Euripides' 'Alcestis,' only one of the six elements of
'ritual form' - the suffering and death of the heroine - retains
its tragic *serio*. Admetus' lament is treated ironically, and two
elements - Apollo's agon with Death and the sobering of the drunken demigod - are clearly farcical. The price of recognition is
betrayal, and the epilogue is only a mock theophany. Tragedy
turns into comedy, and the last scene has the tone and gestures
of satyr drama again. Maurice Regnault's paradox applies to
'Alcestis' as to no other play: 'Comedy is born from the absence
of tragedy in a tragic world.'

Mercury has already changed 'Alcestis.' So let us now read it
as comedy. Following Northrop Frye, one can demonstrate its
model as the succession of three periods: the time of mourning
and parting; the time of general confusion and temporary loss of
identity 'usually portrayed by the stock device of impenetrable
disguise'; (2) and finally, the time of recognition in which the
heroes find themselves and their new place in the reborn community.
'As the hero gets closer to the heroine and opposition is overcome,'
Frye writes in The Argument of Comedy, 'all the right-thinking

people come over to his side. Thus a new social unit is formed on
the stage, and the moment that this social unit crystallizes is the
'moment of comic resolution.' (3)

In the first phase, which corresponds liturgically to the
season of Lent, the lovers are separated and the hero or heroine
undergoes a 'ritual' death. This phase is often dominated by cruel
laws, such as the inhuman condition that Admetus has to find a substitute who will agree to die for him. In the second phase, that
of lost identity, it is not only Alcestis who has assumed the
'impenetrable disguise'; Admetus, too, on his return to the empty
house from the burial, has lost his social place and thereby lost
himself. The third phase, of reconciliation and renewal, consists,
in comedy, of the lovers' finding each other, and ends with the
wedding.

In the Greek marriage ceremony, the most solemn moment was the
lifting of the veil by the bride in the presence of her future husband and the wedding guests. This moment, the anakalypteria, is
represented most expressively in the metope sculptures at Selin-
unte: the bride unveils herself with a ceremonious gesture.

In the epilogue of 'Alcestis,' Heracles brings a veiled woman. The
veil is later lifted. But who has lifted it? At this point Admetus
is holding the Stranger by the hand, his head turned away, as if
from the sight of some horrible Gorgon. It is hardly likely that
he would dare to unveil her. It has been most often assumed that
the veil is lifted by Heracles. But if this scene is to be a repetition of the anakalypteria ceremony, the beautiful Stranger has to
lift the veil herself. In this way Alcestis marries Admetus again,
but does so as his second wife.

Error in persona, in which the wife replaces the mistress, will
later turn out to be a stock comedy situation. Admestus' mistake
will be repeated by Count Almaviva in 'The Marriage of Figaro.'
But in 'Alcestis' this comedy situation has an air of terror about
it. It is the moment when laughter dies on one's lips. Neither
reconciliation nor renewal follows. The marriage is poisoned. Read
as a comedy, anagnorisis, the recognition, is almost tragic in
'Alcestis.' In the prologue Death comes for Alcestis; in the epilogue Alcestis, raised from her grave, comes for Admetus. In
'Alcestis' the theme of Protesilaus returning for Laodamia recurs
again. The mute veiled woman is the image of Death. Only now can
we understand why Admetus was terrified when he took the Stranger by
the hand. Her hand was icy.

Read as a tragedy, 'Alcestis' ends with a mock resurrection;
read as a comedy, 'Alcestis' ends with a deathly marriage. 'I have
never understood the difference people make between the comic and
the tragic,' Ionesco wrote in 'Expérience du Théâtre'. 'The
"comic" ... seems to me more hopeless than the "tragic." The
"comic" offers no escape ...'

The unveiling is an allegory of Truth. 'Time unveiling Truth'
was, following the ancient pattern, a frequent theme in the sculpture and painting of the Renaissance and the Baroque, as well as
a rhetorical adage. '... to unmask falsehood and bring truth to
light,' Shakespeare wrote in 'The Rape of Lucrece.' The lifting
of the veil in 'Alcestis' is the moment of truth. But this final
gesture is ambiguous. The Stranger has unveiled herself, but

'Alcestis' has remained veiled.

NOTES

1 Gilbert Murray, Excursions on the Ritual Forms Preserved in
   Greek Tragedy, in Jane Harrison, 'Themis', Cambridge, 1912,
   p. 363.
2 'A Natural Perspective', Harcourt, Brace & World, N.Y., 1965,
   pp. 76 ff.
3 The Argument of Comedy, 'English Institute Essays', ed.
   D.A. Robertson, jr, Columbia University Press, N.Y., 1944,
   p. 59.

'THE BACCHAE'

2. 4 ROBERT GRAVES

     Dionysus's Nature and Deeds, (*) 'The Greek
     Myths', Penguin, 1955, vol. 1, pp. 103-7

At Hera's orders the Titans seized Zeus's newly-born son Dionysus,
a horned child crowned with serpents and, despite his transforma-
tions, tore him into shreds. These they boiled in a cauldron,
while a pomegranate-tree sprouted from the soil where his blood
had fallen; but, rescued and reconstituted by his grandmother
Rhea, he came to life again. Persephone, now entrusted with his
charge by Zeus, brought him to King Athamas of Orchomenus and his
wife Ino, whom she persuaded to rear the child in the women's
quarters, disguised as a girl. But Hera could not be deceived,
and punished the royal pair with madness, so that Athamas killed
their son Learches, mistaking him for a stag. (1)
    Then, on Zeus's instructions, Hermes temporarily transformed
Dionysus into a kid or a ram, and presented him to the nymphs
Macris, Nysa, Erato, Bromie, and Bacche, of Heliconian Mount Nysa.
They tended Dionysus in a cave, cosseted him, and fed him on honey,
for which service Zeus subsequently placed their images among the
stars, naming them the Hyades. It was on Mount Nysa that Dionysus
invented wine, for which he is chiefly celebrated. (2)
    When he grew to manhood Hera recognized him as Zeus's son,
despite the effeminacy to which his education had reduced him, and
drove him mad also. He went wandering all over the world, accompanied by his tutor Silenus and a wild army of Satyrs and Maenads,
whose weapons were the ivy-twined staff tipped with a pine-cone,
called the *thyrsus*, and swords and serpents and fear-imposing bull-
roarers. He sailed to Egypt, bringing the vine with him; and at
Pharos King Proteus received him hospitably. Among the Libyans of
the Nile Delta, opposite Pharos, were certain Amazon queens whom
Dionysus invited to march with him against the Titans and restore
King Ammon to the kingdom from which he had been expelled.
Dionysus's defeat of the Titans and restoration of King Ammon was

the earliest of his many military successes. (3)

He then turned east and made for India. Coming to the Euphrates,
he was opposed by the King of Damascus, whom he flayed alive, but
built a bridge across the river with ivy and vine; after which a
tiger, sent by his father Zeus, helped him across the river Tigris.
He reached India, having met with much opposition by the way, and
conquered the whole country, which he taught the art of vini-
culture, also giving it laws and founding great cities. (4)

On his return he was opposed by the Amazons, a horde of whom he
chased as far as Ephesus. A few took sanctuary in the Temple of
Artemis, where their descendants are still living; others fled to
Samos and Dionysus followed them in boats, killing so many that
the battlefield is called Panhaema. Near Phloeum some of the ele-
phants which he had brought from India died, and their bones are
still pointed out. (5)

Next, Dionysus returned to Europe by way of Phrygia, where his
grandmother Rhea purified him of the many murders he had committed
during his madness, and initiated him into her Mysteries. He then
invaded Thrace; but no sooner had his people landed at the mouth
of the river Strymon than Lycurgus, King of the Edonians, opposed
them savagely with an ox-goad, and captured the entire army,
except Dionysus himself, who plunged into the sea and took refuge
in Thetis's grotto. Rhea, vexed by this reverse, helped the
prisoners to escape, and drove Lycurgus mad: he struck his own
son Dryas dead with an axe, in the belief that he was cutting down
a vine. Before recovering his senses he had begun to prune the
corpse of its nose and ears, fingers and toes; and the whole land
of Thrace grew barren in horror of his crime. When Dionysus,
returning from the sea, announced that this barrenness would continue unless Lycurgus were put to death, the Edonians led him to
Mount Pangaeum, where wild horses pulled his body apart. (6)

Dionysus met with no further opposition in Thrace, but
travelled on to his well-beloved Boeotia, where he visited Thebes,
and invited the women to join his revels on Mount Cithaeron,
Pentheus, King of Thebes, disliking Dionysus's dissolute appearance, arrested him, together with all his Maenads, but went mad
and, instead of shackling Dionysus, shackled a bull. The Maenads
escaped again, and went raging out upon the mountains, where they
tore calves in pieces. Pentheus attempted to stop them; but,
inflamed by wine and religious ecstasy, they rent him limb from
limb. His mother Agave led the riot, and it was she who wrenched
off his head. (7)

At Orchomenus the three daughters of Minyas, by name Alcithoë,
Leucippe, and Arsippe, or Aristippe, or Arsinoë, refused to join
in the revels, though Dionysus himself invited them, appearing in
the form of a girl. He then changed his shape, becoming success-
ively a lion, a bull, and a panther, and drove them insane.
Leucippe offered her own son Hippasus as a sacrifice - he had been
chosen by lot - and the three sisters, having torn him to pieces
and devoured him, skimmed the mountains in a frenzy until at last
Hermes changed them into birds, though some say that Dionysus
changed them into bats. (8) The murder of Hippasus is annually
atoned at Orchomenus, in a feast called Agrionia ('provocation to
savagery'), when the women devotees pretend to seek Dionysus and

then, having agreed that he must be away with the Muses, sit in a
circle and ask riddles, until the priest of Dionysus rushes from
his temple, with a sword, and kills the one whom he first
catches. (9)

When all Boeotia had acknowledged Dionysus's divinity, he made
a tour of the Aegean Islands, spreading joy and terror wherever
he went.   Arriving at Icaria, he found that his ship was unsea-
worthy, and hired another from certain Tyrrhenian sailors who
claimed to be bound for Naxos.   But they proved to be pirates and,
unaware of his godhead, steered for Asia, intending to sell him
there as a slave.   Dionysus made a vine grow from the deck and
enfold the mast, while ivy twined about the rigging; he also
turned the oars into serpents, and became a lion himself, filling
the vessel with phantom beasts and the sound of flutes, so that
the terrified pirates leaped overboard and became dolphins. (10)

It was at Naxos that Dionysus met the lovely Ariadne whom
Theseus had deserted, and married her without delay.   She bore him
Oenopion, Thoas, Staphylus, Latromis, Euanthes, and Tauropolus.
Later, he placed her bridal chaplet among the stars. (11)

From Naxos he came to Argos and punished Perseus, who at first
opposed him and killed many of his followers, by inflicting a madness on the Argive women: they began devouring their own infants
raw.   Perseus hastily admitted his error, and appeased Dionysus by
building a temple in his honour.

Finally, having established his worship throughout the world,
Dionysus ascended to Heaven, and now sits at the right hand of
Zeus as one of the Twelve Great Ones.   The self-effacing goddess
Hestia resigned her seat at the high table in his favour; glad
of any excuse to escape the jealous wranglings of her family, and
knowing that she could always count on a quiet welcome in any
Greek city which it might please her to visit.   Dionysus then
descended by way of Lerna, to Tartarus where he bribed Persephone
with a gift of myrtle to release his dead mother, Semele.   She
ascended with him into Artemis's temple at Troezen; but, lest
other ghosts should be jealous and aggrieved, he changed her name
and introduced her to his fellow-Olympians as Thyone.   Zeus
placed an apartment at her disposal, and Hera preserved an angry
but resigned silence. (12)

NOTES

1   Euripides: 'Bacchae' 99-102; Onomacritus, quoted by
    Pausanias: viii. 37.3; Diodorus Siculus: iii. 62; 'Orphic
    Hymn' xlv. 6; Clement of Alexandria: 'Address to the Greeks'
    ii. 16.
2   Apollodorus: iii. 4. 3; Hyginus: 'Fabula' 182; Theon on
    Aratus's 'Phenomena' 177; Diodorus Siculus: iii. 68-69;
    Apollonius Rhodius: iv. 1131; Servius on Virgil's Eclogues'
    vi. 15.
3   Apollodorus: iii. 5. 1; Aeschylus: 'The Edonians, a Fragment';
    Diodorus Siculus: iii. 70-71.
4   Euripides: 'Bacchae' 13; Theophilus, quoted by Plutarch: 'On
    Rivers' 24; Pausanias: x. 29. 2; Diodorus Siculus: ii. 38;

Strabo: xi. 5. 5; Philostratus: 'Life of Apollonius of Tyana'
ii. 8-9; Arrian: 'Indica' 5.
5   Pausanias: vii. 2. 4-5; Plutarch: 'Greek Questions' 56.
6   Apollodorus: iii. 5. 1; Homer: 'Iliad' vi. 130-40.
7   Theocritus: 'Idylls' xxvi.; Ovid: 'Metamorphoses' iii. 714 ff.;
     Euripides: 'Bacchae', passim.
8   Ovid: 'Metamorphoses' iv. 1-40; 390-415; Antoninus Liberalis:
     10; Aelian: 'Varia Historia' iii. 42; Plutarch: 'Greek
     Questions' 38.
9   Plutarch: loc. cit.
10   'Homeric Hymn to Dionysus' 6 ff.; Apollodorus: iii. 5. 3; Ovid:
     'Metamorphoses' iii. 577-699.
11   Scholiast on Apollonius Rhodius: iii. 996; Hessiod: 'Theogony'
     947; Hyginus: 'Poetic Astronomy' ii. 5.
12   Apollodorus: iii. 5. 3; Pausanias: ii. 31. 2.
*   The literary ancestry of the myth.

2. 5   D.J. CONACHER

Dramatic Analysis, 'Euripidean Drama', University
of Toronto Press, Toronto and London, 1967,
pp. 59-72

[...] The 'Bacchae' is first and foremost the tragedy of King
Pentheus. As such, it shows what happens, and *why* it must happen,
to a king who denies Dionysus and declares that his people shall
live without him. The revelation of Dionysus, first of his meaning and then of his power, is, of course, fundamental to this
demonstration. But it is the tragedy of Pentheus which determines
the dramatic action of the play and the significant changes in its
choral themes.
    The dramatic movement of the 'Bacchae' expresses the gradual
shift from the good to the bad potentialities of Dionysianism, a
change which arises from the continued suppression of the religion
by King Pentheus and which results in the ruin of the oppressor.
The crucial conflict is presented in a series of tense scenes between the disguised god and his persecutor, which occupy the middle
portions of the play. However, it is through the Chorus and
through the reports of off-stage happenings that the full significance of this conflict is grasped. The Chorus is particularly
well suited to the expression of the group emotionalism of the
cult, and it is chiefly through this instrument that the poet
indicates the declension from a state of holy equilibrium to one
of violent outrage which the persecution of Pentheus brings about.
    In the opening passages of the play itself, the Chorus and
Teiresias express, the one in poetic terms, the other in rational,
the positive and beneficent aspects of Dionysianism. The *parodos*
(in content suggestive of what the dithyramb, the cult song in
honour of Dionysus, may once have been) expresses the vigorous
happiness, the innocent, even controlled, exhaltation of the
initiate. Here the bacchant is one 'who purifies his life and
delights his soul with worship among his fellows'; here the maenads

are exhorted, for all their revelling, to be 'reverent in the handling of the violent thyrsus.' The vivid description of the *oreibasia* [frenzied dancing and racing in the mountains] in the epode and particularly of the leader's thirst for blood of the slain victim provides a moment of sinister anticipation. But the main, and certainly the overt, emphasis of this lyric is on the joyous abandon of Dionysian worship and on the gifts ('the land flowing with milk and wine and honey') which it brings.

To the lyric extravagances of this exotic chorus, the two aged Bacchants who now appear provide a grotesquely striking contrast. Cadmus and Teiresias, royal grandfather and aged yet ageless priest, have important functions to fulfil vis-à-vis Pentheus, but the purpose of the preliminary 'duet' between them is surely to indicate, not without comic overtones (Dionysus is not a solemn god), that the mysterious power of Dionysus extends to the old and wise as well as to the young and female. Such at any rate is the effect of sprightly decisions of the aged pair to dispense with chariots and to dance all night on the mountain in honour of the god.

From the beginning of the scene, the wisdom of Teiresias is emphasized: three times in Cadmus' opening speech he is called *sophos* in himself or in his attributes. Thus even before the King can voice his suspicions, an association between Dionysianism and wisdom is established and this is rendered the more explicit by Teiresias' own warning (the context is the new religion):

> About the gods, we apply no subtle reasoning. Ancestral teach-
> ings, coeval with time itself, no argument will overthrow,
> whatever cleverness has been devised by lofty minds.

(Through the timeless personage Teiresias, the poet skilfully removes us from the specific historical context, for what the new religion *signifies,* which is what we are concerned with here, is 'coeval with time itself.')

The first speech of the young King Pentheus (who now confronts the aged initiates) is a masterpiece of characterization: each disclosure with which he thinks to unveil the new religion reveals the King himself:

> ... Our women, I hear, have abandoned our homes for feigned
> Bacchic revels scampering about in bushy hiding-places in the
> hills.... Full stand the wine bowls midst their revelling
> bands, as now one and now another girl goes slinking off to
> serve some master's lusts, pretending (would you believe it?)
> to be 'inspired maenads'! Not Bacchus but Aphrodite is their
> leader!

Of the alleged god, it is his 'newness' (contrast the wise Teiresias' complete disregard for this aspect) and his suspected attraction for women ('blond scented hair, fresh face and bedroom eyes!') which particularly arouse Pentheus' ire. Throughout the speech, the telling choice of words, the vivid images reveal the heart of Pentheus and serve to anticipate the scene in which the god will lure him to his doom: the King's righteous wrath, here

misapplied, assails the very deeds to which he would be privy.
  The action of the whole central portion of the play, from this
manifesto of Pentheus' till his dreadful 'seduction' by Dionysus
presents a series of tests or 'revelations' by which the King is
given ever stronger and more compelling inducements to believe in
the divinity of the god he is rejecting. The first of these is the
quietest, though morally and 'philosophically' the most persuasive:
the favourable witness of Cadmus and more particularly of Teiresias, which carries the weight of family authority and of traditional religious wisdom.
  The ambiguity of Teiresias' role lies in the paradox that Teiresias the wise man (the initial emphasis on his wisdom has already
been remarked) is here used as a champion of Dionysianism, the
realm of irrational ecstasy. On the one hand, the prophet, in
revealing that the new religion is allied with the traditional,
instinctive 'wisdom of the ages,' indicates the proper limits of
more sophisticated thought. [...] On the other hand, in contrast
with the more 'manic' effects of the Chorus (not to mention the
off-stage maenads and indeed the whole terrifying action of the
play), Teiresias does not represent the philosophic, the intellectual acceptance of Dionysianism.   Thus, even as he deprecates the
over-confident rationalism which would reject this mysterious
force, he allows the King (and us) to look at Dionysianism in
something like the light of reason. In so doing, it is inevitable
(considering his poet and the times) that he should blend the
mythical tradition, in which 'dramatically' he speaks, with the
language of fifth century sophistic thought.
  As one of the inducements to acceptance of the new religion,
Teiresias 'rationalizes' - or at least reduces the absurdity of -
certain incredible stories of Dionysus' birth at which he imagines
certain hard-headed rationalists like Pentheus may laugh. True to
the role we have described as his, he shows that this kind of fun-
damentalism is not in question; he provides instead another 'myth'
explaining how the first 'impossible story' arose - a 'pseudo-
scientific' account, perhaps, but one in which the details
(whether we accept them or not) have no bearing on Dionysus himself. More impressive, however, is the prophet's explanation of
the real meaning of Dionysus, especially in his positive and beneficent aspect, for man. He tells us, in effect, that man cannot
live by bread alone; that to Demeter's 'dry element' Dionysus adds
the moist draught of the grapes as a complementary portion, that
draught 'which brings to weary men relief from pain, which brings
sleep, a release from the ills of every day and which is the only
cure for all our woes.' For the rest, Teiresias adds one or two
of the enthusiastic 'manic' effects of Dionysus, by which the god
will be a boon to the state and a bane to her enemies: prophecy
(a significant admission from Apollo's priest) and, in battle,
panic affecting whole armies before they can even touch the spear.
The King's suspicions, too, are simply answered: self-control
lies in the worshipper's own nature and so the chaste initiate
will not be corrupted by the Bacchic revels. [...]
  Whatever Pentheus (or we) may think of the sophistic aspects of
Teiresias' defence of Dionysianism, dramatically the important
point must still be that, with all his traditional authority, he

has defended it. In these terms, it is the prophetic warning of
the wise man which is most significant for Pentheus and for the
action of the play:

> ... this god you will see ... great throughout Greece.
> Pentheus, mark my words: Don't boast that force has real
> power in mortal affairs and don't, if you have some opinion
> which is really sick and false, mistake that thought for
> wisdom.

It is the Chorus which, in the ensuing *stasimon,* picks up the
essential thematic material in Teiresias' statements about wisdom,
cleverness and the Dionysian spirit. Throughout the play, the
Chorus is, of course, the instrument which conveys the essential
Dionysian ecstasy, first in joy and then in fury, just as it is
the recorder of the Dionysian reaction to the various successive
stages in the King's long battle with the god. Now, therefore,
the Chorus combines its plaint against the *hybris* and impious
cleverness with a vivid account of the joy and peace which Dionysus can bring to the humble heart. In all this, the lyric extends
and deepens Teiresias' meaning in a way which, for all his powers,
is quite beyond the prophet: the joys of Dionysianism can here be
expressed with an immediacy possible only in the choral song and
dance. In the cries of the Maenads, the praise of the traditional
earthy wisdom at which the philosophic Teiresias has hinted
acquires a more authentic ring.

> [Dionysus]...
> Whose gifts are joy and union of soul in dancing,
> Joy in music of flutes,
> Joy when sparkling wine at feasts of the gods
> Soothes the sore regret,
> Banishes every grief,
> When the reveller rests, enfolded deep
> In the cool shade of ivy-shoots,
> On wine's soft pillow of sleep.

> Cleverness is not wisdom, nor is it wisdom to ponder matters
> beyond mortal ken. Life is short: who would pursue such
> lofty thoughts would miss the present pleasure. Not for me
> the mad and foolish ways of such as these.

As the King persists in the persecution of the god and his
followers, there follows a sequence of miracles, awesome proofs,
in an ascending scale, of the divinity which Pentheus questions.
In a series of 'cat-and-mouse' scenes between these miracles, the
'captive' Dionysus, disguised as his own priest, makes trial of
Pentheus and gently leads him on. Each of these miracles suggests
a different aspect of the god, while the irony of the intervening
dialogues reflects a potentially sinister combination of gentleness and power.
    The first miracle symbolizes the liberating force of Dionysus.
Even as the servant leads in the captive Dionysus, 'this beast
gentle and submissive towards us,' he announces the miraculous

escape of the Theban maenads from Pentheus' chains. This irony
(which is lost on Pentheus) is sustained throughout the scene by
the god's quiet confidence before the bullying threats of his tor-
mentor. The themes of the preceding episode and chorus are
sounded once again. First, there is the old quarrel about 'wisdom'
(here the play on the words for 'wisdom,' 'moderation' and 'right
conduct' clearly indicates the ethical overtones of Dionysus'
claims); then come the usual suspicions about sexual license
afforded by the Dionysian rites (here the King's insistent curiosity about the *night-time* orgies is itself a little suspect); at
the end of the episode, Pentheus' threat to strip Dionysus of his
sacred accoutrements (the *thyrsus,* the flowing locks of hair)
anticipates the subsequent unmanning of Pentheus himself in his
later attempts to strip the veil of secrecy from the Dionysian
rites.

In the following *stasimon,* the Chorus continues its celebration
of Dionysian myth and cult, but now the note of joy begins to give
way to the plaintive fear of the oppressor as the maenads ponder
the imprisonment of their leader. The description of Pentheus as
a chthonic, dragon-sired monster is suggestive both of the 'gigantic' qualities of a theomachist and, perhaps, of a latent Dionysianism; this 'monstrous' aspect of Pentheus reappears in his own
distorted image of himself when he has fallen completely under the
sway of Dionysus. And in the prayers of the Chorus the *thyrsus*
appears for the first time as a weapon against the *hybris* of the
oppressor.

If the first miracle, the freeing of the Theban women, is
meant to suggest the liberating power of Dionysianism, the 'palace
miracles' must surely symbolize its destructive force within any
individual who would suppress it. Dionysus' account of his escape,
in which Pentheus is described as struggling and panting to ensnare
a phantom bull, underlines, perhaps, the sexual aspect of Pentheus'
private struggle. The earthquake which, again according to Dionysus, 'destroys the palace of King Pentheus,' is a continuation, on
a larger, less intimate scale, of this portent of the god's destructive power; and the springing up of the flame over Semele's
tomb is yet another manifestation of his divinity. That this destruction did not occur in any completely literal sense has been
well established by various scholars. The 'Bacchae' is not realistic drama, and here, as Winnington-Ingram has well observed, 'it
is essential to hold fast to the symbolic interpretation.' No one
has any difficulty in believing in the phantom quality of the bull
which Dionysus describes Pentheus as struggling with, and whose
effect on Pentheus, as well as on ourselves, is real enough. It
is the same with the alleged destruction of the palace. The fact
that Pentheus emerges from the palace with no mention of this destruction indicates, as Winnington-Ingram has shown, that 'he has
come less from a scene of real cataclysm than from a nightmare of
terrors and phantoms and futile struggles in the dark.' Now some
spectacular or theatrical manifestation of these powerful effects
is needed, just as, on the literal level, a messenger speech is
often supported by the subsequent showing of a murdered or a dying
hero. Such a need would here be satisfied by a sheet of flame
from the tomb of Semele and by the Chorus's onstage observation of

cracks (not necessarily visible to the audience) in the lintels of
the temple columns.

The herdsman's account of the bacchantes on the mountain presents the last of the miracles by which the *amathia* [ignorance] of
Pentheus is tested. This time the revelation is effected on a
still broader and more terrifying scale, including yet transcending the partial revelations already made and anticipating the
horrors still to come.

So far the Chorus has shown us something of the peaceful libera-
tion of the Dionysian urge, and the characterization of Pentheus,
together with his hopeless struggles to imprison the god, has suggested the dangers, within the individual, of suppressing it. Now
we are given a first-hand account of what happens within the
thiasos itself (that *group* manifestation of Dionysianism which is its
only true fulfilment) when the impulse of the god is interfered
with. The most striking feature of this account is, of course, the
contrast between the *thiasoi* (or bands of maenads) before and after
they are hunted by the herdsmen of the King. By his description of
the modest, sleeping maenads, the messenger specifically gives the
lie to Pentheus' prurient suggestions. ('With limbs relaxed in
slumber, they lay in random yet modest postures on the ground, just
as they'd fallen; not as *you* say, drunk and seeking Cypris in the
forest's solitude.') This impression continues as, through the
Herdsman's eyes, we watch the maenads wake and rise up ('a spectacle of wondrous grace to see'), don their ritual garb and go
about their Bacchic activities. These include suckling the young
of wild gazelles and wolves and breakfasting in the woods on milk,
honey and wine secured by the mere tap of the *thyrsus* - a nice
symbol of escape for women from the mundane activities of their
'real' world.

Not until the herdsmen attempt to capture them do the maenads
go berserk. Now for the first time the dread *thyrsus* is raised in
violence and, as the herdsmen flee (a vivid illustration of that
'panic' effect of Dionysus which Teiresias has mentioned), there
follow the rending of the cattle and the plundering of the villages
at the hands of the rampaging women. In this brilliant passage we
have, of course, a representation of the ritual Dionysian *sparagmos*
[tearing to pieces of the sacrificial animal], as well as an indication of the terrible catastrophe awaiting Pentheus. As in the
case of the *sparagmos* of Pentheus, we see what happens when the
Dionysian instinct surges wildly out of control in reaction to such
dangerous repression.

The Bacchae is a drama of tensions, external and internal, and
so we may expect violent changes in direction on the part of its
warring elements, as one force yields suddenly to another, or as
one aspect of character suddenly reappears in a different and more
powerful guise. One such volte-face we have just encountered in
the terrifying transformation of the Theban *thiasoi*. Another now
occurs in the soul of Pentheus. After summoning the troops against
the raging maenads and rejecting with suspicion Dionysus' last
attempts to dissuade him, Pentheus suddenly finds himself agreeing
to follow Dionysus to the hills, there to indulge in the guilty joy
of spying on the bacchantes.

Critics have tended to attribute Pentheus' sudden yielding to

Dionysus simply to the supernatural mesmerization of the god.   It
is true that Dionysus, when he finally decides to lure Pentheus to
his destruction, radically changes his approach: instead of seeking to dissuade the King, he now appears to abet his efforts to
circumvent the maenads.   But in bringing the suspicious King
within his power, Dionysus makes use of tendencies already present
in the psyche of Pentheus.   The most startling break in the King's
resistance to the god comes with his sudden admission of a desire
to see the maenads at their secret revels.   Even here, the policeman in Pentheus still masks the guilty puritan voyeur and the
unconscious blend of motives is brilliantly illustrated in the
assertions, wrung from him by the god, first of the pain, then of
the pleasure, which the prospective sight will bring him.   Thus,
in the first of these so-called mesmerizing scenes, it is the
natural rather than the supernatural element which dominates.   In
the *last* scene between the god and the King this emphasis is
reversed.   In this grimly comic sequence, Pentheus, dressed as a
bacchante, titivates like a girl before a party and shows in other
ways that he is beside himself, that the god has now 'possessed'
him.   Dionysus himself has indicated the kind of difference we may
expect between the two scenes we are discussing: for at the end
of the first (as he leads Pentheus indoors) he cries:

> Dionysus, to your work ... first cast him from his wits,
> setting a touch of madness on him: while sane, he'll never
> willingly don female garb, but mad, he will.

Even so, this divine madness, this 'possession' of the King by the
god, is not completely contrary to his nature.   We have already
seen signs of the suppressed Dionysian in Pentheus, and Teiresias
has told us that true *sophrosyne* [intelligence, wisdom, know-
ledge] will not be corrupted by the god.   Under Pentheus' suppression, Dionysianism has turned perverse - in the King himself as in
his female subjects.   On stage, it takes the maddening of the King
to make this manifest.
    Thus the maddening of Pentheus has its *beginnings,* at least, in
psychological realism.   This blending of the natural and the supernatural is, on occasion, a very typical Euripidean device.   The
power and meaning of Dionysianism finds its best dramatic expression in mythical terms, but it is by such means as these that the
poet lets us see the reality beneath the symbol.
    The ironic effect of the 'cat-and-mouse' scenes between Pentheus
and Dionysus reaches a new height in this last encounter.   Previously, that effect has depended on our awareness of the *real* contrast in power between the bullying King and the gently submissive
god.   Now the tragic delusion on which Pentheus' personality is
based takes on a new and more terrifying dimension: the inspired
King acquires a Dionysian urge for effeminate grace even as he
feels the strength within himself to overthrow the mountain with
his own bare hands.   In both these aberrations the subtle deceptions of Dionysus (an Iago to Pentheus' noble, self-deluding
Othello) encourage him, till finally the King's responses blend
with the god's to bring the irony to its excruciating climax:

DIONYSUS: You will come home borne aloft...
PENTHEUS: What luxury you forecast for me!
DIONYSUS: ...in your mother's arms.
PENTHEUS: You'll spoil me with such treatment!
DIONYSUS: What a spoiling that will be!
PENTHEUS: And yet it is my due.

The choral odes which complement the various exchanges between
Pentheus and Dionysus trace a gradual declension from the serene
joy of the early odes to savage fury as the destructive power of
Dionysianism is finally unleashed. We have already noted in the
second stasimon the beginnings of the Chorus's fear of the 'monster' Pentheus and the first hints at violence and vengeance.
This destructive note recurs with more sinister emphasis in the
third stasimon which follows the gods' decision to end the trial
and begin the punishment of Pentheus.

In the opening strophe, the maenad's rapture in the all-night
revels is likened, in a brilliant image, to the delight of a fawn,
who has finally escaped the huntsman's pack; here, too, the fawn's
joy in the leafy stillness beyond the river reflects the Chorus's
own relief at the coming deliverance from Pentheus.

In the antistrophe the theme changes from escape to retribution: the slow and secret hunting down of the unholy, of those
who seek to know more than what tradition has sanctified as
natural for men. Even here the hint of vengeance is restrained:
the Chorus dwells rather on the impersonal working out of divine
justice.

Only in the refrain which follows both strophes do we catch a
note of triumph more personal and violent:

What, then, is 'cleverness'? Or, mid mortals, what prize from
the gods is nobler than to hold a triumphant hand over the
heads of one's enemies? And what is noble is forever dear.

Thus the violent joy of vengeance replaces, for a moment, the old
distinctions between true and false wisdom which the Chorus had
picked up from Teiresias. It is only a flash - the concluding
epode returns to the 'escape theme' on an almost platitudinous
level - but it shows us in what direction the Chorus, and so the
Dionysiac spirit, is turning as a result of Pentheus' suppression.
[...]

The last song of the Chorus comes after the Messenger's
announcement of the terrible *sparagmos* of Pentheus at the hands of
his mother and the Theban maenads. It is a pure song of triumph
without pity for the violent destruction of Pentheus and nothing
more. The Chorus has come full cycle in its declension from
innocent joy to savage delight in the destruction of the enemy.

The Messenger's account of Pentheus' destruction needs little
comment. Perhaps the most striking feature of this splendid passage is the skill with which the poet has adapted these traditional
and symbolic features of the Bacchic *sparagmos* to the dramatic
requirements of his narrative. Thus Agave's madness creeps on her
gradually: at first she sees both beast and human spy, later, only
the beast; as for the tree, it is Pentheus himself who, ever his

own worst enemy, requests this vantage-point for spying on the maenads.   Throughout the speech, the poet succeeds in repeating,
without loss of dramatic power, themes basic to the meaning of the
play: witness the brief glimpse we are given of peaceful and
joyous maenads, *before* they are disturbed; witness, too, the
mysterious inability of Pentheus to see them in this state!   And
finally, when the whole dread tale is told, the Messenger himself
answers the Chorus's earlier questions about what is the wisest
and what the fairest thing for man:

> Humility and reverence in matters divine: this is fairest,
> and I think too that this is the wisest practice for men who
> follow it.

This is precisely the lesson which Teiresias the wise had sought to
teach Pentheus.

The *exodos* of this play draws together its human and divine
elements in a remarkably successful blend of realistic drama and
effective 'theatre.'   In the savage little *kommos* preceding it, the
chorus has cruelly played on the delusion of Agave as she carries
on-stage the head of Pentheus.   In sharp contrast with this cruelty
is the gentle ministering of Cadmus who now leads his daughter step
by step back to reality.   The psychological subtlety of this passage greatly enhances its pathos: the climax of Agave's dreadful
recognition is, perhaps, the play's most poignant moment.   Hard on
this discovery comes the spectacular appearance of Dionysus, who
states, in the pitiless terms typical of Euripidean gods, the reasons for all this suffering.   Since the god had been present in
disguised form throughout the play, this appearance in the full
authority and glory of the godhood which he has so awesomely
established strikes one as dramatically more appropriate than many
of Euripides' theophanies.

The role of Cadmus throughout the *exodos* is interesting and
important.   It is through Cadmus, the least guilty member of his
family, that the dramatist expresses most fully an awareness of the
family's collective guilt. [...] Again it is the gentleness of
Cadmus, both in his ministering to Agave and in his homely but
effective little encomium of Pentheus which is set up as a contrast
with the insensitive cruelty of the god and his followers, the
Chorus.   Thus it is fitting that it should be Cadmus who rebukes
the god.   Three times, even as he recognizes the element of justice
in the punishment, he stresses that this punishment is too extreme.
Echoing the words of the servant in the 'Hippolytus,' he declares,
'Gods should not be like men in their passions.'

2. 6   WOLE SOYINKA (*)

On this Adaptation, programme note, National Theatre
Company, Old Vic, 1973

'The Bacchae' belongs to that sparse body of plays which evoke
awareness of a particular moment in a people's history, yet imbues

that moment with a hovering eternal presence. [...]

The Dionysiac impulse was not new. Essentially agrarian in origin, it was the peasant's natural evocation of, and self-immersion in, the mysterious and forceful in Nature. The Dionysiac is present, of course, in varied degrees of spiritual intensity in all religions. But Dionysiac cults found suddenly fertile soil in Greece, after centuries of near-complete domination by state-controlled Mysteries, because of peasant movement in the wake of urban expansion. Attachment to a suitable deity - in this case Dionysus - was nothing more than the natural, historic process by which populist movements (religious or political) identify themselves with mythical heroes at critical moments of social upheaval.

Dionysus was eminently suited to the social and spiritual needs of the new urban classes. His history was rich in all the ingredients of a ravaged social psyche - displacement, suppression of identity, dissociation, dispossession, trials, and the goal of restoration. He fulfilled the visceral link of the peasant personality to the rhythms of nature - growth, decay and rejuvenation. [...]

'The Bacchae' is not a play of accommodation but of group challenge and conflict. The Dionysiac religion had a powerful social impact on the slave-sustained economy of Greece. Punishment for 'economic sabotage' - malingering, rebelliousness, quota failure, etc. - was, in a sense, a disciplinary perversion of the nature-propitiation principle in traditional religion. At least it must have appeared so to the classes who provided the scapegoat in times of plague or famine. The selected sacrifice was ritualistically fed, whipped on the genitals and led in procession through the city. He was then burnt to death and his ashes were scattered to the winds. This effort to stimulate growth must have struck the oppressed groups as hardly different from the 'public deterrent' - flogging, breaking on the wheel, etc. - meted out to the mine-worker who had ruined a piece of machinery, attempted to foment labour unrest or reduced the week's profit in some other way. Both forms of imposed penance were designed to stimulate greater productivity. What the class-conscious myth of Dionysus achieved was to shift the privilege of supplying scapegoats to the class that had already monopolised all other privileges. The magic munificence of Nature requires both challenge and sacrifice in all Nature renewal myths. Pentheus the aristocrat provides both in the highly seditious version of the myth by Euripides.

I see 'The Bacchae', finally as a prodigious barbaric banquet, a manifestation of man's universal need to match himself against Nature. The more-than-hinted-at cannibalism corresponds to the periodic need of humans to swill, gorge and copulate on a scale as huge as Nature in her monstrous cycle of regeneration. The Dionysiac cult is both social therapy and reaffirmation of group solidarity. It is a celebration of life, bloody and tumultuous, an extravagant rite of the human and communal psyche.

NOTE

* Wole Soyinka is a Nigerian poet and Africa's main contemporary

playwright.   His version of 'The Bacchae' was directed by
Roland Joffé with Martin Shaw as Dionysus, John Shrapnel as
Pentheus and Constance Cummings as Agave.

SHAKESPEARE: 'TWELFTH NIGHT','MACBETH' AND 'THE WINTER'S TALE'

'TWELFTH NIGHT'

3. 1 JOHN RUSSELL BROWN

Directions for 'Twelfth Night', 'Shakespeare's
Plays in Performance', Arnold, 1966, pp. 207-10,
213-17

This play might have been designed for an age when each director
must make his name and register his mark. Yet there is one difficulty: in most productions some part of the play resists the
director's control. In Sir John's elegant 'Twelfth Night',
Malvolio yielded Sir Laurence Olivier a role in which to exploit
his impudent and plebeian comedy, and in his last line - 'I'll be
revenged on the whole pack of you' - an opportunity for the cry
of a man unmade. The grey and urban setting of the Old Vic's
production in 1950 was enlivened by an untrained ballet of sailors
and riffraff, but Peggy Ashcroft's clear, white voice was an
unechoed reminder of other directions the comedy can be given.
More commonly, without such trained stars to cross the director's
intentions, robust comics can usurp more attention than their part
in the last Act is allowed to satisfy, an intelligent Sebastian
may deny his own words, a too gentle Orsino devalue Viola's
ardour. There is need for vigilance. [...] What happened, one
wonders, before there were directors to give directions?
    For if we refer back, from the theatre to the text of the
play, we shall observe a similar lack of simplicity and uniformity.
Malvolio can be a 'turkey cock', a. common 'geck and gull' who is
told to 'shake his ears'; or a fantastic who asks what 'an alpha-
betical position portends' and speaks repeatedly 'out of his
welkin'. Yet Olivier's petty, ambitious vulgarian is also true to
the text when he addresses his mistress with 'Sweet lady, ho,ho!'
and with tags from popular ballads. Even Michael Hordern's
tortured Malvolio at the Old Vic in 1954, 'dried up, emaciated,
elongated ... (as) an El Greco' - his hands, reaching out of the

pit in the scene where Feste visits him as Sir Topas, the curate,
suggested to one critic 'the damned in the "Inferno"'- is autho-
rized by Feste's disguise, by his own first words of 'the pangs of
death' and 'infirmity', his account of how 'imagination' jades him,
and his physical and psychological isolation at the end. And yet
again, Olivia's high regard for Malvolio - she 'would not lose him
for half her dowry' - justifies Eric Porter's performance at
Stratford-upon-Avon in 1960, as a solid, efficient steward waking
with practical good sense to worlds unrealized.

   Actors seeking to express their originality will find that
'new' interpretations rise unbidden from a straightforward study
of the text. Sir Toby is usually a domesticated Falstaff, but at
the Old Vic in 1958 with tumultuous 'gulps and shouts', he was
seen as a plain 'boor'; and for this there is plenty of support
in his name, Belch, and in his talk of 'boarding and assailing',
making water and cutting 'mutton'. And the same year, at
Stratford-upon-Avon, Patrick Wymark made him young and spry with
a sense of style; for this, 'she's a beagle, true-bred' was most
appropriate language, and his easy confidence in 'consanguinity'
with Olivia and expertise in swordplay were natural accomplishments. One might imagine, too, a melancholy Sir Toby, tried in
true service and knowing from experience that 'care's an enemy
to life': his tricks upon Sir Andrew would then be a compensation
for his own retirement, his wooing - off-stage and presumably
brief - of Maria, a just and difficult tribute to her service for
him; lethargy comes with drunkenness and he 'hates a drunken
rogue'; he needs company, even that of a fool, an ass, and a
servant.

   Olivia is another role which can be seen to be of different
ages - either mature years or extreme youth; and she can be melancholy or gay. Maxine Audley at Stratford-upon-Avon in 1955 presented a gracious lady, truly grieving for the death of her
brother and strong enough to recognize an absolute passion for a
boy; this Olivia had the 'smooth, discreet and stable bearing',
the majesty, to which Sebastian and Orsino testify. And three
years later, at the same theatre, Geraldine McEwan presented her
as kittenish and cute, saved from triviality by fine timing of
movement and verse-speaking, the dignity of 'style'. And yet
another Olivia may be suggested by the text: a very young girl,
at first afraid of meeting the world and therefore living in a
fantasy capable of decreeing seven years of mourning; then a girl
solemnly repeating old saws with a new understanding of their
truth;

   Even so quickly may one catch the plague..... I do I know
   not what, and fear to find Mine eye too great a flatterer
   for my mind..... What is decreed must be ... how apt the
   poor are to be proud ... youth is bought more oft than
   begg'd or borrowed,

and forgetting her 'discreet' bearing in breathless eagerness:

   How does he love me? ... *Why,* what would you? ... not too
   fast: soft, soft! ... Well, *let* it be.... That's a degree

to love.... Yet *come* again.... I have sent after him: *he says*
he'll come.... *What* do you say? ... *Most wonderful*!

Feste, the fool, can be melancholy, or bitter, or professional,
or amorous (and sometimes impressively silent), or self-contained
and philosophical, or bawdy and impotent. Sir Andrew Aguecheek can
be patient, sunny, feckless, gormless, animated or neurotic. (In
1958 Richard Johnson gave an assured performance of this knight as
a 'paranoid manic-depressive, strongly reminiscent at times of
Lucky in "Waiting for Godot"'.) Orsino can be mature or very
young; poetic or weak; or strong but deceived; or regal and distant. The text can suggest a Viola who is pert, sentimental,
lyrical, practical, courageous or helpless. Shakespeare's words
can support all these interpretations, and others; there are few
plays which give comparable scope for enterprise and originality.
The characters, the situations and the speeches are protean. [...]
    'Twelfth Night' has received many visual interpretations: the
elegant, controlled and overtly dramatic, as a Tiepolo fresco, is
a common one; or domestic with dark shadows, like the Jacobean
interiors in Joseph Nash's 'Mansions of England in the Olden
Times'; or Italianate, free and colourful in the fashion of the
commedia dell'arte. Or the stage may be spacious and clean, like
one modern notion of what an Elizabethan platform stage was like,
or pillared, tiered and substantial, like another. Some designers
have introduced the satins and laces of Restoration England, and
others the boaters and billows of the theatre of 'Charley's Aunt'.
The main difficulty is that all these, and others, are in some
degree appropriate, usually in different parts of the play; and
yet it would be distracting to a modern audience to move from one
to another during a single performance, even if this were technically possible. If a mature production of 'Twelfth Night' is to
be considered, this problem will have to be solved in a single
way - the more urgently because the proscenium arches and lighting
devices of modern theatres have made the visual embodiment of a
play, in setting, costumes and effects, a dominating - often *the*
dominating - element of a production. [...]
    Illyria, the world of 'Twelfth Night', is obviously a land of
love, music, leisure, servants, a Duke and a Countess; it must have
dwellings, a garden, a seacoast and a 'dark house' or temporary
prison. Its institutions include a church and a chantry, a captain and officers of the law, an inn; and there must be doors or
gates. Thus far the choice of a setting is not circumscribed; it
might be English, Italian, French, Russian (before the revolution), or, with some adaptation, American or Utopian; medieval,
renaissance or modern. But incidental details of speech and
action at once limit the setting to something resembling, or
representing, English countryside and domesticity. In the first
scene there are mentioned a bank of violets, a hunt, sweet beds
of flowers, and these are followed by wind and weather, a squash
and a peascod, a willow, the hills, a beagle, roses, a yew, a
cypress and box tree, and more flowers; familiar living creatures
are a hart, a sheep-biter, a horse, a trout, a turkey-cock and a
wood-cock, a raven, lamb and dove, and hounds; daylight, champaign
(or open fields), harvest, ripeness, and oxen and wainropes easily

come to mind; the songs of nightingales, daws and owls have been
heard. The characters of the play do not talk of an elegant or
fanciful scene, although the violets and beds of flowers might be
interpreted in that way; their wain-ropes, sheep-biter and daws
belong to a countryside that knows labour and inconvenience,
as well as delights. Speaking of horrors and danger, they are
neither sophisticated nor learned; they refer to tempests, the
sea, fields, mountains, barbarous caves, and hunger. The domestic
note is almost as persistent as that of the countryside: early
in Act I, canary-wine, beef, a housewife and a buttery-bar are
mentioned; even the Duke, Orsino, speaks of knitters in the sun;
there is talk of pilchards and herrings (fresh and pickled) and
of vinegar and pepper. If a director is to attempt a responsible production of the play, he should give substance to these
references in his setting - not in an illustrative way which
provides objects for the actors to point at, but in a manner
which echoes, extends and, where appropriate, contrasts with the
dialogue and stage business. This is the mental and emotional
world of the *dramatis personae* as revealed by their language, and
the stage picture can help to establish this, not insistently,
but with subtlety.

It is the world of the play's action too, and its visual
recreation will, therefore, aid the director towards an appropriate rhythm and acting style: an Italianate setting, which is
often chosen, suggests the wrong tempo - the wrong temperature,
even - and insists on distracting contrasts between dialogue and
visual effect. An English summer takes three months to establish
itself, through April, May and June, and so does the action of
this play - as Orsino states explicitly in the last scene. It
would be convenient, therefore, to show this passage of time in
modifications to the setting during the course of the play: the
first Acts green and youthful, the last coloured with roses in
bloom and strong lights; the same setting but at different times
of the year. In the first scene Orsino would be seeking the
earliest violets; later 'beauty's a flower', 'women are as roses',
'youth's a stuff will not endure' would sound properly precarious
in view of the visual reminder of the changing seasons; a 'lenten
answer' would seem more restrictive and 'let summer bear it out'
a fuller and more inevitable judgement. Orsino might stand in
white, as the young lover in Nicholas Hillyarde's miniature
(dated about 1590), over against frail, twining roses: this
association represented for the painter his motto - '*Dat poenas
laudata fides*', or 'My praised faith procures my pain' - and it
might serve in much the same way today. 'Midsummer madness' and
'matter for a May morning', which are spoken of in Act III, would
be in key with the setting, and the talk of harvest, the grave
and the immutable yew-tree would sound in significant contrast.

The course of single days might also be suggested in the
lighting of the stage picture. Talk of hunting in the first
scene establishes the time as early morning. In the third,
Maria's remonstrance to Sir Toby about returning late 'a'nights'
belongs to the first meeting of a new day, and then coming
'early' by one's 'lethargy' implies preprandial drinking. In
II.3, the chaffing about 'being up late', Malvolio's chiding

about 'respect of ... time', and ''tis too late to go to bed now'
all suggest midnight; so one 'day' is completed in due order.
(Again Feste's song in this last mentioned scene, about 'present
mirth' and 'what's to come' and 'youth's a stuff will not endure'
will be more poignant if it seems indeed to have been sung just
before the 'night-owl', nature's reminder of death, is roused.)
The following scene, II.4, is clearly a new day with its first
lines of 'good morrow' and 'we heard last night'; and the truth
that '... women are as roses, whose fair flower Being once
display'd doth fall that very hour' is more fully expressed if
spoken in the transitory light of dawn. The next scene, II.5,
beginning with 'Come thy ways...' and with news that Malvolio has
been 'i' the sun practising behaviour to his own shadow this half
hour', is still early morning. Act III, Scene 1, which follows
with Feste speaking of the sun shining everywhere, may be at noon,
and later, when Malvolio supposes Olivia invites him to bed, his
outrageous presumption would be more apparent if it were obviously
not that 'time of day'. At the end of IV.2, Feste visits Malvolio
in prison and sings:

> I'll be with you again,
> In a trice,
> Like the old Vice,
> Your need to sustain;
> Who, with dagger of lath,
> In his rage and his wrath,
> Cries, ah, ha! to the devil....

here stage lighting could simulate a sudden, passing storm, such
as interrupts an easy summer's afternoon in England; it might
culminate in thunder. This would be an elaboration impossible to
stage in an Elizabethan theatre, but it would be appropriate in a
play which is continually concerned with the summer countryside
of England, with 'beauty that can endure wind and weather' and
which ends with a song of the rain that 'raineth every day'. Sir
Toby and Maria could take shelter from the storm, while the fool
is left to bear it out and 'pursue the sport'. The sun would shine
fully again for Sebastian's 'This is the air; that is the glorious
sun; This pearl she gave me ...', and for the high afternoon of the
ending of the comedy. Towards the close shadows might lengthen
and, as the marriages are postponed till 'golden time convents,'
the sky might become golden with a sunset's promise of another
fair day. Then as the other characters leave, to enter perhaps a
lighted house, Feste might be left in the grey-green light of early
evening to sing alone of time and youth, and of the beginning of
the world and the conclusion of a play.
   (There is in fact a double time scheme in 'Twelfth Night':
three months for the development and fulfilment of the action, and
two consecutive days for the sequence of scenes. The representation of both schemes in the setting and in the lighting may help
an audience to accept this double sense of time which suits, on
the one hand, the rapid fairy-tale transitions and the 'changeable'
characterizations, and, on the other hand, the play's suggestion of
the season's alterations and the endurance and maturing of affections.)

3. 2 C.L. BARBER

> On 'Twelfth Night', 'Shakespeare's Festive Comedy',
> Princeton University Press, Princeton, N.J., 1959,
> pp. 245-7

The most fundamental distinction the play brings home to us is the
difference between men and women. To say this may seem to labor
the obvious; for what love story does not emphasize this difference? But the disguising of a girl as a boy in 'Twelfth
Night' is exploited so as to renew in a special way our sense of
the difference. Just as a saturnalian reversal of social roles
need not threaten the social structure, but can serve instead
to consolidate it, so a temporary, playful reversal of sexual
roles can renew the meaning of the normal relation. One can add
that with sexual as with other relations, it is when the normal
is secure that playful aberration is benign. This basic security
explains why there is so little that is queazy in all Shakespeare's
handling of boy actors playing women, and playing women pretending
to be men. This is particularly remarkable in 'Twelfth Night,'
for Olivia's infatuation with Cesario-Viola is another, more fully
developed case of the sort of crush Phebe had on Rosalind. Viola
is described as distinctly feminine in her disguise, more so than
Rosalind:

> ... they shall yet belie thy happy years
> That say thou art a man. Diana's lip
> Is not more smooth and rubious; thy small pipe
> Is as the maiden's organ, shrill and sound,
> And all is semblative a woman's part.

When on her embassy Viola asks to see Olivia's face and exclaims
about it, she shows a woman's way of relishing another woman's
beauty - and sensing another's vanity: "Tis beauty truly blent...'
'I see you what you are - you are too proud.' Olivia's infatuation with feminine qualities in a youth takes her, doing 'I know
not what,' from one stage of life out into another, from shutting
out suitors in mourning for her brother's memory, to ardor for a
man, Sebastian, and the clear certainty that calls out to 'husband'
in the confusion of the last scene.

We might wonder whether this spoiled and dominating young
heiress may not have been attracted by what she could hope to dominate in Cesario's youth - but it was not the habit of Shakespeare's
age to look for such implications. And besides, Sebastian is not
likely to be dominated; we have seen him respond to Andrew when the
ninny knight thought he was securely striking Cesario:

> ANDREW: Now, sir, have I met you again? There's for you!
> SEBASTIAN: Why, there's for thee, and there, and there!

To see this manly reflex is delightful - almost a relief - for we
have been watching poor Viola absurdly perplexed behind her disguise as Sir Toby urges her to play the man: 'Dismount thy tuck,

be yare in thy preparation ... Therefor on, or strip your sword
naked; for meddle you must, that's certain.' She is driven to the
point where she exclaims in an aside: 'Pray God defend me! A
little thing would make me tell them how much I lack of a man.'
What she lacks, Sebastian has. His entrance in the final scene
is preceded by comical testimony of his prowess, Sir Andrew with
a broken head and Sir Toby halting. The particular implausibility
that there should be an identical man to take Viola's place with
Olivia is submerged in the general, beneficent realization that
there is such a thing as a man. Sebastian's comment when the confusion of identities is resolved points to the general force which
has shaped particular developments:

> So comes it, lady, you have been mistook.
> But nature to her bias drew in that.

Over against the Olivia-Cesario relation, there are Orsino-Cesario
and Antonio-Sebastian. Antonio's impassioned friendship for
Sebastian is one of those ardent attachments between young people
of the same sex which Shakespeare frequently presents, with his
positive emphasis, as exhibiting the loving and lovable qualities
later expressed in love for the other sex. Orsino's fascination
with Cesario is more complex. In the opening scene, his restless sensibility can find no object: 'naught enters there .../
But falls into abatement .../ Even in a minute.' Olivia might
be an adequate object; she at least is the Diana the sight of whom
has, he thinks, turned him to an Acteon torn by the hounds of
desires. When we next see him, and Cesario has been only three
days in his court, his entering question is 'Who saw Cesario, ho?'
and already he has unclasped to the youth 'the book even of [his]
secret soul.' He has found an object. The delight he takes in
Cesario's fresh youth and graceful responsiveness in conversation
and in service, is one part of the spectrum of love for a woman,
or better, it is a range of feeling that is common to love for a
youth and love for a woman. For the audience, the woman who is
present there, behind Cesario's disguise, is brought to mind
repeatedly by the talk of love and of the differences of men and
women in love. 'My father had a daughter loved a man ...'

> She never told her love,
> But let concealment, like a worm i' th' bud,
> Feed on her damask cheek.

This supremely feminine damsel, who 'sat like patience on a monument,' is not Viola. She is a sort of polarity within Viola,
realized all the more fully because the other, active side of
Viola does not pine in thought at all, but instead changes the
subject: '... and yet I know not. / Sir, shall we to this lady? -
Ay, that's the theme.' The effect of moving back and forth from
woman to sprightly page is to convey how much the sexes differ
yet how much they have in common, how everyone who is fully alive
has qualities of both. Some such general recognition is obliquely
suggested in Sebastian's amused summary of what happened to Olivia:

You would have been contracted to a maid;
Nor are you therein, by my life, deceiv'd:
You are betroth'd both to a maid and man.

The countess marries the man in this composite, and the count
marries the maid. He too has done he knows not what while nature
drew him to her bias, for he has fallen in love with the maid
without knowing it.

3. 3 PETER HALL

Introduction to 'Twelfth Night', published by the
Folio Society for its members, 1966, pp. 5-6

I have space only to talk of one character in depth. I pick what
is to me the most important character in the play - Feste. He is
a deliberate enigma, poised uneasily between the two worlds of the
court and the great house:

A fool that my Lady Olivia's father took much delight in.

He is bitter, insecure, singing the old half-forgotten songs to the
Duke (for nostalgia is predictably the Duke's favourite musical
companion), his jokes now tarnished and not very successful. He is
the creation of a professional entertainer, and we may perhaps
remotely relate him to John Osborne's Archie Rice, or to that
fearful misanthropy which overtakes most comics when they begin to
despise their audience. He is suffered by all, and liked by few.
He is the most perceptive and formidable character in the play.
Viola brings reality to the play by her instinct, but Feste could
often do it if he wished by his shrewdness. I believe he penetrates Viola's disguise:

Now Jove, in his next commodity of hair, send thee a beard!

He is left alone at the end of the play singing bitterly, and more
obscenely than most people realize, about the transient nature of
life.
And he is the main character of the play's most extraordinary
scene. He is a strange kind of fool, when disguised as Sir Topas
he cruelly tortures the imprisoned Malvolio. He is very perceptive about Orsino, and offers a penetrating judgement:

Now the melancholy god protect thee, and the tailor make thy
    doublet of changeable taffeta,
For thy mind is a very opal.

Feste is the critical centre of the play, the Thersites, the
Jacques without eloquence, the malcontent, the man who sees all
and says little, the cynic. It takes an indealist to be such a
cynic.
I would like now to speculate. It is known that many of the

professional fools were, in fact, defrocked priests. If the poor
boy who was educated up to be a cleric failed to get a benefice,
or if his reason or his morals dragged him away from the true
faith, there was not much open to this medieval outsider except
professional foolery. The education, the mental agility, and the
Latin tags could all find a professional use. The destructive
resentment of the failure could help his professional personality.
Such a hypothesis is impossible to prove, but it is certainly a
useful background to the actor playing Feste. It leads him without difficulty to the malice of Sir Topas's scene. Men are very
bitter about the professions that fail them.

Only one of the other characters of the play, in my opinion,
lacks three dimensions, and the life-enhancing inconsistency with
which Shakespeare regularly surprises us. This is Malvolio -
after Viola, the most famous character in the play. I find the
character drawn from the outside and slightly caricatured. The
plot makes it appear a great part - or at least offers an actor of
genius the opportunity of making it flesh. But it is two-
dimensional. Shakespeare's professional enemies were plagues and
puritans. Perhaps he could not be objective; perhaps his hatred
was too intense.

3. 4 ANNE BARTON

Programme note for 'Twelfth Night', (*) Royal
Shakespeare Company, Stratford-upon-Avon, 1969

[...] Children separated at sea, a heroine forced to disguise herself as a boy, the wise fool, a girl who reluctantly woos her own
rival in love, ill-considered vows, confusion between twins:
these are only a few of the themes which 'Twelfth Night' picks up
and elaborates from its predecessors. At the same time, this
comedy prefigures the final romances. Like Marina in 'Pericles',
or Perdita in 'The Winter's Tale', Viola simply accepts her
strange situation. She does not attempt to transform it, as
Rosalind and Julia did. Although she knows that 'youth's a stuff
will not endure', that her beauty is wasting away in boy's disguise, she insists that Time 'must untangle this, not I'. Even
when the plot seems to demand her interference, as it does at the
end of Act 3, she sits still, placing her faith in the mysterious
symmetries of a universe whose 'tempests are kind, and salt waves
fresh in love'. This trust is justified. In depicting Viola's
reunion with the brother she thought dead, her own fairy-tale
marriage with the Duke Orsino, or Sebastian's splendid match.
'Twelfth Night' is deliberately unrealistic but emotionally highly
charged in the manner of Shakespeare's last plays.

For Elizabethans, the very title of this comedy would have
stirred associations with an annual period of revelry: a feast
at which the world turned upside down, pleasure became a kind of
obligation, and ordinary rules of conduct were reversed. The sea-
captain who firsts tells Viola about Illyria might justly have
said to her what the Cheshire Cat says to Alice: 'They're all

mad here'.   Orsino and Olivia are both in abnormal states of mind
at the beginning of the play, and there are even madder characters
to come: the drunken Sir Toby, the hare-brained Andrew Aguecheek,
or Feste, the man whose profession is folly.   Even Sebastian and
Antonio will admit to temporary insanity.   Malvolio alone tries to
check this prevailing atmosphere of abandon, this abdication from
common sense.   As soon as he does so, he becomes the enemy: the
churl, the sober-sides at the carnival who refuses to yield himself to the extraordinary.   As a comedy audience, we naturally
side·with Sir Toby, Feste and Maria against this Puritan, as they
trick him into the service of just that world of play-acting and
lunacy he so loftily despised.   Thereafter, carnival will do with
him what it chooses - until the moment of awakening.

By its very nature, holiday is not eternal.   It is only an
interval in the everyday, destined to yield in the end to the
sober order it has momentarily overthrown.   In the final act of
'Twelfth Night', fantasy fights against the cold light of day.
For some characters, it is true, holiday perpetuates itself.   Viola
and Orsino, Olivia and Sebastian remain, by the special dispensa-
tion of art, in a romance world that never falters.   They recover
their sanity.   They have even gained a certain self-knowledge from
their experiences.   But it is clear that they remain privileged
inhabitants of Illyria: that place of idealistic friendships and
sudden, irrational loves, where people are shipwrecked into good
fortune, and the dead return.   Orsino does not even need to behold
Viola in her own person as a girl before accepting her as 'Orsino's
mistress, and his fancy's queen'.   The other characters of the
comedy, by contrast, are exiled into reality.   For most of them,
holiday is paid for in ways that have real life consequences.
Aguecheek creeps back to his depleted lands, rejected both by
Olivia and by the friend he trusted.   Sir Toby exits crying (in
vain) for a surgeon to dress his wounds.   His marriage to Maria is
the coldest of off-stage bargains.   Malvolio rushes away invoking
a futile vengeance 'on the whole pack of you'.   None of these
characters, in striking contradiction to Shakespeare's usual practice, can be absorbed into the harmony of the romantic plot.   They
are not even allowed to remain on stage with the happy lovers at
the end.

'Twelfth Night' denies us the complete resolution of 'A
Midsummer Night's Dream' or 'As You Like It'.   Instead, it con-
signs some of its characters to a fairy-tale world while jolting
others into reality.   The audience leaving the theatre faces its
own jolt into reality, but at least it is given Feste and not
Malvolio as its guide.   Left alone on the stage, Feste sings his
song about the ages of man, part of which will re-appear in 'King
Lear' in the mouth of another and more tragic fool.   Feste does
not attempt to judge, or even to reason. He simply states those
facts which he has known all along.   The child is permitted his
fancies: 'a foolish thing was but a toy'.   When he grows up, he
discovers that his self-deceptions are easily penetrated by the
world: 'by swaggering could I never thrive'.   The reality of wind
and rain wins out, the monotony of everyday.   The passing of time
is painful, may even seem unendurable, but there is nothing for it
but resignation, the wise acceptance of the Fool.   All holidays

come to an end. All revels wind down at last. Only in the
theatre can some people be left in Illyria. For the rest of us,
at a certain point, the play is done and we return to normality
along with Sir Toby, Aguecheek and Malvolio. 'Twelfth Night'
is over, and we have been dismissed to a world beyond holiday,
where 'the rain it raineth every day'.

NOTE

* The production was directed by John Barton with Donald Sinden
  as Malvolio and Judi Dench as Viola.

'MACBETH'

3. 5 SARAH SIDDONS (*)

     Remarks on the Character of Lady Macbeth, 'Life of
     Mrs. Siddons', Thomas Campbell, Effingham Wilson,
     1834, vol. 2, pp. 10-11, 13-34

In this astonishing creature one sees a woman in whose bosom the
passion of ambition has almost obliterated all the characteristics
of human nature; in whose composition are associated all the sub-
jugating powers of intellect and all the charms and graces of personal beauty. You will probably not agree with me as to the
character of that beauty; yet, perhaps, this difference of opinion
will be entirely attributable to the difficulty of your imagination disengaging itself from that idea of the person of her representative which you have been so long accustomed to contemplate.
According to my notion, it is of that character which I believe is
generally allowed to be most captivating to the other sex, - fair,
feminine, nay, perhaps, even fragile. [...] Such a combination
only, respectable in energy and strength of mind, and captivating
in feminine loveliness, could have composed a charm of such
potency as to fascinate the mind of a hero so dauntless, a character so amiable, so honourable as Macbeth. [...]
     Lady Macbeth, thus adorned with every fascination of mind and
person, enters for the first time, reading a part of one of those
portentous letters from her husband. [...] She then proceeds to
the investigation of her husband's character. [...]
     In this development, we find that, though ambitious, he is yet
amiable, conscientious, nay pious; and yet of a temper so irreso-
lute and fluctuating, as to require all the efforts, all the
excitement, which her uncontrollable spirit, and her unbounded
influence over him, can perform. [...]
     Shortly Macbeth appears. He announces the King's approach; and
she, insensible it should seem to all the perils which he has
encountered in battle, and to all the happiness of his safe return
to her, - for not one kind word of greeting or congratulation does
she offer, - is so entirely swallowed up by the horrible design,

which has probably been suggested to her by his letters, as to
have entirely forgotten both the one and the other. It is very
remarkable that Macbeth is frequent in expressions of tenderness
to his wife, while she never betrays one symptom of affection
towards him, till, in the fiery furnace of affliction, her iron
heart is melted down to softness. For the present she flies to
welcome the venerable gracious Duncan, with such a shew of eagerness, as if allegiance in her bosom sat crowned with devotion and
gratitude.

The Second Act

There can be no doubt that Macbeth, in the first instance, suggested his design of assassinating the king, and it is probable
that he has invited his gracious sovereign to his castle, in order
the more speedily and expeditiously to realize those thoughts [...]
Yet, on the arrival of the amiable monarch who had so honoured him
of late, his naturally benevolent and good feelings resume their
wonted power. [...] All those accumulated determents, with the violated rights of sacred hospitality bringing up the rear, rising all
at once in terrible array to his awakened conscience, he relin-
quishes the atrocious purpose, and wisely determines to proceed no
further in the business. But. now, behold his evil genius, his
grave-charm, appears, and by the force of her revilings, her contemptuous taunts, and, above all, by her opprobrious aspersion of
cowardice, chases the gathering drops of humanity from his eyes,
and drives before her impetuous and destructive career all those
kindly charities, those impressions of loyalty, and pity, and
gratitude, which, but the moment before, had taken full possession
of his mind. [...]
    Her language to Macbeth is the most potently eloquent that
guilt could use. It is only in soliloquy that she invokes the
powers of hell to unsex her. To her husband she avows, and the
naturalness of her language makes us believe her, that she had
felt the instinct of filial as well as maternal love. But she
makes her very virtues the means of a taunt to her lord: - 'You
have the milk of human kindness in your heart,' she says (in substance) to him, 'but ambition, which is my ruling passion, would
be also yours if you had courage. [...] Look to me, and be
ashamed of your weakness,' Abashed, perhaps, to find his own
courage humbled before this unimaginable instance of female
fortitude, he at last screws up his courage to the sticking-place,
and binds up each corporal agent to this terrible feat. [...] In
the tremendous suspense of these moments, while she recollects
her habitual humanity, one trait of tender feeling is expressed,
'Had he not resembled my father as he slept, I had done it.' [...]
    Then instantaneously the solitary particle of her human feeling
is swallowed up in her remorseless ambition, and, wrenching the
daggers from the feeble grasp of her husband, she finishes the act
which the infirm of purpose had not courage to complete, and
calmly and steadily returns to her accomplice with the fiend-like
boast,

My hands are of your colour;
But I would scorn to wear a heart so white.

[...] In a deplorable depravation of all rational knowledge, and
lost to every recollection except that of his enormous guilt, she
hurries him away to their own chamber.

The Third Act

The golden round of royalty now crowns her brow, and royal robes
enfold her form; but the peace that passeth all understanding is
lost to her for ever, and the worm that never dies already gnaws
her heart.

Nought's had - all's spent,
Where our desire is had without content,
'Tis safer to be that which we destroy,
Than by destruction dwell in doubtful joy.

Under the impression of her present wretchedness, I, from this
moment, have always assumed the dejection of countenance and manners which I though accordant to such a state of mind; and, though
the author of this sublime composition has not, it must be acknowledged, given any direction whatever to authorize this assumption,
yet I venture to hope that he would not have disapproved of it.
It is evident, indeed, by her conduct in the scene which succeeds
the mournful soliloquy, that she is no longer the presumptuous,
the determined creature, that she was before the assassination of
the King: for instance, on the approach of her husband, we behold
for the first time striking indications of sensibility, nay tenderness and sympathy; and I think this conduct is nobly followed
up by her during the whole of their subsequent eventful intercourse. It is evident, I think, that the sad and new experience
of affliction has subdued the insolence of her pride, and the
violence of her will; for she comes now to seek him out, that she
may, at least, participate his misery. [...]
Far from her former habits of reproach and contemptuous taunt-
ing, you perceive that she now listens to his complaints with
sympathizing feelings. [...] Yes; smothering her sufferings in
the deepest recesses of her own wretched bosom, we cannot but
perceive that she devotes herself entirely to the effort of supporting him.
Let it be here recollected, as some palliation of her former
very different deportment, she had, probably, from childhood commanded all around her with a high hand; had uninterruptedly, perhaps, in that splendid station, enjoyed all that wealth, all that
nature had to bestow; that she had, possibly, no directors, no
controllers, and that in womanhood her fascinated lord had never
once opposed her inclinations. But now her new-born relentings,
under the rod of chastisement, prompt her to make palpable
efforts in order to support the spirits of her weaker, and, I
must say, more selfish husband Yes; in gratitude for his
unbounded affection, and in commiseration of his sufferings, she

suppresses the anguish of her heart, even while that anguish is precipitating her into the grave which at this moment is yawning to receive her.

The Banquet

Surrounded by their court, in all the apparent ease and self-complacency of which their wretched souls are destitute, they are now seated at the royal banquet; and although, through the greater part of this scene, Lady Macbeth affects to resume her wonted domination over her husband, yet, notwithstanding all this self-control, her mind must even then be agonized by the complicated pangs of terror and remorse. [...]

Dying with fear, yet assuming the utmost composure, she returns to her stately canopy; and, with trembling nerves, having tottered up the steps to her throne, that bad eminence, she entertains her wondering guests with frightful smiles, with over-acted attention, and with fitful graciousness; painfully, yet incessantly, labouring to divert their attention from her husband. Whilst writhing thus under her internal agonies, her restless and terrifying glances towards Macbeth, in spite of all her efforts to suppress them, have thrown the whole table into amazement; and the murderer then suddenly breaks up the assembly, by the confession of his horrors [...]

What imitation, in such circumstances as these, would ever satisfy the demands of expectation? The terror, the remorse, the hypocrisy of this astonishing being, flitting in frightful succession over her countenance, and actuating her agitated gestures with her varying emotions, present, perhaps, one of the greatest difficulties of the scenic art, and cause her representative no less to tremble for the suffrage of her private study, than for its public effect.

It is now the time to inform you of an idea which I have conceived of Lady Macbeth's character, which perhaps will appear as fanciful as that which I have adopted respecting the style of her beauty; and, in order to justify this idea, I must carry you back to the scene immediately preceding the banquet, in which you will recollect the following dialogue:

Oh, full of scorpions is my mind, dear wife;
Thou knowest that Banquo and his Fleance live.
LADY MACBETH: But in them Nature's copy's not eterne.

Now, it is not possible that she should hear all these ambiguous hints about Banquo without being too well aware that a sudden, lamentable fate awaits him. Yet, so far from offering any opposition to Macbeth's murderous designs, she even hints, I think, at the facility, if not the expediency, of destroying both Banquo and his equally unoffending child, when she observes that, 'in them Nature's copy is not eterne.' Having, therefore, now filled the measure of her crimes, I have imagined that the last appearance of Banquo's ghost became no less visible to her eyes than it became to those of her husband. Yes, the spirit of the noble

Banquo has smilingly filled up, even to overflowing, and now com-
mends to her own lips the ingredients of her poisoned chalice.

The Fifth Act

Behold her now, with wasted form, with wan and haggard countenance, her starry eyes glazed with the ever-burning fever of
remorse, and on their lids the shadows of death. Her ever-
restless spirit wanders in troubled dreams about her dismal
apartment; and, whether waking or asleep, the smell of innocent
blood incessantly haunts her imagination. [...]
   During this appalling scene, which, to my sense, is the most
so of them all, the wretched creature, in imagination, acts over
again the accumulated horrors of her whole conduct. These dreadful images, accompanied with the agitations they have induced,
have obviously accelerated her untimely end; for in a few moments
the tidings of her death are brought to her unhappy husband. It
is conjectured that she died by her own hand. Too certain it is,
that she dies, and makes no sign. I have now to account to you
for the weakness which I have, a few lines back, ascribed to
Macbeth; and I am not quite without hope that the following observations will bear me out in my opinion. Please to observe, that
he (I must think pusillanimously, when I compare his conduct to
her forbearance,) has been continually pouring out his miseries
to his wife. His heart has therefore been eased, from time to
time, by unloading its weight of woe; while she, on the contrary,
has perseveringly endured in silence the uttermost anguish of a
wounded spirit.

   The grief that does not speak
   Whispers the o'erfraught heart, and bids it break.

Her feminine nature, her delicate structure, it is too evident,
are soon overwhelmed by the enormous pressure of her crimes. Yet
it will be granted, that she gives proofs of a naturally higher
toned mind than that of Macbeth. The different physical powers of
the two sexes are finely delineated, in the different effects which
their mutual crimes produce. Her frailer frame, and keener feelings, have now sunk under the struggle - his robust and less sensitive constitution has not only resisted it, but bears him on to
deeper wickedness, and to experience the fatal fecundity of crime
[...]
   In one point of view, at least, this guilty pair extort from us,
in spite of ourselves, a certain respect and approbation. Their
grandeur of character sustains them both above recrimination (the
despicable accustomed resort of vulgar minds,) in adversity; for
the wretched husband, though almost impelled into this gulph of
destruction by the instigations of his wife, feels no abatement of
his love for her, while she, on her part, appears to have known no
tenderness for him, till, with a heart bleeding at every pore, she
beholds in him the miserable victim of their mutual ambition.
Unlike the first frail pair in Paradise, they spent not the fruit-
less hours in mutual accusation. [...]

NOTE

* Sarah Siddons (1755-1831) first played Lady Macbeth at Drury Lane
  in 1785.

3. 6   G. WILSON KNIGHT

The Ideal Production (1936), 'Shakespearian
Production', Faber, 1964, pp. 131-42

We have referred continually in this book to 'Macbeth'. Here is
an outline of my ideal production. The general purpose will be:
(i) to use a more or less permanent set; (ii) to arrange a rich
production to bring out and solidify *with the help of the action*
layers in the play's imagery and symbolism which it usually takes
years of sensitive appreciation to remark and hold in the mind;
and (iii) to give at last the element of supernature an adequate
projection. [...]
     The stage will be mostly draped in black. There will be a
semi-circular background with a ledge half-way up, and two or more
high entrances there. There are entrances below variously as may
be convenient. A flight of steps leads down from the ledge C, or
possibly a little L of C, so that it points inward at a slight
angle. There is a big dais R supporting a heavy and elaborate
golden throne. Opposite the throne there is, L, a niche containing a raised Madonna-figure and Child and an altar-like level,
having a step in front, but none of it too definitely ecclesi-
astical. Possibly the black drapes all round are streaked with
gold zig-zags here and there. Two of the entrances to the ledge
show red curtains, but these and other gaps can also disclose sky
for out-door effects. The stairway is carpeted first in green,
later in crimson, and finally again in green. The lighting will
be subtly used throughout: especially important will be its varied
play on the Madonna and the throne. These will, however, nearly
always remain visible. There will be no obvious stress on coloured
lights.

Act I

The first scene is given on the fore-stage: I assume that we
should have a good one. Next Duncan stands before the throne, the
bloody Sergeant entering down L. The Madonna is well lit and wide
patches of sky show above the ledge.
     The lights would then change for Macbeth's meeting with the
Weird Sisters, dimming on the Madonna. Through the openings over
the ledge irregular patches of sky-sheet could show to suggest a
mountainous and craggy gorge. Our set lends itself to effects of
descent which can be used to suggest a Dantesque circle of Hell.
Having a very definite permanent set we need be less afraid of dimming corners, since the audience are conscious of what is there and
have a feeling for the proper limits. The throne and Madonna are

dim. The Weird Sisters meet and circle C. Macbeth and Banquo
enter on one of the ledge openings, silhouetted for a second
against sky, and walk round and descend the steps. They are coming
over mountain crags. The Weird Sisters prophesy grouped in front of
the throne, and facing Macbeth and Banquo, who have walked down L.
Macbeth advances: they melt away, and he finds himself confronted
significantly by the throne, ón which the lights have slightly
risen. Macbeth gazes on it, as he says 'Your children shall be
kings'; then starts at Banquo's 'You shall be king'. and turns away
from it as though uninterested: 'And Thane of Cawdor, too ...'
During his soliloquy he stands near, and on appropriate lines
regarding, the throne. Banquo and the lords group down L. Macbeth
comes down to meet them, while the curtain closes behind. They go
off together.

The curtain is drawn and Duncan is discovered on the throne, his
sons on either side. No sky is visible: it is an interior. The
Madonna and Child are bright. Macbeth and Banquo enter down L -
not down the steps - and approach the dais. The King's proclamation of Malcolm's accession must be done ceremoniously, Macbeth and
the others kneeling before the throne--group; this will be effective, and brings out the meaning of the situation, besides throwing
forward to a later group.

The lights change and direct the eye to Lady Macbeth appearing
through one of the ledge-entrances. Morning sky might show, as
through windows. She is on the steps, reading the letter. At
'Glamis thou art ...' she swiftly descends, facing the throne from
the bottom step at' ... shalt be what thou art promis'd'. The
servant tells of the messenger. 'He brings great news' takes Lady
Macbeth up-stage. She refers to her 'battlements', arms raised to
the sky openings, back to the audience; then swings round to face
the Madonna and Child. She deliberately challenges the figure for
a second, then scornfully turns and invokes the spirits of evil
against her sex and motherhood; or she might speak boldly facing
the image. Macbeth enters down R crossing the throne, and does
not look on it until his wife urges him. They go out.

Duncan and his following enter down L, and look up to the ledge
as to a battlemented castle. After Duncan's 'martlet' speech,
Lady Macbeth descends the green stairway to meet him. He confronts
her standing with his sons and lords grouped before the throne.

The curtains are drawn and the feast procession passes to music
across the fore-stage.

Next the full set is discovered with now a *red* carpet on the
stairs. Macbeth is standing on the lower steps of the stairway
for his soliloquy. His references to Duncan are made looking at
the throne. As his speech grows impassioned he rises, walks down-
stage, and faces the Madonna for his lines on 'pity like a naked
new-born babe' and 'heaven's cherubin'. Finally he falls on his
knees on the steps before the Madonna, looking back at the throne
for the words 'vaulting ambition'; then prays. At Lady Macbeth's
entry he rises. She draws him down L, away. Laughter is heard
from the feast, from time to time, during their dialogue. Then we
have a ceremonious procession. Duncan and the rest enter R.
There is business of some sort between the King and his hosts. He,
with his sons, ascends the red stairs and, half-way, turns and

holds his arms in blessing over the crowded stage. The grouping
tends to mask the throne. Then all go out, some up the stairs and
at different openings on the ledge, others at up-stage ground entrances, others at the wings. You should see the red-curtained door
of Duncan's exit on the ledge.

The lights change. Night sky is seen at openings over the ledge.
Banquo enters below with Fleance; then Macbeth and a servant.
During this subtle dialogue the throne, close to Macbeth, can catch
Banquo's eye on the words 'To you they have show'd some truth'.
Macbeth stands with his back to it, for 'I think not of them'. The
Madonna is dim. Macbeth is left alone. The air-drawn dagger points
up the red stairs. He follows it a step or two. Then he banishes
it, turning, and facing the darkly glowing throne with lustful eye.
He now succumbs utterly to evil and speaks the Tarquin lines. He regards the throne again at 'Whiles I threat, he lives'. The bell
sounds. He crouches up the stairs and along the ledge to Duncan's
room. [...]

Act II

Banquo enters in the full set and uses reference to the throne
freely to point his words, standing C. Then Macbeth and Lady
Macbeth enter from above with a couple of attendants, and come down
the crimson-carpeted stairs. Banquo draws R to the throne-step.
The stage fills from lower entrances LC and down L. Macbeth is
again the apex of a crowd, as he comes down C. The repetition is
significant. Banquo, with Fleance, is R, and seems for a second to
be barring Macbeth's approach to the throne. Then he bows and the
incident melts, as he steps aside and Macbeth and Lady Macbeth
cross. This is the second of a series of incidents where Banquo is
related to the throne. Now we have a small wooden throne for Lady
Macbeth down-stage of the gold one, beside it: which points the
proper quality of Lady Macbeth's position, subsidiary to Macbeth's
kingship. Her unselfishness is a platitude of commentary. Macbeth
in his throne looks lost. It is so big. An all but ludicrous
effect is wanted; for which there is authority in the text:

Now does he feel his title
Hang loose about him, like a giant's robe
Upon a dwarfish thief.

After Banquo's exit, the others go and leave Macbeth alone. He
rises quickly from the throne as if with relief. 'To be thus is
nothing ...' Referring to Banquo's royal descendants he looks on
it, bringing to our minds the two incidents when Banquo has, as
it were by chance, seemed positionally to possess it. Macbeth
asserts himself as he defies fate. He can, as it were, attack the
image of Banquo, sweeping it from the throne, banishing it like the
air-drawn dagger: then swiftly turns, nervous, at 'Who's there?'
He stands on the throne steps as he addresses the murderers; then
goes out. Lady Macbeth returns. The Servant goes out down-stage.
Lady Macbeth sees her husband re-enter and stand gazing at the
Madonna. She quickly draws him away, telling him to banish

'sorriest fancies' and all thoughts that should die with the dead.
She leads him to his throne, would put him there, and try to love
seeing him there, as a mother puts her baby to rest. He sits in it
for 'We have scotch'd the snake, not killed it ...' She kneels,
and caresses him. 'Gentle my lord, sleek o'er your rugged looks
...' Macbeth breaks from her, but still sitting, and hints
aside of some 'deed of dreadful note'. She, anxious, rises and
importunately draws to him, holds his arm. 'What's to be done?'
Now he breaks from her altogether, rises, and from the throne steps
invokes night and evil. She is fearful, bereft of speech.

The murder of Banquo is done as a front-scene.

For the feast we have our full set. There is one big table running diagonally down L at whatever exact angle may be most convenient. Macbeth and Lady Macbeth are in their thrones. Guests are
at the table. Macbeth's other chair is at the table's up-stage end,
which is near the base of the stairs. Macbeth talks to the murderer on the stairs where the Ghost is to come from. Then he comes
down R. On his lines referring to Banquo the Ghost walks slowly
and deliberately down the red stairs and sits in Macbeth's table-
chair, which is slightly raised, giving the Ghost a dominant position. Lady Macbeth comes down R and talks to Macbeth aside. The
Ghost exits into the shadows up R behind the throne. On its next
entrance it appears down R, stalks to the dais and *sits in the
throne*. Macbeth on his second reference to Banquo has taken
possession of the table-chair as if to make sure of no more accidents, but only finds that he has driven the Ghost to a still
more terrible position: the very one he most hates to associate
with Banquo. Macbeth finally advances to the throne steps and
violently banishes it, repeating the movement I introduced
earlier. Note Macbeth's *courage in face of the supernatural*.
Every time he shakes portentous nightmares from him. It was the
same with the dagger; and he curses the Weird Sisters later. He
treats them like dirt. His humanity never bends under these sub-
human horrors. He never abrogates his human status. This is
important and forms, or should, a large part of our admiration.
His bark is thus 'tempest-toss'd' but 'cannot be lost'. The
Ghost's exit is a simple turn left and round along the dais into
shadows, quickly obscured behind the tall throne. The guests go
out L and up R. Alone together Macbeth and Lady Macbeth stay by
the thrones; Macbeth is sunk on the dais, his wife kneels, ministering to him. At 'Come, we'll go to sleep' they cross and start to
ascend the stairs, slowly, like Adam and Eve, hand-in-hand. Half-
way up, Macbeth stops and speaks his last couple of lines, looking
on the disordered remains of the banquet: 'My strange and self-
abuse ...' Again they move up, slowly, laboriously.

The Hecate scene is done on the fore-stage. Then we go back to
the feast scene. All is just as we left it, overturned chairs and
all. But the lights have changed. The Madonna-figure is picked
out brilliantly. Lennox and a Lord enter looking surreptitious
and stealthy, up-stage. Their dialogue is done more or less C.
They speak softly. At Lennox' lines 'Some holy angel ...' they
come down, perhaps kneel, to the Madonna. The advantages of doing
this dialogue from our full set are obvious. The Lord can point
to the disarranged remnants, tumbled cups, and so on for his words:

We may again
Give to our tables meat, sleep to our nights,
Free from our feasts and banquets bloody knives ...

The words point the moral of the Banquet scene; let the action do
so, too.

We cannot run on at once to the Cauldron scene, as the table has
to be moved. I suggest that we draw the curtain, and all lights
are down. In the darkness we hear the thunder and the Weird
Sisters' first speeches; this can go on as long as may be necessary. Then the lights come up on our full set showing the cauldron C and the three figures at their work around it. The sky
shows in craggy strips above. We are in one of the lowest circles
of Hell, the 'pit of Acheron'. The Madonna figure is dim for this
Black Mass: if we use Hecate's entrance, she will appropriately
obscure it, down L. The Weird Sisters between their chants can
variously twirl away a little up the stairs or on to the dais.
Macbeth appears above and speaks from half-way down the steps:
'What is't you do?' The throne is not clearly visible. Macbeth
stands before it. The Sisters are now down-stage of the cauldron
and when the Apparitions are to appear group themselves diagonally
LC facing up-stage, close to the cauldron. The Apparitions come
from the cauldron C, very solid and distinct. They could be dummy
figures and their words spoken in turn by each of the Sisters:
this may be the original intention. The thunder is very loud.
Macbeth cowers instinctively before the Crowned Child: though part
of the little conflict-drama it is itself a powerful life-symbol.
The words, however, reassure him. Macbeth demands to know more.
The Weird Sisters get C above the cauldron. Macbeth, back to the
audience, fiercely advances, and the cauldron sinks, obeying the
text. It almost seems as if Macbeth has stamped it out of existence. The Sisters and Hecate draw back, moving backwards, up the
stairs as though fearful, as they should be, of what follows.

Macbeth, C, sees the throne loom out, the lights coming up on
it and the Madonna. Music sounds. The kings enter up R and down
R variously, each pausing before Macbeth, and in turn grouping
themselves round the throne, like a photograph group. Pauses are
no difficulty: let it be all done with deliberation and ceremony.
Balls and sceptres and the glass should be visibly solid. Last
the Ghost of Banquo enters and takes his place in the throne itself.
Banquo's continual possession of the throne during the middle action
is most significant. His royalty is spiritual, creative, and real;
Macbeth's selfish, lustful, and unreal. This is why Banquo worries
Macbeth so much. Now the whole group is complete. Macbeth stands C
between it and the bright Madonna. The effect is splendid and
solid. The kings as they enter must give Macbeth a good look:
usually they just peep at him through gauze. The group then melts
away, ceremoniously, moving with dignity, the lights on them dimming. Lights could for once go down all round the stage leaving
Macbeth alone illuminated C, a pin-point of burning consciousness in
Hell. [...]

Act III

The murder of Lady Macduff can be best done before simple curtains.
Generally it gets laughter. It is, however, not meant to hold any
grandeur of action. Macbeth's exploits get less and less dignified
and more mad. They are meant to. Duncan's murder was tragically
grand; Banquo's melodramatic; and this is almost ludicrous. The
producer must bring out its quality of ghoulish horror fearlessly
and no one will laugh. He must avoid a lot of screams at the end.
     The English scene is done also before a plain curtain: a green
background would do well.
     We return to our main set for the sleep-walking. Lady Macbeth
comes down the red stairs and later reascends them. Her candle
will be put on the throne dais, or the stairs. She fingers the
throne with the action of blindness. At one point she comes near
the Madonna, perhaps touches the altar-level in front, and shrinks
away whimpering. She moves about the stage, living its signifi-
cances. The Doctor's 'God, God, forgive us all!' can be spoken
with some reference to the Madonna, which should be palely lit.
     From now the action speeds up. A short military front-scene,
accompanied by martial drums, shows troops gathering to meet
Malcolm. Then we have our full set: the sky-sheet shows in
places above to give some effect of battlements, but lights are
gloomy and autumnal for Macbeth's passage of tragic loneliness
and the Doctor's lines on Lady Macbeth. The stairway is now green
again. Now follows a second short scene, martial music getting
louder and nearer for Malcolm's and Macduff's approach. The play
is growing brighter. We want our lights to grow sensibly brighter
during this last movement, but this does not mean that all the
middle action must be done in half darkness. All that is necessary is for this movement to start dark; quickly get bright enough
for clear expression but with a certain toning of atmospheric and
autumnal suggestion; and gradually increase to a brilliant conclusion. Notice the repeated direction 'drum and *colours*' for Malcolm
and his supporters; also for Macbeth; and Macbeth's 'Hang out our
banners on the outward walls'. Both sides share in the awakening.
Macbeth is reckless and flings himself in the throne. He is almost
happy. There is action, colour and sane purpose at last, replacing
nightmare and actions that beat only the dark and torment the doer.
Macbeth no longer fears a night-shriek; he has all but won through.
Hearing of his wife's death he first moves towards the Madonna, as
if to pray, but turns away:

     She should have died hereafter;
     There would have been a time for such a word...

The messenger announcing the movement of Birnam Wood comes from
above. Martial music sounds louder and very close for another
front-scene: 'Now near enough: your leavy screens throw down ...'
I think these are best suggested off-stage. Then our full set, for
the last time. The sky-sheet shows more than ever before. The
stage is bright. Macbeth fights Young Siward, and goes off.
Macduff enters. During his short speech - 'My wife and children's
ghosts will haunt me still' - he might get some business with the

Madonna-altar, dedicating his sword to her and praying. He goes
off up the stairs. Malcolm and Siward enter from down L and cross,
going out down R. Macbeth re-enters, and is by his throne as Macduff confronts him coming down the stairs. He is killed finally
below the Madonna and Child. The body lies on the steps before it,
sacrificed. We remember Macduff's slaughtered wife and children,
and Lady Macbeth's speech invoking the desecration of motherhood.

The rest is easy. At the conclusion Malcolm ascends the throne,
or at the least stands on its step. Macduff remains close to the
Madonna for the final group. Malcolm might in some way use the
Madonna for his phrase 'the grace of Grace'; as might Old Siward
earlier. The lights are bright, the sky above as brilliant as
possible, for the first time exposed all the way round the curving
ledge, crowning the stage with a wide circle of light.

I have hurried these last descriptions, not because the last
scenes are weak or unimportant, but because they depend more on a
quick time sequence and martial sounds than on spatial signifi-
cances.

Such is my outline. I have used a permanent set for all big
scenes and have preserved an impression of weight and solidity.
The main impressions used are:

(i) *The throne,* which covers the various royalty-symbolism of
our play, gold crowns and sceptres, etc.; and the whole matter of
kingship, rightful for Duncan and Malcolm, wrongful for Macbeth,
spiritual and prophetic for Banquo.

(ii) *The red stairway,* mainly suggesting blood, which is a
powerful impression throughout. My arrangement of the carpets
will be best understood by considering that the play moves from
social and natural order through nightmare and blood to daylight
sanity and a new harmony.

(iii) *The green stairway* at the beginning and end, suggesting
nature and social harmony generally, an integral conception to be
contrasted with the unnatural and nightmarish evil and related to
the child-with-a-tree, the martlet's nest, the wren passage, the
Birnam Wood incidents, and numerous other nature references; and
also thoughts of honour and integrity generally.

(iv) *The Madonna and Child,* relating to the frequent Christian
imagery of purity, angels and divine grace, closely associated
with child-thoughts, Lady Macbeth's invocation of evil to dry up in
her breasts the milk of human and feminine tenderness, her 'I have
given suck ...', the 'naked new-born babe', the two child apparitions, Macduff's family. The symbolism blends with the creative
royalty of Banquo and his descendants.

3. 7 W.H. AUDEN

The Dyer's Hand, 'Listener', 16 June 1955,
pp. 1064-5

[...] Let us compare a work in which the poet has no historian to
contend with, and one in which they fight it out between them:

for instance, Sophocles's 'Oedipus Rex' and Shakespeare's 'Macbeth'
I have selected these because in both of them there is a prophecy
about the future which comes true. The notion presupposed by the
Greek Oracle is that the future is pre-ordained; that is to say,
there is no real future because it is already latent in the present. If one asks, therefore, what would have happened if Oedipus
had remained in Corinth instead of running away, the only answer
can be that, although the actual events would have been different,
the results would have been the same; in the end he would have
murdered his father and married his mother. What the Oracle says
may be put in a riddle form, but, once this is deciphered, what it
says is not a promise but a statement of fact like a statement of a
scientific law, and there is no question of belief or disbelief.
[...]
    In 'Macbeth', the witches prophesy that Macbeth shall become
king. If he had listened to them as a Greek would have listened to
the Oracle, then he would have been able to sit and wait until by
necessity it came to pass. But he takes it as a promise with which
he has to co-operate and which, in consequence, brings about his
downfall, so that it is legitimate to say that Macbeth should not
have listened to them, in which case he would not have become
king, and they would have been proved to be what they were, lying
voices.
    One might say that, though there is a history of Oedipus,
Oedipus himself has no history, for there is no relation between
his being and his acts. When the play opens he has already committed parricide and incest, but he is still the same person he was
before he had done so; it is only when he finds out that the old
man whom he killed in a quarrel about precedence, a deed which
neither he nor his audience are supposed to think wrong, was, in
fact, his father, and that the Queen of Thebes to whom he has been
happily married for years is, in fact, his mother, that there is
a change, and even then this is a change not in him but in his
status. He who formerly was a happy king beloved by his subjects
is now a wretched outcast. In 'Macbeth', on the other hand, every
action taken by Macbeth has an immediate effect upon him so that,
step by step, the brave bold warrior we hear of in the first scene
turns before our eyes into the guilt-crazed creature of the
'tomorrow and tomorrow and tomorrow' soliloquy.
    At no point during the Greek tragedy is Oedipus faced with a
choice so that one could say that he made the wrong one. If, for
example, he accepts Tiresias's advice and drops his inquiry into
who the criminal is who is responsible for the plague, the plague
will continue. But Macbeth not only makes a series of wrong
choices which he should not have made, but also, though the past
exerts an increasing pressure on the present, at no point does it
become necessity; however difficult it might have been, for instance, after the murder of Duncan, to repent and refrain from
murdering Banquo, it was not impossible.
    The parricide and incest committed by Oedipus are not his acts
but things that happen to him without his knowledge and against
his desire, presumably as a divine punishment for his *hubris*; for
thinking, that is, that he is so fortunate he is a god whom misfortune cannot overtake. Macbeth's acts are his own and not a

punishment for, but the outcome of, his pride; of his believing,
not that he is a god, but that he can do what he pleases irrespec-
tive of God's will.

Watching 'Oedipus', there is no question of the audience identifying themselves with the hero - all psychoanalytical explanations
of the play are nonsense - for what they see is a unique case of
spectacular misfortune. The majority know, like the members of
the chorus, that they will never be great men, so such a thing
could not happen to them: if there is an exceptionally fortunate
man in the audience, the most he will say is, 'I hope nothing like
that ever happens to me', and has quite good grounds for his hope.
Watching 'Macbeth', every member of the audience knows that the
possibility of becoming a Macbeth exists in his nature. One cannot imagine Sophocles arriving at the idea of a play about Oedipus
except from a knowledge of the myth, but the germ of Macbeth in
Shakespeare's mind could perfectly well have been what Kipling
suggests in his poem, 'The Craftsman'.

> How at Bankside, a boy drowning kittens
> Winced at the business; whereupon his sister
> Lady Macbeth aged seven - thrust 'em under,
> Sombrely scornful.

[...] It is possible to imagine a Shakespearian type of play
using the premise of Oedipus. If Oedipus is to make certain of
not fulfilling the prophecy, then he must take two vows: never to
strike a man and never to sleep with a woman. Let us imagine,
then, a man by nature highly choleric and passionate, and place
him in two situations in which he is greatly tempted to break
these vows; in the first, some man has done him a mortal injury,
some serious treachery, perhaps; in the second, he falls violently
in love with a woman who reciprocates equally violently. Naturally, he will do his best to persuade himself that the man could
not possibly be his father or the woman his mother, but in this
kind of play the author must show us the process of self-
deception; that is to say, there must be elements in both situations which would make any impartial observer suspect that the
man and the woman could very well be what anger and lust would
persuade Oedipus they are not.

Such a treatment demands not only a different plot, but also a
different formal structure and a different poetic style. In the
original play it is natural that there should be only one place
and no breaks in time, for the function of both is external: the
action is the revelation of what has already happened, and all
that is needed is a place where and a certain length of time in
which this can occur.

In our new version such unities are highly unnatural and can be
retained, if at all, only by a technical *tour de force,* for the
decisive events and choices by which the innocent Oedipus becomes
guilty cannot occur all at the same time and it is improbable that
they could all occur in the same place. As to style, the unbroken
elevation of the Greek version becomes unsuitable and needs to be
replaced by something far more mixed, now high, now low like the
porter in 'Macbeth'. In a world of being, where people are what

they are by fate, the more intense the moment and the more magnificent their verbal response to it, the more they manifest their being, and every relaxation weakens the effect and should be eliminated. But in a world where people become by their choices what they previously were not, a moment in which the characters are emotionally relaxed may be just as significant as one in which they are emotionally stirred.

Further, while in the first world there is no essential difference between man and other creatures of nature, in the second man is unique as a conscious creature who is changed by his acts and at the same time as a physical being subject to the necessities of nature. He cannot choose to feel hungry or not hungry, sleepy or not sleepy, full of or free from sexual desire, and one function of a lowering of style is to express this creaturely framework within which his freedom of will operates. [...]

Returning to our imaginary version of 'Oedipus', let us suppose it is written by Shakespeare himself at the height of his powers, equal in poetic splendour to 'King Lear' and 'Antony and Cleopatra'. Compared with Sophocles it will be a more interesting, possibly more profound, play but it will be a less beautiful and less perfect work of art; for no matter how great the genius of its author, it will lack that exact correspondence of form and content which the Greek play possesses. The modern dramatist is faced with an insoluble problem: how to present a character who by a combination of circumstances and his own free choices becomes different. Becoming and choice are continuous processes, not a series of jumps from one state to another, but it is only as a series of jumps that the dramatist can portray becoming at all, and any answer to the question 'How many different stages do I need to show?' must be arbitrary: there is no Shakespeare play which one cannot imagine either longer or shorter than it is.

3. 8 JAN KOTT

> 'Macbeth', or Death-Infected, 'Shakespeare our
> Contemporary', trans. B. Taborski, Methuen, 1965,
> pp. 74-8

In its psychology, 'Macbeth' is, perhaps, the deepest of Shakespeare's tragedies. But Macbeth himself is not a character, at least not in the sense of what was meant by a character in the nineteenth century. Lady Macbeth is such a character. Everything in her, except craving for power, has been burnt out. She is empty, and goes on burning. She is taking her revenge for her failure as lover and mother. Lady Macbeth has no imagination; and for that reason she accepts herself from the outset, and later cannot escape from herself. Macbeth does have imagination, and from the moment of the first murder he asks himself the same sort of questions that Richard III has asked himself:

> To be thus is nothing;
> But to be safely thus.

From the first scenes onwards Macbeth defines himself by negation.
To himself he is not the one who is, but rather the one who is not.
He is immersed in the world as if in nothingness; he exists only
potentially. Macbeth chooses himself, but after every act of
choice he finds himself more terrifying, and more of a stranger.
'.... all that is within him does condemn itself for being there'.
The formulas by which Macbeth tries to define himself are
amazingly similar to the language of the existentialists. 'To be'
has for Macbeth an ambiguous, or at least a double, meaning; it is
a constant exasperating contradiction between existence and
essence, between being 'for itself' and being 'in itself'.
    He says:

    ... and nothing is
    But what is not.

    In a bad dream we are, and are not, ourselves, at the same
time. We cannot accept ourselves, for to accept oneself would
mean accepting nightmare for reality, to admit that there is
nothing but nightmare, that night is not followed by day.
    Says Macbeth after the murder of Duncan: 'To know my deed,
'twere best not know myself.' Macbeth recognizes that his existence is apparent rather than real, because he does not want to
admit that the world he lives in is irrevocable. This world is to
him a nightmare. For Richard 'to be' means to capture the crown
and murder all pretenders. For Macbeth 'to be' means - to escape,
to live in another world, where:

    Rebellion's head, rise never ...
    ... and our high-plac'd Macbeth
    Shall live the lease of nature, pay his breath
    To time and mortal custom.

The plot and the order of history, in Shakespeare's Histories and
in 'Macbeth', do not differ from each other. But Richard accepts
the order of history and his part in it. Macbeth dreams about a
world where there will be no more murders, and all murders will
have been forgotten; where the dead will have been buried in the
ground once and for all, and everything will begin anew. Macbeth
dreams of the end of nightmare, while sinking in it more and more.
He dreams of a world without crime, while becoming enmeshed in
crime more and more deeply. Macbeth's last hope is that the dead
will not rise:

    LADY MACBETH: But in them nature's copy's not eterne.
    MACBETH: There's comfort yet; they are assailable;
            Then be thou jocund.

But the dead do rise. The appearance at the banquet of murdered
Banquo's ghost is one of the most remarkable scenes in 'Macbeth'.
Banquo's ghost is visible to Macbeth alone. Commentators see in
this scene an embodiment of Macbeth's fear and terror. There is
no ghost; it is a delusion. But Shakespeare's 'Macbeth' is not
a psychological drama of the second half of the nineteenth century.

Macbeth has dreamed of a final murder to end all murders. Now he knows: there is no such murder. This is the third and last of Macbeth's experiences. The dead do return. 'The sequence of time is an illusion ... We fear most the past that returns.' This aphorism by S.J. Lec has something of the atmosphere of 'Macbeth':

> If charnel-houses and our graves must send
> Those that we bury back, our monuments
> Shall be the maws of kites.

Macbeth, the multiple murderer, steeped in blood, could not accept the world in which murder existed. In this, perhaps, consists the gloomy greatness of this character, and the true tragedy of Macbeth's history. For a long time Macbeth did not want to accept the reality and irrevocability of nightmare, and could not reconcile himself to his part, as if it were somebody else's. Now he knows everything. He knows that there is no escape from nightmare, which is the human fate and condition, or - in more modern language - the human situation. There is no other.

> They have tied me to a stake; I cannot fly,
> But, bear-like, I must fight the course.

Before his first crime, which was the murder of Duncan, Macbeth had believed that death could come too early, or too late. 'Had I but died an hour before this chance, I had liv'd a blessed time.' Now Macbeth knows that death does not change anything, that it cannot change anything, that it is just as absurd as life. No more, no less. For the first time Macbeth is not afraid. 'I have almost forgot the taste of fears.'

There is nothing to be afraid of any more. He can accept himself at last, because he has realized that every choice is absurd, or rather - that there is no choice.

> Out, out, brief candle!
> Life's but a walking shadow; a poor player,
> That struts and frets his hour upon the stage,
> And then is heard no more: it is a tale
> Told by an idiot, full of sound and fury,
> Signifying nothing.

In the opening scenes of the tragedy there is talk about the thane of Cawdor, who had betrayed Duncan and become an ally of the King of Norway. After the suppression of the rebellion he was captured and condemned to death.

> ... nothing in his life
> Became him like the leaving it; he died
> As one that had been studied in his death,
> To throw away the dearest thing he owed,
> As 'twere a careless trifle.

The thane of Cawdor does not appear in 'Macbeth'. All we know of him is that he has been guilty of treason and executed. Why is his

death described so emphatically and in such detail? Why did
Shakespeare find it necessary? After all, his expositions are
never wrong. Cawdor's death, which opens the play, is necessary.
It will be compared to Macbeth's death. There is something Senecan
and stoic about Cawdor's cold indifference to death. Faced with
utter defeat Cawdor saves what can still be saved: a noble atti-
tide and dignity. For Macbeth attitudes are of no importance; he
does not believe in human dignity any more. Macbeth has reached
the limits of human experience. All he has left is contempt.
The very concept of man has crumbled to pieces, and there is
nothing left. The end of 'Macbeth', like the endings of 'Troilus
and Cressida', or 'King Lear', produces no catharsis. Suicide is
either a protest, or an admission of guilt. Macbeth does not
feel guilty, and there is nothing for him to protest about. All
he can do before he dies is to drag with him into nothingness as
many living beings as possible. This is the last consequence of
the world's absurdity. Macbeth is unable to blow the world up.
But he can go on murdering till the end.

> Why should I play the Roman fool, and die
> On my own sword? whiles I see lives, the gashes
> Do better upon them.

'THE WINTER'S TALE'

3. 9 NORTHROP FRYE

> The Triumph of Time, 'A Natural Perspective',
> Columbia University Press, New York, 1965,
> pp. 113-17

'The Winter's Tale' is a diptych, in which the first part is the
'winter's tale' proper, the story of the jealousy of Leontes, the
slandering of Hermione, and the perilous exposure of Perdita. The
second part, the last two acts, is the story of Florizel's love,
Perdita's recognition, and the revival of Hermione. Shakespeare's
main source, Greene's 'Pandosto,' is almost entirely confined to
the first part; for the rest Shakespeare appears to be on his own.
There are parallels and contrasts in the construction: the contrast
in imagery, the first part full of winter and storm and chaos and
the second all spring and revival and fertility, is not easily
missed. The first part begins with Archidamas speaking of how the
old people in Sicilia would wish to live until the king had a son,
and proceeds to the court of Sicilia, where an attempt is made to
delay a return to Bohemia. Then Leontes becomes a jealous *senex*
[old man], after which Camillo flees to Bohemia. The second part
begins with Time telling us that a generation has passed, proceeds
to the court of Bohemia and an attempt to delay a return to Sicilia,
and exhibits Polixenes in the role of a jealous and suspicious
senex, after which Camillo flees to Sicilia. In the first part
Mamillius dies and Perdita is very near death; in the second part

Florizel, who reminds Leontes of Mamillius and becomes his heir,
marries Perdita, after (as Bottom says when he has died in the role
of Pyramus and sprung up again) 'the wall is down that parted their
fathers.'

The jealous Leontes is [...] the focus of the anticomic mood,
and the first part of the action is the anticomedy that his jealousy
constructs. We begin with references to an innocent childhood when
Leontes and Polixenes were 'twinned lambs,' and then suddenly plunge
from the reminiscence of this pastoral paradise into a world of
superstition and obsession. Leontes has a great fear of becoming
an object of ridicule or comic butt, though, as Antigonus mutters
in an aside, that is precisely what he does become. The horror of
the world he creates is expressed mainly in the imagery of sacrifice: he wants to gain rest by burning Hermione alive; his courtiers offer to be or provide sacrifices in her place, and eventually the sacrificial role settles on Mamillius. The first part
ends in a storm which, like the storm in 'Lear' (which it echoes
in its bear and sea), is described in such a way as to suggest an
unsettling of the order of nature. We are told later that 'all the
instruments which aided to expose the child were even then lost
when it was found,' as though a new generation had to grow up in
the desert before the festival world could be reached. Some very
curious echoes indicate the starting of a new action: part one
ends with the clown hearing the cries of Antigonus as the bear
tears out his shoulder bone; part two begins with the same clown
hearing the cries of Autolycus pretending that his shoulder blade
is out.

The normal action of a comedy moves from irrational law to
festivity, which symbolizes a movement from one form of reality to
another. The world of tyranny and irrational law is a world where
what is real is given us arbitrarily as a datum, something we
must accept or somehow come to terms with. This is a spectator's
reality, the reality we see to be 'out there.' The world of the
final festival is a world where reality is what is created by
human desire, as the arts are created. There is something of this
in 'The Winter's Tale': Leontes takes a morbid pleasure in facing
what he thinks are facts, and insists on the tangible external
reality of his world: 'I do smell't and feel't,' he says. The
creative arts are also deeply involved in the recognition scene:
painting, sculpture, poetry, and music are all introduced or
referred to, and several conceptions of art, from the idealism of
Polixenes and the realism of Romano to the nonsense of Autolycus'
ballads, are mentioned.

But the action of 'The Winter's Tale' is clearly something
other than a movement from external to created reality. In the
first place, the world of Leontes' jealousy does not exist at all:
only the consequences of believing in it exist. In the second
place, the power of human desire that revives Hermione and brings
the lovers together is identical, first, with the power of nature
to bring new life out of death, and second, with the will of
Apollo, whose oracle is being fulfilled. The action, therefore,
moves from appearance to reality, from mirage to substance. Once
the real world is reached, the mirage becomes nothingness. The
real world, however, has none of the customary qualities of reality.

It is the world symbolized by nature's power of renewal; it is the
world we want; it is the world we hope our gods would want for us
if they were worth worshiping.   But it is 'monstrous to our human
reason,' according to Paulina, and its truth 'is so like an old
tale that the verity of it is in strong suspicion.' Such things
happen in stories, not in life, and the world 'The Winter's Tale'
leaves us with is neither an object of knowledge nor of belief.
    It would be an object of belief, of course, or symbolize one,
if we could feel that 'The Winter's Tale' was an allegory. I have
been assuming that it is not: that in Shakespeare the meaning
of the play is the play, there being nothing to be abstracted
from the total experience of the play. Progress in grasping the
meaning is a progress, not in seeing more in the play, but in
seeing more of it. Further progress takes us from the individual
plays to the class of things called plays, to the 'meaning' of
drama as a whole. That meaning, again, is our total experience of
drama. The center of that experience is the fact that drama is
doing, through the identity of myth and metaphor, what its ritual
predecessors tried to do by the identity of sympathetic magic:
unite the human and the natural worlds. But the world where this
unity can be achieved is clearly not the world of ordinary experience, in which man is an alienated spectator.   The world we are
looking at in the conclusion of 'The Winter's Tale' is not an
object of belief so much as an imaginative model of desire. The
last words, 'Hastily lead away,' summon us like a beckoning to a
new and impossible world, and our cue is to say, like Antipholus
of Syracuse when confronted by a wife he never saw before: 'I'll
entertain the offered fallacy.'

3. 10 NEVILL COGHILL

        Six Points of Stage-Craft in 'The Winter's Tale',
        'Shakespeare Survey', ed. A. Nicoll, Cambridge
        University Press, vol. 2, 1958, pp. 31-3, 35-6,
        39-40.

[...] charges of creaking dramaturgy have been made against 'The
Winter's Tale', severally, by Bethell and the Cambridge editors.
Let us consider them one by one, with this thought in mind, that
if Shakespeare has demonstrably told his story in certain rather
unusual ways, he may well have had some special, and perhaps dis-
cernible, intention in doing so: the careful consideration of how
a contrivance works may often guide us to an understanding of its
purpose.

THE SUPPOSED SUDDENNESS OF THE JEALOUSY OF LEONTES

    In 'Pandosto' (we shall use Shakespeare's names) Leontes'
jealousy is made slow and by increase plausible. Shakespeare
weakens the plausibility of it as well by ennobling Hermione -
after his way with good women - as by huddling up the jealousy

in its motion so densely that it strikes us as merely frantic
and - which is worse in drama - a piece of impossible improb-
ability.   This has always and rightly offended the critics....
(Sir Arthur Quiller-Couch). (1)

Then suddenly with no more hint of preparation - and no hint
at all on the psychological plane - Leontes' jealousy comes
full upon him. (S.L. Bethell). (2)

In an appendix devoted to this subject Bethell adds the conjec-
ture that if Shakespeare had intended Leontes to be jealous from
the start he would have brought him on alone 'to deliver an
appropriate soliloquy'. (3)   This would indeed have been 'a naïve
and outmoded technique', one at least as old-fashioned as that
which, long before, had so brilliantly opened 'Richard III'.
But in 'The Winter's Tale' Shakespeare went about his business
with new subtlety of dramatic invention.   To understand it we
must begin at the opening scene, a dialogue between Archidamus and
Camillo, asking ourselves certain questions in dramaturgy.
What is the reason for this dialogue?   What information does it
convey?   What is it supposed to do to an audience? [...]

CAM.:   Sicilia cannot show himself over-kind to Bohemia.   They
were trained together in their childhoods; and there rooted
betwixt them then such an affection, which cannot choose but
branch now...they have seemed to be together, though absent,
shook hands, as over a vast, and embraced, as it were, from the
ends of opposed winds.   The heavens continue their loves!
ARCH.:   I think there is not in the world either malice or
matter to alter it.   You have an unspeakable comfort of your
young prince Mamillius....

[...] Camillo and Archidamus prepare it [the audience] for what
it is about *not* to see (technique of the prepared surprise):
directed to expect a pair of happy and affectionate friends, the
audience is startled by seeing exactly the opposite: the two
monarchs enter separately, and one, perceived to be the other's
host, wears a look of barely controlled hostility that may at any
moment blacken into thundercloud.   The proof of this is in the
dialogue, which contains all the stage-directions necessary;
Polixenes leads in with his elaborate lines:

Nine changes of the watery star hath been
The shepherd's note since we have left our throne
Without a burthen: time as long again
Would be fill'd up, my brother, with our thanks;
And yet we should, for perpetuity,
Go hence in debt: and therefore, like a cipher,
Yet standing in rich place, I multiply
With one 'We thank you' many thousands moe
That go before it.

Polixenes is an artist in the language of court compliment, at
once flowery and formal, like Jacobean embroidery.   All the

flourish of his opening lines conveys no more information than
this: *'I am visiting the King and have been here nine months.'*
His closing lines, however, make it certain that he is standing
beside Hermione (she is perhaps upon his arm?) and addressing her.
With self-deprecating paronomasia, and a bow no doubt, he pays her
compliment:

>   And therefore, *like a cipher,*
>   *Yet standing in rich place*.....

To a visiting King there can be no richer place than next to the
Queen. This Queen, however, has something specially remarkable
about her: she is *visibly pregnant,* and near her hour, for a day
later we hear the First Lady tell Mamillius:

>   The queen your mother rounds apace.

This fact about her has been grasped by the audience at her first
entry, because they can see it is so; they hear the visiting King
say he has been there nine months; who can fail to wonder whether
the man so amicably addressing this expectant mother may not be
the father of her child? For what other possible reason can
Shakespeare have contrived the conversation so as to make him
specify nine changes of the inconstant moon? These things are not
done by accident; Shakespeare has established a complex situation
with the same inerrant economy, swiftness and originality that he
used to open 'Hamlet' or 'Macbeth'.
   How then is Leontes to bear himself? Again the clue lies in
the dialogue, in the calculated contrast between the flowery language of Polixenes and the one-syllabled two-edged utterances of
his host. To the airy conceits of his boyhood's friend, Leontes
replies with ironic brevity, sprinkled with equivocation:

>   Stay your thanks awhile;
>   And pay them when you part.

[...] The *équivoques* [prevarications] of Leontes continue to alternate with the flourishes of Polixenes, mannerly on the surface,
menacing beneath:

>   We are tougher, brother,
>   Than you can put us to't.

>   Tongue-tied, our queen? speak you.

'Our queen' are cold vocables for married love and 'tongue-tied'
is a familiar epithet for guilt. It is clear that Leontes, as in
the source-story which Shakespeare was following, has long since
been jealous and is angling now (as he admits later) with his sardonic amphibologies, to catch Polixenes in the trap of the invita-
tion to prolong his stay, before he can escape to Bohemia and be
safe. All this [...] is easy for an actor to suggest, facially
and vocally, and it is the shock we have been prepared to receive
by the conversation of Archidamus and Camillo. We have witnessed

a little miracle of stage-craft.

FATHER TIME

> In this play of ours, having to skip sixteen years after Act 3,
> he desperately drags in Father Time with an hour-glass ... which
> means on interpretation that Shakespeare, having proposed to
> himself a drama in which a wronged woman has to bear a child,
> who has to be lost for years and restored to her as a grown
> girl, simply did not know how to do it, save by invoking some
> such device (Sir Arthur Quiller-Couch). (4)

> Time the Chorus is not central at all but a necessary mechanism
> of the plot ... (S.L. Bethell). (5)

Both critics essentially regard Time as a mechanism for over-
leaping sixteen years and therefore necessary to the plot. But in
fact, if that is all he is there for, he is redundant. His choric
soliloquy makes three plot-points: first, that we are to slide
over sixteen years, second, that Leontes has shut himself away in
penitence for his great sin, and, third, that we are about to hear
of Florizel and Perdita. As all these points are clearly made in
the scene immediately following (between Camillo and Polixenes),
Time and his speech, so far as mere plot is concerned, could be
cut without much loss; but the loss to the theme and quality of
the play would be enormous, for Time is absolutely central to both
and if he were not a character in the play, it would be necessary
to invent him. His function is as follows: he shows us we are
being taken beyond 'realism' into the region of parable and fable,
adumbrated in the title of the play. Time stands at the turn of
the tide of mood, from tragedy to comedy, and makes a kind of
pause or poise at the play's centre; coming to us from an
unexpected supernatural or mythological region, yet he encourages
us (in spite of that solemnity) to enter with confidence, by the
easy-going familiarity of his direct address, into that mood of
comedy initiated by the no less unexpected bear. The same unique
imagination envisaged both Time and bear for the great moment
necessary to the narrative and to the theme it bears, when the
hour-glass turns and the darkness passes. To take a further step
in the defence of Time's presence in the play will perhaps lead
me into the subjective interpretations I believe myself so far to
have avoided; but the risk must be taken. Few will deny that the
central theme is the sin of Leontes, which has its wages in the
death, and seeming death or dispersion of all that he loves; but,
under the guidance of Paulina, this sin is long and truly repen-
ted, and the self-inflicted wound, given, as Camillo says, by one
who is 'in rebellion with himself' is healed. But repentance and
healing both take *time*; Time is the tester:

> I, that please some, try all.

Time is at the heart of the play's mystery; why should his visible
presence offend? We do not take offence at Time with his hour-

glass in a Bronzino or a Van Dyck; why then in Shakespeare? He
who holds too tenaciously in the study of Shakespeare to 'realism'
and the Unities, has left the punt and is clinging to the pole.
[...]

THE STATUE SCENE

Of all Shakespeare's *coups de théâtre,* the descent of Hermione
from her pedestal is perhaps the most spectacular and affecting;
it is also one of the most carefully contrived and has indeed been
indicted for its contrivance: 'Hermione's is not a genuine
resurrection...The very staginess of this 'statue' scene acknow-
ledges the inadequacy of the dramatic means' (S.L. Bethell). (6)
These dramatic means (Bethell seems to argue) are inadequate to
certain religious ends he senses in the play. I had hoped in this
essay to avoid those private, still more metaphysical interpretations, to which even the best of us are liable; but since, by
drawing attention to the fineness of Shakespeare's stage-craft in
this scene, I may be aggravating the charge of staginess, let it
be admitted certainly that Hermione is not a Lazarus, come from
the dead, come back to tell us all; that she is *believed* dead is
one of those errors which Time makes and unfolds. The spiritual
meaning of the play in no way depends on her being a Lazarus or
an Alcestis. It is a play about a crisis in the life of Leontes,
not of Hermione, and her restoration to him (it is not a 'resurrection') is something which happens not to her, but to *him*. He
had thought her dead by his own hand ('She I kill'd') and now finds
her unexpectedly alive in the guardianship of Paulina. (So a man
who believed himself to have destroyed his soul by some great sin
might, after a long repentance under his Conscience, find that
that very Conscience had unknown to him kept his soul in being and
could at last restore it to him alive and whole.) That is the
miracle, it seems to me, for which Shakespeare so carefully
prepared.
    It had to be a miracle not only for Leontes, but for the
audience. His first dramaturgical job, then, was to ensure that
the audience, like Leontes, should *believe her dead*. For this
reason her death is repeatedly reasserted during the play by a
number of characters, and accepted by all as a fact. Shakespeare's next care was to give credentials to the statue. The
audience must accept it *as a statue,* not as a woman; so the Third
Gentleman names its sculptor, an actual man, Giulio Romano; a
novel trick to borrow a kind of authenticity from the 'real'
world of the audience, to lend solidity to the imaginary world of
the play; it seems to confer a special statueishness. For the
same reason Paulina warns Leontes that the colour on it is not
yet dry.
    But above all Shakespeare stretched his art in creating for his
'statue' a long stillness. For eighty lines and more Hermione
must stand, discovered on her pedestal, not seeming to breathe;
that is, for some four long minutes. Those among the audience who
may think her a living woman, encouraged by Paulina's promise to
'make the statue move indeed', must be *reconvinced against hope*

that she is a statue if the miracle is really to work excitingly
for them. So when at last Hermione is bidden to descend Shakespeare does not allow her to budge; against all the invocations of
Paulina, he piles up colons, twelve in five lines; it is the most
heavily punctuated passage I have found in Folio. It can be no
other than his deliberate contrivance for this special effect;
only at the end of the long, pausing entreaty, when the suspense
of her motionlessness has been continued until it must seem
unendurable, is Hermione allowed to move:

> Musick; awake her: Strike:
> 'Tis time: descend: be Stone no more: approach:
> Strike all that looke vpon with meruaile: Come:
> Ile fill your Graue vp: stirre: nay, come away:
> Bequeath to Death your numnesse: (for from him,
> Deare Life redeemes you) you perceiue she stirres...

There is nothing antiquated or otiose in stage-craft such as this.

NOTES

1 Sir Arthur Quiller-Couch and John Dover Wilson, 'The Winter's
   Tale' (Cambridge, 1931, p. xvi). This work hereafter will be
   referred to as 'WT' (Camb.).
2 'The Winter's Tale: A Study' (1946), p. 78. This important
   work is a contribution to the imaginative and philosophical
   understanding of the play; although in my essay I have only
   quoted from it to disagree, the disagreements are largely of
   a technical kind on relatively minor matters.
3 ibid., p. 122.
4 'WT' (Camb.), p. xix.
5 op. cit., p. 89.
6 op. cit., p. 103.

3. 11 JOHN RUSSELL BROWN

> Playing for Laughs: the Last Plays,
> 'Shakespeare's Plays in Performance',
> Arnold, 1966, pp. 104-6

A full clown's performance in 'The Winter's Tale' importantly
affects the theatrical life of the play. In a story that moves
from prosperity through destruction to regeneration, from separation to reconciliation, the clown presents a character who is
both a failure and a success. In an intensely felt narrative he
evokes from the audience laughter, connivance and appreciation,
relaxation and admiration. In a drama about the influences of
time, he provides a timeless artistry and remains unchanged at
the conclusion. He brings topicality to a fantastic tale, an
escape from the consequences of knavery to a moral confrontation,
and a grotesque embodiment of irresponsible fears and aggressions,

of vigorous and sexual activity, to a shapely and often refined
romance.

The relevance of his role can be gauged partly through particular verbal contact with the rest of the play: Florizel calls
Perdita a goddess, as Autolycus sings his wares 'as they were
gods and goddesses'; Polixenes calls her a 'knack', the word he
used for Autolycus' pedlar's wares; Perdita's 'blood looks out'
at Florizel's whisperings, after Autolycus had hailed 'red blood'
that reigns in 'winter's pale'; and Florizel had disappeared from
court, as Autolycus' ballad promises:

Get you hence, for I must go
Where it fits not you to know.

So the clown's disguise, trickery, thieving and easy excitement
of 'summer songs....While we lie tumbling in the hay' are shown
to be relevant to the affairs of the main plot. Later the very
clothes for disguising Florizel are taken from Autolycus' disguise, and the fearful trembling of this clown is a reminder of
the dangers the King's son is risking.

But Autolycus' contribution to the play is greatest at its most
general. His heightening of the 'mirth of the feast' - the
licence of instinctive and irresponsible enjoyment - enables
Shakespeare to present Florizel and Perdita without stiffness and
yet with contrasting carefulness; it also enables the dance of the
wild 'men of hair' to make its contrast with the earlier decorous
dance with immediate acceptance as another divertissement. The
last exit for Autolycus in Act V, with its climactic and possibly
silent humour, is an important device to relax the critical
attention of the audience immediately before Hermione is revealed
as a painted statue. Grock used to play Verdi on a diminutive
concertina at the end of his act, and it always seemed powerfully
seductive to the audience; and so here, the audience's content-
ment at the invincible humour and roguery of Autolycus disposes
it to accept the strange, severe and sweetened theatricality of
the concluding scene. Laughter and dreams alike release our fan-
tasies from the restrictive control of our censoring minds; so,
having joined everyman's laughter at the undeserved and unfounded
resilience of Autolycus, the audience will more readily accept
the dreamlike conditions of the final scene, the living statue
that

Excels whatever yet you look'd upon
Or hand of man hath done.

Laughter has contrived the relaxed and uncritical condition suitable for the acceptance of a further and solemn fantasy.

'Dreams are toys' argues Antigonus in III.3, and at the end of
'A Midsummer Night's Dream' Puck asks that the whole comedy should
be accepted as an idle dream. So much Shakespeare certainly knew
about the connexions between fantasy and humour, and his contemporaries accepted it too. The total solemnity of much crticism
of the last plays that is current today would strike Elizabethans
and Jacobeans as pompous and restrictive. Romance, for them,

spelt wonder, delight, *and* mirth.   The prologue to the romantic
comedy 'Mucedorus' expresses this directly:

> Mirth drown your bosom, fair Delight your mind,
> And may our pastime your contentment find.

And 'The Winter's Tale' has more 'pastime' than Autolycus.   The
two shepherds are traditional rustic comics, with muddled meetings and muddled speeches; they mix comedy and pathos in discovering the disastrous end of Antigonus; they mistake meanings, labour
slowly in witticisms, attempt mimicry, and, like Autolycus, leave
the play with more troubles obviously to come.   There is comedy,
too, in the earlier scenes of the main plot, especially in the
contrasts between the forthright Paulina and the timid jailer and
courtiers, and the two husbands, Antigonus and Leontes.   All the
comedy contributes to the final effect of the play, by its fantasy and freedom, obviously; but also by the individuality, topicality and robust vitality that are required to perform the more
comic roles.

3. 12 G. WILSON KNIGHT

> Great Creating Nature: an Essay on 'The Winter's
> Tale', 'The Crown of Life', Methuen, 1948, pp. 120-6

Now 'The Winter's Tale' is hammering on the threshold of some
extraordinary truth related to both 'nature' and 'eternity'.
Hence its emphasis on the seasons, birth and childhood, the continual moulding of new miracles on the pattern of the old; hence,
too, the desire expressed for youthful excellence perpetuated
and eternal; the thought of Perdita's every action as a 'crowned'
thing, a 'queen', in its own eternal right; and also of art as
improving or distorting nature, in the flower-dialogue, in Julio
Romano's uncanny, eternity-imitating, skill.   And yet no metaphysics, no natural philosophy or art, satisfy the demand that the
lost thing, in all its nature-born warmth, be preserved; that it,
not only its descendant, shall live; that death be revealed as a
sin-born illusion; that eternity be flesh and blood.
  The action moves to the house of the 'grave and good Paulina'.
The scene is her 'chapel', recalling the chapel of death at
III. ii. 240, where Leontes last saw Hermione's dead body.
Paulina shows them the statue, which excels anything 'the hand of
man hath done'; and they are quickly struck with - again the
word - 'wonder'.   Leontes gazes; recognizes Hermione's 'natural
posture'; asks her to chide him, yet remembers how she was tender
as infancy and grace':

> O! thus she stood,
> Even with such life of majesty - warm life
> As now it coldly stands - when first I woo'd her.
> I am asham'd: does not the stone rebuke me
> For being more stone than it?   O, royal piece!

Sweet though it be, it remains cold and withdrawn, like Keats'
Grecian Urn. Yet its 'majesty' exerts a strangely potent 'magic'
before which Perdita kneels almost in 'superstition'. Leontes'
grief is so great that Camillo reminds him how 'sixteen winters'
and 'so many summers' should by now alternately have blown and
dried his soul clean of 'sorrow'; why should that prove more persistent than short-lived 'joy'? Leontes remains still, his soul
pierced by remembrance. Paulina, however, speaks realistically of
the statue as art, saying how its colour is not dry yet; half
apologizing for the way it moves him, her phrase 'for the stone is
mine' re-emphasizing her peculiar office. She offers to draw the
curtain, fearing lest Leontes' 'fancy may think anon it moves'.
The excitement generated, already intense, reaches new impact and
definition in Paulina's sharp ringing utterance on 'moves'.

But Leontes remains quiet, fixed, in an other-worldly consciousness, a living death not to be disturbed, yet trembling with
expectance:

    Let be, let be!
    Would I were dead, but that, methinks, already -
    What was he that did make it?

A universe of meaning is hinted by that one word 'already' and
the subsequent, tantalizing, break. Now the statue seems no
longer cold:

    See, my lord,
    Would you not deem it breath'd, and that those veins
    Did verily bear blood?

As the revelation slowly matures, it is as though Leontes' own
grief and love were gradually infusing the thing before him with
life. He, under Paulina, is labouring, even now, that it may
live. The more visionary, paradisal, personal wonder of Pericles
(who alone hears the spheral music) becomes here a crucial conflict, an *agon,* in which many persons share; dream is being
forced into actuality. 'Masterly done', answers Polixenes,
taking us back to common-sense, and yet again noting that 'the
very life seems warm upon her lip'. We are poised between motion
and stillness, life and art:

    The fixure of her eye has motion in't,
    As we are mock'd with art.

The contrast drives deep, recalling the balancing of art and
nature in Perdita's dialogue with Polixenes; and, too, the
imaging of the living Marina as 'crown'd Truth' or monumental
Patience ('Pericles'). Paulina reiterates her offer to draw the
curtain lest Leontes be so far 'transported' (a word strongly toned
in Shakespeare with magical suggestion) that he actually think it
'lives' - thus recharging the scene with an impossible expectation.
To which Leontes replies:

No settled senses of the world can match
The pleasure of that madness. Let't alone.

He would stand here, spell-bound, forever; forever gazing on this
sphinx-like boundary between art and life.
   Paulina, having functioned throughout as the Oracle's implement,
becomes now its priestess. Her swift changes key the scene to an
extraordinary pitch, as she hints at new marvels:

I am sorry, sir, I have thus far stirr'd you: but
I could afflict you further.

She has long caused, and still causes, Leontes to suffer poignantly;
and yet his suffering has undergone a subtle change, for now this
very 'affliction has a taste as sweet as any cordial comfort'.
Already we have found joy and sorrow in partnership, as, too, in
the description of Cordelia's grief ('King Lear'). So Leontes
endures a pain of ineffable sweetness as the mystery unfolds:

Still, methinks,
There is an air comes from her: what fine chisel
Could ever yet cut breath?

However highly we value the eternity phrased by art (as in Yeats'
'monuments of unaging intellect' in Sailing to Byzantium and
Keats' Grecian Urn), yet there is a frontier beyond which it and
all corresponding philosophies fail: they lack one thing,
breath. With a fine pungency of phrase, more humanly relevant
than Othello's 'I know not where is that Promethean heat...', a
whole world of human idealism is dismissed. The supreme moments
of earlier tragedy - Othello before the 'monumental alabaster'
of the sleeping Desdemona, Romeo in Capel's monument, Juliet and
Cleopatra blending sleep and death - are implicit in Leontes'
experience; more, their validity is at stake, as he murmurs, 'Let
no man mock me', stepping forward for an embrace; as old Lear,
reunited with Cordelia, 'a spirit in bliss', says 'Do not laugh
at me'; as Pericles fears lest his reunion with Marina be merely
such a dream as 'mocks' man's grief. Those, and other, supreme
moments of pathos are here re-enacted to a stronger purpose.
Leontes strides forward; is prevented by Paulina; we are brought
up against a *cul-de-sac*. But Paulina herself immediately
releases new impetus as she cries, her voice quivering with the
Sibylline power she wields:

Either forbear,
Quite presently the chapel, or resolve you
For more amazement. If you can behold it,
I'll make the statue move indeed, descend,
And take you by the hand; but then you'll think -
Which I protest against - I am assisted
By wicked powers.

The 'chapel' setting is necessary, for we attend the resurrection
of a supposedly buried person; the solemnity is at least half

funereal. Much is involved in the phrase 'wicked powers': we
watch no act of necromancy. The 'magic', if magic it be, is a
white magic; shall we say, a natural magic; the living opposite of
the Ghost in 'Hamlet' hideously breaking his tomb's 'ponderous and
marble jaws'. The difference is that between Prospero's powers
in 'The Tempest' and those of Marlowe's Faustus or of the Weird
Sisters in 'Macbeth'. The distinction in Shakespeare's day was
important and further driven home by Paulina's:

> It is requir'd
> You do awake your faith. Then, all stand still;
> Or those that think it is unlawful business
> I am about, let them depart.

The key-word 'faith' enlists New Testament associations, but to it
Paulina adds a potency more purely Shakespearian: music. Shakespeare's use of music, throughout his main antagonist to tempestu-
ous tragedy, reaches a newly urgent precision at Cerimon's restoration of Thaisa and Pericles' reunion with Marina. Here it functions as the specifically releasing agent:

> PAULINA: Music, awake her: strike! (*Music sounds*)
>   'Tis time; descend; be stone no more; approach;
>   Strike all that look upon with marvel. Come;
>   I'll fill your grave up: stir, nay, come away;
>   Bequeath to death your numbness, for from him
>   Dear life redeems you. You perceive she stirs:
> (*Hermione comes down*)
>   Start not; her actions shall be holy as
>   You hear my spell is lawful: do not shun her
>   Until you see her die again, for then
>   You kill her double. Nay, present your hand:
>   When she was young you woo'd her; now in age
>   Is she become the suitor?
> LEONTES: O! she's warm.
>   If this be magic, let it be an art
>   Lawful as eating.

'Redeems', 'holy' and 'lawful' continue earlier emphases. The
concreteness of 'fill your grave up' has analogies in Shelley's
Witch of Atlas and the empty sepulchre of the New Testament.
Such resurrections are imaged as a re-infusing of the dead body
with life. Hermione's restoration not only has nothing to do with
black magic; it is not even transcendental. It exists in warm
human actuality: hence our earlier emphases on warmth and
breath; and now on 'eating' too. It is, indeed, part after all of
'great creating nature'; no more, and no less; merely another
miracle from the great power, the master-artist of creation, call
it what you will, nature or eternity, Apollo or - as in the New
Testament - 'the living God'.
    The poet carefully refuses to elucidate the mystery on the
plane of plot-realism. When Polixenes wonders where Hermione 'has
liv'd' or 'how stol'n from the dead', Paulina merely observes that
she *is* living, and that this truth, if reported rather than

experienced, would 'be hooted at like an old tale'. Perdita's
assistance is needed to unloose Hermione's speech; whereupon she
speaks, invoking the gods 'sacred vials' of blessing on her
daughter and referring to the Oracle. Leontes further drives home
our enigma by remarking that Paulina has found his wife, though
'how is to be question'd'; for, he says,

> I saw her
> As I thought, dead, and have in vain said many
> A prayer upon her grave.

We are not, in fact, to search for answers on this plane at all:
the poet himself does not know them. Certainly our plot-realism
is maintained: Paulina reminds us that her husband is gone; and
we may remember Mamilius. It is the same in 'Pericles'. The
subsidiary persons are no longer, as persons, important: the per-
functory marrying of Paulina and Camillo to round off the ritual
might otherwise be a serious blemish.

MOLIÈRE: 'TARTUFFE'*

4. 1 HARDOUIN, ARCHBISHOP OF PARIS

Ordinance Against 'Tartuffe' (1667),
trans. S. Khin Zaw

HARDOUIN, by the grace of God and the Holy Apostolic See Arch-
bishop of Paris, to all Parish Priests and Curates of this town
and suburbs, GREETINGS in Our Lord. Seeing that it has been
pointed out to us by our Fiscal Procurator that on the fifth
Friday of this month, there was performed in one of the Theatres
of this Town, under the name of 'The Impostor', a very dangerous
Comedy, which is all the more apt to harm Religion in that under
the pretext of condemning hypocrisy, or false devotion, it lays
open to such condemnations all those who profess the most solid
piety, and thereby exposes them to the continual mockeries and
calumnies of Libertines; so that to stay the course of so great
an evil, which could tempt away weak souls and turn them from the
path of virtue, our said Fiscal Procurator has prayed us to forbid
all persons of our Diocese to perform the aforesaid Comedy under
any name whatsoever, to read it, or to hear it recited, whether in
public or in private, on pain of Excommunication ...

NOTE

* Molière's 'Le Tartuffe' was first performed privately in Paris
  in 1664 and publicly in 1667 in an altered version titled
  'L'Imposteur'.

4. 2 MOLIÈRE

Preface to 'Tartuffe' (1669), trans. C.J. Raab

There has been a good deal of fuss about this comedy, which has
been under attack for a long time; the sorts of people it pillories

have made it very apparent that they are more powerful in France than those I have satirized so far. The nobility, the bluestockings, the cuckolds and the doctors have calmly accepted their characterization, and they have pretended to be as amused as everyone else at their stage portraits. The hypocrites, however, would not stand for it; they were at first furious and could not understand why I was bold enough to show up their dissimulations and why I wanted to disparage an occupation practised by many worthy people. It was an unforgivable crime, and they have all risen in arms against my comedy with a frightful rage. They have very carefully not attacked it on the front from which they received their wounds - they are too wily for that and too much men of the world to disclose their innermost feelings. Following their usual habit, they have cloaked their interests under the guise of God's cause and, according to what they say, 'Le Tartuffe' is a play offensive to piety. From beginning to end it is full of abominations, and the whole work should be put on the bonfire. Every syllable is a desecration, even the gestures are criminal - the least flutter of an eyelid, the slightest movement of the head, the smallest step to left or right conceal mysteries for which they find means to attribute low motives on my part.

In vain did I show it to my friends to criticize and to everyone to disapprove. The revisions I made, the opinion of the king and queen (who have seen it), the approval of the great princes and the ministers who have openly honoured it by their presence, the evidence of worthy people who have found it valuable - none of this has helped in any way. None of my detractors would budge - and still their ardent champions make daily proclamations of pious defamation and condemn me in the name of charity.

I would not mind at all what they say, were it not for their ruses in making enemies out of people I respect and in gathering into their ranks truly worthy people whom they make misjudge their own honest opinion and accept the views of others. This is what forces me to defend myself. It is to the truly devout that I want to justify the direction of my comedy: I beg them, with all my heart, not to condemn things before they have seen them, to get rid of any preconceived opinions and in no way to fall a prey to the passion of those whose dissimulations do them no credit.

If one takes the trouble to examine my comedy disinterestedly, it will be found that my intentions are manifestly innocent throughout, and that it never mocks things that should be reverenced; I have taken the utmost precautions in dealing with the delicate subject-matter, and I have used all my skill and taken the greatest possible care to distinguish between the character of the hypocrite and that of the truly holy man. Thus I have taken up two whole acts in preparing the entrance of my scoundrel. The listener in the audience is not in doubt for a single moment; the man is immediately recognizable from the distinguishing marks I have given him - from start to finish every word, every action, depicts for the spectators a wicked man and shows the true worthy man in shining contrast.

I know very well that these gentlemen, by way of response, try to imply that these matters have nothing to do with theatre, but

I would like to ask them, with their permission, to tell me the
foundation for this fine maxim. It is a proposition that is only
surmise and that cannot be proved. And yet it should not be difficult to make them admit that, in olden times, comedy arose out
of religion and played a part in its mysteries: the Spaniards,
our neighbours, incorporated comedy into almost all their festivals; in our own country, even, it originated thanks to a guild
to which the Hotel de Bourgogne still belongs - a place which was
set aside for the representation of the most important mysteries
of our faith; comedies are still printed in Gothic letters in the
name of a doctor of the Sorbonne; an immediate example here at
hand is that the holy plays of M. de Corneille have been performed
to the admiration of France as a whole.

If the aim of comedy is to correct the vices of men, I see no
reason why there should be privileged exceptions. For the state,
this can have more dangerous consequences than any other - we have
seen that the theatre has an important moral influence. The
finest features of a serious moral piece are less effective, more
often than not, than those of satire; nothing so affects most men
as the depiction of their faults. Vices are under great attack
when they are exposed to general ridicule. Criticism may be
easily borne; scorn, never. A man may not mind being a scoundrel;
he can never abide being a laughing stock.

I have been accused of putting words of piety into the mouth of
my impostor. Well, how could I do otherwise if I were to show the
character of a hypocrite accurately? I think it is enough that I
explain the criminal motives behind what he says, and that I have
cut out those religious expressions which would have been badly
received had he used them. Act IV begins with a pernicious
moral - but has not this moral been dinned into the ears of
everyone? Is my comedy the first to express it? Is it to be
feared that people's minds will be influenced by matters so universally loathed? Do I make them dangerous by introducing them
onto the stage? Will they receive any seal of approval by being
expressed by a scoundrel? There is not the least indication of
that, and either my comedy 'Le Tartuffe' ought to be approved or
all comedies ought to be banned altogether.

This is what people have been concentrating on for some time,
and never before have such feelings against the theatre burst
forth. I cannot deny that some churchmen have indeed condemned
comedy; on the other hand, it must be admitted that others have
treated it rather more gently. Thus the so-called authority upon
which this criticism is based is negated by this division of
opinion. The only conclusion to be drawn from this lack of unani-
mity among men who have received their enlightenment from the same
sources is that they have fastened upon different aspects of
comedy: some have seen only its purity, while others have considered it only as a vehicle for corruption and have lumped it
together with those infamous shows that are rightly called
degrading.

And, indeed, since argument concerns things, not words, and
since most contradictions arise out of misunderstandings and using
the same word to express opposite meanings, all that is needed
is to lift the veil of equivocation and look at comedy in itself

to see whether it should be condemned. It can doubtless be easily
seen that because it is no more than an ingenious poem that
points out men's faults through painless lessons, it does not
deserve to be unjustly criticized. Further, if we want to learn
from antiquity, we will find that the most famous philosophers
praised comedy – these were men of the most rigorous scholarship
who were constantly protesting against the vices of their time.
We will find that Aristotle devoted his labours to the theatre and
took the trouble to construct principles for the art of writing
comedy. We will discover that some of the greatest men of olden
time, and the most esteemed, prided themselves on writing
comedies; that others of them did not disdain to recite in public
those they had composed. In Greece this brilliant art was greatly
enhanced by prizes of glory and the superb theatres dedicated to
its honour; later, in Rome, the most outstanding honours were
heaped upon it – I am not talking about Rome in decline, under
licentious emperors, but about her period of order under wise
consuls, when Roman virtue flourished.

I agree that there have been times when comedy has been
corrupt. But does anything in the world exist that is not corrupted daily? There is nothing so innocent that something criminal cannot be found in it, no art so healthy that its intentions
may not be turned upside down, nothing so intrinsically good that
it may not be put to evil use. Medicine is a worth-while art and
is universally revered as one of the most excellent things we
have, and yet there have been times when it has become hateful;
often it has been turned into a means of poisoning people. Philosophy is a gift from heaven – it was bestowed upon us in order that
our spirits might be brought to the knowledge of a God through contemplation of the wonders of nature – although it must not be forgotten that it has frequently been deflected from its proper use
and publicly made use of in order to uphold impiety. Even the
most holy things are not sacrosanct from corruption by men, and
every day we see scoundrels who abuse piety and wickedly put it at
the service of the greatest crimes. But, none the less, there are
distinctions that must be made. One must never falsely confuse the
goodness of corrupted things with the wickedness of the corrupters.
A distinction must always be made between the evil usage and the
good intentions of art, and as one does not go so far as to defend
the banishment of medicine from Rome or the public condemnation of
philosophy at Athens, so one should not wish to forbid comedy
because it has been criticized at certain times. The reasons for
this censorship are not valid here; it was limited by what it
could see, and we should certainly not try to drag it out beyond
those limits that it set for itself, to stretch it unreasonably
and make it embrace the innocent together with the guilty. The
comedy that it aimed to attack has nothing to do with the comedy
I am defending. One must take care not to confuse the one with
the other. They are like two people whose ways of life are dia-
metrically opposed. The only connection between them is a similarity of names; it would be utterly unjust to want to condemn
Olympia, who is a good woman, because there is an Olympia who is
immoral. (1) Surely such judgments would make for much confusion
in the world. Nothing anywhere would be safe from condemnation,

and as we are not nearly vigilant enough about many things we criticize every day, we ought to treat comedy with the same courtesy and applaud those plays where moral instruction and honesty are seen to triumph.

I know very well that some people are too refined to endure any comedy at all, who say that the most honest ones are the most dangerous, that the passions portrayed are the more moving, the more virtuous they are, and that these sorts of portrayals have a bad moral influence. I do not see that it is such a crime to be influenced by the sight of an honest passion or that this complete insensibility to which they would have us aspire is such an elevated state of virtue. I doubt whether such great perfection exists within the forces of human nature, and I am not sure whether it is not better to try to modify and elevate the passions of men than to cut them out entirely. I know that there are places more worthy to be visited than the theatre, and, if one wants to condemn everything that does not lead directly to God and our salvation, that comedy must be included and I am not averse to its being condemned with everything else. Given, however (and it is true), that one may take a rest from piety, and that men need amusement, I declare that no amusement is more innocent than comedy. But I have wandered too far from the point. Let me finish with the words of a great prince (2) about the comedy 'Le Tartuffe'.

Eight days after 'Tartuffe' had been banned, a play called 'Scaramouche the Hermit' was put on in the presence of the court. (3) On leaving, the king said to the prince I have mentioned: 'I would really like to know why the people who were so shocked at Molière's comedy say nothing about "Scaramouche".' The prince replied: 'The reason is that "Scaramouche" pillories heaven and religion, for which these people don't care tuppence; they themselves are pilloried by Molière, and that they cannot bear.'

NOTES (*)

1 It has been said that Molière, in mentioning the name of Olympia, wished to hit at Olympia Maldachini, a sister-in-law of Pope Innocent X. This Pope died in 1655, and was the author of the bull against the five propositions of Jansenius. The life of the lady, who was far from a saint, had only lately been translated from the Italian into French.
2 The Prince de Condé.
3 The farce of 'Scaramouche the Hermit' contained many indecent situations; amongst others, that of a monk entering by the balcony into the house of a married woman.
* Notes quoted from Preface to 'Tartuffe', trans. H. van Laun, 'Reader's Encyclopedia of World Drama', ed. J. Gassner and E. Quinn, Methuen, 1970, p. 973.

4. 3 ERICH AUERBACH

The *Faux Dévot*, 'Mimesis: the Representation of
Reality in Western Literature', trans. W.R. Trask,
Princeton University Press, Princeton, N.J., 1953,
pp. 359-62

The portrait of the *faux dévot* [religious hypocrite] in the chap-
ter 'De la mode' [On Fashion] in La Bruyère's 'Caractères' contains
a number of polemic allusions to Molière's 'Tartuffe'. The *faux
dévot*, La Bruyère says at once, does not speak of '"my hair shirt
and my scourge"; on the contrary; he would pass for what he is,
for a hypocrite, and he wants to pass for what he is not, for a
devout man: it is true that he behaves in a way which makes
people believe, without his saying so, that he wears a hair shirt
and scourges himself.' Later he criticizes Tartuffe's behaviour
in Orgon's house:

> If he finds himself on a good footing with a wealthy man, whom
> he has been able to take in, whose parasite he is, and from
> whom he can draw great assistance, he does not cajole his wife,
> at least he does not make advances nor a declaration to her;
> he will run away, he will leave his cloak in her hands, if he is
> not as sure of her as of himself. Still less will he employ the
> jargon of devotion to flatter her and seduce her; he does not
> speak it from habit, but from design and according as it is
> useful to him, and never when it would serve only to make him
> extremely ridiculous ... He has no idea of becoming his sole
> heir, nor of getting him to give him his entire estate, especi-
> ally if it is a case of taking it away from a son, the legiti-
> mate heir: a devout man is neither avaricious nor violent nor
> unjust nor even interested: Onuphre is not devout, but he
> wants to be thought so and, by a perfect, though false, imita-
> tion of piety, to take care of his interests secretly: hence
> he never ventures to confront the direct line and he never
> insinuates himself into a family where there are both a daugh-
> ter to be provided for and a son to be set up in the world;
> such rights are too strong and too inviolable: they cannot be
> infringed without scandal (and he dreads scandal), without such
> an attempt coming to the ears of the Prince, from whom he hides
> his course because he fears to be exposed and to appear as what
> he is. He has designs on the collateral line: it is more
> safely to be attacked; he is the terror of cousins male and
> female, of nephew and niece, the flatterer and declared friend
> of all uncles who have acquired fortunes; he claims to be the
> legitimate heir of every old man who dies wealthy and child-
> less ....

Here La Bruyère is apparently thinking of the perfect, one might
say, the ideal, type of the *faux dévot*, who is nothing but a hypocrite and who, without any human weakness or inconsistency, constantly vigilant, constantly rational, steadily pursues the coolly
premeditated plan which goes with his part. But Molière cannot

possibly have intended to bring a perfect incarnation of the term
faux dévot on the stage. He needed strong comic effects for the
stage, and he found them, most ingeniously, by contrasting the part
played by his Tartuffe with the man's natural character. This
strong, healthy fellow, [...] with his big appetite [...] and his
other no less strongly developed physical needs, has not the
slightest talent for piety, not even for a feigned piety. Everywhere the ass looks out from under the lion's skin. He plays his
part execrably by exaggerating it beyond all reason; and he loses
control over himself as soon as his senses are aroused. His
intrigues are crude and simple-minded, and no one except Orgon and
his mother can be taken in by him even for a moment - neither the
other actors in the play nor the audience. Tartuffe is not at all
the embodiment of an intelligent self-disciplined hypocrite, but a
coarse-grained fellow with strong, crude instincts who tries to
assume the attitude of a bigot because it seems to promise results
and despite the fact that it is not becoming to him at all and
clashes with his inner nature and outward appearance. And this is
precisely what impresses us as overwhelmingly comic. The critics
of the seventeenth century who, like La Bruyère, accepted only the
rationally plausible as probable would naturally wonder how it was
possible that even Orgon and Madame Pernelle should be taken in by
him. However, experience teaches us that even the crudest deception and the silliest temptation will succeed at times if they
flatter the habits and instincts of their victims and satisfy
their secret cravings. Orgon's most deeply instinctive and secret
craving, which he can indulge precisely by selling himself and his
soul to Tartuffe, is the sadism of a family tyrant. What he would
never dare to do without piety making it legitimate, for he is as
sentimental and uncertain of himself as he is choleric, he can now
give himself up to with a clear conscience. [...] He loves Tartuffe and lets himself be duped by him because Tartuffe makes it
possible for him to satisfy his instinctive urge to tyrannize over
and torment his family. This further weakens his power of judgment, which in itself is not too highly developed. A very similar
psychological process takes place in Madame Pernelle. And again
it is extremely ingenious how Molière makes use of piety itself to
remove the obstacles which impede the free development of Orgon's
sadism.
　　Here, as in many of his other plays, Molière is much less concerned with character types, he is much more intent upon rendering
the individual reality, than the majority of the moralists of his
century. He did not present 'the miser' but a perfectly specific
coughing old monomaniac; not 'the misanthropist' but a young man
of the best society, an unyielding fanatic of sincerity, who is
steeped in his own opinions, sits in judgment upon the world, and
finds it unworthy of himself; not 'the hypochondriac' but a
wealthy, extremely robust, healthy, and choleric family tyrant who
keeps forgetting his role of invalid. And yet no one can help
feeling that Molière fits perfectly into his moralizing and typi-
fying century, for he seeks the individually real only for the
sake of its ridiculousness, and to him ridiculousness means devi-
ation from the normal and customary. For him too a character
taken seriously would be 'typical.' He wants stage effects; his

genius is livelier and requires freer play. The short-winded and
finicky technique of La Bruyère, who builds up the abstractly
moral type from a mass of traits and anecdotes, is unsuited to the
stage; for the stage requires striking effects and greater homo-
geneity in the realm of the concrete and individual than in that
of the abstract and typical. But the moralistic attitude is
essentially the same.

4. 4 TYRONE GUTHRIE (*)

   Programme, National Theatre Company, Old Vic, 1967

It has been our aim to present 'Tartuffe' as comedy rather than
farce; to suggest the meaning underlying the goings-on rather
than just to make them as funny as we could. The meaning, we
believe, concerns the maintenance of order. The universe is seen
by Molière as a hierarchy with Almighty God at the top; under God
there are various degrees of authority. Kings are God's deputies
in the political sphere. At domestic level, the father of a
family represents the power, and should represent the loving
wisdom, of the Almighty Father.
   Tartuffe, although the name-part and a great creation, is not
the central figure of the play. Rather it is Orgon, who, by his
inordinate affection for, and foolishly misplaced trust in, Tartuffe, betrays the divine authority and belies the divine wisdom
which a father should embody. Terrible consequences are only
averted by the intervention of a higher power. Following the Greek
convention of a *deus ex machina,* Molière introduces a Messenger
from the King, a sort of secular cousin of the Archangel Raphael.
   The play is concerned with the results rather than the causes
of Orgon's lapse. Modern drama is apt to explore the psychic
causes of error. We are prone to believe that, if we uncover
its cause, the fruits of error will not ripen. Molière, unlike
Shakespeare, but like Shaw and like Sophocles, is less interested
in the causes than the wages of sin.

NOTE

* The production was directed by Tyrone Guthrie with Robert
  Stephens as Tartuffe and John Gielgud as Orgon.

4. 5 W.G. MOORE

   Mask, 'Molière: a New Criticism', Oxford University
   Press, 1949, pp. 49-50

It is remarkable that for many people this great play has ceased
to be a comedy at all; it is often read as if it were a realistic satire. No one could deny that sinister forces are here

suggested in powerful fashion. The mask of hypocrisy is an almost perfect fit, and ensures a steady increase of power to the wearer. It is probable that in a first three-act version of the play the mask was never removed and was completely successful. But that hypocrisy is a mask there should be no doubt. The sub-title of 'L'Imposteur' settles the question. The play is about a man who gives himself out to be what he is not; he wears the mask of piety and that is not in itself a comic proceeding, unless or until it be shown to be ... a mask, and not the man.

This elementary contrast within the man who plays a part is surely a basic feature of the role of Tartuffe. The part he plays is of vital importance to him. It assures his well-being and his domination over his fellows. It is the mask of a pious attitude, ascetic, world-renouncing, sanctimonious: 'Cover your bosom, I can't bear to see it.' But this part is not kept up all the time. We see more than the mask, at times, when for one reason or another he is not hypocritical but sincere. In any judgement of the part it would seem vital to ask when the mask falls. Can anything be deduced from the alternation of hypocrisy and sincerity? In the case of a classical dramatist this may reveal the dramatic purpose. The mask falls at four points of the action, twice with Orgon and twice with Elmire. Nowhere else in the play, as far as I can see, does Tartuffe pretend to be other than a holy man. These four points of the action are worth close scrutiny.

The first is the famous third scene of the third act. 'My bosom doesn't enfold a heart of stone'; with this statement the hypocrite seems to me to be leaving his role. It is the first of a series of ambiguous statements, which are true of his real nature as well as of the mask he has assumed. The point is more evident when he says: 'Ah, but being devout doesn't make me any less a man.' He intends surely to convey by this that humanity is not incompatible with piety. But his statement is true of himself as a natural and evil man: that his piety has not (in the least) affected his humanity, a statement which as a lover he may sustain, but which as an ascetic he would not. The same double echo is heard in a moment: 'But madam, after all, I'm no angel.' From this Tartuffe proceeds to something which is not ambiguous at all, to an avowal of sharp practice and trickery which he would not for the world have anyone but Elmire overhear:

> But people like us burn with a hidden fire,
> And with us one can be sure that it will remain a secret ...
> With us, if real intimacy is achieved, one can find
> Love without scandal and pleasure without fear.

This is the complete avowal, by the *masqué*, that his mask is a mask. It may not be funny; it is deeply comic.

The second glimpse of Tartuffe's sincerity seems to me even more instructive for the aesthetics of this play. Three scenes later (III. vi) Tartuffe, accused of seducing his employer's wife, pleads guilty, as indeed he was. His statements are all true:

> Each moment of my life is heavily blemished ...
> Do you trust me only by my appearance, my brother?

And from what you see, do you believe me to be any better?
No, no. You are letting yourself be taken in by outward
    appearances,
And I am even less, I am afraid, than one might think.
The world takes me for a good man;
But the simple truth is that I am worth nothing.

How can one escape the comedy of hearing, from one whose profession and practice it was to disguise the truth, 'the simple
truth'? With extreme ingenuity Molière forces his impostor into
a second situation where he can drop the mask, a situation quite
different from the first. For here to tell the truth is not the
result of natural, animal desire; it is the fruit of policy. To
tell the truth in that context is the highest and most successful
deception. He is not believed. So he can assume the mask once
more and cover his own advantage with the will of heaven: 'May
Heaven's will be done in everything.'
    It is, I suppose, highly unlikely that the first version of
the play contained a second interview between Tartuffe and
Elmire. There must have been strong reasons for making the impostor walk a second time into an obvious trap. Before we assume a
weakness on the part of the dramatist let us note what is gained
by the repetition. The force of the satire is not increased. The
character of Orgon is not affected. But the impostor is this time
not only completely exposed by his words, but actually discovered
beyond hope of justification. The mask is, so to speak,
almost torn off his face. To the objection that a clever scoundrel would have foreseen and avoided a second encounter there is a
plain answer. That Tartuffe does not foresee it is a feature of
his character; it is the final proof that he was not in that connexion wise, cautious, or cunning any longer; that, in a word, he
was infatuated. Once again the impostor is sincere, sincere in
his hesitation, in his professions of pleasure at her words which
he longs to hear:

    Their honey-sweetness sets my senses tingling all over -
    It's a sensation I have never had before.

Sincere also in his application to her of religious terms describing the happiness he may never have really felt before God
but does actually feel before her, and sincere above all in his
gross sensuality, that demands more than words, what she calls
'the ultimate favours' and he 'the realities'. This is the real
world in which he moves, and having admitted it he scoffs at
morality:

    If it is only Heaven which stands in the way of my vows,
    That is only a small obstacle for me to overcome.

To fear God is a ridiculous fear; casuistry can cover anything.
Sin does not count when concealed: 'It is no sin to sin in pri-
vate.' The new morality is to follow one's director blindly:
'You have only to let yourself be guided.'
    In the following scene there is a final glimpse of the real

man. When his pious excuses are cut short he claims that he is
master of the house, in the eyes of the law, that he will be a
match for all of them, and thus (picking up the mask again)
avenge heaven. In his last scene the mask is slightly adjusted
to that of the good citizen. He regards as his first duty the
good of the State. It is of some aesthetic importance to note
that he ends, as he began, by provoking Dorine's pungent comment,
'The impostor.'

If the foregoing analysis be sound, we are faced in this play
with a character at once more profound and more comic than has
been made clear. There is, to begin with, no doubt of its
realism. The author himself had in a significant stage-direction
to call attention to the fact that his impostor was a scoundrel.
He is indeed a sinister figure, 'a scoundrel whom the police are
seeking', as Vedel says, whom we fear rather than laugh at.
Brunetière expressed the typical reaction of the intelligent
spectator: 'If we laugh at his discomfitures, he is nevertheless
a famous rogue whom we fear, on the whole, rather than laugh at,
and if he is found to be a comic figure, then without doubt,
gentlemen, he is certainly that, but only in his own individual
way.' What for Brunetière was a grudging admission is roundly
denied by Michaut, as by so many readers. He admits that but for
a single passage he does not find Tartuffe comic at all. Agreed,
if comedy be limited to the pleasant things on the surface of
life, if 'comic' be more or less equated with 'funny' and thus
barred from dealing with mystery and evil. But there is no evidence that Molière held this view, nor that the wiser of his contemporaries thought his play less profound that the tragedies of
Racine.

The view that 'Tartuffe' is a comedy does not imply any softening of the character of the impostor. We may admit him to be a
sinister figure, but we should at the same time notice that
Molière has stressed this aspect far less than others. As a dangerous man he is kept in the background and hardly ever seen at
work. As a contrast in and to himself he is exhibited in an endless variety of pose. Molière was apparently not satisfied with
the contrast in the nature of an impostor, that his acts are at
variance with his professions. He carries the contrast to a much
deeper level, to situations which force the impostor to be himself, to drop the mask, as we have shown. It is vital to notice
how close is the connexion between Tartuffe's sincerity and his
undoing. He is unmasked, not primarily by others, not by Damis,
or the police, but (in our eyes, and it is after all for the
audience that the dramatic spectacle is staged) by himself. More
than this, he is not unmasked by his slips, or by a faulty technique, but because, and whenever, he wants to be. His scheme, in
fact, of being an impostor will not work. At times he does not
want it to work. Where intellectual ends are involved it works
to perfection; where more elementary and more human ends are
involved, such as the satisfaction of his animal desires, the
scheme does not work at all; it breaks down, because he is too
human to allow it to work. Brunetière has seen something of the
connexion between his skill and his weakness: 'Each attempt that
is made to unmask him or to kick him out only succeeds in

anchoring him more deeply and more firmly in Orgon's affections.
We wouldn't be able to deal with him at all, in fact, had he not -
happily for us - one weak spot: his sensuality.' But why should
this cardinal point be ascribed to luck? Nothing is lucky in
classical drama; all is design. Tartuffe fails, as M. Michaut has
made clear, precisely because he was over-confident of his powers,
because he reckoned without his appetites. 'His misfortune is
that success has intoxicated him; he has too much confidence in
his power of seduction. His sensuality, which he does not keep in
control, has made him blind; he makes his declaration ... he falls
into the trap ... his true wickedness standing out even in the
midst of his various passions.' It is not far from such a conception to discovery of the comic principle lying at the root of such
a character. Is it so much a misfortune that Tartuffe's human
nature escapes his calculation? Is this not the real nerve of the
play?

NOTE

* Quotations in the text translated by Richard Wilson.

CONGREVE: 'THE WAY OF THE WORLD'

5. 1   CONGREVE

Letter to John Dennis, 10 July 1695,
'William Congreve: Letters and Documents', ed.
J.C. Hodges, Macmillan, 1964, pp. 182-4

I should be unwilling to venture even on a bare Description of
Humour, much more, to make a Definition of it, but now my hand
is in, Ile tell you what serves me instead of either. I take it
to be, *A singular and unavoidable manner of doing, or saying any
thing, Peculiar and Natural to one Man only; by which his Speech
and Actions are distinguish'd from those of other Men.*
   Our *Humour* has relation to us, and to what proceeds from us,
as the Accidents have to a Substance; it is a Colour, Taste, and
Smell, Diffused through all; thô our Actions are never so many,
and different in Form, they are all Splinters of the same Wood,
and have Naturally one Complexion; which thô it may be disguised
by Art, yet cannot be wholly changed: We may Paint it with other
Colours, but we cannot change the Grain. So the Natural sound
of an Instrument will be distinguish'd, thô the Notes expressed
by it, are never so various, and the Divisions never so many.
Dissimulation, may by Degrees, become more easy to our practice;
but it can never absolutely Transubstantiate us into what we would
seem: It will always be in some proportion a Violence upon
Nature. [...]
   I dont doubt, but you have observed several Men Laugh when
they are Angry; others who are Silent; some that are Loud: Yet
I cannot suppose that it is the passion of *Anger* which is in it
self different, or more or less in one than t'other; but that it
is the *Humour* of the Man that is Predominant, and urges him to
express it in that manner. Demonstrations of pleasure are as
Various; one Man has a Humour of retiring from all Company, when
any thing has happen'd to please him beyond expectation; he hugs
himself alone, and thinks it an Addition to the pleasure to keep
it Secret. Another is upon Thorns till he has made Proclamation
of it; and must make other people sensible of his happiness

before he can be so himself. So it is in Grief, and other Passions. Demonstrations of Love and the Effects of that Passion upon several Humours, are infinitely different. [...]

One might think that the Diversity of Humour, which must be allowed to be diffused throughout Mankind, might afford endless matter, for the support of Comedies. But when we come closely to consider that point, and nicely to distinguish the Difference of Humours, I believe we shall find the contrary. For thô we allow every Man something of his own, and a peculiar Humour; yet every Man has it not in quantity, to become Remarkable by it: Or, if many do become Remarkable by their Humours; yet all those Humours may not be Diverting. Nor is it only requisite to distinguish what Humour will be diverting, but also how much of it, what part of it to shew in Light, and what to cast in Shades; how to set it off by preparatory Scenes, and by opposing other humours to it in the same Scene. Thrô a wrong Judgment, sometimes, Mens Humours may be opposed when there is really no specific Difference between them; only a greater proportion of the same, in one than t'other; occasion'd by his having more Flegm, or Choller, or whatever the Constitution is, from whence their Humours derive their source.

5. 2 CHARLES LAMB

On the Artificial Comedy of the Last Century
(1823), 'The Essays of Elia', Dent, 1906,
pp. 167-8

The Fainalls and the Mirabels, the Dorimants and the Lady Touchwoods, in their own sphere, do not offend my moral sense; in fact they do not appeal to it at all. They seem engaged in their proper element. They break through no laws, or conscious restraints. They know of none. They have got out of Christendom into the land - what shall I call it? - of cuckoldry - the Utopia of gallantry, where pleasure is duty, and the manners perfect freedom. It is altogether a speculative scene of things, which has no reference whatever to the world that is. No good person can be justly offended as a spectator, because no good person suffers on the stage. Judged morally, every character in these plays - the few exceptions only are *mistakes* - is alike essentially vain and worthless. The great art of Congreve is especially shown in this, that he has entirely excluded from his scenes, - some little generosities on the part of Angelica perhaps excepted, - not only anything like a faultless character, but any pretensions to goodness or good feelings whatsoever. Whether he did this designedly, or instinctively, the effect is as happy, as the design (if design) was bold. I used to wonder at the strange power which his 'Way of the World' in particular possesses of interesting you all along in the pursuits of characters, for whom you absolutely care nothing - for you neither hate nor love his personages - and I think it is owing to this very indifference for any, that you endure the whole. He has spread a privation of

moral light, I will call it, rather than by the ugly name of palpable darkness, over his creations; and his shadows flit before
you without distinction or preference. Had he introduced a good
character, a single gush of moral feeling, a revulsion of the
judgment to actual life and actual duties, the impertinent Goshen
would have only lighted to the discovery of deformities, which
now are none, because we think them none.

    Translated into real life, the characters of his, and his
friend Wycherley's dramas, are profligates and strumpets, - the
business of their brief existence, the undivided pursuit of law-
less gallantry. No other spring of action, or possible motive of
conduct, is recognised; principles which, universally acted upon,
must reduce this frame of things to a chaos. But we do them
wrong in so translating them. No such effects are produced in
their world. When we are among them, we are amongst a chaotic
people. We are not to judge them by our usages. No reverend
institutions are insulted by their proceedings, - for they have
none among them. No peace of families is violated, - for no
family ties exist among them. No purity of the marriage bed is
stained, - for none is supposed to have a being. No deep affections are disquieted, - no holy wedlock bands are snapped asunder,
- for affection's depth and wedded faith are not of the growth of
that soil. There is neither right nor wrong, - gratitude or its
opposite, - claim or duty, - paternity or sonship. Of what consequence is it to virtue, or how is she at all concerned about it,
whether Sir Simon, or Dapperwit, steal away Miss Martha; or who
is the father of Lord Froth's, or Sir Paul Pliant's children.

    The whole is a passing pageant, where we should sit as uncon-
cerned at the issues, for life or death, as at a battle of the
frogs and mice. But, like Don Quixote, we take part against the
puppets, and quite as impertinently. We dare not contemplate an
Atlantis, a scheme, out of which our coxcombical moral sense is
for a little transitory ease excluded. We have not the courage
to imagine a state of things for which there is neither reward nor
punishment. We cling to the painful necessities of shame and
blame. We would indict our very dreams.

5. 3 BONAMY DOBRÉE

        'Restoration Comedy 1660-1720', Oxford University
        Press, 1924, pp. 140-4, 146-8

'The Way of the World' naturally failed at its first appearance on
the stage [...] Downs said that 'it had not the success the company expected because it was too keen a satire', but in reality,
it was too civilized for an age that revelled in the scribblings
of Mrs. Pix, and applauded the burlesque of Farquhar's 'Love and
a Bottle'. But there was also the fact that in many passages Congreve had ceased to write the ordinary comedy. While his secondary characters in his previous plays, his Lord and Lady Froth and
his Lady Plyant, are made of that flimsy material which could
enable Lamb to call them creatures of a sportive fancy, this is

not so with Mrs. Marwood and the Fainalls in this play. Fainall
is a repulsive villain, but Mrs. Fainall, whom Mirabell had once
loved, is more sinned against than sinning. She remains loyal to
Mirabell, and even helps him in his advances to Millamant (what
profound psychology is here!), but at the same time her heart
aches at not being loved by her husband. 'He will willingly dispense with the hearing of one scandalous story, to avoid giving
an occasion to make another by being seen to walk with his wife,'
she says with an affectation of lightness. But how bitter it is!
How full of unnecessary pain is the way of the world!

She and Mrs. Marwood are figures of an intense realism, driven
by that insane jealousy which is often more bitter and nearer to
the surface in illicit love than in the marriage tie. Mrs. Marwood is Fainall's mistress; but she also loves Mirabell, so that
Mrs. Fainall has double reason to be jealous of her; yet it is
rather on account of Mirabell she is jealous, and this also is
true to life. Fainall, again, is jealous of Mirabell, and goads
Mrs. Marwood into a very frenzy of despair, and though all the
time he is wounding himself, he cannot resist the impulsion.
[...] To say that these are puppets animated by no real passions
is to misunderstand Congreve; one might as well say the same of
Richardson's women.

But he could still be comic when he wished; take this little
inset:

MIRABELL: Excellent Foible! Matrimony has made you eloquent
in love.
WAITWELL: I think she has profited, sir. I think so.

Delicious ridicule! O complacency of the satisfied male!

But in spite of such passages, in spite of the drunken scenes
of Sir Wilful Witwoud and Petulant, and the masquerading of Waitwell as Sir Rowland, which are calculated to appeal to the most
stupid elements in an audience, the whole play needs close following sentence by sentence. It is this which makes it everlasting
literature. But even that glorious farcical scene between Lady
Wishfort and 'Sir Rowland' is too fine for immediate appreciation.
When Lady Wishfort hopes Sir Rowland will not 'impute her complacency to any lethargy of continence', nor think her 'prone to
any iteration of nuptials', or believe that 'the least scruple of
carnality is an ingredient', he assures her, 'Dear Madam, no.
You are all camphire and frankincense, all chastity and odour.'
On the stage? No, one must repeat it, laughing, to oneself -
'all camphire and frankincense, all chastity and odour'. Like
good poetry, it speaks to the inward ear.

Although much of this play is the pure presentation of the
artist to whom all life is material, and whose attitude towards
it must be guessed through the quality of the words rather than
by their surface meaning, in the main personages we feel Congreve
coming to more direct grips with his inmost self. And the theme
in which this is apparent is, inevitably in that age, the theme
of love. Millamant, 'Think of her, think of a whirlwind!'
From the first we know that she and Mirabell really love each
other. Mirabell thinks it was for herself she blushed when he

blundered into the 'cabal night'; but it was for him, at seeing
the man she loved make a fool of himself in company vastly
inferior to him. For the first time in his life he is jealous for
a woman, 'not of her person, but of her understanding', and he
feels that for a 'discerning man' he is 'somewhat too passionate
a lover; for I like her with all her faults; nay, like her for
her faults'. And when they meet, how exquisite they are together,
how tenderly she chaffs him:

> MIRABELL: You are no longer handsome when you've lost your
> lover; your beauty dies upon the instant: for beauty is the
> lover's gift; 'tis he bestows your charms - your glass is all
> a cheat ....
> MILLAMANT: O the vanity of these men!...Beauty the lover's
> gift! Lord! what is a lover, that it can give? Why, one
> makes lovers as fast as one pleases, and they live as long as
> one pleases, and they die as soon as one pleases; and then, if
> one pleases, one makes more.

Mirabell is too serious a lover to take her remarks as fun, or as
affectionate teasing; he is goaded into gibes, and although Millamant gets bored with them, she sees the love behind. But she
wants light and air, the freshness of spring and a clear gaiety -
charming, lovable Millamant, no wonder the young men in the pit
would gladly marry her in spite of Macaulay's sneer - she is the
incarnation of happiness, or at least of the desire for it.
'Sententious Mirabell! - Prithee don't look with that violent and
inflexible wise face, like Solomon at the dividing of the child
in an old tapestry hanging.' Life is serious, but let us at least
be gay while we can. [...]
     [...] For Millamant is a woman; she has the inestimable power
of giving, but she is rightly jealous of herself, and is not to be
undervalued. She is alive and breathing, hiding a real personality behind the only too necessary artifices of her sex. Once
assured of Mirabell's love, she divests herself of her armour, and
shows a perfect frankness. Meredith, in giving Congreve praise
for the portraiture, does not do her justice; she is only a
'flashing portrait, and a type of the superior ladies who do not
think, not of those who do'. Millamant not think! when on the
face of it she has thought a great deal, and thought very clearly,
about the living of her own life. She needed to be certain of
Mirabell before taking the plunge and dwindling into a wife, for
she had all the fastidiousness of a woman of experience. 'If
Mirabell should not make a good husband, I am a lost thing.'
     The only other figure at all comparable to Millamant is Lady
Wishfort, but she is not in the round, and her presentation too
nearly approaches satire. 'Her flow of boudoir Billingsgate',
says Meredith, 'is unmatched for the vigour and pointedness of the
tongue. It spins along with a final ring, like the voice of
Nature in a fury, and is indeed the racy eloquence of the educated
fishwife.' [...]
     Her *De Arte Amandi* passage ripples along with unthinkable
skill. After scolding Mirabell, 'Frippery! Superannuated frippery! I'll frippery the villain!' she turns to a more agreeable
subject.

LADY W: But art thou sure Sir Rowland will not fail to come?
or will he not fail when he does come? Will he be importunate, Foible, and push? For if he should not be importunate, -
I shall never break decorums - I shall die with confusion,
if I am forced to advance! - I shall swoon if he should
expect advances. No, I hope Sir Rowland is better bred, than
to put a lady to the necessity of breaking her forms. I
won't be too coy, neither - I won't give him despair - but a
little disdain is not amiss; a little scorn is alluring.
FOIBLE: A little scorn becomes your ladyship.
LADY W: Yes, but tenderness becomes me best - a sort of
dyingness - you see that picture has a sort of a - ha, Foible!
a swimmingness in the eyes - yes, I'll look so - my niece
affects it; but she wants features. Is Sir Rowland handsome?
Let my toilet be removed - I'll dress above. I'll receive Sir
Rowland here. Is he handsome? Don't answer me. I won't
know: I'll be surprised. I'll be taken by surprise.
FOIBLE: By storm, madam, Sir Rowland's a brisk man.
LADY W: Is he! O then he'll importune, if he's a brisk man.
I shall save decorums if Sir Rowland importunes. I have a
mortal terror at the apprehension of offending against
decorums.

Yet such a current of sympathy seems to flow from Congreve even
into this subject, that she becomes almost pathetic, and one
feels a touch of the tragic mingled with the comic vision.

5. 4 VIRGINIA WOOLF

Congreve's Comedies (1937), 'Collected Essays',
ed. L. Woolf, Hogarth Press, 1966, vol. 1,
pp. 78, 82

[...] Never was any prose so quick. Miraculously pat, on the
spot, each speaker caps the last, without fumbling or hesitation;
their minds are full charged; it seems as if they had to rein
themselves in, bursting with energy as they are, alive and alert
to their finger-tips. It is we who fumble, make irrelevant observations, notice the chocolate or the cinnamon, the sword or the
muslin, until the illusion takes hold of us, and what with the
rhythm of the speech and the indescribable air of tension, of
high breeding that pervades it, the world of the stage becomes
the real world and the other, outside the play, but the husk and
cast-off clothing. To attempt to reduce this first impression to
words is as futile as to explain a physical sensation - the slap
of a wave, the rush of wind, the scent of a bean field. It is
conveyed by the curl of a phrase on the ear; by speed; by stillness. It is as impossible to analyse Congreve's prose as to distinguish the elements - the bark of a dog, the song of a bird,
the drone of the branches - which make the summer air. But then,
since words have meaning, we notice here a sudden depth beneath
the surface, a meaning not grasped but felt, and then come to

realize something not merely dazzling in this world, but natural,
for all its wit; even familiar, and traditional. It has a
coarseness, a humour something like Shakespeare's; a toppling
imagination that heaps image upon image; a lightning swiftness
of apprehension that snatches a dozen meanings and compacts them
into one. [...]
   But it is the Valentines, the Mirabells, the Angelicas, and the
Millamants who keep us in touch with truth and, by striking a
sudden serious note, bring the rest to scale. They have sharpened their emotions upon their wits. They have flouted each
other; bargained; taken love and examined it by the light of
reason; teased and tested each other almost beyond endurance.
But when it comes to the point and she must be serious, the swift-
est of all heroines, whose mind and body seem equally winged, so
that there is a rush in the air as she passes and we exclaim with
Scandal, 'Gone; why, she was never here, nor anywhere else', has
a centre of stillness in her heart and enough emotion in her
words to furbish out a dozen pages of eloquent disquisition.
'Why does not the man take me? Would you have me give myself to
you over again?' The words are simple, and yet, after what has
already been said, so brimming with meaning that Mirabell's reply,
'Ay, over and over again', seems to receive into itself more than
words can say. And this depth of emotion, we have to reflect,
the change and complexity that are implied in it, have been
reached in the direct way; that is by making each character speak
in his or her own person, without addition from the author or any
soliloquy save such as can be spoken on the stage in the presence
of an audience. No, whether we read him from the moralist's angle
or from the artist's, to agree with Dr. Johnson is an impossibility. To read the comedies is not to 'relax those obligations
by which life ought to be regulated'. On the contrary, the more
slowly we read him and the more carefully, the more meaning we
find, the more beauty we discover.

5. 5   NORMAN N. HOLLAND

        'The Way of the World', 'The First Modern
        Comedies: the Significance of Etherege,
        Wycherley and Congreve', Harvard University
        Press, Cambridge, Mass., 1959, pp. 176-80

A number of critics think this play a witty but unstageable closet
drama, largely because the plot is so intricate. Of course, this
is a difficult play to stage, like most plays worth doing, but it
is not unstageable. In fact, the play is almost inconceivable
apart from a stage - its speech demands a speaker. The supposed
complexity of the plot, as we shall see, is intended to be confusing; the confusion is an essential part of the dramatic impact.
In part the complication comes from the standard Restoration convention about intrigue. That is, as long as there is an inconsistency between appearances and emotions, power is given to the
person who knows this inconsistency. The power ceases if the

inconsistency ceases, if there are no secrets left to be discovered. More important, the plot becomes complex because Congreve deals out the secrets of the play so slowly, so gradually,
that they assume an intricacy far beyond that of the actual
situation. [...]

'The Way of the World' deals with a typical family situation -
a fight for the control of an estate. Presiding over the family
at the beginning of the play is the absurd Lady Wishfort who
holds in a 'Cabal', a gossip club, her daughter Mrs. Fainall and her
niece Millamant. She controls all of Mrs. Fainall's estate and
part of Millamant's as well. As the plot thickens, a contest
develops as to who shall get these estates from Lady Wishfort:
Mr. Fainall or Millamant's lover, Mirabell.

So far, so simple. But Congreve seems to complicate these
fairly straightforward family relations by such statements as this
by Fainall, '[Sir Wilfull Witwoud] is half Brother to this
Witwoud by a former Wife, who was Sister to my Lady *Wishfort*, my
Wife's Mother. If you [Mirabell] marry *Millamant*, you must call
Cousins too.' Congreve has added (and one wonders why) the confusing brothers Witwoud. Anthony, a town fop, is one of Lady
Wishfort's cabal; his half-brother and Lady Wishfort's nephew,
Sir Wilfull, comes to town from the country (where he has been a
bumpkin these many years) on his way abroad. Lady Wishfort forces
him into a half-hearted courtship of Millamant. This terribly
complicated family tree can be diagramed (as in the accompanying
figure, where the characters in the play are italicized). To an

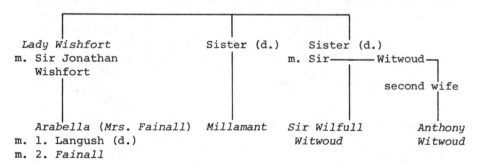

audience, however, only two facts emerge: that Mrs. Fainall is
Lady Wishfort's daughter and that Lady Wishfort has control over
Millamant's estate. The other relationships, particularly the
confusion of Witwouds, serve only to create the impression of a
welter of consanguinity. Congreve is confusing his audience gratuitously, and we must infer he has some reason for doing so.

He does the same thing with the emotional relations that he
does with the family structure. Behind the already complicated
dynastic relations lie even more complicated emotional affairs.
In Act I we learn that Mirabell has made advances to Lady Wishfort to cover his wooing of Millamant. Mrs. Marwood, another
member of the cabal, betrayed him to the old lady, who, naturally
enough, despises him now. Act II tells us that Mirabell had been
Mrs. Fainall's lover when she was a widow, and, when she seemed
pregnant, he married her off to Fainall. We learn, too, that Mrs.

Marwood is now Fainall's mistress, but yearns for Mirabell.

The discrepancy between the family structure and the emotional structure plays into the Restoration convention about intrigue: a discrepancy between appearances (the overt family relations) and 'nature' (the hidden emotional facts) gives power to the man who knows the discrepancy. At the beginning of the play, Mirabell is trying to set up such a situation. He has married his servant Waitwell to Lady Wishfort's maid Foible and plans to have Waitwell disguise himself as a nobleman, court, *and marry* Lady Wishfort. Then Mirabell plans to reveal the disguise, show Lady Wishfort that she has married a servant, and offer to release her if she will let him marry Millamant *cum* estate. Unfortunately, Mrs. Marwood (who for at least two reasons wants to spike Mirabell's courtship of Millamant) discovers the plan and tells Lady Wishfort. Mrs. Marwood also tells Fainall of his wife's former affair with Mirabell; he threatens to publish it to the world unless Lady Wishfort signs over to him not only his wife's but also Millamant's estate and even the reversion after her life of Lady Wishfort's own estate. Mrs. Fainall then ineffectually reveals that she knows Mrs. Marwood is having an affair with her husband. Finally, however, Mirabell wins the contest by knowing the ultimate discrepancy between appearance and nature. He produces a deed by Mrs. Fainall conveying all her estate to him as her trustee; she made it when she was a widow (and could execute a valid conveyance of her property), and it therefore predates any deed Fainall could now obtain. These various deeds at the end of the play combine and fuse the two kinds of reality, dynastic and emotional, from which the play is built.

Congreve, even though the plot is complicated enough, makes it seem even more complicated. There are certain hidden facts – we could call them quanta of knowledge – and a large part of the so-called complexity simply involves revealing these facts, slowly unraveling the appearances which cover them over. There are only four such quanta in the play: Marwood's desire for Mirabell, Marwood's relationship with Fainall, Mirabell's past affair with Mrs. Fainall, and Mirabell's plot with his disguised servant. But Congreve gives the impression of far greater complexity by measuring out each secret slowly, person by person, until the final complete revelation. He adds even more complexity by having each of these underlying motives and relationships refer back into the group instead of expanding to include outsiders; he makes it seem as though these five people knew only these five people.

An example of the way Congreve uses these quanta of knowledge is his treatment of Mrs. Marwood's and Fainall's liaison. In the first act, there are only a few hints: Fainall reveals he doesn't know his wife's doings; Mirabell describes Marwood ironically to Fainall as 'your Friend, or your Wife's Friend'; he remarks to Fainall, who is suggesting Marwood is overfond of Mirabell, 'You are conscious of a Concern for which the Lady is more indebted to you, than is your Wife.' Act II, scene iii, fully reveals the affair to the audience in the dialogue between Fainall and Marwood. Act III contains only a hint by Mrs. Marwood that Foible, the maid, knows the secret: 'Why this Wench is the *Pass-partoute*, a very Master-Key to every Body's strong Box.' Nothing

further is done with this knowledge until Act V, when Foible
tells Mrs. Fainall, who tells Mirabell, who tells all. At the
last, the revelation, the complete knowledge, contributes virtually nothing to the denouement, because Fainall plays his trump -
the threat of scandal - immediately after it.

It is in revealing these hidden facts that Congreve deals with
the basic Restoration theme of the contrast between appearance
and nature. The first act serves to define the outer, obvious
social framework of family relationships, admitted loves, and
professed friendships. It is, however, riddled with hints of the
underlying currents of emotion, unrevealed until the second act,
which is primarily devoted to unmasking - to the audience only -
the emotional involvements of Mirabell, the Fainalls, and Mrs.
Marwood. In Act III, the characters gain partial awareness of the
undercurrents: Marwood and Fainall learn of Mirabell's plan and
of his past affair with Mrs. Fainall. The fourth act does not
appreciably change the quanta of knowledge the several characters
have, but contrasts the decorous, moderated honesty of Mirabell
and Millamant with the indecorous openness of Sir Wilfull and the
deceptions and pretenses of Lady Wishfort and the other characters. In Act V, all pretenses are destroyed with Fainall's and
Mirabell's revelations and the bringing out from a black box of the
deed that renders Fainall powerless. The pattern is that the difference between visible and invisible factors gives power to him
who knows it; breaking down the difference, i.e., revealing the
hidden facts, destroys that power.

Congreve has unduly complicated both kinds of relationship,
dynastic and emotional, and in both cases some of the complica-
tions are not essential to the plot. We must look for the reason.
The confusion which is the prevailing atmosphere of the play
becomes almost a kind of symbol for one of the points Congreve
wants to make. That is, the confusion asks the question that
underlies almost every facet of the play: What is the true inter-
action between these two kinds of relationships? To some extent,
I think, we are meant to be aware simply of the idea 'family' and
the idea 'emotion,' without necessarily following through the
involved details. The technique is much the same as that in
T.S. Eliot's 'The Confidential Clerk,' where emotional and dynastic
relations proliferate in the same way to define two kinds of
reality and test their relative 'realness.' As it develops, 'The
Way of the World' does just exactly that; act after act tests the
relative realness of dynastic and emotional relations. In Act I,
only the family relations and Mirabell's love for Millamant are
particularly evident, and they artificially overshadow the
implicitly more 'real' relations developed in Act II. As the play
develops, however, the undercurrents of emotion assume greater and
greater force. In Act III, Marwood's role becomes increasingly
important. She has no family connection to the central group, but
is related instead by her affair with Fainall and resentment of
Mirabell, emotional connections. Her overhearing Mirabell's plan
and learning of his past affair with Mrs. Fainall are crucial to
the plot development. The entrance at this point of Sir Wilfull
Witwoud as a country bumpkin ridiculed by the fops reveals the
ultimate irrelevance of the dynastic tie that brings him there,

compared to the importance of Marwood's emotional tie. Linguistically, there is the contrast between the superficial banter on Sir Wilfull's entrance and the urgent plotting by Marwood and Fainall immediately after. Act IV continues to set off Sir Wilfull's blunt openness against the duplicity of the social situation. His entrance, which was like a breath of fresh air from the country, becomes, when he is drunk, a 'Breath like a Bagpipe.' His stillborn courtship of Millamant, with only the family tie for a basis, contrasts with Mirabell's supremely urbane wooing, derived from an emotional attachment. Mirabell, in turn, establishes a mean between the knight's willfulness and the social pretenders. In the last scene, the emotional undercurrents seem to have established final dominance over the family relations. Marwood and Fainall have complete control, and are manipulating the family relations as a lever to gain their ends. Lady Wishfort's plaintive remark, 'Ah! her first Husband, my Son *Languish*, wou'd not have carry'd it thus,' seems to mark the nadir of dynastic strength. Sir Wilfull's sword, though on the side of family and good-nature, is powerless; it is Mirabell's deed that saves the day.

The unraveling with its final clue, the deed, suggests the relation between the two complex realities of family and emotional ties: that the 'real' reality is the inward, emotional nature; this reality is a changing flux that gives birth to a more stable framework of overt social facts (dynastic relations); when, for whatever reason, these social facts are not true reflections of the underlying emotional relations (Mrs. Fainall's marriage, the projected 'marriage' of Lady Wishfort to Mirabell's servant, and the like) a situation of power results in favor of one who knows the inconsistency; the antidote to such situations is to create an overt, social situation which will truly reflect the underlying realities. [...]

BÜCHNER: 'WOYZECK'

6. 1 RICHARD SCHECHNER

Notes Toward an Imaginary Production, in Büchner,
'Woyzeck', trans. H.J. Schmidt, Avon Books, New
York, 1969, pp. 11-23

Friedrich Johann Franz Woyzeck, soldier, rifleman in the second
regiment, second battalion, fourth company, born on the Feast of
the Annunciation. Today I'm thirty years, seven months, and
twelve days old. (Scene 17)

1.
Or whatever scene you want to make it. Woyzeck, so precise about
his own status, proclaims in opposition to Büchner's play. That
play is a masterpiece of indeterminacy. Each scene stands by
itself, even the incomplete scenes. These scenes don't 'go' anywhere. Each is hard and fast, like a stone. Arrange them as you
please.
    The structure is in the totality, in the relentless exposing and
probing of Woyzeck and the society that makes and undoes him.
    Nothing but peas for a year. That diet can kill.
2.
Woyzeck knows how old he is to the day. It's all written out for
him on a paper someone gave him. A confirmed, official identity.
Woyzeck is also: a cuckold, a murderer, a father, a guinea pig, a
barber, a visionary who hears voices and sees things, a poor man.
He is implosive, inarticulate - the object rather than the subject
of the drama.
    Büchner is as hard on Woyzeck as the doctor is.
3.
Indeterminacy. The murder could come first, absolutely first.
Each event has happened; everything is in the past. Time is a
thing, and 'Woyzeck' has a geography rather than a temporality.
    Film is the perfect medium. As many projectors as there are
scenes. Each scene wound onto its projector. Many screens. Ran-
domly one scene follows another. The showing continues until the

audience chooses to leave.

Such a vision of Woyzeck would, I think, approach Büchner's
(unconscious) intention. The work is unfinished, fragmented, not
ordered with finality. Only a film can accurately project this
kind of indeterminacy.

How many possible permutations could 27 scenes yield?

4.

Woyzeck himself is crushed by so many possibilities.

5.

Is Woyzeck, caught, tried, convicted, executed?

The 'real' Woyzeck was. His head rolled in Leipzig on August
27, 1824. A large crowd watched.

What do you do with a bad dog? Or a pet monkey who kills your
pet canary?

Are members of the classes that read, write, produce, and
view plays capable of approaching members of Woyzeck's class without contempt?

Woyzeck is not one of 'us.' Therefore we can see in him only
an object of our contempt, our pity, our sentimentality, or our
horror. We cannot look straight across into Woyzeck's eyes.
Büchner knew this.

6.

Büchner's letter to his family, February 1834: 'I scorn no one:
the least of all for his reason or his education, for it lies in
nobody's power not to become an idiot or a criminal, because in
similar circumstances we would all be equal and because the circumstances lie outside of ourselves.'

What utter, unremitting scorn! This rhetoric of intellectualism!

'Whoever accuses me of such scorn maintains that I would kick
a man because he was wearing a shabby coat. This brutality,
which one would not be accused of in the physical sense, is here
transposed into the sphere of the intellect where it is all the
more base. I can call someone an idiot without scorning him for
that. Idiocy belongs to the general characteristics of human
affairs. I can't change their existence, but no one can prevent
me from calling everything that exists by its rightful name or
from avoiding whatever I don't like.'

I repeat: Büchner knew that he, a doctor, a man of intellect
and social privilege, a university lecturer, could *never* look
straight across at Woyzeck. Thus the bitterness of the play.

7.

Pity is the death of revolution. Thus look at Woyzeck coldly if
you wish to do him justice.

8.

See Woyzeck stumbling among the high marsh grass looking for the
knife. Marie's body is close by, with its necklace and jewels
of blood. But she is dead. Woyzeck has no more interest in her.
The knife is important to him. Marie can no longer talk - the
knife is eloquent.

Woyzeck's face is tormented. Crawling in the marsh, he knows
he is stupid. He knows that he should have gotten rid of the
knife at once.

And all the while he searches, more evidence cakes on his pants.

The mud will speak as eloquently as the Jew's ransomed knife.

You can't wipe blood off your right elbow with your right hand.
9.
What does it mean: 'Let us piss crosswise, so that a Jew will
die'?

A commonplace, I'm told. Something that 19th-century Germany
was full of.

I remember a friend of mine from Montgomery, Alabama, telling
me how he and his friends would go into Niggertown to 'egg
niggers.' That was, to throw stones at them. This was long ago,
in the forties.

And how many Jews died? When was that?

The magic of micturating. Many film clips of men pissing
like crossed swords, and Jews dying.
10.
If 'Woyzeck' is done in a theatre it is important that Woyzeck
gets very close to the audience. Close enough so that the audience smells his sweat, his fear. He is marked from the very
beginning. He is hot, very hot. He sweats, as his son does, even
in his sleep.

Woyzeck smells like a hunted man. Hunted men smell like
frightened animals.
11.
Büchner wrote 'Woyzeck' at 23, when he was less than a year from
death. This is an adolescent play: morbid, teetering on sentimentality, at loose ends, sexually raw, relentless.

Take the poetry of Keats. Invert it as the French Revolution
inverted the politics/values of Europe. Upside down Keats-Büchner.
12.
Büchner to his fiancée: 'I studied the history of the [French]
Revolution. I felt myself crushed by the terrible fatalism of
history. I find in human nature a horrifying sameness, in the
human condition an inescapable force, granted to all and to no
one. The individual merely foam on the waves, greatness sheer
chance, the mastery of genius a puppet play, a ludicrous struggle
against an iron law: to recognize it is our utmost achievement, to
control it is impossible.'
13.
Konrad Lorenz: 'The dark side of pseudospeciation is that it makes
us consider the members of pseudospecies other than our own as not
human, as many primitive tribes are demonstrably doing, in whose
language the word for their own particular tribe is synonymous with
"Man." From their viewpoint it is not, strictly speaking, cannibalism if they eat fallen warriors of an enemy tribe.'

It is not 'exploitation' for the doctor to experiment on Woyzeck,
nor is it 'cruelty' for the captain to mock him. [...]

The carnival barker doubts the animality of his animals, attri-
buting to them 'double *raison*' - the ability to ratiocinate, if not
to articulate fully their thoughts and emotions. Conversely, Woyzeck is denied full humanity by the captain and the doctor.

The struggle in 'Woyzeck' is not simply between classes, but
between species.

It is an absolute struggle, signaled by the absolute gap between
Woyzeck and those above him.

14.
Uniquely, Büchner shows pseudospeciation from Woyzeck's point of
view. Woyzeck is 'different' than the captain. It is not simply
a question of being poor.
    Poverty is the symptom, the mark of a difference so profound
that it creates its own values.
15.
In 1836 Büchner wrote 'Woyzeck.' How swiftly had the glow of
English romanticism faded and the audacity of Goethe's all-
challenging Faust collapsed inward. Büchner forefeels the exist-
ential crisis. His poetry is of our century.
16.
What kind of man is Woyzeck? What does he look like? Is he a big
brute?
    There is, strangely, a hint that Woyzeck is (somewhat) an
intellectual. That Büchner could not prevent a projection of himself from emerging.
    Othello - who also knows what blind jealousy is - is a noble
savage: big, black, articulate to sublimity, graceful, gifted,
superb.
    But Woyzeck lives Othello's life negatively. Woyzeck's
jealousy is not a grand illusion. Marie makes love to the drum
major. Woyzeck does not murder a sleeping innocent but a wakeful
woman who struggles against the knife. Woyzeck does not kill
with the silken pillow and then kiss his corpse-bride adieu. He
stabs again and again with a two-penny knife.
    Where, then, is the intellectualism? In the scenic structure.
In the geography that Büchner arranges around, within, and
throughout Woyzeck.
    It is wrong to think that Woyzeck is inarticulate. When words
are necessary - as in his correlation between cash and morality -
words are there. And when he speaks with gestures, he speaks
with authority, How many of us can kill?
17.
Woyzeck is not Karl, a dwarfed idiot. But he is passing ugly.
A little squat maybe, and a touch fat. All those peas. A man for
whom black-haired, deep-eyed Marie would be a catch.
    Woyzeck is not young. Thirty. But in 1836, when the common
people did not live much past sixty.
    The sergeant, the drum major are the best of Woyzeck's species.
The ruffians at the tavern are the meanest of them. Woyzeck is
not a leader. He is like Andres.
    Except that Andres is satisfied.
    Woyzeck is interesting because he is restless. The revolution-
ists can point to Büchner's play with pride because Woyzeck is
restless. Later in the century millions of Woyzecks were 'organized.'
18.
Drum major, sergeant, captain, doctor, carnival barker. Everyone,
in fact, but Woyzeck, Marie, Karl, and the child are caricatures.
Partial people. Aspects. Elements pressing in on Woyzeck. Not
'real' people as Ibsen understood them, but characters from a fable
about predatory animals.
    How everyone loves to torture Woyzeck, as if his misery was
their salvation.

19.
'Woyzeck' is a sacrifice, a bullfight, a slaughterhouse dance done
by the lowest class for the entertainment and edification of the
higher classes.
20.
Marie quotes Christ because in atavistic christianity whores are
welcomed into the kingdom of God.
    'Franz hasn't come, not yesterday, not today. It's getting hot
in here. "And stood at his feet weeping, and began to wash his feet
with tears, and did wipe them with the hairs of her head, and kissed
his feet, and anointed them with ointment." It's all dead!
Savior, Savior, I wish I could anoint your feet!'
    Marie witnesses Woyzeck's torment, identifiying him with Christ.
Not for our benefit, but for hers. And then Woyzeck kills Marie;
not for her benefit, but for ours.
21.
Marie is sensual. Wet, hot, black-eyed, black-haired. For her,
appearances are essences. She can stare through leather pants.
Having borne Woyzeck a child, she wishes to spawn a whole race of
drum majors.
    Marie's earrings are not trifles. They are everything. She
isn't a casual woman. Each time she makes love with a new man she
gives herself totally, anew. The murder is justified.
    Marie likes Woyzeck, but is getting bored with him. He is no lon-
ger shiny like a new earring. She is tied to him through their child
    She wonders: Has Woyzeck slept with anyone else?
    He would, of course. But he doesn't have the time. He spends
his spare time with the doctor, earning money for Marie and the baby
Or hearing voices and seeing things. Once Woyzeck began his commerce
with the world of supernature his very mundane sexuality dried up.
    To Marie, appearances are essences; and Woyzeck sees things.
Marie screws with the drum major, while Woyzeck is unfaithful with
the grass.
    She knows that her infidelity is justified.
22.
Hegel wrote that the best tragedies emerge from conflicts between
two 'good' forces. In other words, Marie is justified in sleeping
with the drum major, and Woyzeck is justified in killing her.
23.
Should the murder be bloody, or performed with clean and delicate
grace?
    She sees the knife, knows what's going to happen. She thinks
it's retribution. Her soul aches for the stabs, but her body
resists. It is the opposite with Woyzeck. His soul says, 'Don't
kill Marie,' but his body is relentless.
    Such murders are mangles, all blood and pulpy flesh.
24.
'Woyzeck' was written during the first decades of politicized
Europe. The French Revolution made it perfectly clear that the
masses wished to have power.
    There is no aristocracy in 'Woyzeck.' Only the weakened silly
middle classes, and the stupid serious masses. A play in which
both the middle and lower classes are treated with contempt, but
in which a small store of compassion is spent on a character of the
lower classes, is a work of art made by an intellectual.

Büchner is among the first modern intellectuals: A man without
a class who finds it necessary to identify with the lower classes.

'Woyzeck' is a politicized play, not a political play. Poli-
tics, the struggle for power among masses and elites worked out
through statecraft and revolution - these shimmer deep in 'Woyzeck,' never rising to its surface.

Yet in the doctor we see a foreview of Auschwitz' lovely
experimenters. And in Woyzeck himself we can identify the
naïveté that permitted so many Germans to support Hitler. Woyzeck
believes in discipline. He likes order and is menaced by the
chaos he feels around and underneath him. He is willing to take
orders from captain and doctor even if those orders bestialize him.

There is a sexual counterpart to the doctor's experiments and
Woyzeck's submission. The connection between them is dark but
unmistakable. There isn't much difference between political and
sexual manipulation. That is why the scene which ends with the
students handling Woyzeck is both brutal and sensuous.

The doctor watches Woyzeck piss against the wall, out in the
open, and then rebukes him for it. To the actor playing the
doctor: What are you thinking while watching Woyzeck piss?
25.
A film of 'Woyzeck' must look back to the French Revolution and
forward to the Nazi Revolution. That is the historical span of the
play, these two bloody ambivalent brackets of European history.
26.
Of Marxism, little can be said with regard to Büchner, who would
have understood Nietzsche sooner than Marx. But they were all
Germans.

The sideshow, the animal show, the reified intellectualism, the
inn with its loud music and dark beer, the marching band, the drum
major's leather pants, heavy boots, monkeys dressed as men, horses
answering questions, men treated like animals.

A confusion between the animal and the human worlds. Not the
naked ape, but the dressed ape and the naked man. To those who
rule there is little difference between a lower-class man and an
animal.

Woyzeck, the German soldier, accepts this. Büchner asks the
questions, not Woyzeck.
27.
It would be appropriate to have all the animals played by men.
28.
To what degree is Woyzeck different from the captain? Pseudospeciation, merely a hint when one first confronts 'Woyzeck,' emerges
more and more clearly the closer one comes to the heart of the play.

Why not have the animals of the' sideshow come to the inn for the
dance? Why not have them watch the murder in the woods?
Watch with muted amusement, excited chatter. Blood smells?

'And then the giant said: I smell, I smell, I smell human
flesh.'

'A good murder, a real murder, a beautiful murder. As good a
murder as you'd ever want to see. We haven't had one like this for
a long time.'
29.
And a good murder is double blood. After the first victim there is
a second. The courts see to that.

6. 2 RAYMOND WILLIAMS

Georg Büchner: a Retrospect, 'Drama from Ibsen
to Brecht', Chatto & Windus, 1968, pp. 233-6

[...]'Woyzeck' is very difficult to judge, because its arrangement is uncertain, and the modern edited versions differ in important respects. Though very powerful, it is then in an essential
way fragmentary; indeed there seem to me to be signs in it of two
or three related but different conceptions, which exist at different levels of realization. Interpretation can compound them,
but the more relevant exercise is their distinction, since this
shows us much more clearly the major experimental quality in
Büchner's art. At a simple level, it is in effect a ballad-play,
in which Woyzeck is the poor soldier, exploited and cheated, who
kills his wife when she is unfaithful to him. The scenes of the
dance, the killing at the pond, the wading into the pond to get
rid of the knife (in the common version, the wading until he
drowns) are in that mode of romantic drama which derives, not
from the sophisticated romances, but from the folk-tale. It is
simple, effective and limited, because it draws on the resources
of common intense experience, in which the individual is not even
representative; he is so integrated with ordinary humanity, and
with its normal crises, that neither representation (an individual
standing for others) nor individuality (in its modern sense, a man
distinct from others) arises. This is clearly an important part
of Büchner's inheritance, some of it directly through folk-song;
but though in a technical sense experimental it is not innovating:
the crisis of popular literature was not the transposition of
folk-literature, that experience of a stable world in which certain
traditional crises occur (husband, wife, **lover**); but was the
redefinition of common experience in a changing, socially and
philosophically conscious world. The nostalgia for ballad-
experience is a nostalgia for pre-revolutionary society; it is
understandable and powerful, and some kinds of literature can be
made from it. But the point about Büchner is that though he
received this tradition, and drew strength from it, he lived also,
consciously, in a revolutionary period, philosophically and
socially.
    The ballad-play is there, as a late action. But the defining
scenes of 'Woyzeck' are in a different mode. The fact of exploitation is made actual, in a major originality. In the presence of
the captain and the doctor, Woyzeck is the man being used like a
trained animal: 'yes, sir, Captain'; 'yes, sir, Doctor': the
Captain's body-servant and the Doctor's experimental creature.
Woyzeck is presented in a rigidity of response against the fluent
dominance of his trainers and exploiters; but he is given also -
the convention gives him - an ironic radical consciousness:

Our kind is miserable only once: in this world and the next.
I think if we ever got to Heaven we'd have to help with the
thunder.
    Us common people, we haven't got virtue. But if I could be

a gentleman, and if I could have a hat and a watch and a cane,
and if I could talk refined, I'd want to be virtuous, all
right.

Woyzeck is not, that is to say, singly defined: he is the rigid
servant, and the ironic critic: And this is not a question of
complexity of character; it is a process of variation of dramatic
viewpoint (what Brecht, whom these scenes indicate, called a
century later 'complex seeing'). The point can be reinforced by
a characteristic scene which, like the social naming of Captain
and Doctor, anticipates clearly an expressionist mode. The captain and doctor are projected in a self-defining, self-exposing
mode, and this is extended to the scene at the fair in which the
charlatan presents a trained monkey:

> You see before you here a creature as God created it. But it
> is nothing this way. Absolutely nothing. Now look at what art
> can do. It walks upright, wears coat and trousers, even
> carries a sabre. This monkey here is a regular soldier. So
> what if he isn't much different!

As Woyzeck, the trained soldier, is shown watching this presentation of the trained animal, there is a characteristic shift of
dramatic viewpoint and method: the isolation and conscious inspec-
tion of a distortion which repeats, in an acted image, a distortion
already directly presented. In scenes like this, Büchner is
pioneering an objective-critical mode which is a deeply innovating
dramatic response to a changed position in popular experience. It
is what he had expressed in simple argument in his revolutionary
pamphlet 'The Hessian Courier'.
  These two modes - of the folk-tale and of conscious and self-
conscious criticism - are interwoven with a third: the confused
relation between Nature and man's nature - the animal and the
social being. This association of themes is a particular structure
of feeling, which is as much historical as it is personal: the
three themes commonly occur, in very complex relations, in romantic
literature (they are all present, for example, in Wordsworth). At
the same time, Büchner's intensity is so great that each element,
as it is expressed, rises to a temporary dominance. It is interesting that he does not express the complicated relations to nature in
the consciously recovered simplicity of the ballad. Where Woyzeck
speaks traditionally in his folk-role, and with a clear bitter
irony in his critical role, he speaks, in this natural relation, in
a desperate inarticulate imagery:

> Like when the sun stops at noon, and it's like the world was
> going up in fire? That's when I hear a terrible voice saying
> things to me.
>   Did you ever see the shapes the toadstools make when they
> grow up out of the earth? If only somebody could read what they
> say.
>   A fire's sailing around the sky and a noise coming down like
> trumpets.

And he passes through this imagery - of an unrealizable relation
to natural forces - into a self-questioning, a general questioning, which is the philosophical revolt:

> What is Man? Bones. Dust, sand, dung. What is Nature? Dust,
> sand, dung. But poor stupid Man, stupid Man. We must be
> friends. If only you had no courage, there would be no
> science. Only Nature: no amputation, no articulation. What
> is this? Woyzeck's arm, flesh, bones, veins. What is this?
> Dung. Why is it rooted in dung? Must I cut off my arm? No,
> Man is selfish, he beats, shoots, stabs his own kind.

And he arrives through this at an alienation and a despair:

> Every man's a chasm. It makes you dizzy when you look down in.
>   Look, a beautiful, hard, grey sky. You'd almost like to
> pound a nail in up there and hang yourself on it.

He becomes, in this despair, what the Captain had taunted him with
being:

> Running through the world like an open razor, you're liable to
> cut someone.

What Büchner is then doing, in 'Woyzeck', is reaching out,
through an intense association of themes and images, to the dramatization of a complicated process which he seeks to embody in this
single figure: materializing him first this way, then that. The
fertility of the play, in later minds, is not only the persistence
of this intense inquiry; it is also, in the main tradition, a separation of elements that were there historically united, so that
each of the themes can be taken up and taken further. Woyzeck is
a 'raid on the inarticulate' in the full sense: that what is
created and connected out of intense feeling is only later available for deliberate explanation. Dramatically, the excitement of
'Woyzeck' is its reaching in so many directions at once; not the
grasp of a single vision, from which new total conventions could
be built; but the tumbling experimental touching of one intense
vision after another, and the achievement of conventions which for
a scene, for a group of scenes, express and control this, and then
this. When the play is used, by later writers and critics, any
one of these achievements can be isolated and abstracted; indeed
this is commonly so, in the process of tradition, and especially,
as here, when it leaps a historical gap.

6. 3   CHARLES MAROWITZ (*)

> Introduction to 'Woyzeck' Adaptation,
> 'Gambit', 6 (23), October 1973, pp. 83-4

What interests me about Woyzeck (and what is never explained in the
play) is precisely what it is his voices are saying. What is it

that is being communicated to Woyzeck through the walls, through the sounds he monitors into his mind from the natural world about him? Whatever these voices are telling him, it is clearly opposed to the sentiments and shibboleths of his external social life. Like Joan of Arc, there is a superior moral intelligence at work inside the man, but unlike Joan, the man is incapable of articulating its message.

The inner voice of Woyzeck is free from the fetters of social convention. It tells him that he loves a woman and so he sleeps with her. A baby is born and he accepts it, wedlock or no. He finds himself without money and with small means of bettering himself, and although he resents it, he also accepts it. Perhaps because greater materialism would only plunge him deeper into the outer world; the world which stands in furthest opposition to his inner world; his true world. He asks only for the fruits of his labour. A woman, a child, a microcosm containing himself and his family which will cocoon him from the pronged world around him; that world to which he is temperamentally opposed. When these things are taken away, when Marie is appropriated by an emissary from that other world, when his child becomes a useless, unmoored object which violates the natural arrangements as he understands them, he loses tangible proof of his existence.

The murder of Marie is a *crime passionel* and a *crime passionel* implies a degree of emotional intensity irreconcilable with the restrictions and conventions of social life. Marie has been seduced, not only by a Drum-Major, but by the world which Woyzeck has always tried to keep at bay; the world that Marie and the child, so long as they *were* his, also resisted. Marie never understood about the 'voices', but neither did she reject them. Woyzeck could discuss his inner life with her, and it didn't matter then whether she 'understood' or not; the main thing was having her there to relate to. But when she was no longer a listener, the only 'Other Person' in his world, he could no longer ignore the evil in the outer world - for it had reached out and taken away everything which was uniquely his.

The murder of Marie is an act of revenge against a terrible defector; a person who, by being lured into the world of material-ism and sensuality, delivered a terrible rebuff to the integrity of Woyzeck's private world; that state in which a purer morality prevailed - even if its only outer manifestation were 'hallucina-tion'. Marie must die not for infidelity, but for forcing Woy-zeck out of his cocoon; for forcing him to confront the realities of the real world; a world in which the twin driving imperatives were exploitation and corruption. In Woyzeck's inner world, there is God and nature; elemental forces hold dialogues and he is privy to them. In the real world, there is conformity, deprivation, malice and subterfuge. There are specific orders to obey and a larger, Social Order to maintain. But instinctively, Woyzeck knows this has been imposed upon the 'natural order' and in cling-ing to the instinct for his own world, he becomes an outsider and a misfit in the world around him. Still, this is a small price to pay for maintaining contact with the essential varieties of life.

NOTE

* Charles Marowitz directed 'Woyzeck' at the Open Space Theatre in
  1973 with David Schofield as Woyzeck and Carol Drinkwater as
  Marie.

IBSEN:
'PEER GYNT', 'THE WILD DUCK'
AND 'ROSMERSHOLM'

'PEER GYNT'

7. 1 IBSEN

Letters, 'The Oxford Ibsen',trans. and ed.
J.W. McFarlane, Oxford University Press,
vol. 3, 1972, pp. 486, 490-3, 497

I have completed a new dramatic work which will be published at
Christmas; it will interest me greatly to know what you think about
it. The work is called 'Peer Gynt' after the main character, about
whom one reads in Asbjørnsen's folk-tales. I had not very much to
build on; but then I could be all the freer to play with the
material as I wanted. [...]
(Letter of 15 Oct. 1857 to Magdalene Thoresen, his stepmother.)

How is it going with 'Peer Gynt'? As far as I can tell from the
newspaper reports, it has been well received in Sweden; but are the
sales commensurate?
    I hear that the work had caused a lot of upset in Norway; this
worries me not in the slightest; but both there and in Denmark
people have found much more satire in it than I intended. Why
can't they read the book like any ordinary poem? For that was
how I wrote it. The satirical bits are fairly isolated. But if,
as seems to be the case, the present-day Norwegians recognize
themselves in the person of Peer Gynt, that is those good people's
own business. [...]
(Letter of 24 Feb. 1868 to Frederik Hegel.)

After 'Brand', 'Peer Gynt' followed as it were of its own accord.
It was written in Southern Italy, in Ischia and in Sorrento. When
one is so far away from the intended readers, one becomes reckless.
This work contains much that was occasioned by my own youth; my

mother served, with necessary exaggerations, as the model for
Aase. (Similarly for Inga in 'The Pretenders'.)
    The locality has a great influence on the forms within which
the imagination creates. Can I not, rather like Christoff in
[Holberg's play] 'Jakob von Tyboe', point to 'Brand' and 'Peer
Gynt' and say: 'Look, that was when intoxicated with wine'?
(Letter of 28 Oct. 1870 to Peter Hansen.)

'Peer Gynt' is Brand's opposite; it is regarded by many as my best
work. How far you will find pleasure in it, I don't know. It is
wild and formless, recklessly written in a way that I could only
dare to write while far from home. [...]
(Letter of 30 April 1872 to Edmund Gosse.)

Nor am I in a position to give any further details of the circumstances that led to 'Peer Gynt' being written. If any account of
that were to be intelligible, I would have to write a whole book
about it; and the time for that has not come yet. Everything I
have written has a close connection with what I have experienced -
not to say observed; every new work has for me had the purpose of
serving as a process of spiritual liberation and purification; for
one never stands quite without complicity and responsibility within
the society one belongs to. That is why I once wrote in a copy of
one of my books by way of dedication the following lines:

    To *live* is to war with trolls
    In the vaults of the heart and brain;
    To write - that is to pass
    Judgement upon one's self.

    The meaning of the lines you ask about is as follows: Peer
Gynt pleads, when trying to get admittance to hell, that he has
been a slave-trader. To this the 'Thin Man' replies that many
people have done worse things, e.g. suppressed the spiritual, the
will and the mind in their surroundings; but if this is done
'våset' [stupidly], i.e. without demonic intent, then this is no
qualification for getting into hell but only into the 'casting-
ladle'.
(Letter of 16 June 1880 to Ludwig Passarge.)

Of course, 'Peer Gynt' is in no way designed to be performed, and
you will remember that I myself had grave doubts about publishing
this work in Germany.
(Letter of 17 Aug. 1881 to Ludwig Passarge.)

It is self-evident that 'Peer Gynt' can only be produced in the
theatre in a cut version. When I first wrote to Grieg concerning
the music, I sketched out for him how I had imagined the fourth
Act might be replaced by a tone-poem which would indicate the
content and would be accompanied by a few living pictures or

tableaux presenting the most appropriate situations in the Act
which had been omitted, e.g. Peer Gynt and the Arab girls,
Solveig waiting at home in the cottage, etc. I communicated this
plan to Herr Josephson, but he did not agree with me; instead he
proposed certain cuts in the dialogue - cuts which seemed to me to
have been made very conscientiously, and to which I gave my
approval. [...]
(Letter of 16 Aug. 1875 to Hartvig Lassen.)

7. 2 G.B. SHAW

> 'Peer Gynt' (1891), 'The Quintessence of Ibsenism',
> Constable, 1929, pp. 47-8, 53-4

Brand dies a saint, having caused more intense suffering by his
saintliness than the most talented sinner could possibly have done
with twice his opportunities. Ibsen does not leave this to be
inferred. In another dramatic poem he gives us a rapscallion
named Peer Gynt, an idealist who avoids Brand's errors by setting
up as his ideal the realization of himself through the utter satisfaction of his own will. In this he would seem to be on the path
to which Ibsen himself points; and indeed all who know the two
plays will agree that whether or no it was better to be Peer Gynt
than Brand, it was beyond all question better to be the mother or
the sweetheart of Peer, scapegrace and liar as he was, than mother
or wife to the saintly Brand. Brand would force his ideal on all
men and women: Peer Gynt keeps his ideal for himself alone: it is
indeed implicit in the ideal itself that it should be unique - that
he alone should have the force to realize it. For Peer's first
boyish notion of the self-realized man is not the saint, but the
demigod whose indomitable will is stronger than destiny, the
fighter, the master, the man whom no woman can resist, the mighty
hunter, the knight of a thousand adventures, the model, in short,
of the lover in a lady's novel, or the hero in a boy's romance.
Now, no such person exists, or ever did exist, or ever can exist.
The man who cultivates an indomitable will and refuses to make way
for anything or anybody, soon finds that he cannot hold a street
crossing against a tram car, much less a world against the whole
human race. Only by plunging into illusions to which every fact
gives the lie can he persuade himself that his will is a force that
can overcome all other forces, or that it is less conditioned by
circumstances than a wheelbarrow is. [...]
  Peer Gynt has puzzled a good many people by Ibsen's fantastic
and subtle treatment of its metaphysical thesis. It is so far a
difficult play, that the ideal of unconditional self-realization,
however familiar its suggestions may be to the ambitious reader, is
not understood by him. When it is stated to him by some one who
does understand it, he unhesitatingly dismisses it as idiotic; and
because he is perfectly right in doing so - because it is idiotic
in the most accurate sense of the term - he does not easily recognize it as the common ideal of his own prototype, the pushing,
competitive, success-craving man who is the hero of the modern
world.

There is nothing novel in Ibsen's dramatic method of reducing
these ideals to absurdity. Exactly as Cervantes took the old ideal
of chivalry, and shewed what came of a man attempting to act as if
it were real, so Ibsen takes the ideals of Brand and Peer Gynt, and
subjects them to the same test. Don Quixote acts as if he were a
perfect knight in a world of giants and distressed damsels instead
of a country gentleman in a land of innkeepers and farm wenches;
Brand acts as if he were the perfect Adam in a world where, by
resolute rejection of all compromise with imperfection, it was
immediately possible to change the rainbow 'bridge between flesh
and spirit' into as enduring a structure as the tower of Babel was
intended to be, thereby restoring man to the condition in which he
walked with God in the garden; and Peer Gynt tries to act as if he
had in him a special force that could be concentrated so as to
prevail over all other forces. They ignore the real - ignore what
they are and where they are, not only, like Nelson, shutting their
eyes to the signals a brave man may disregard, but insanely steer-
ing straight on rocks no man's resolution can move or resist.
Observe that neither Cervantes nor Ibsen is incredulous, in the
Philistine way, as to the power of ideals over men. Don Quixote,
Brand, and Peer Gynt are, all three, men of action seeking to
realize their ideals in deeds. However ridiculous Don Quixote
makes himself, you cannot dislike or despise him, much less think
that it would have been better for him to have been a Philistine
like Sancho; and Peer Gynt, selfish rascal as he is, is not
unlovable. Brand, made terrible by the consequences of his
idealism to others, is heroic. Their castles in the air are more
beautiful than castles of brick and mortar; but one cannot live in
them; and they seduce men into pretending that every hovel is such
a castle, just as Peer Gynt pretended that the Trold king's den
was a palace.

7. 3 W.H. AUDEN

       The Shield of Perseus: Genius and Apostle, 'The
       Dyer's Hand and other Essays', Faber, 1948,
       pp. 436-41

In order to become an artist, a man must be endowed with an
exceptional talent for fabrication or expression, but what makes
it possible for him to exercise this talent and for his public to
appreciate it is the capacity of all human beings to imagine anything which is the case as being otherwise; every man, for
example, can imagine committing a murder or laying down his life
for a friend's without actually doing so. Is there, one can
picture Ibsen asking himself, perhaps subconsciously, any figure
traditionally associated with the stage who could be made to stand
for this imaginative faculty? Yes, there is: the actor. Keats'
famous description of the poet applies even more accurately to the
actor.

As to the poetic character itself, it is not itself: it has no

self - it is everything and nothing. The Sun, the Moon, the
sea, and men and women who are creatures of impulse, are
poetical and have about them an unchangeable attribute - the
poet has none: no identity.

Throughout 'Peer Gynt,' one question keeps being asked and
answered in various ways, namely, *Who am I? What is my real
self?* For the animals, the question does not arise.

> What innocence is in the life of beasts.
> They perform the behest of their great creator.
> They are themselves.

The nearest human approximation to this animal selfhood is the
'second nature' a man acquires through heredity and social custom.

> My father thieves,
> His son must steal.
> My father received,
> And so must I.
> We must bear our lot,
> And be ourselves.

So, too, with the drowning cook who gets as far in the Lord's
Prayer as *Give us this day our daily bread* and then sinks.

> Amen, lad,
> You were yourself to the end.

Next comes the social 'idiot' in the Greek sense, the individual
whose life is as conditioned by one personal overriding interest as
the conventional individual's is by social habit. In the first act
Peer sees a young peasant cutting off a finger in order to escape
conscription; Peer is fascinated and shocked:

> The thought perhaps - the wish to will,
> That I can understand, but really
> To do the deed. Ah me, that beats me.

In the last act he hears a funeral sermon about the same peasant
in which the parson says:

> He was a bad citizen, no doubt,
> For Church and State alike, a sterile tree -
> But up there on the rocky mountain side
> Where his work lay, *there* I say he was great
> Because he was himself.

Neither of these human ways of being oneself, however, satisfy
Peer. He tells his mother he means to be a King and Emperor, but
there is only one kind of empire which nobody else can threaten or
conquer, the empire of one's own consciousness, or, as Peer defines
it:

> The Gyntian Self - An army that,
> Of wishes, appetites, desires!
> The Gyntian Self - It is a sea
> Of fancies, claims, and aspirations.

But the Peer we see on stage has no appetites or desires in the ordinary sense; he plays at having them. Ibsen solves the problem of presenting a poet dramatically by showing us a man who treats nearly everything he does as a role, whether it be dealing in slaves and idols or being an Eastern Prophet. A poet in real life would have written a drama about slave trading, then another drama about a prophet but, on the stage, play acting stands for making.

The kinship of the poet to the dreamer on the one hand and the madman on the other and his difference from them both is shown by Peer's experiences, first in the kingdom of the trolls and then in the asylum. The kingdom of dreams is ruled by wish or desire; the dreaming ego sees as being the case whatever the self desires to be the case. The ego, that is to say, is the helpless victim of the self; it cannot say, 'I'm dreaming.' In madness it is the self which is the helpless victim of the ego: a madman says, 'I am Napoleon,' and his self cannot tell him, 'You're a liar.' (One of the great difficulties in translating 'Peer Gynt' is, I understand, that Norwegian has two words, one for the I *which is conscious* and another for the self *of which it is conscious,* where English has only one. *Myself* can mean either.)

Both the dreamer and the madman are in earnest; neither is capable of play acting. The dreamer is like the moviegoer who writes abusive letters to the actor he has seen playing a villain; the madman is like the actor who believes the same thing about himself, namely, that he is identical with his role.

But the poet pretends for fun; he asserts his freedom by lying - that is to say, by creating worlds which he *knows* are imaginary. When the troll king offers to turn Peer into a real troll by a little eye operation, Peer indignantly refuses. He is perfectly willing, he says, to swear that a cow is a beautiful maiden, but to be reduced to a condition in which he could not tell one from the other - that he will never submit to.

The difference between trolls and men, says the king, is that the Troll Motto is *To Thyself Be Enough,* while the Human Motto is *To Thyself Be True.* The Button-Moulder and the Lean One both have something to say about the latter.

> To be oneself is: to slay oneself.
> But on you that answer is doubtless lost;
> And therefore we'll say: to stand forth everywhere
> With Master's intention displayed like a sign-board.

> Remember, in two ways a man can be
> Himself - there's a right and wrong side to the jacket.
> You know they have lately discovered in Paris
> A way to take portraits by help of the sun.
> One can either produce a straightforward picture,
> Or else what is known as a negative one.

In the latter the lights and the shades are reversed.

But suppose there is such a thing as a poetic vocation or, in terms of Ibsen's play, a theatrical vocation; how do their words apply? If a man can be called to be an actor, then the only way he can be 'true' to himself is by 'acting,' that is to say, pretending to be what he is not. The dreamer and the madman are 'enough' to themselves because they are unaware that anything exists except their own desires and hallucinations; the poet is 'enough' to himself in the sense that, while knowing that others exist, as a poet he does without them. Outside Norway, Peer has no serious relations with others, male or female. On the subject of friendship, Ibsen once wrote to Georg Brandes:

> Friends are a costly luxury, and when one invests one's capital in a mission in life, one cannot afford to have friends. The expensiveness of friendship does not lie in what one does for one's friends, but in what, out of regard for them, one leaves undone. This means the crushing of many an intellectual germ.

But every poet is also a human being, distinguishable from what he makes, and through Peer's relations to Ase and Solveig, Ibsen is trying to show us, I believe, what kind of person is likely to become a poet - assuming, of course, that he has the necessary talent. According to Ibsen, the predisposing factors in childhood are, first, an isolation from the social group - owing to his father's drunkenness and spendthrift habits, he is looked down on by the neighbors - and second, a playmate who stimulates and shares his imaginative life - a role played by his mother.

> Ay, you must know that my husband, he drank,
> Wasted and trampled our gear under foot.
> And meanwhile at home there sat Peerkin and I -
> The best we could do was to try to forget ....
> Some take to brandy, and others to lies;
> And we - why, we took to fairy-tales.

It is not too fanciful, I believe, to think of laboring as a neuter activity, doing as masculine, and making as feminine. All fabrication is an imitation of motherhood and, whenever we have information about the childhood of an artist, it reveals a closer bond with his mother than with his father: in a poet's development, the phrase *The milk of the Word* is not a mere figure of speech.

In their games together, it is the son who takes the initiative and the mother who seems the younger, adoring child. Ase dies and bequeaths to Solveig, the young virgin, the role of being Peer's Muse. If the play were a straight realistic drama, Peer's treatment of Solveig would bear the obvious psychoanalytic explanation - namely, that he suffers from a mother-fixation which forbids any serious sexual relation: he cannot love any women with whom he sleeps. But the play is a parable and, parabolically, the mother-child relationship has, I believe, another significance: it stands for the kind of love that is unaffected by time and remains unchanged by any act of the partners. Many poets, it would seem,

do their best work when they are 'in love,' but the psychological
condition of being 'in love' is incompatible with a sustained
historical relationship like marriage. The poet's Muse must
either be dead like Dante's Beatrice, or far away like Peer's
Solveig, or keep on being reincarnated in one lady after another.
Ase's devotion gives Peer his initial courage to be a poet and
live without an identity of his own, Solveig gives him the courage
to continue to the end. When at the end of the play he asks her,
'Where is the real Peer?' - the human being as distinct from his
poetic function - she answers, 'In my faith, in my hope, in my
love.' This is an echo of his own belief. Ibsen leaves in doubt
the question whether this faith is justified or not. It may be
that, after all, the poet must pay for his vocation by ending in
the casting-ladle. But Peer has so far been lucky: 'He had
women behind him.'

The insoluble difficulty about the artist as a dramatic character
is that, since his relations with others are either momentary or
timeless, he makes any coherent plot impossible. 'Peer Gynt' is a
fascinating play, but one cannot say its structure is satisfying.
Practically the whole of the drama (and nearly all of the best
scenes) is a Prologue and an Epilogue: the Prologue shows us how
a boy comes to be destined for the vocation of poet rather than a
career as a statesman or an engineer, the Epilogue shows us the
moral and psychological crisis for a poet in old age when death
faces him and he must account for his life. Only in the Fourth
Act are we shown, so to speak, the adult poet at work, and in this
act the number of scenes and the number of characters introduced
are purely arbitrary. Ibsen uses the act as an opportunity to
make satirical comments on various aspects of Norwegian life, but
Peer himself is only accidentally related to the satire.

7. 4 ROLF FJELDE

        Foreword to 'Peer Gynt', Signet edition, New
        American Library, New York and Toronto, 1964,
        pp. xix-xxiv

What wearies Peer Gynt most is, in all his wandering, having
missed so completely the springs of life; but his failure certainly stems in part from his mode of quest. Anyone who reads the
text with some care is struck by the number of modulated repetitions of motifs from Peer's youth in the later action. His harsh
treatment at the hands of the troll-imps, for example, is dupli-
cated in his encounter with the Moroccan monkeys and again in the
final chaos of the asylum scene. His invocation of the inviolable
Anitra snoring in her tent repeats, in satiric reduction, his
original refusal to approach Solveig in the hut. The enormous pig
becomes the miraculous horse. He begins to quote the Bible, the
classics, proverbs, acquaintances, himself, incessantly - and
never quite accurately. The Memnon statue seems like the Dovre
King; the Sphinx is like the Boyg.

In this mosaic of repeating patterns, Ibsen suggests that experience takes its shape primarily from the set of the personality, and that the world we never made is, often to a surprising extent, an outgrowth of our own human powers or a denial thereof, and not, as Peer passively claims, of Fate. But the repetitions, we also see, are veiled, disguised, off key, inaccurate; and in this fact are further implications. The Gyntian mode of procedure in all things, large or small, is roundabout. To go by roundabouts - or by the Rotation Method, to use the comparable term from *Either/Or,* one of the works of Kierkegaard read by Ibsen in his Grimstad days - is to compromise between two extremes. One extreme would be to break the cycle of repetitions, to strike out, through struggle and suffering, for genuine novelty, for a new contribution to the life of man. But this would be to enter the refining creative matrix of the universe and have one's ego shrunk to scale and eventually lost, becoming only a moment in the evolution of intelligence. The other direct route would be to face repetition undisguised, head on. To confront one's life as repetition is to confront oneself; to confront oneself in such terms is to confront despair; but to accept despair would be to affirm at least the potentiality of self-transcendence in other dimensions of existence. In either case, there would be a risk, a leap, but this time the real would be grounded in the real and the Button-molder sent packing. Peer's flirtation with pure research, however, is no more than another transitory bit of role-playing; and the first time he really knows despair is when the shooting star flashes down and out, and the mists shattered by his imaginary leap in the opening scene threaten to close in again. So, for the Gyntian personality, the cycle must hold; and the effective function of fantasy, in proceeding by roundabouts, we see, is to throw just enough of a veil over repetition to persuade the self that no really fundamental change or effort is necessary.

The great arc of the play's action, then - from Gudbrandsdal throughout the world and back again - though framed in the archetypal pattern of the hero's life, his adventure and return, is far from the fulfillment of a heroic destiny. In the three aspects of the play discussed above, comprising the hero's choice, his initiation and his quest, each is presented in terms of its inverse, its antithesis, the negative - or, as the Lean One makes clear, not even that, since, photographically speaking, Peer Gynt is an undeveloped plate on which nothing has really registered. In this antiromantic work that employs the full resources of the romantic theater, the nonheroic hero is the pilot model of the hollow man of our own time, rendered perplexed and anxious by problems of identity and direction.

'If the modern age has been rightly called the age of anxiety,' Erich Fromm has written, 'it is primarily because of ... anxiety engendered by the lack of self.' To the extent that we *are* all brothers in old Peer Gynt, Ibsen's image of the human condition takes its place as one of the invaluable reference points in mapping the present world and one of the major landmarks indicating the course of the past. Again, as Georg Groddeck remarks, there is so much to learn from this play, it is quite impossible to refer to everything.

Deficient as he is in a strong sense of self, Peer has a personality that picks up and reveals the pressures and conflicts of an
age of transition the way iron filings strewn on paper bring out a
magnet's lines of force. In his young manhood, Peer's life is
outwardly restricted; he is the son of a *bondemand*, a peasant
farmer, tied to his limited milieu of parish, village, and farm.
The bent of his mind is feudal and romantically medieval; women
are princesses, mountains are castles, trees are warriors cloaked
in chain mail. He sees himself as a knight-at-arms, needing only
an unapproachable lady to serve [...]
    Then, with a masterfully bold stroke, Ibsen opens Act Four on
his middle-aged protagonist suavely presiding over the banquet
years of the latter nineteenth century as an exemplar of the
international, cosmopolitan world of finance capitalism. Peer has
made his fortune, after the manner of the empire builders, in
slaves and idols, the two logical products of reductive Gyntian
opportunism, which turns even the essence of the human and the
divine into commodities. (Appropriately, it is as an Americanized
European that Peer engages in the slave trade, the shame of
Europe and the guilt of America.)
    The transition from an organic community based on land and
blood ties, from which Peer Gynt is outlawed, to a collective
based on abstract contractual relationships - the company of self-
made men among whom he finds an insecure perch - is accompanied by
the loosening, the blurring of traditional sanctions and prohibi-
tions. The result is a state of inner disorientation and drift,
the background of which can be traced through a number of literary
antecedents. For, quite as much as the community defines for
Oedipus what he has to do ('Now, Oedipus, Greatest in all men's
eyes/here falling at your feet we all entreat you,/find us some
strength for rescue'), so the Ghost in 'Hamlet' lays his charge
upon the prince ('If thou hast nature in thee, bear it not'). But,
by the time of 'Faust,' the bonds are clearly in dissolution; the
hero has saved the community a long while back, and his present
ties are rather with Mephistopheles, the destructive principle,
conceived still in its traditional form. 'Peer Gynt,' however,
brings us up to date, as the hero wanders the whole world over,
trying to discover what it is he ought to be or do. The community,
the ancestors, even self-knowledge, are no longer sufficient
guides. Life becomes a feat, or a series of feats, of subjective
choice.
    In this awareness, Kierkegaard had already modified the original
Greek imperative accordingly. '"Know thyself" cannot be the real
goal of life, he wrote, 'if it is not also the beginning. The
ethical individual knows himself; but this knowledge is no mere
contemplation.... It is a reflection about oneself, which is
itself an action, and therefore I have purposely used the expression "choose yourself" instead of "know yourself."' The transformation of the classic hero of reason and virtue, or the tragic
departure therefrom, into the modern hero of the will, or the
lack thereof, implies a new conception of tragedy, which Ibsen then
strives to articulate. In the later plays, he is ceaselessly preoccupied with the question: To what extent *is* one free to choose,
oneself, and to what extent is self-knowledge, the uncovering of

the obstinate past, a determinant in making that choice?

What is made clear in this earlier work is the fact that the
hero is not free *not* to choose himself, not free to expand his
personality in the romantic or Faustian pattern to include all
knowledge, all experience, all phases of consciousness. It is
part of its significance that 'Peer Gynt' stands as a cenotaph for
the Renaissance man. At some time in the progressive nineteenth
century with its immense and varied innovations in fact and
theory, the Goethes, the Ben Franklins, the leisured men of parts,
cease to be possible; and, with that abruptness that struck Henry
Adams, the eighteenth-century man who was, at his best, still the
Renaissance man, the microcosm of all learning, becomes the speci-
alized twentieth-century man, locked in the pressure chamber of
his career, seeking fulfillment in the utilitarian ethic. Peer
experiments with that ethic briefly, after his manner, by
envisioning himself as a canal builder, but the solution for the
aged Faust is not for him. It is after this that he sees that, if
he cannot be one thing, he must be all things; that he is, in
reality, the sum of man, the whole of the past, the Emperor of all
Human Life - but this last and greatest of his visions, which is
essentially the Renaissance belief in the plenitude and perfect-
ibility of the individual, is, by itself and in this advanced age,
only one more waystage on the road to the Cairo asylum. Like his
brother under the skin, Don Quixote, two and a half centuries
before, Peer Gynt is a dreamer patching together the tatters of
an outworn ideal, no longer of medievalism and *courtesie* - he has
graduated from that - but of an aspiration that has its origins in
Castiglione and Petrarch.

And what is Peer left with in the last analysis, under the
tatters, under the patchwork coat of many colors? Only his life,
his having lived, the fountain of his vitality. Every peeling of
the onion - if one is looking for more in life - is a detour, a
delusion; and yet at the same time, every peeling was himself,
some part of himself that he could not deny: To give him due
credit, we have to say of Peer that, in this one sense, he holds
nothing back. There is no staid bourgeois façade, as in the
later plays, in which chink after chink of the truth will open.
And for this reason Groddeck is right when he speaks of him as
sincere. For this is exactly what Peer Gynt is. This chronic
liar whose life blows away like the desert wind, this clump of
nothing who creeps back to the beginning and the end of everything in Solveig's lap, is amazingly sincere, amazingly significant. He was hardly far wrong about what he should do - what
Ibsen did do with him - when, in the passage projecting the
Renaissance ideal, he first thought of writing his life story
down as a guide to others. But we, more fortunate, scarcely need
his book when we have him alive in the theater. And with his
flamboyance, his roguish variability, his innumerable masks and
emotions, the theater is where he belongs, along with all the
chiaroscuro of his motley world. Aase scolding on the hill, Peer
spellbinding his mother into death, the near-blind Solveig speaking forgiveness at the end - in a theater of authentic, not
counterfeit, greatness, they would prove unforgettable. The
shifting illusions and realities of the stage are the counterpart

and fit medium of the selfsame shifts within Peer's life, by
which we are eventually brought up to that last and most impressive
change of scene when, for him as perhaps for us, before the ultimate hour, a light breaks; and out of the strange mercy of the
universe, the sun rises still one more time.

'THE WILD DUCK'

7. 5 MARY McCARTHY

   The Will and Testament of Ibsen, 'Sights and
   Spectacles', Heinemann, 1959, pp. 166-9, 174

   GINA: Wasn't that a queer thing to say - that he'd like to be
   a dog?
   HEDWIG: I tell you what, Mother. I think he meant something
   else by that.
   GINA: What else could he mean?
   HEDWIG: Well, I don't know; but it was as though he meant
   something else all the time - and not what he said.

This short catechism - from the second act of 'The Wild Duck' -
is at first sight only a sort of road sign to the audience to
look out for curves ahead. Hjalmar Ekdal's wife and daughter are
discussing his friend, Gregers, the meddling fanatic who has
inserted himself into the family, speaking a dark language and
pressing what he calls the claim of the ideal. In the scene just
before, he has expressed the wish to be a dog - an 'extraordin-
arily clever dog. The kind that goes to the bottom after wild
duck when they dive down and bite fast hold of the weeds and the
tangle down in the mud'. Translated out of this idiom into plain
speech, this means that Gregers sees himself as the rescuer of the
household which his father (the hunter) has wounded and sent down
into the depths. These depths, ironically, are located in an
attic, where Hjalmar, who plays the flute and has a windy,
'artistic' personality, also plays at being a professional photographer and inventor while his wife does the hard work. In the
neighbouring garret room, behind a curtain, Hjalmar's disgraced,
drunken old father, wearing a brown wig and his lieutenant's
uniform, plays at being a hunter with an old double-barrelled
pistol, some barnyard fowls, pigeons, rabbits, and a real wild
duck. Father and son 'go hunting' in this make-believe forest,
which is rather like photographer's scenery. Hedwig, the perci-
pient little girl, who is not Hjalmar's real daughter but the
illegitimate child of Gregers's father, is going blind. This
blindness is a metaphor for the state of darkened self-deception
in which the little family lives. Gregers believes that he has
the duty to *open Hjalmar's eyes* to the true facts of his marriage.
At the house of Gregers's father, who is also losing his sight,
they are drinking Tokay wine and playing Blind Man's Buff.
   In short, as Hedwig indicates to her uninstructed mother, the

dramatist means something else all the time and not what he says.
Everything, Hedwig precociously understands, is symbolic. The
real wild duck is the child, Hedwig, who picks up Gregers's
'loaded' suggestion and shoots herself. The tragic climax of
'The Wild Duck' is brought about, thus, by an act of over-
interpretation. Gregers, for once, was speaking literally when
he said to the little girl: 'But suppose, now, that you of your
own free will sacrificed the wild duck for *his* sake?' But
Hedwig, confused and terrified the next morning by her supposed
father's harshness (for Hjalmar's eyes have at last been
opened), thinks that she has finally grasped Gregers's under-
meaning and, presuming that she is the 'sacrifice' alluded to,
goes into the garret room and puts the pistol to her breast.
    This ending, like so many of Ibsen's dramatic finales ('The
mill race! The mill race!'), seems a little heavy and strained,
like the last crashing chords of movie music. Yet it is utterly
just. The child's suggestibility has a semantic grounding. She
has been led by the Higher Critics around her to look for the
real reality under the surface of language - that is, to schema-
tise her life as she lives it. Gregers, with his 'claim of the
ideal', Hjalmar, with his talk of 'a task in life', are both
inveterate schematisers, one a truth-speaker, the other an
aesthetician. As his wife says of Hjalmar, 'Surely you realise,
Mr. Werle, that my husband isn't one of those ordinary photo-
graphers.' Everything has conspired to make Hedwig distrust the
ordinary way of looking at things. In a peculiarly sinister
scene in the third act, Gregers has been talking to Hedwig about
the garret room where the wild duck lives. She tells him that
sometimes the whole room and all the things in it seem to her
like 'the ocean's depths', and then she adds: 'But that's so
silly.'

    GREGERS: No, you mustn't say that.
    HEDWIG: It is, because it's only an attic.
    GREGERS (*looking hard at her*): Are you so sure of that?
    HEDWIG (*astonished*): That it's an attic?
    GREGERS: Yes, Do you know that for certain?
    (*Hedwig is silent, looking at him with an open mouth.*)

Gregers preaches mysteries. Hjalmar's daily conversation is a flow
of oratory. He always speaks of his brown-wigged bald father as
'the white-haired old man'. And his pretended 'purpose in life' is
a sort of parody of Gregers's 'purpose to live for'. Hjalmar too
conceives of himself as a saviour, the rescuer of his father.
'Yes, I will rescue that ship-wrecked man. For he was ship-
wrecked when the storm broke loose on him.... That pistol there, my
friend - the one we use to shoot rabbits with - it has played its
part in the tragedy of the House of Ekdal.' Again, a flight of
metaphors, more disjointed and *ad libitum* in Hjalmar's case, a fact
which points to the difference between the two rhetoricians.
Hjalmar improvises idly on the instrument of language, but Gregers
is in earnest, with his single unifying metaphor, of the duck and
the bird dog and the hunter, which he pursues to the fearful end.
    The men are poet-idealists; Hedwig is a budding poetess. Gina,

the uneducated wife, belongs to the prosy multitude that was
patronised earlier in the century by Wordsworth: 'A primrose by
the river's brim, A yellow primrose was to him. And it was
nothing more.' 'That there blessed wild duck,' she exclaims.
'The fuss there is over it!' When Gregers, true to his metaphor,
speaks of the 'swamp vapour' that is morally poisoning the Ekdal
household, Gina retorts: 'Lord knows there's no smell of swamps
here, Mr. Werle; I air the place out every blessed day.'
[...]
      [...] But the temptation of this new, allusive method (the
method described by Hedwig in the passage quoted) was that it led
to grandiosity and cunning or, more precisely, to the kind of
schematic thinking exemplified by Gregers Werle, this schematic
thinking being really a form of God-identification, in which the
symbolist imposes on the concrete, created world his own private
design and lays open to question the most primary facts of
existence, i.e., whether an attic is 'really' an attic or is not
in fact a swamp or something else. The allusive, hinting language employed by Gregers is the 'language of all messianic individuals and interfering, paranoid prophets. And, like Hjalmar's
sentimental flow of metaphor, it is the language of bad art, art
that is really religion or edification. This type of symbolism
is often found in sermons and in addresses by college presidents,
who liken the institution to a ship, themselves to the pilot at
the helm, etc.
      Ibsen sees all this in Gregers, and he sees, furthermore, that
Gregers is incurable. In his last speech of the play, Gregers
has merely shifted metaphors: 'GREGERS (*looking in front of him*):
In that case, I am glad that my destiny is what it is. RELLING:
May I ask - what *is* your destiny? GREGERS (*on the point of
going*): To be thirteenth at table.' This cryptic and portentous
remark means something more than it says, evidently - either that
the speaker is going to commit suicide or that he sees himself
from henceforth as the odd, unassimilable man, the bird of ill
omen, and that he finds a mysterious satisfaction in the picture.

7. 6 F. ANSTEY

      'The Wild Duck', Act 5, 'Mr. Punch's Pocket Ibsen',
      Heinemann, 1893, pp. 145-51

Gregers enters, and finds Gina retouching photographs.
GREGERS (*pleasantly*): Hialmar not come in yet, after last night,
I suppose?
GINA: Not he! He's been out on the loose all night with Relling
and Mölvik. Now he's snoring on their sofa.
GREGERS (*disappointed*): Dear! - dear! - when he ought to be
yearning to wrestle in solitude and self-examination!
GINA (*rudely*): Self-examine your grandmother!
(*She goes out; Hedvig comes in.*)
GREGERS (*to Hedvig*): Ah, I see you haven't found courage to
settle the Wild Duck yet!

HEDVIG: No - it seemed such a delightful idea at first. Now it strikes me as a trifle - well, *Ibsenish*.
GREGERS (*reprovingly*): I *thought* you hadn't grown up quite unharmed in this house! But if you really had the true, joyous spirit of self-sacrifice, you'd have a shot at that Wild Duck, if you died for it!
HEDVIG (*slowly*): I see; you mean that my constitution's changing, and I ought to behave as such?
GREGERS: Exactly, I'm what Americans would term a 'crank' - but *I* believe in you, Heavig.
(*Hedvig takes down the pistol from the mantelpiece, and goes into the garret with flashing eyes; Gina comes in.*)
HIALMAR (*looking in at door with hesitation; he is unwashed and dishevelled*): Has anybody happened to see my hat?
GINA: Gracious, what a sight you are! Sit down and have some breakfast, do (*She brings it.*)
HIALMAR (*indignantly*): What! touch food under *this* roof? Never! (*Helps himself to bread-and-butter and coffee.*) Go and pack up my scientific uncut books, my manuscripts, and all the best rabbits, in my portmanteau. I am going away for ever. On second thoughts, I shall stay in the spare room for another day or two - it won't be the same as living with you! (*He takes some salt meat.*)
GREGERS: *Must* you go? Just when you've got nice firm ground to build upon - thanks to me! Then there's your great invention, too.
HIALMAR: Everything's invented already. And I only cared about my invention because, although it doesn't exist yet, I thought Hedvig believed in it, with all the strength of her sweet little shortsighted eyes! But now I don't believe in Hedvig! (*He pours himself out another cup of coffee.*)
GREGERS (*earnestly*): But, Hialmar, if I can prove to you that she is ready to sacrifice her cherished Wild Duck? See!
(*He pushes back sliding-door, and discovers Hedvig aiming at the Wild Duck with the butt-end of the pistol. Tableau.*)
GINA (*excitedly*): But don't you *see*? It's the pigstol - that fatal Norwegian weapon which, in Ibsenian dramas, *never* shoots straight! And she has got it by the wrong end too. She will shoot herself!
GREGERS (*quietly*): She will! Let the child make amends. It will be a most realistic and impressive finale!
GINA: No, no - put down the pigstol, Hedvig. Do you hear, child?
HEDVIG (*still aiming*): I hear - but I shan't unless father tells me to.
GREGERS: Hialmar, show the great soul I always *said* you had. This sorrow will set free what is noble in you. Don't spoil a fine situation. Be a man! Let the child shoot herself!
HIALMAR (*irresolutely*): Well, really, I don't know. There's a good deal in what Gregers says. H'm!
GINA: A good deal of tomfool rubbish! I'm illiterate, I know. I've been a Wild Duck in my time, and I waddle. But for all that, I'm the only person in the play with a grain of common-sense. And I'm sure - whatever Mr. Ibsen or Gregers choose to say - that a screaming burlesque like this ought *not* to end like a tragedy -

even in this queer Norway of ours! And it shan't, either! Tell
the child to put that nasty pigstol down, and come away - do!
HIALMAR (*yielding*): Ah, well, I am a farcical character myself,
after all. Don't touch a hair of that duck's head, Hedvig.
Come to my arms and all shall be forgiven!
(*Hedvig throws down the pistol - which goes off and kills a
rabbit - and rushes into her father's arms. Old Ekdal comes out
of a corner with a fowl on each shoulder, and bursts into tears.
Affecting family picture.*)
GREGERS (*annoyed*): It's all very pretty, I dare say - but it's
not Ibsen! My real mission is to be the thirteenth at table. I
don't know what I mean - but I fly to fulfil it! (*He goes.*)
HIALMAR: And now we've got rid of *him*, Hedvig, fetch me the deed
of gift I tore up, and a slip of paper, and a penny bottle of gum,
and we'll soon make a valid instrument of it again.
(*He pastes the torn deed together as the Curtain slowly
descends.*)

7. 7 JOHN NORTHAM

      'The Wild Duck', 'Ibsen: A critical Study',
      Cambridge University Press, 1973, pp. 136-41,
      145-6

The lighting of Act V sets the emotional tone of the play now that
Gregers has had his effect on events. Cold grey morning light;
wet snow lies on the large panes of the skylight. A dreary scene.
    Gina takes a resolutely sensible view of the hullabaloo of the
previous night but Hedvig shows her need for her father. It is
not his master, Gregers, who brings news of Hjalmar, but Relling.
Hjalmar has not lived up to Gregers' image of the spiritual gladi-
ator; he has been very drunk. In the analysis of his personality,
Relling has far more evidence on his side than Gregers; he provides information about Hjalmar's upbringing that we have to take
on trust, but we are prepared to do so because of Relling's deadly
accuracy when he describes details that can be checked: Hjalmar's
skill in declaiming other people's ideas, for example. And we
accept his estimate of Gregers too, as a sufferer not merely from
'rectitudinal fever' but from the need to worship something that
doesn't concern him.
    And yet Relling is not a distinguished person, not a distin-
guished doctor. His regimen has made neither him nor his patients
into specimens of radiant health. Gregers may be absurd in his
obstinate search for the absolute but Relling is depressing in his
estimate that just about everybody is sick and that the only thing
to do is keep each going with his own life-lie. In Relling's analysis, Hjalmar and old Ekdal are at best the equivalents of the
actual crippled wild duck, damaged beyond repair and contented
with captivity, saved as much as they can ever be saved - his nos-
trum is the antithesis to Gregers'. And yet his method works;
illusion can make people happy. And Relling will not allow that
ideals are any better than lies. The opposition between the two

men is absolute and irreconcilable. They stand for two antithetical views of life, the ideal and the pragmatic; each has some
virtue and many vices. Their discussion ends, as it must, in a
declaration of war from Gregers: 'Doctor Relling, I shall not
give up until·I have rescued Hjalmar out of your clutches!' So
much the worse for Hjalmar, is Relling's reply and he immediately
begins to exercise his kind of therapy on Hedvig when she comes
on: 'Well, little wild-duck mother, I'm going down now to see if
your dad is still lying and pondering on that marvellous invention.' Those few words are carefully chosen to cheer and
reassure.

Gregers sets to work in his own way. He thrusts himself at
Hedvig physically and mentally. His first words to her are portentous: '(draws close to Hedvig) I can see from your face that
it is not finished.' 'It is [not] finished' is the phrase from St
John - 'when Jesus therefore had received the vinegar, he said
It is finished'. The emphasis, the intensity, are quite frightening; it seems a let-down to be reminded of what is involved - that
business with the wild duck, as Hedvig calls it.

She has slipped away from him. Last night she had accepted his
symbolism: in the light of day her sense of fact has reasserted
itself. Gregers takes this as evidence that she too has been
ruined by her environment; like her grandfather and her father,
she has lost her courage at the critical moment. He implies that
she is yet another version of the wild duck, but again it is a
resistible interpretation; it follows from his theory but it does
not match up to the impression Hedvig has made.

Gregers makes a last, emotional appeal to win her back to his
way of thinking: 'Oh, if only you'd had your eyes opened to what
makes life really worth-while, - had the genuine, joyful, courageous spirit of self-sacrifice, then you would soon see how he would
come up to you - But I still have faith in you, Hedvig.' Those
insistently rhetorical words, those accumulated, loaded terms, are
the last words that Hedvig hears from him, the final message to
remember.

They are enough to make her return to the plan she accepted
under Gregers' domination the night before. When old Ekdal comes
out of the attic - where, incidentally, he has virtually lived
since the beginning of Act III so far as his stage existence is
concerned; and where Hedvig has never yet been seen to enter in
behind the net - she coaxes out of him the best way to shoot a duck
and seems about to do so when she is interrupted by the return of
Hjalmar.

The comic scene takes a stomach-turning lurch into agony. It
is quite extraordinary. There are five brief lines of conversation
between husband and wife; Hedvig runs in and cries out with joy
'Oh, Daddy, Daddy!', Hjalmar waves her off with 'Go away, go away,
go away. Take her away from me, I tell you', and Hedvig goes in
silence. That is all, and yet a child's agony (the word will stand
repetition) is compressed into that moment of rejection. It is not
obliterated, indeed its painfulness for us is sharpened by the
comic egocentricity that Hjalmar goes on to display. He thinks
only of himself and his self is worthless. And yet Hedvig loves
him. She has to endure his callousness again in a scene of even

greater pain when Hjalmar hounds her out of the kitchen. His
words about 'intruders' reduce her to frightened confusion. She
cannot respond with words; all she can say is 'The wild duck', but
that is enough to show that she is determined now to put Gregers'
precepts into action. But as she enters the attic for the first
time, wounded, bitterly wounded by these terrible events, the
symbol seems to expand. This wild duck is plunging to the sea-
deeps in a totally different way.

She is not forgotten while she is in there behind closed doors.
The dialogue sets up an acute tension between the girl who has been
revealed and the girl who is described so wrongly by Hjalmar
luxuriating in self-pitying cynicism. It is not as though he can
be taken seriously. His fury seems no more substantial than his
other emotions and resolutions. He is not the man Gregers took him
for. But Gregers can gain some hope when at last Hjalmar turns his
mind away from his piddling affairs to his child; he is able to say
that perhaps from that quarter Hjalmar will receive proof of genuine love. Then the shot is heard. Gregers is ecstatic; when it
is all explained to him, Hjalmar is filled with the appropriate
emotion. They look for the girl in her room.

Old Ekdal's appearance on stage does more than heighten the
tension - after all it was assumed that it was he who shot the
duck, yet here he is, coming from his room. He makes a striking
spectacle. He is more fully clad in his past, so to speak, than
ever before. In Act II he wore his uniform cap; now he wears full
uniform, with sword. It looks like a grotesque fancy-dress on
this old wreck, a faintly mad obsession with the past.

The discovery of Hedvig dead in the attic drives him further
back. He repeats the strange phrase he let fall in Act II
denoting the effect his ruin has had on his mind. It is an idea
that obsesses him, and it is this which comes to the surface, not
any direct response to the immediate situation, under the shock:
'The forest avenges.' On this wild duck at least Gregers has had
an effect opposite to what he intended. Instead of bringing him up
out of the swamp he has driven him deeper. What has he done to
Hedvig, that other wild duck? Here the play leaves an open doubt
except insofar it is certain that this is not what Gregers meant
to happen.

Did she die by accident, fumbling for the bird she intended to
shoot? Relling's evidence seems to dispose of that; it was no
accident. Did she, as some have thought, shoot herself in despair
when she heard Hjalmar say: 'If I asked her then: Hedvig, are you
willing to give up your life for me (*laughs scornfully*). Yes,
thank you, - you'd soon hear what answer I got! (*a pistol shot is
heard* ...)' The balance of evidence is against this. All through
the play the attic doors seem thick enough to prevent overhearing.
And in any case, the timing is wrong. This interpretation demands
that Hedvig should hear Hjalmar, register what he says, decide on
her action and perform it in an instant.

There is a more probable reconstruction that makes her death not
the reaction of a moment but the culmination of a process in keeping with her character. Hedvig is a thoughtful child. She has
listened to her elders and has understood that they, and especially
Gregers, mean something different from what they say. She trusts

Gregers because he shares part of her imaginative world and
because he knows what should be done. She starts by thinking that
she understands what he intends her to do - shoot a bird - but
when she finally enters the attic after the second terrible
assault on her feelings she is no longer sure. All she has to go
on are those final words of his. Is the willing sacrifice the
bird, or she herself who is like the bird? She accepts the latter;
it is her final surrender to an adult symbolism that she does not
fully comprehend.

Uncomprehending or not, and even though for an ignoble father,
Hedvig dies for love. Her entry into the attic and her death there
suddenly makes her seem the one and only person in the play for
whom a wild duck is an apt symbol. Not the damaged, contented
creature in the attic, but the wild duck in nature, wounded and
choosing death rather than accept the outrage. The wild duck in
the play is a travesty of nature; the wild duck Hedvig becomes is
nature itself.

Gregers seems to sense this when he repeats that poetic phrase
that equates the attic with the 'sea-deeps'. She has gone wounded
to the bottom to die. But he cannot feel proud of this outcome;
she has coined her own symbol, not followed his. He has rescued
nobody, but caused another and fatal casualty. Old Ekdal he has
driven deeper into a fantasy world. 'The forest avenges. But I'm
not afraid,' he says, and we see him go back into the attic, for
him a world of fantasy that has suddenly become terribly real.
Hjalmar he has driven to a sickening display of facile emotion.
Gina, thank God, he has not been able to change. She stands as a
rebuke to his idealistic inhumanity, thinking all the time, as he
has never thought, of the dignity of the dead child.

Hedvig is carried off by her parents, but she is not forgotten
during the bitter scene that ends the play. Nothing can obliter-
ate the impact of the past few minutes. Her death and its conjectured reasons hover in the air as the unspoken alternative to
Relling and Gregers. Each puts his case. Relling has fact on his
side, but what his philosophy leads to is merely the preservation
of Hjalmar as he is; Gregers has idealism,but his philosophy leads
to death. They speak from their fixed positions, each seeing himself as spokesman, the one of empiricism, the other of idealism.
Neither is justified in this assumption. Ibsen has not created
spokesmen but individuals. Relling is an empirical whose rough
and lax experience has led him to conclude that all men are sick;
Gregers is an idealist whose vision and drive have been distorted
by the peculiar deprivations of his own youth. It is not a matter
of choosing between them, but of recognising how different men,
and women, can be as a result of their previous lives. If we had
to choose, and choose one of these, then the play would be dismal.
Hedvig supplies the alternative. Her act of love, for however
unworthy an object and performed in whatever confusion of spirit,
is one that Relling's philosophy cannot account for. Nor Gregers'.
She provides the human dignity that Relling cannot understand, and
the deep, untheoretical integrity of emotion that is lacking in
Gregers. Gregers goes off, probably to suffer, as he always felt
he would, the fate of being the unlucky thirteenth at table;
Relling stays to curse. Neither has changed. But Hedvig has; and

with her has changed our conception of what it is possible for a
human being to become. [...]

[...] Hedvig is not the protagonist though she is a vital con-
tributor to the final effect. Ibsen seems only to be beginning to
understand the importance of this subterranean life of the individual, but that in itself marks a decisive advance over his earlier
work. It can be defined as a broadening of Ibsen's concept of
idealism. In all of the earlier plays, even in 'Love's Comedy',
idealism is conceived of as heavy with ethical and moral content,
and for that reason accessible to discussion, debate and explanation. Gregers' idealism is of this sort and it is now presented
for condemnation; what Hedvig offers is more elusive yet more com-
prehensive. It is difficult to define in terms of morality and
yet it seems to deserve that description more than does Gregers'
systematising. It amounts to a passionate conviction of feeling
rather than of intellect about one essential value upon which depends the quality of life as a whole. Love is, for Hedvig, the
value without which her life would be intolerable. Through it she
demonstrates a beauty of character, not a mere mental strength or
rigidity, an intuitive fineness that leads her to make essential
rather than superficial discriminations. Ibsen has begun to see
that moral choice of this kind can only be conducted from the
centre of feeling and must necessarily, in a society that places
so many impediments in the way of self-expression, be less readily
accessible to any formal kind of articulation than he had earlier
conceived. Hedvig is the first of Ibsen's inarticulate poets of
living. She is handicapped by her social circumstances: by her
immaturity, blindness, lack of education, of intellectual challenge and stimulus. She could never express her poetry. Yet the
play convinces us that the impulse towards a poetry of living,
though frustrated of utterance, is not killed in her. In one
person at least there is an integrity of purpose towards a finer
morality that is, in the crisis, invincible.

That is all that Ibsen chooses to set against the defeat and
despair and scepticism generated by the rest of the play. That
little is further diminished by the circumstance that only an
adolescent girl is capable of this integrity; all the adults have,
in one way or another, suffered corruption of the spirit. Had
Hedvig lived on... but the play does not invite this surmise. It
is enough that the small affirmation has been made. Ibsen has
lost his old type of hero, the moral stalwart; he has not fully
developed the new kind, but the intimations are there, affirming
the persistent faith that in some rare persons at least, heroism
is possible even in the modern world.

'ROSMERSHOLM'

7. 8 IBSEN

> Letters, 'The Oxford Ibsen', trans. and ed.
> J.W. McFarlane, Oxford University Press, vol. 6,
> 1960, pp. 445, 447

Eight days ago I came home again to Norway after being away for eleven years. During these eight days at home I have known more happiness than in all the eleven years abroad. I have found immeasurable progress in many matters, and I have seen how the people I most closely belong to have approached much closer to the rest of Europe than ever before. But my visit home has also provided disappointments. I have found that even the most neces- sary rights of the individual are still not as secure under the new régime as I felt I might hope and expect them to be. The majority of those in control do not permit the individual either freedom of faith or freedom of expression beyond a certain arbit- rarily fixed limit. Much remains to be done here before we can be said to have achieved real freedom. But our democracy, as it now is, is hardly in a position to deal with these problems. An element of nobility must find its way into our public life, into our government, among our representatives and into our press. Of course I am not thinking of nobility of birth, nor of money, nor a nobility of learning, nor even of ability or talent. What I am thinking of is a nobility of character, of mind and of will. That alone can liberate us. This aristocracy which I hope our people will be provided with, will come to us from two direc- tions. It will come to us from two groups which so far have not suffered any irreparable damage under party pressure. It will come to us from our women and from our workers. The transforma- tion of social conditions which is now being undertaken in the rest of Europe is very largely concerned with the future status of the workers and of women. That is what I am hoping and waiting for, that is what I shall work for, all I can. Permit me with these few scattered remarks to express my most heartfelt thanks for the honour and pleasure which the Trondheim Workers' Union have given me this evening. And in expressing my thanks, I salute the Working Class and its future.
(Speech to a workers' procession, Trondheim, 14 June 1885.)

Certainly, the call to work is something that runs right through 'Rosmersholm'. But apart from that, the play deals with the struggle that every serious-minded man must wage with himself to bring his way of life into harmony with his convictions. The different functions of the spirit do not develop uniformly or comparably in any one individual. The acquisitive instinct rushes on from one conquest to the next. Moral consciousness, however, 'the conscience', is by comparison very conservative. It has its roots deep in tradition and in the past generally.

From this comes the conflict within the individual. But naturally
the play is first and foremost a work about people and their destiny.
(Letter to Bjornson's nephew, Bjorn Kristensen, 13 Feb. 1887.)

The only advice I can give you is to read the whole play several
times through very carefully, and pay particular attention to what
the other characters say about Rebecca. Our actors often used to
make the mistake, in earlier days at any rate, of studying their
parts in isolation and without paying sufficient regard to the
character's position in and relation to the whole work.... No
declamation. No theatrical emphasis. No pomposity at all!....I
don't think Rebecca's character is difficult to get into and understand. But there are difficulties in the way of presenting and
rendering this character because it is so concentrated.
(Letter to Sofie Reimers, actress at the Kristiania Theatre, 25
March 1887.)

7.   9   SIGMUND FREUD

> Some Character Types Met With in Psychoanalytic
> Work (1916), 'Standard Edition of the Complete
> Psychological Works of Sigmund Freud', rev. and
> ed. J. Strachey, vol. 14, Hogarth Press, 1957,
> pp. 328-31

The enigma of Rebecca's behaviour is susceptible of only one
solution. The news that Dr. West was her father is the heaviest
blow that can befall her, for she was not only his adopted
daughter, but had been his mistress. When Kroll began to speak,
she thought that he was hinting at these relations, the truth of
which she would probably have admitted and justified by her
emancipated ideas. But this was far from the Rector's intention;
he knew nothing of the love-affair with Dr. West, just as she
knew nothing of Dr. West's being her father. She *cannot* have had
anything else in her mind but this love-affair when she accounted
for her final rejection of Rosmer on the ground that she had a
past which made her unworthy to be his wife. And probably, if
Rosmer had consented to hear of that past, she would have con-
fessed half her secret only and have kept silence on the more
serious part of it.
   But now we understand, of course, that this past must seem to
her the more serious obstacle to their union - the more serious
crime.
   After she has learnt that she has been the mistress of her own
father, she surrenders herself wholly to her now overmastering
sense of guilt. She makes the confession to Rosmer and Kroll
which stamps her as a murderess; she rejects for ever the happiness to which she has paved the way by crime, and prepares for
departure. But the true motive of her sense of guilt, which
results in her being wrecked by success, remains a secret. As we

have seen, it is something quite other than the atmosphere of
Rosmersholm and the refining influence of Rosmer.

At this point no one who has followed us will fail to bring
forward an objection which may justify some doubts. Rebecca's
first refusal of Rosmer occurs before Kroll's second visit, and
therefore before his exposure of her illegitimate origin and at a
time when she as yet knows nothing of her incest - if we have
rightly understood the dramatist. Yet this first refusal is energetic and seriously meant. The sense of guilt which bids her
renounce the fruit of her actions is thus effective before she
knows anything of her cardinal crime; and if we grant so much, we
ought perhaps entirely to set aside her incest as a source of
that sense of guilt.

So far we have treated Rebecca West as if she were a living
person and not a creation of Ibsen's imagination, which is always
directed by the most critical intelligence. We may therefore
attempt to maintain the same position in dealing with the objection that has been raised. The objection is valid: before the
knowledge of her incest, conscience was already in part awakened
in Rebecca; and there is nothing to prevent our making the influence which is acknowledged and blamed by Rebecca herself responsible for this change. But this does not exempt us from recognizing the second motive. Rebecca's behaviour when she hears what
Kroll has to tell her, the confession which is her immediate reaction, leave no doubt that then only does the stronger and decisive motive for renunciation begin to take effect. It is in fact a
case of multiple motivation, in which a deeper motive comes into
view behind the more superficial one. Laws of poetic economy
necessitate this way of presenting the situation, for this deeper
motive could not be explicitly enunciated. It had to remain concealed, kept from the easy perception of the spectator or the
reader; otherwise serious resistances, based on the most distressing emotions, would have arisen, which might have imperilled
the effect of the drama.

We have, however, a right to demand that the explicit motive
shall not be without an internal connection with the concealed
one, but shall appear as a mitigation of, and a derivation from,
the latter. And if we may rely on the fact that the dramatist's
conscious creative combination arose logically from unconscious
premises, we may now make an attempt to show that he has fulfilled this demand. Rebecca's feeling of guilt has its source in
the reproach of incest, even before Kroll, with analytical perspi-
cacity, has made her conscious of it. If we reconstruct her past,
expanding and filling in the author's hints, we may feel sure that
she cannot have been without some inkling of the intimate relation
between her mother and Dr. West. It must have made a great
impression on her when she became her mother's successor with this
man. She stood under the domination of the Oedipus complex, even
though she did not know that this universal phantasy had in her
case become a reality. When she came to Rosmersholm, the inner
force of this first experience drove her into bringing. about, by
vigorous action, the same situation which had been realized in the
original instance through no doing of hers - into getting rid of
the wife and mother, so that she might take her place with the

husband and father. She describes with a convincing insistence
how, against her will, she was obliged to proceed, step by step,
to the removal of Beata.

'You think then that I was cool and calculating and self-
possessed all the time! I was not the same woman then that I am
now, as I stand here telling it all. Besides, there are two sorts
of will in us, I believe! I wanted Beata away, by one means or
another; but I never really believed that it would come to pass.
As I felt my way forward, at each step I ventured, I seemed to
hear something within me cry out: No farther! Not a step
farther! And yet I *could* not stop. I *had* to venture the least
little bit farther. And only one hair's-breadth more. And then
one more - and always one more. And then it happened. - That is
the way such things come about.'

That is not an embellishment, but an authentic description.
Everything that happened to her at Rosmersholm, her falling in
love with Rosmer and her hostility to his wife, was from the first
a consequence of the Oedipus complex - an inevitable replica of
her relations with her mother and Dr. West.

And so the sense of guilt which first causes her to reject
Rosmer's proposal is at bottom no different from the greater one
which drives her to her confession after Kroll has opened her
eyes. But just as under the influence of Dr. West she had become
a freethinker and despiser of religious morality, so she is trans-
formed by her love for Rosmer into a being of conscience and
nobility. This much of the mental processes within her she herself understands, and so she is justified in describing Rosmer's
influence as the motive for her change - the motive that had
become accessible to her.

The practising psycho-analytic physician knows how frequently,
or how invariably, a girl who enters a household as servant, companion or governess, will consciously or unconsciously weave a
day-dream, which derives from the Oedipus complex, of the mistress of the house disappearing and the master taking the newcomer
as his wife in her place. 'Rosmersholm' is the greatest work of
art of the class that treats of this common phantasy in girls.
What makes it into a tragic drama is the extra circumstance that
the heroine's day-dream had been preceded in her childhood by a
precisely corresponding reality.

7. 10 GORDON CRAIG

> A note on 'Rosmersholm', programme, Teatro della
> Pergola Rappresentazioni di Elenora Duse, Florence,
> December 1906, British Library

[...] There is the powerful impression of unseen forces closing
in upon the place: we hear continually the long drawn out note of
the horn of death.

It is heard at the commencement, it mingles with the cries
towards the end.

Here and there hurries the figure of Life, not merely a little

photographic figure of Rebecca West - not even a woman - but the
very figure of Life itself - and all the while we hear the soft
crescendo of the Death Horn as its player approaches.   Therefore
those who prepare to serve Ibsen, to help in the setting forth of
his play, must come to the work in no photographic mood, all must
approach as artists. [...]

We are not in a house of the 19th or 20th century built by
Architect this or Master Builder that, and filled with furniture
of Scandinavian design - That is not the state of mind Ibsen
demands we shall be in.   Let us leave period and accuracy of
detail to the museums and to curiosity shops.

Let our common sense be left in the cloak room with our umbrel-
las and hats.   We need here our finer senses only, the living part
of us.   We are in Rosmersholm, a house of shadows.

Then consider the unimportance of custom and clothes - remember
only the colour which flows through the veins of life - red or
grey as the sun or the moon will it, dark or fair as we will.
[...]

Do you think you see a sad and gloomy picture before you.   Look
again.   You will find an amazingly joyous vision.

You will see Life as represented by Rebecca West, the will to
do, free until the end.

That in itself is inspiration without limit.

You will see fools surrounding this figure of Life, fools who
are either cowards or knaves - that is to say maimed examples
of live beings, but not alive creatures.   You will hear these fools,
knaves and cowards talking, hoping to entrap Life, to bind it, to
control it - and you will see Life triumphant and folly destroyed.

I do not know where except in Ibsen we can today find such
faithfulness to the old creed or such an advocate for the individuality of Flame. [...]

7. 11   MAURICE VALENCY

Ibsen, 'The Flower and the Castle', Macmillan, New
York, 1963, pp. 179, 181, 183-7

Rosmer is interesting.   He is the end-product of a long line of
high-bred people, one of those sickly souls which Chekhov also,
and Thomas Mann, considered the special objects of literary
interest.   Rosmer is sensitive; his conscience is queasy; he is
full of self-doubt and self-criticism.   In him we have not so much
the protagonist, as the battleground of the evolutionary process.
He is not a strong man like Kroll.   His faith in God was easily
shaken; so too is his new-found faith in man.   He is, in short, a
man of shaky faith, and his tragedy proceeds from the fact that he
can accept no certainty, and yet must have certainty in order to
live.

Rebecca West is Ibsen's first version of the fascinating woman
who brings death to the man who loves her. [...]

In the cycle of plays which deal with this theme, the form
varies only slightly.   The protagonists of these plays - Rosmer,

Lövborg, Solness, Rubek - are all, for one reason or another, delicately poised men. Each is peculiarly susceptible to the influence of the woman who comes to set him free, and each is destroyed by the effort he is forced to make. They are all examples of highly talented men who are incapable, because of some characterological flaw, of reconciling within themselves their need for freedom and their fear of its consequences, which in each case turns out to be justified.

The narrative patterns conformable with so exigent a formula necessarily varied within relatively narrow limits. The protagonists of these plays are all tied in some way to a woman who gives them no joy. Rosmer cannot extricate himself from the dead Beata. Thea is indispensable to Lövborg. Solness is tied to the desiccated Aline by his imaginary obligation. Borkman - if he may be admitted to this company - is shackled to Gunhild through his crime. Rubek, who rejected Irene, is bound to Maja, who neither loves nor understands him. Into these loveless lives comes, in each case, a beautiful woman whose function it is to save, inspire, and bless - and eventually to kill.

From a metaphysical viewpoint, these ladies are unwittingly in the service of a power which uses them, and, in most cases, uses them up, for purposes beyond their own: their mysterious fascination is attributable to a force outside themselves, with which the soul of the hero is in precise accord. The human wreckage that piles up in the wake of these angels is, accordingly, the debris of the cosmic dialectic which works through the souls of men, presumably toward the betterment of mankind. The lives of these men and women may therefore be considered phenomena of transition, examples that illustrate the cosmic process through which the future grows out of the ruins of the past. It was chiefly to such transitional figures - the 'delicate children of life,' to use Mann's phrase - caught up in the clash of titanic forces, that Ibsen looked for the characters of modern tragedy. [...]

[...] The type of tragic hero developed by Ibsen, and after him by Strindberg, Chekhov, and the rest, is a sensitive and neurotic individual whose spiritual malaise is the motor of the action in which he is spent. The contrast between such a concept of the tragic hero and that of the Greek dramatists is obvious. The hero of Greek tragedy is, in general, a strong man in sound health who is for some reason at odds with fate. He has no spiritual problems. His pressures are external, and would be ended if he had his will. The Greek gods take little notice of meagre types. The man marked out for tragedy is hybristic through his stature, and there is something stimulating in his struggle and his overthrow by a superior power. In a type of drama based on such characters, there is no need for psychological analysis. The interest centers on the contest, and the issues are moral and ethical, involving choices which depend upon reason. Though the answers may not be simple, the questions are.

The heroes of modern tragedy, on the contrary, are ill with a disease of the soul which mirrors the illness of our culture. The adversary is not an external power. The enemy is within themselves. To enter into their struggles, it is necessary to achieve a degree of intimacy which is entirely foreign to classic drama. The

tendency in the modern theatre has been, accordingly, for analysis
to take the place of poetry; but the great masterpieces are always
those which transmit grandeur. It is no accident, then, that of
the great figures of seventeenth-century drama the two which seem
to us most 'modern' are Phèdre and Hamlet, the prototypes of the
modern tragic protagonist. Rosmer seems classic to us only insofar as we do not understand him.

In 'Rosmersholm,' as in most of his later work, Ibsen made use
of an analytic technique in which a pre-existent situation is
examined in detail until in the end it is clear. Such a method is
essentially expository, not narrative. It consists of a series of
explanations, each of which is precipitated by an event; and the
events of the action are motivated chiefly by the need to elicit
further explanations. In the three days which encompass the
action of 'Rosmersholm,' no event of any importance takes place.
Headmaster Kroll pays several visits to Rosmersholm, and asks some
questions. The old teacher Brendel comes twice to borrow money.
The rest is explanatory. When the exposition is ended, the play
ends, and the principals go out to drown themselves.

These tableaux, which to the eye seem static, derive extraordinary interest from the manner in which the characters little
by little reveal themselves. Everything has happened when the
play begins. What goes on is, accordingly, a rearrangement of the
past, a relocation of events, and re-definition of motives; so
that the significant part of a lifetime is relived in the course
of these days, and brought to a close. Underlying the short
sequence of actual happenings is the very extensive action which
took place before the curtain rose, an action which in a more open
type of drama would have furnished the substance of the play
instead of the exposition. Hardly a detail remains to be added.
'Rosmersholm' is, indeed, no more than the epilogue or, at the
most, the denouement of Rebecca's over-successful intrigue.

This intrigue involves a time-honored situation - the struggle
of two women for a man, and it is described in some detail. In
bringing about the death of Beata, Rebecca is doubtless guilty of
what Strindberg was to call, in connection with the plays of
1887-1888, a psychic murder - but this is not the subject of
'Rosmersholm,' merely its basis. 'Rosmersholm' illustrates
another application of the technique of 'Ghosts.' In keeping the
antecedent action off the stage and concentrating exclusively on
the denouement - that is to say, on the revenge of Beata, with all
that this implies - Ibsen once again resorted to the manner of
regular tragedy; but the effect of the action is different from
that of Renaissance drama, and it is certainly quite different
from that of 'Oedipus Rex,' with which it is sometimes compared.
Rebecca, unlike Oedipus, knows from the beginning that she is
guilty. The dramatic process is therefore not intended to adduce
evidence of a crime, but through the application of spiritual
pressures, to elicit a confession. In 'Rosmersholm' each act
represents another turn of the screw; in each act another revelation is wrung out of Rebecca, until in the end the confession is
complete, and she is ready to expiate her sins.

There is, however, no compulsion upon Rebecca other than that
which arises out of her own psychic situation. Had her conscience

been robust, and her aim purely practical, she might, conceivably, have succeeded admirably in her undertaking, and they might all have lived happily ever after. But the machine which brings about the destruction of Rebecca and Rosmer is in operation from the moment when they first meet. For people constituted as they are, there is no possible happy outcome.

Ibsen leaves Rebecca's original purpose in some doubt; if her ends were sordid in the beginning, they are certainly not so in the end. She represents herself as a woman with a mission; and there is no particular reason to doubt her sincerity. She appears to have insinuated herself into Rosmer's house, like the self-appointed agent of a foreign power, in order to convert Rosmer to her way of thought, and thus to work through him in the liberal cause. When she has gained her ends, she finds herself emotionally implicated, and is thus precisely in the position of the heathen enchantresses we meet in Renaissance *romanzi,* who are sent to corrupt the Christian hero but are converted by him instead. But Rebecca is completely dedicated. It would be logical for a penniless adventuress to give up her missionary purpose at a certain point, and to marry her willing victim. Rebecca, however, does not lose sight of her goal for a moment. She cancels all her material gains by persisting in her wish that Rosmer publish his apostasy and his conversion at the first possible moment. In this manner she brings about a catastrophe which everyone desires to avoid, and most of all, herself.

The tragedy of Rebecca, like that of Rosmer, is thus implicit in her nature. She too suffers from recurrent attacks of that integrity which Dr. Relling calls the national disease of Norway. She stops at nothing and refuses to compromise at any point Even when she understands that Rosmer will demand an All-or-Nothing sacrifice of her, she stands her ground. In consequence, the play includes within the frame of tragedy a *reductio ad absurdum* of the idealistic personality.

There is something especially grotesque in Rosmer, but his pattern of mind is a familiar one with Ibsen's idealistic heroes: in each case the ideal demands a sacrifice. In 'The Wild Duck,' the idealistic Gregers needs a blood-sacrifice to assure himself that humanity is noble. Similarly, Hedda Gabler needs to destroy Lövborg to assure herself that life can be beautiful. Rosmer must have Rebecca die in order to justify his faith in the liberal creed.

Bereft of his faith in God, Rosmer cannot preach his faith in man unless he is convinced of his own goodness. He cannot believe that his influence on Rebecca has been good unless Rebecca proves it to him, and she can prove it convincingly only by dying for him. Before he can save anyone, therefore, he has to kill someone; but, of course, he cannot, in all conscience, survive such an act. He too must die. Obviously, Rosmer is a victim of logic: such are the dangers of idealism. [...]

7. 12   ALRIK GUSTAFSON

> Some Notes on Theme, Character and Symbol in
> 'Rosmersholm', 'Carleton Drama Review', 1 (2),
> 1955-6, pp. 9-11

One of the measures of Ibsen's cunning dramaturgic powers in the
play is the skill with which he employs symbolistic patterns to
suggest largely by indirection the irrational drives of the central characters in the web of their tragic fate. Symbols are, of
course, a commonplace in Ibsen's dramas, but seldom does he employ
them so extensively and with such telling effect as in 'Rosmersholm.' In the social reform plays Ibsen uses symbolistic devices
somewhat too obviously, almost exclusively to clarify his
themes. [...] The symbols convey *ideas* - and little else. They
have few emotional overtones, are invested with little of the
impressive mystery of life, the tragic poetry of existence. They
tend to leave us in consequence cold, uncommitted, like after a
debate whose heavy-handed dialectic has ignored the very pulse-
beat of a life form which it is supposed to have championed. It
is not until 'The Wild Duck' that Ibsen's symbolism manages to
maintain a fine balance between what the dramatist is trying to
say directly and what he wishes to suggest. In 'Rosmersholm' he
goes a step farther in his use of symbolism: not prepared to
offer a final moral judgment on Rosmer and Rebecca, Ibsen dis-
penses entirely with direct statement and allows symbolistic patterns alone to cast their fitful lights and shadows over the
tragic pair, merely intimating by magnificently fragmentary
indirection whatever 'truth' the central action of the play may
seem to yield.
    The symbolistic patterns which Ibsen employs in 'Rosmersholm'
are drawn very largely from primitive folkloristic sources -
sources which spring directly from man's relationship to land and
sea and which inevitably assume a dark-toned, fateful view of
life. As such they are peculiarly adapted to Ibsen's tragic
theme. The central symbolistic patterns are two in number, those
which reflect the Rosmer view of life represented primarily by the
White Horses that haunt the Rosmersholm estate, and those which
reflect Rebecca's emancipated views as represented by the Mermaid
and the Sea Troll. I use the term 'patterns of symbolism' quite
deliberately, for in 'Rosmersholm' Ibsen's central symbols (the
White Horses, the Mermaid, the Sea Troll) are constantly being
joined by related symbolistic material which serves to enrich the
contents of the central symbols and intensify their effects. This
is particularly true of the White Horses symbol, which in itself,
and to begin with, is only vaguely suggestive of the way in which
the dead claim the living at Rosmersholm. But in the course of
the play we come to see in many ways that what this means is that
the Rosmersholm tradition is a sterile, sick tradition, that it
leaves its clammy, debilitating mark upon all who come under its
subtle spell, including at the last even Rebecca.
    The White Horses *are* Rosmersholm, and all that Rosmersholm
stands for - a way of life which once may have nurtured a vital,

living idealism but which has at the last stiffened into a
correct, deadly conformity and conventionalism. In dozens of
different ways we become aware of this, sometimes more or less
pointedly, but more often tangentially in bits of observation or
in deftly suggestive stage properties. When Madam Helseth remarks,
for instance, that at Rosmersholm children never cry and grown-ups
can never bring themselves to laugh we see into the core of the
Rosmersholm psyche. And when we observe in the opening scene the
stern family portraits of many generations of the Rosmer family
staring from the living room walls down upon Rebecca and Madam
Helseth, we immediately sense a world of the strictest conformity
- especially when we note that Rebecca has placed large quanti-
ties of 'fresh birch branches and wild flowers' in this room, as
if to defy the Rosmer spirit hanging grimly on the surrounding
walls. Later we come to learn that Beata could not stand flowers,
their scent and colors were too much for her.
     Though the patterns of symbolism attached to the character and
role of Rebecca are not repeated and varied with the same persis-
tency as those related to Rosmer, they are in their way equally
expressive. They derive with very few exceptions from sea phenomena and folk superstitions connected with the sea, and are
designed to suggest the primitive amoral sources of Rebecca's
character. Brought up near the sea in the sparsely settled semi-
Arctic regions of Finnmarken by a free-thinking doctor, she had
upon first coming to Rosmersholm found everything strange and
stifling. She could neither understand nor accept the gloomy
traditionalism of Rosmersholm. Instinctively she reacted against
this traditionalism, and having no ethical norms except those
provided by instinct she had no particular qualms of conscience
when she became instrumental in causing Beata's death. Beata stood
in the way of her converting Rosmer to her emancipated views of
the social and political order, and Beata must therefore die.
     Rebecca herself confesses all of this, and more - in a language
whose tense laconisms at times breaks out into poetry and symbolism, the poetry and symbolism of the sea. And the commentary of
other characters in the play adds similar symbolical detail in describing Rebecca. At the end, when Rebecca has agreed to follow
Beata into the mill-race, she does so because she otherwise
'should only be a Sea Troll dragging down the ship that is to
carry [Rosmer] forward.' And earlier, when she describes her love
for Rosmer, she says - 'It came upon me like a storm on the sea.
It was like one of the storms we sometimes have in the North in
the winter-time. It seizes you - and whirls you along with it -
wherever it will. There is no resisting it.' And Ulric Brendel
[...] calls her to her face a 'fascinating mermaid.' Rebecca had
in her much of the wild mystery of the sea, its sweeping expan-
siveness and beauty but also its mysterious destructive power.
When she ultimately became tamed by the over-civilized Rosmersholm
spirit she was maimed, she had lost her courage and what she called
her 'power of action.' Shortly before Rosmer at the end proposed
the double suicide in the mill-race she had planned to return to
the North, to the primitive sources of her being, to the wild
fjord country of her childhood and young womanhood.

STRINDBERG: 'MISS JULIE' AND 'THE GHOST SONATA'

'MISS JULIE'

8. 1 STRINDBERG (1909)

>'Letters to the Intimate Theatre', trans.
>W. Johnson, Peter Owen, 1967, p. 296

Since the beginning of the Intimate Theater can be said to be
Falck's successful production of 'Lady Julie' (at the Folk Theater)
three years ago, it is understandable that the young director feels
he has been influenced by the Preface, which recommended that one
try to achieve reality. But I wrote that twenty years ago, and, if
I do not exactly need to attack myself on that point, [I may say]
that all that scribbling about stage properties was unnecessary.
The play itself, which in its day was received as an act of a villain in Sweden, has now had time to be accepted, and August Palme,
who resurrected it, noticed that it was a 'Figaro' which contained
more than an unusual seduction story. In it are the struggle between races and classes, the renewal of society from the roots up,
the patrician and the plebeian, woman's foolish attempt to free
herself from nature, the whole raging modern revolt against tradition, customs, and common sense.
    Falck, faithful to the program, had [as his set] a kitchen com-
plete in all details, which I got to see later on for the first
time, however. And everything was as it should be!

8. 2 ROBERT BRUSTEIN

>August Strindberg, 'The Theatre of Revolt',
>Methuen, 1965, pp. 115-19

The dramatic design of 'Miss Julie' is like two intersecting lines
going in opposite directions: Jean reaches up and Julie falls

down, both meeting on equal grounds only at the moment of seduction, in the arms of the great democratizer, sex. Both are motivated by strong internal (in Julie's case, almost unconscious)
forces which propel them towards their fate - underscored by
social-sexual images of rising and falling, cleanliness and dirt,
life and death. These images inform the entire play but are uni-
fied in two contrasting poetic metaphors: the recurring dreams
of Jean and Julie. In Julie's dream, she is looking down from
the height of a great pillar, anxious to fall to the dirt beneath,
yet aware that the fall would mean her death; in Jean's, he is
lying on the ground beneath a great tree, anxious to pull himself
up from the dirt to a golden nest above.

The crossover is the crux of the action: Jean seduces Julie
during the Midsummer Eve festivities, and then induces her to cut
her throat in fear that their impossible liaison will be discovered. Julie's descent, therefore, is a movement from spirit to
flesh, motivated by her attraction to dirt and death. She unconsciously desires to degrade herself, to be soiled and trampled on,
and when she falls, she ruins her entire house. Born, like
Strindberg, of an aristocratic father and a common woman (her
mother is associated with dirt through her fondness for the kitchen, the stables, and the cowsheds), Julie finds in her parent-
age the source of her problems. Her father's weakness has taught
her to despise men, and the influence of her mother, an emancipated woman, has encouraged her to dominate and victimize them.
Jean has seen her with her weakling fiancé, forcing him to jump
over her riding crop like a trained dog; and in the torrent of
abuse which pours from her after she has been seduced, her hatred
of men is further underlined. On the other hand, neither her
class arrogance nor her sex hatred is total. Her fiancé has
filled her with egalitarian ideas, so that she tempers her aristocratic impudence with democratic condescension ('Tonight we're all
just happy people at a party,' she says to Jean. 'There's no
question of rank'). And her natural sexuality, heightened by suggestions of masochism, weakens her masculine resolve ('But when
that weakness comes, oh .... the shame!') Like Diana, her wayward
bitch, she is a thoroughbred who consorts with the local mongrels,
since her unconscious impulses lead her, against her will, to roll
herself in dirt.

By contrast, Jean's ascent is associated with cleanliness and
life, and is a movement from the flesh to the spirit. He wishes
to be proprietor of a Swiss hotel; and his highest ambition is to
be a Rumanian count. Like Julie, he is trying to escape the con-
ditioning of his childhood - a childhood in which filth, muck, and
excrement played a large part. As we learn from his story of the
Turkish outhouse, his strongest childhood memory is of himself on
the ground yearning towards cleanliness. Having escaped from the
Turkish pavilion through its sewer, he looked up at Julie in 'a
pink dress and a pair of white stockings' from the vantage point
of weeds, thistles, and 'wet dirt that stank to high heaven.' At
that time, he went home to wash himself all over with soap and
warm water. Now he is still washing himself, in a metaphorical
sense, by trying to rise above his lowly position and aping the
fastidious manners of the aristocracy. For just as Julie is

attracted to his class, so he is impelled towards her. He has
become a lower-class snob through his association with his
betters, wavering between an aristocratic affectation of French
manners and tastes, and a slavish servility amidst the Count's
boots.

The contrast between the two characters is further emphasized
by their conflicting views of the sexual act and the concept of
'honor.' Despite her mother's influence, Julie believes rather
strongly in Romantic love and Platonic ideals, while Jean, despite his rather pronounced prudishness, regards love merely as
an honorific term for a purely animal act - as Iago would put it,
as 'a lust of the blood and a permission of the will.' Jean,
indeed, is the Elizabethan Naturalist come to life in the modern
world, though, unlike the Elizabethan dramatists, Strindberg does
not make the Naturalist a villain. Jean is superstitious, and
pays lip service to God (a sign, Strindberg tells us, of his
'slave mentality'), but, in effect, he is a complete materialist,
for whom Platonic ideals have no real meaning whatsoever. Though
he admires Julie's honor, he knows it is only a breath; truth,
like honesty, is wholly at the service of his ambition, for he
will lie, cheat, and steal to advance himself; and as for conscience, he might say, had he Richard III's eloquence, 'It is a
word that cowards use.' It is because of his pragmatic material-
ism that Jean so values reputation, whereas Julie, the idealist,
seems to scorn it. For like the Elizabethan Machiavel, Jean
knows that it is external appearances rather than personal integrity that determines one's success in the world. Strindberg
undoubtedly views this unscrupulous valet as a link in the evolution of the Superman. And though he secretly disapproves of all
his values, he is willing to countenance Jean, in spite of his
basenesss, because of his effective masculine power.

Jean, therefore, differs from the Captain in his toughness,
self-sufficiency, and total lack of scruples; but Strindberg has
apparently decided that Iago's ruthlessness, rather than Othello's
romantic gullibility, is the necessary element in achieving victory over the female. Yet, if Jean is no Othello, then Julie is
no Desdemona either; and just as Julie learns that Jean is not a
shoe-kissing cavalier, so Jean is disillusioned in his expectations of Julie. Jean's disenchantment is signified by his growing
realization that the aristocracy is also tainted. For, in getting
a close look at Julie, he sees that she, too, has 'dirt on your
face,' and that the inaccessible golden nest is not what he had
hoped:

I can't deny that, in one way, it was good to find out that
what I saw glittering above was only fool's gold ... and that
there could be dirt under the manicured nails, that the
handkerchief was soiled even though it smelled of perfume.
But, in another way, it hurt me to find that everything I was
striving for wasn't very high above me after all, wasn't even
real. It hurts me to see you sink far lower than your own
cook. Hurts, like seeing the last flowers cut to pieces by
the autumn rains and turned to muck.

Julie, in short, has achieved her unconscious desire. She has
turned to muck, and been cut to pieces by the rain. And now
there is nothing left for her but to die.

In this act of expiation, Jean serves as Julie's judge and
executioner; but it is in her death that she proves her social
superiority to Jean, even though she has been sexually defeated
by him. In the most obvious sense, of course, her suicide signifies his victory; just as he chopped off the head of Julie's
pet songbird, so he must chop off hers, lest she decapitate him
(the sermon in church that morning, significantly, concerned the
beheading of John the Baptist). But if Jean triumphs as a male,
he is defeated as a servant, for her honorable suicide, a gesture he is incapable of, makes his survival look base. Strindberg
dramatizes Jean's ignobility by his servile cringing at the sound
of the Count's bell. Slobbering with uncontrollable fear, he
hypnotizes Julie into going into the barn with his razor. But
despite this display of will, it is Julie, not Jean, who is
finally redeemed. Hitherto convinced of her own damnation
because of the biblical injunction that the last shall be first
and the first last, Julie discovers that she has unwittingly
attained a place in paradise through her fall. For she learns
that 'I'm among the last. I *am* the last' - not only because she
is last on the ladder of human degradation, but because she is
also the last of her doomed and blighted house. As she walks
resolutely to her death, and Jean shivers abjectly near the
Count's boots, the doubleness of the play is clarified in the
conclusion. She has remained an aristocrat and died; Jean has
remained a servant and lived; and Strindberg - dramatizing for
the first time his own ambiguities about nobility and baseness,
spirit and matter, masculine and feminine, purity and dirt - has
remained with them both to the very end.

8. 3   PATRICK ROBERTS

> Strindberg: the Long and Cruel Struggle, 'The
> Psychology of Tragic Drama', Routledge & Kegan
> Paul, 1975, pp. 63-6

[...] Strindberg's second realistic play, 'Miss Julie', is much
subtler [than 'The Father'] in its presentation of sexual conflict
in the adult here-and-now. It too contains remarkable insights
into the primitive constituents of the psyche and their power to
direct the conscious life of the adult. In this play, where the
servant possesses and in so doing destroys the 'decadent' upper-
class woman, the aggressive feelings against women take a more
thoroughly sadistic form, culminating in the beheading of the finch
and Miss Julie's suicide. Although Jean does not consciously wish
for Julie's death, there is a coarseness and cruelty in him that
allow him to derive satisfaction from bringing Julie down to his
level, and from the subsequent survival of the fittest; moreover,
he directly incites her to her death. At this level the play
appears to be a riposte to 'The Father'; if women are potentially

stronger, and wish to dominate and destroy us, then we must hoist them with their own petard. There is an identification here with Strindberg's father, who seems to have dominated the women in his life. However, the impression the play makes on us is very dif- ferent from this; it is as though the triumph over the woman rel- eases Strindberg's sympathy with her, and enables him to portray her as a tragic victim, despite his talk (in the foreword) about the 'degeneracy of the half-woman, the man-hater'. If there is an element of self-portraiture in Jean - like Strindberg the servant's son who seduces the aristocratic girl but 'sexually is himself the aristocrat because of his virility' - there is more of Strindberg in Julie, the child fatally divided by the divi- sions between her parents; and whereas Jean is described by Strindberg in his introduction to the play, correctly, as callous, vulgar, and with a slave mentality, Julie as presented by him is a tragic figure, unconsciously bent on self-destruction. Just as Strindberg himself was a woman-hater who at the same time was powerfully drawn towards women, a conflict originating as he him- self was aware in his attitude towards his mother, so Julie is portrayed as a man-hater whose sexual urge, as powerful as Strindberg's, is similarly and even more fatally turned to self- destructive ends. For Jean is more the occasion than the cause of her ruin, whose origins, as the play specifically demonstrates [...] lie far in the past, in the child's relations with her parents. It is here that we find Strindberg's finest insight into primitive aggression and persecution: Julie's sexual initiative towards Jean, seemingly based on appetite, supported by the acci- dent of physical circumstances, is really self-destructive in nature and design. Although she believes herself to be in love, and although their situation, admittedly difficult, is not des- perate, she kills herself when her father returns, because (to quote Strindberg himself in the foreword) her 'repressed instincts break out uncontrollably'. (1) What these repressed instincts are is shown partly in description and partly in action: her sexual intercourse with Jean is experienced by her in the fantasy light of her original incestuous feelings for a father defeated and humiliated in the sexual struggle with her mother. Miss Julie had been brought up by her mother 'to loathe the whole male sex'; more recently, her breach with her fiancé has been brought about by her insistence on 'training' him, an activity that involved sexual humiliation. To give herself to a man is thus an act undertaken against powerful resistance, and is experienced as an enactment of this forbidden incestuous passion for the father; to give her- self to her father's servant is felt as an act of defiance and revenge against him, the fruit, perhaps, of envy and a sense of rejection. As she says to Jean near the end:

> My father will come back ... find his desk broken open
> ... then he'll ring the bell ... send for the police ...
> and I shall tell him everything. Everything. Oh how
> wonderful to make an end of it all - a real end! He
> has a stroke and dies and that's the end of all of us ...

Both aspects of her sexual union with Jean - the enactment of an

incestuous wish and the act of revenge against her father whom, in
her own words, she 'loved deeply but hated too, unconsciously'
- provoke in her an overwhelming sense of guilt. In the passage
quoted above, Strindberg shows how closely she is identified with
her father. He will die, she says, from the shock of what she has
done 'and that's the end of all of *us*'. By a similar process of
identification, his sexual defeat has imposed a like defeat on
her. (At the same time Strindberg shows her identification with
the mother, when she says, contemplating what she has done and
what she has yet to do, '... my mother is revenged again, through
me'.) She is herself the desk that should have been kept closed
for her father but has been broken open and violated - in this
image the two contradictory aspects of her sexual guilt are simultaneously expressed. When the bell finally rings, warning her
that her father is in the house, and she prepares in a trance-
like state for the final act of suicide, she says to Jean,

> ...the whole room has turned to smoke - and you look like
> a stove - a stove like a man in black with a tall hat -
> your eyes are glowing like coals when the fire is low -
> and your face is a white patch like ashes.

In this superb image of destructive sexuality father and lover
coalesce as a single avenging persecutory figure. The figure
also beckons her to peace - the peace of death, suggesting the
seemingly reparatory aspect of suicide, and thus the magnitude of
the preceding guilt. It is very striking that she needs Jean's
help in order to perform the act. He has to instruct her 'like a
hypnotist at the theatre' and actually puts the razor into her
hand; no less striking is the timing, and nature, of her appeal to
Kristin, the elder woman. In revulsion against Jean at the
killing of the goldfinch (she rightly identifies herself with the
bird) she appeals frantically to Kristin for protection against
him. The tone and manner of her speech is that of a frightened
child, repelled by and terrified of a brutal father, whose desperate pleas to a hostile, jealous mother fall on deaf ears. It
may be noted that the cold hypocritical pietism of Kristin's final
dismissal of Julie's appeal recalls the pietism of Strindberg's
parents, especially his mother, against which he rebelled so violently in adolescence. Significantly, Strindberg has made Kristin
Jean's regular mistress, and made Julie aware of this fact; the
child in Julie is thus appealing to a woman who, like her (or any
child's) mother is in sexual relation to the man in her life.
Julie's failure to placate Kristin leads directly to the despair
which culminates in suicide once her father's bell is heard. Her
first open reference to suicide immediately follows Kristin's smug
departure. Rejected by the mother, she is left alone with the man
in black - lover and father - whose persecutory threat derives
both from guilt and from her own hostile projections, stimulated
as these have been by Jean's cruelty to the finch: 'I should like
to see the whole of your sex swimming ... in a sea of blood', she
says to Jean after he has killed the bird. Her suicide is both
reparation and identification; her death is what the avenging male
figure desires - Jean puts the razor into her hand - for in so

acting she both makes amends for what she has done - obtaining
what she calls the 'gift of grace' - and joins him in his defeat
and disgrace. The father, whose 'unhappy spirit is kept above
and behind the action', in the words of the author's foreword, had
earlier attempted to shoot himself. It is insights such as these
that give 'Miss Julie' so deservedly honoured a place in the
beginnings of modern drama. They demonstrate Strindberg's understanding of some of the mechanisms of aggression and persecution,
as yet unexplored by psychoanalysis, whose nature he divined by
an introspective understanding of his own experience, with its
conflicts and obsessions. [...]

NOTE

1 All quotations from 'Miss Julie', trans. E. Sprigge, New York,
   1955, pp. 107-8, 113.

8. 4 MICHAEL ELLIOTT (*)

   Programme, National Theatre Company, Old Vic, 1966

Miss Julie cuts her throat, it is said, after sleeping once with a
servant. Since such behaviour must be ridiculous, it has been
used as an excuse to dismiss the play as out of date. Disingenu-
ously, of course. It then becomes possible to ignore Strindberg's
clinical analysis of some of our own least palatable and most carefully disguised motives. When the play first scandalised the
theatre-going society of the nineties the sympathies of the audience must have been almost entirely with Miss Julie - not because
they liked her behaviour but because she was their social equal,
being casually destroyed by a coarse, vicious, dishonest and
worthless animal. It was the unpardonable suggestion that such
things could happen, or if they could that they should be mentioned in public, that caused the play to be banned. But now that
situation has changed. The audience seems to identify itself more
easily with Jean. We are mostly his descendants, and it gives us
pleasure to see a degenerate aristocrat get her come-uppance.
   When Jean says to Miss Julie, 'Do you know what the world looks
like from down there? No, you don't!' the words could have been
written by any of a dozen English playwrights of the last ten
years. The difference is in the context. Strindberg does not
identify himself exclusively with one side of the conflict. He
uses it only as a fragment in his obsession with the great revolution in whose shadow we live. The power that is passing to Jean,
or to Lopakhin, has been in the hands of Miss Julie's predecessors
since the beginnings of civilisation. There are centuries of
oppression to poison Jean's mind with thoughts of destruction and
revenge when at last he finds, unbelievably, that he has the power.
He wants, as his dream tells us more clearly, to 'plunder the
bird's nest up there, where the golden eggs lie.'
   As for Miss Julie, she 'wants to fall', to bury herself deep in

the earth. Life is for her unbearable. She is as much deformed
by the past as Jean. The position in society that she inherits
from her family has been made increasingly hollow by history. She
hates herself for the way in which she has been crippled. She
hates the humiliation of finding herself a woman. She hates her
continual crucifixion by desires that she wishes to reject. She
is completely lonely. She has a vivid sense of her own degeneracy, of being a member of a decadent and dying race. And when
she does fall, she finds the new hell of living with a member of
a class that must always despise and torment her equally unthinkable. Is it strange that death seems a better alternative?
    Perhaps they really are great lovers. The greatest service
that Jean can do for her is to destroy her. She longs to be destroyed. Chained together in some profound sense, their egos cut
and scrape against each other until one of them breaks. This is
no chance midsummer-night encounter. It has been preparing for
centuries. The old social order must die. At this crossroads
Miss Julie finds relief at last in being freed from herself, and
Jean finds the opportunity to fulfil his desires. We are their
heirs. We must not disown them. The likeness is unmistakable.

NOTE

* Michael Elliott's production of 'Miss Julie' (in a double bill
  with Peter Shaffer's 'Black Comedy') was first performed at the
  Chichester Festival Theatre in 1965 with Maggie Smith as Miss
  Julie and Albert Finney as Jean.

'THE GHOST SONATA'

8. 5   MILTON A. MAYS

       Strindberg's 'Ghost Sonata': Parodied Fairy Tale
       on Original Sin, 'Modern Drama', 10 (2), September
       1967, pp. 189-94

[...] The many readers who find 'The Ghost Sonata' one of the most
exciting pieces in modern drama - however much avoided by pusil-
lanimous directors - are surely correct. The play, that is to
say, for all its admitted redundancies and even symbolic nonsequi-
turs, must have a thematic and symbolic coherence. The thesis
here advanced - which by no means explains everything - is that
'The Ghost Sonata' takes as its main structural mode the fairy
tale, that it is in fact a parodied fairy tale of sorts, and that
this form is the means of saying something about Original Sin.
    Strindberg's was a basically religious consciousness, and a
fascination with the concept of Original Sin would seem a natural
corollary of his known obsessive fascination with guilt, especially
marked in the chamber plays. 'The Burned House,' which immediately
precedes our play in the group, and is closely associated with it

in the writing, turns on a question of the guilty past, and is
full of allusions to the Garden, the Tree of Knowledge, and the
loss of an (equivocal) childhood innocence. 'The Ghost Sonata,'
with that hallucinatory clarity peculiar to the surrealistic work,
focuses on the universality and inescapability of guilt, bearing
down on 'innocent' and 'sinful' alike in a debacle which seems
fully as terrible as the pagan retribution rejected by the play -
and this despite the concluding unction of the Student's words on
patience and hope, accompanied by 'a white light,' Böcklin, and
'soft, sweet, melancholy' music.

Early in Scene I when the Old Man begins to open out the
insanely complicated relationships binding the inmates of the
Colonel's house, the Student says, 'It's like a fairy story.'
Hummel, in replying, 'My whole life's like a book of fairy
stories ... held together by one thread, and the main theme constantly recurs,' seems to corroborate their genre and hints that
his story - and our play - is about something specific. Seen in
broad relief, 'The Ghost Sonata' contains all the elements of
the fairy story, and it is this which gives it a kind of structural cohesiveness not found in the other chamber plays, which seem
to spill their symbols into a void. We have a poor but heroic
youth, and one, moreover, especially blessed or singled out by
destiny (a 'Sunday child' with the gift of second sight). Our
Student is enraptured of a beautiful and highborn maiden, who
lives in a 'castle' imagined by the Student to enclose all his
life's desires. He thinks his suit is hopeless, but a 'fairy godfather' with an aura of immense and mysterious powers appears and
promises him an entrée to 'doors and hearts.' In Scene II we discover, as we might have expected, that there are 'ogres' in the
castle who have the maid in thrall; but the fairy godfather is
prepared to do them battle. In the third scene we would further
expect the fairy princess and hero to be united and 'live happily
ever after.' Just how true - and false - to the facts of the
play this outline is should be apparent; yet in the play's relation
to this submerged paradigm, I am suggesting, lies much of its meaning.

For the fairy tale, after all, is a projection of the return-
to-Paradise wish. Whatever his ill fortune (symbolic of the fallen
world), the hero's desert is always good (he is naturally good, an
erect Adam), and the powers that be, somehow always recognizing
this, return him and his Eve, the princess (who has suffered her
trials as well), to Paradise, shutting the golden doors of 'they
lived happily ever after' firmly before our inquisitive eyes. In
'The Ghost Sonata' Strindberg uses parody and distortion of the
fairy tale to make it say the opposite thing: that guilt is contagious, innocence non-existent, or, if in some sense real (the
girl), it is 'sick' and 'doomed,' 'suffering for no fault' of its
own. In Adam's fall, sinned we all. Nor is there any Paradise to
be regained in the last act. The Student says of the girl's
house: 'I thought it was paradise itself that first time I saw you
coming in here.' But the flowers in the 'paradise' are poisonous;
it is in fact a place of ordeals, where no dreams come true. In
sum, despite the vague appeal of the Student [...] to a 'Liberator'
who will waken the innocent girl to 'a sun that does not burn, in

a home without dust, by friends without stain, by a love without
a flaw' - despite this perhaps rather sentimental gesture, the
force of the play is compacted into a metaphor for Original Sin:
it is expressive of the agony of 'this world of illusion, guilt,
suffering, and death ... endless change, disappointment, and pain.'

Strindberg's meaning in the play is put both abstractly and
concretely: both in discursive 'talk,' such as we have rather too
much of in the Student's last speeches, and in the most vivid symbols, such as the vampire cook - a disturbing contribution of
paranoia to art. The Student *says* that 'The curse lies over the
whole of creation, over life itself'; but this allusion to the
fallen world is only effective because we have seen the 'haunted'
old house, in which the very air is tainted, 'charged with crime,'
so that its inmates, guilty and innocent alike, are withering away.

It has been said that 'the fairy tale's miracles occur on the
material plane; on the spiritual plane (affections; characters;
justice; love) law abides.' (1) 'The Ghost Sonata' is a fairy tale
parodied and distorted. We have not witnessed this play for long
before getting a disturbing sense that nothing is quite right,
that even a 'spiritual logic' is being tampered with. Is the Old
Man, Hummel, a benefactor, or a self-serving user of other people,
after power - or what? That is, is he good fairy or wicked witch?
There are abundant hints to shake our confidence in Hummel, the
most startling of which is the first sounding of the vampire-
motif when Hummel takes the Student's hand in his icy hand, and
the Student struggles to free himself, saying, 'You are taking all
my strength. You are freezing me.' Variations on this theme
occur throughout the play, of course: 'vampirism' is a multiplex
symbol for vicarious gratification ('enjoy life so that I can
watch., at least from a distance'), for enslaving others by a knowledge of their guilty secrets (Johansson, the Colonel), or by a
sense of obligation (the Student) or by usury. Hummel is a
'blood-sucker' both metaphorically, on the surreal level of 'sucking the marrow out of the house,' and economically (the debts of
the Consul and the Colonel).

There is, if anything, a redundancy of suggestion of evil
identity for the Student's ostensible benefactor: he is a pagan
god in a chariot, a wizard, an 'old devil.' Hummel's Mephistophe-
lean character is underlined by his saying to the Student, 'Serve
me and you shall have power.'

STUDENT: Is it a bargain? Am I to sell my soul?

And when the Student, after hearing something disturbing about
Hummel from Johansson, his servant, decides to escape from him,
the girl drops her bracelet out of the window, the Student returns
it, and there is no more talk of escape. The girl serves Hummel's
purpose in a sense as Gretchen does Mephisto's. (And both women
are destroyed, though I am not suggesting the parallel be taken
any further.)

The question of the essential nature of Hummel remains a difficult one. He is clearly the most dynamic character in the play,
the one who seems to make everything happen. With the Student as
the 'arm to do [his] will' Hummel will enter the Colonel's house

and 'expose the crimes' there so that the girl (his daughter by the Colonel's wife), withering away in the evil atmosphere, can live again in health with the Student. All is for the young couple; Hummel's cleansing revenge is to involve the 'ghosts' only. But by Scene II we are as suspicious of Hummel's intention as is the Mummy. In any case, realistic criteria of character consistency and continuity of action are mostly irrelevant in this play. If we are unsure what Hummel's 'real' purpose with regard to the 'innocents' is, we are no more sure how his defeat by the Mummy has influenced the outcome of the play in Scene III. Are the Mummy, the Colonel, and the others versus the Old Man two groups of equally evil figures who mutually destroy each other? This would seem to leave the field clear for the blossoming of young love, the ghost house purged. But before we can understand more fully why this is not the case, the Student must be considered.

The role of the Student in 'The Ghost Sonata' also has its curious features. Does the play's conclusion leave him saved or damned? A survivor - the only one - or a victim? Or is he, by the conclusion of the play, not a protagonist at all, but dramatist's *raisonneur*, as suggested above? It seems to me that in his final speeches he does assume the function of authorial surrogate, but that there is a certain fitness to this: like Strindberg, the Student is an innocent trying to believe in an unfallen world in the face of the horrors of real existence. He is an Adam-figure, a 'Sunday child,' who, when he first saw the house of his beloved on Sunday morning - the 'first day of creation' - thought it was paradise. But he is a fairy tale hero ejected from his fairy tale world - and a cruelly parodied hero at that. His dream of bliss is all bourgeois: '"Think of living up there in the top flat, with a beautiful young wife, two pretty little children and an income of twenty thousand crowns a year."' The conclusion of Scene I is also parodistic, and splendid theater: Hummel, standing in his wheel chair which is drawn in by the beggars, cries: 'Hail the noble youth who, at the risk of his own life, saved so many in yesterday's accident. Three cheers for Arkenholtz!' This scene is followed by a nice tableau of the beggars baring their heads, the girl waving her hankerchief, the old woman rising at her window, and the maid hoisting the flag. Strains of a bizarre slapstick are found throughout the play; the audience should laugh, but not overconfidently.

The girl and the Student - fairy tale hero and princess - do not figure in Scene II, where the ogres or witches fight. At least one consequence of Hummel's defeat follows the fairy tale pattern: Johansson, his servant, is 'freed from slavery' by his death, as the victims of the enchanter or wicked witch always are. Alone with his beloved in the Hyacinth Room in Scene III, the Student's expectations are clearly for speedy achievement of his heart's desire. 'We are wedded,' he says; but his Eve must disillusion him. This place is not what it seems; it is no paradise, and no fairy-tale 'ever-after,' but is 'bewitched' - 'bedeviled' we might more literally call the post-lapsarian world. Hummel - 'old Adam' as well as 'old Nick'? - may be dead (literally by his own hand, as Adam was in effect), but his influence lives on after him. 'This room is called the room of ordeals,' says the girl; 'It looks

beautiful, but it is full of defects.' We are placed on earth to
work out our salvation; and earth's beauties are no end in themselves, but illusory, mutable ('defective'). The metaphor for
this in 'The Ghost Sonata' is domestic - if insane. The Student's
'paradise' was domestic; his fate is the domestic demented; instead
of 'they lived happily ever after,' we see the fairy princess at
the kitchen sink, in effect. It is not the real world, but the
domestic-surreal, this house with servants who un-clean, cooks who
un-feed; but the surreal can be taken as measure of the recoil of
the tender soul (Strindberg, the Student) from real life. As the
Student says in closing, only in the imagination is there anything
which fulfills its promise. The Student, rather like his creator,
is Adam who refuses to accept his ejection, symbolically as well
as psychologically the child who refuses to grow up. ('Where are
honor and faith? In fairy-tales and children's fancies.') 'I
asked you to become my wife in a home full of poetry and song and
music. Then the Cook came...' says the Student. 'What have we
to do with the kitchen?' he asks the girl, who replies, 'realistically,' 'We must eat.' The Student reflects Strindberg's neurotic
fastidiousness, well known, toward the 'lower functions'; and
eating, by the mechanism known to psychologists as 'displacement,'
can represent the sexual function, also profoundly disturbing to
Strindberg: 'It is always in the kitchen quarters that the seed-
leaves of the children are nipped, if it has not already happened
in the bedroom.' The Student wants to live in a garden with his
bride, but this garden is 'poison': 'You have poisoned me and I
have given the poison back to you,' says the Student. But perhaps
the 'sickness' is in fact the 'Student's': It is the recoil of a
pathological romanticism upon itself which sees the earth as 'this
madhouse, this prison, this charnel house.' Strindberg, like his
surrogate, the Student, desires the fairy-tale princess in a 'home
full of poetry and song and music' - a home with no 'kitchen
quarters,' only conservatory. That this whole fairy-tale gone
crazy is a projection of the Student's we may take as admitted in
his saying that he is a man born with one of those 'poisons that
open the eyes' - or does it 'destroy the sight'? - 'for I cannot
see what is ugly as beautiful, nor call evil good.'

As the girl enumerates all the tasks which weigh her down, the
Student cries out again and again for 'Music!' - music to drown
out the sounds of real life. But it is no more possible to do so
than it is for Strindberg to ring in 'soft, sweet, and melancholy'
music at the end of his play in order to effect a resolution. The
emotion we depart with is fear trembling on the brink of hysteria,
the image that of the grinning vampire cook. No vague promises of
a 'Liberator,' a waking to a 'sun that does not burn, in a home
without dust, by friends without stain, by a love without a flaw'
can salve over the fact, of which 'The Ghost Sonata' is the grip-
ping symbol, that 'a curse lies over the whole of creation, over
life itself.' Out of his own conflict between paradise and the
fallen world, fairy-tale and reality, Strindberg has made stunning
drama.

NOTE

1 J.T. Shipley, ed., 'Dictionary of World Literary Terms', 1955,
   p. 155.

8. 6 EGIL TÖRNQVIST

Ingmar Bergman Directs Strindberg's 'Ghost Sonata',
'Theatre Quarterly', 3 (11), 1973, pp. 6-7, 9-14

[...] Bergman gives some indication of what he will be aiming at in
his production. Act III, he points out, has always been a
stumbling-block on stage, not least in his own earlier productions.
Bergman: 'We must relate it organically to the preceding acts. The
whole play is a dream - fairly realistic at the beginning, but
growing more and more grotesque as the action develops. It is not
a dream of any one of the characters, although in my Malmö production the assumption was that the Student was the dreamer - but that
didn't make sense, because he is not always on the stage. No, it
is the dream of Strindberg himself. Notice how we move inwards
in the play, from the street to the round room and from there to
the hyacinth room. Strindberg takes us by the hand and we enter
deeper and deeper into the dream.
   'Everything in this production must be close to us, immediate,
naked, simple. Simple costumes, hardly any make-up. The characters are no monsters, but human beings. And if some of them - the
Cook for example - are evil, this does not mean that they need to
look evil. The point is that they are evil to the characters on
the stage, and we must sense their evil nature through the reactions of these characters. We must never underrate the audience's
sensitivity to the reactions of the characters.'

WEDNESDAY 1 NOVEMBER

The scene designer, Marik Vos, has built a model of the stage.
Bergman: 'One of the problems in Act I has always been that Hummel
and the Student have to turn away from the audience every time the
old man tells the Student about the people in the house. And so we
don't see much of their faces, of their reactions. In this production we shall place the house - the imaginary house, that is - in
the auditorium, so that Hummel and the Student constantly keep
facing the audience.' (In his recent production of 'The Wild
Duck,' Bergman resorted to the same device, placing the 'imaginary'
attic in the auditorium.)
   'The people in the house will appear at either side of the
proscenium arch. At the back of the stage will be two huge white
concave screens, with an opening in the middle - a pair of tongs,
an embrace, a womb. On these screens we shall project the scenery
and the properties: houses of the turn of the century type at
first, later the marble statue, the clock, and so on. These things
appear when they are needed, then fade out again. For the

Milkmaid's appearances - she was lured out onto the ice in
Hamburg - we shall project a snowfall. The stage itself will be
practically empty, slightly slanting. Even the advertisement
kiosk I have managed to get rid of. There must be nothing to
block the action and make it heavy-going.'
    Later Bergman tells me: 'We have few properties, very few
things, nothing that can distract from the faces. The important
thing is what happens to the bodies. They must make a choreo-
graphic pattern which must be completely disengaged from the room
and from the scenery.'

TUESDAY 7 NOVEMBER

[...] 'The Ghost Sonata' is written in a kind of telegram style.
The text is pregnant with meaning and much is written between the
lines. Some passages are quite obscure. For example:

    THE OLD MAN: Are you a sportsman?
    THE STUDENT: Yes, that was my bad luck...

Bergman repeats the Student's line, limping across the stage.
Everybody laughs. Bergman: 'This is my third production of this
play, but I've never understood those lines.'
    At one point the Woman in Black makes (silent) conversation with
the Superintendent's Wife. Strindberg does not tell us what the two
are talking about. To tell the actresses to improvize some small-
talk would be to ignore the dramatic possibilities of their meeting.
'After all,' Bergman explains, 'the Woman in Black is waiting in
vain for a man who has made her pregnant. She is desperate. And
the Superintendent's Wife, who is her mother, is trying to calm
her down.' [...]

WEDNESDAY 8 NOVEMBER

Act II. Four chairs are on stage, at the right a vertical piece
of wood representing the marble statue. Gertrud Fridh, who
yesterday did the part of the Young Lady, now plays the Mummy, while
a stand-in - a ballet dancer - does the (silent) part of the Young
Lady. By having the same actress do both parts, Bergman hopes to
bring out more clearly not only the similarity between mother and
daughter but also - and especially - the idea that the Mummy has
once been an attractive young lady (as the statue bears witness),
and that the Young Lady is doomed to turn into the living dead.
Bergman: 'The fact that the Young Lady is slowly turning into
another Mummy is a fundamental idea in my production. That is what
is so horrifying in the whole situation. My original idea was that
the actors doing the Mummy and Hummel should play the parts of the
Young Lady and the Student in the last act, but that proved technically impossible.'
    One of the pre-absurdist effects of the play is the parrot
language spoken by the Mummy. 'This language,' Bergman explains,
'is but an extreme form of the kind of endearing nonsense talk that

you can often find between married partners. The Mummy has been
brought up to please her husband, to pose before him.'

'Another Nora,' Gertrud exlaims. 'Exactly!'

For the famous ghost supper Bergman gives the following memo:
'When Hummel, in his long speech, reveals the secret signs of
everyone present, the audience must be able to feel how he grows
and grows, like a frog blowing himself up, while the others keep
shrinking. Then comes the counter-attack from the Mummy. She
gives Hummel three pricks. Now it is his turn to shrink. When
he has just received the third prick, he thinks: all right, I can
stand all this, just don't you start talking about the Milkmaid
I've murdered. At this point the Milkmaid appears. Produced by
Hummel's anguish.' [...]

THURSDAY 9 NOVEMBER

Act III. From the very beginning it has stood clear that Bergman
wants to build the action toward this final act, so that it
becomes a true climax, instead of the anti-climax it has usually
proved on stage. 'And this we must remember,' he tells the
actors at the beginning of the rehearsal, 'that the Student kills
the Young Lady. And that it is a frightening, horrifying scene of
unmasking and murder. It corresponds to the Mummy's unmasking of
Hummel in the second act, but here the scene is shorn of nearly
every remnant of reality. In the second act we still have the rope
with which Hummel is to hang himself. We still have the idea of
apoplexy. Here it is only the fact that the Student attacks the
Young Lady with frightening words, that he grabs hold of her, that
he tears her dress off. And it kills her.' Bergman is describing
his own version of the act: with Strindberg the Lady's dress
stays in place. [...]
In Act II the Mummy speaks the following lines, perhaps the
most central to the play: 'We are poor miserable creatures, we
know that. We have erred, we have transgressed, we, like all the
rest. We are not what we seem to be. At bottom we are better than
ourselves, since we abhor and detest our misdeeds.' It is a speech
breathing compassion for mankind; we recognize the key note of the
'Dream Play': 'Mankind is pitiable.' Since the final lines of the
play are in much the same spirit, it seems quite natural that they
too are spoken by the Mummy. Commenting on this, Bergman tells me:
'In the end, I have stressed the fact that the only thing that can
give man any kind of salvation - a secular one - is the grace and
compassion which come out of himself.'

TUESDAY 14 NOVEMBER

Act I. When Hummel takes the Student's hand, he is acting the part
of a vampire, sucking the Student's blood. Bergman: 'The movements
must be soft, slow here - as in a dream. A quiet atrocity.'

THURSDAY 16 NOVEMBER

Act III.   Bergman: 'There must be a tension between the Student
and the Young Lady from the very beginning. The first part of the
act must be at once soft and charged. No physical contact between
the two in the beginning, everything light, fragile.'
   The actress playing the part of the gigantic Cook (Hjördis
Peterson), one of the grotesque elements of the play, is instructed
'You must work your way out of the wall terribly slowly, first a
hand, then a shoulder, finally a bottom.' In this way Bergman
seeks to indicate the nightmarish character of the cook, her dream
reality.
   In the fifteen-minute pause [...] Bergman indicates his idea
for the colouring of the three acts: in the first, only black,
white and grey; darkish colours in the second - 'it must bleed' -
and a blue haze in the third.

FRIDAY 17 NOVEMBER

[...] Since yesterday he has been considering how to shape the
Student's monologue at the end. When Mathias Henrikson comes to
the line, 'Why are beautiful flowers so poisonous?' he demonstrates
to the actor how he might pull the Young Lady from her chair, drag
her to the forestage, and brutally take her face between his hands
while she, in anguish, sinks down on her knees. 'Well, we'll work
that out tomorrow.'
   Marik Vos shows her costume designs. Bergman is playing with the
idea of putting a Semitic mask on Hummel, the Mummy and the Young
Lady; in this way their blood relationship could be indicated. But
how will a post-Nazi audience interpret the fact that the most
mephistophelian character in the play looks like a Jew? Indeed,
Bergman's idea would not have been alien to Strindberg, who was a
bit of an anti-Semite - Hummel is, in fact, partly fashioned after
a well-known Jew in Stockholm. Much more important, however, is
the fact that by providing Hummel with a Semitic mask - in the
final production he merely wears a Jewish skull-cap - Bergman could
stress his resemblance to a punishing Jehovah as well as his position as an outcast in society, who (therefore) takes his revenge.
Bergman: 'I think it would have been more embarrassing if one did
not dare to turn Hummel into a Jew. He is a kind of Shylock -
conceived, as is Shakespeare's Jew, with a strange kind of compassion
and a deep aversion at the same time.'

TUESDAY 21 NOVEMBER

Act I. So far the Superintendent's Wife has been sprinkling real
spruce twigs in front of the house in the background as a token
that the Consul has just died. Now she has to rest content with
imaginary spruce twigs. The twigs are transferred from the stage
to our imagination.
   The beginning of the act is still problematic, still too expository. The conversation between Hummel and the Student, Bergman

points out, must not be merely informative.   'You must be more
active, Toivo.   Remember, you are a spider spinning that little
fly, the Student, into your web.'

THURSDAY 23 NOVEMBER

Johansson's part is examined.   Bergman: 'When Johansson talks to
the Student, he swells with self-importance.   He hates his master
(Hummel), but here he identifies himself with him, uses him as a
weapon against the Student.'   To make the actor (Axel Düberg) get
the right feel of this, Bergman has him momentarily say 'I' every
time there is a 'he' (referring to Hummel) in his speeches.

WEDNESDAY 29 NOVEMBER

Act I.   The Student's report about the collapse of a house is
shaped.   'This is an important passage.   Here we have a kind of
dream atmosphere.'   The actors who are on the stage during this
passage are instructed to freeze their positions.   Later the dream
atmosphere is indicated also by a softening of the light surrounding
the Student.   General memo from the director: 'Remember, we don't
play psychological theatre but something higher.   The rhythm of the
play is tremendously important.   There are no intermediate joints
here, as in Ibsen's plays, which are much easier to do.'   Later
Bergman points out to me that the characters in 'The Ghost Sonata'
abruptly oscillate between their social roles and their true human
nature, between mask and face, and that this must clearly be brought
out in production.

FRIDAY 1 DECEMBER

Bergman specifies the lighting for the third act: a blue haze
gradually changing into a shadowy, dead grey light.   It is obvious that the change of the light is meant to visualize the Lady's
gradual mummification.

TUESDAY 5 DECEMBER

How should the Student recite the Song of the Sun at the end of
the play?   Some of the lines read:

     The pure in heart
     Have none to fear.
     The harmless are happy.
     The guileless are good.

Traditionally, the actor playing the Student reads these lines in
much the same way in both acts: tenderly, idealistically.   Bergman
wants to reserve this manner for the second act.   At the end of the
play they must be read quite differently.   'You must try to read

against the rhythm of the poem, break up the verse,' he tells
Mathias Henrikson. Commenting on the lines, Bergman later points
out to me: 'What nonsense to a modern audience, which every day
witnesses how true criminals don't harbour any fear at all, and
how the innocent must suffer. If the Student the second time he
reads the poem feels that it turns to dust, then it seems to me
meaningful.' In the eventual production, Henrikson did not so
much break up the metre as read the lines in a highly sceptical
manner. When he had finished his recital, he repeated the word
'guileless' in a questioning tone - and then disappeared into the
darkness. By giving some of the Student's speeches to other
characters, and by having him recite the poem in this way, Bergman
clearly seeks to solve one of the major difficulties of the last
act as written by Strindberg: the Student's sudden turn-about
from nihilistic despair to a newly gained faith in a benevolent
God. [...]

THURSDAY 7 DECEMBER

Act III. At the end of the play, the Student, referring to the
Young Lady, asks: 'Where can one find virginity?' Is the Young
Lady pure or not? The text is vague on this point. Bergman
suggests the following interpretation: 'His question is, intel-
lectually, preposterous. But if you regard it as a shameful gesture, expressing the urge of a man to rape the girl he desires
but who refuses him, then it makes sense.' In accordance with
this, Bergman has the Student violently part the Lady's thighs and
put his hand against her pudenda as he asks this question.

WEDNESDAY 3 JANUARY

Costume rehearsal. All the characters appear in black or grey
costumes in the first act. In the second, their costumes have
glowing colours - light green for Hummel, dark green and black for
his former Fiancée, scarlet for the Colonel and his servant Bengts-
son (resembling the scarlet velvet of the chairs in the round room),
scarlet changing into yellowish white and grey for the Mummy, a
poisonous violet for the Baron. Bergman is not quite satisfied with
a few of the costumes. 'They are too dead. They must be more
saturated, have more mystery about them. Give the sense of
beetles: it is a world of insects, this!'

CHEKHOV: 'THE THREE SISTERS' AND 'THE CHERRY ORCHARD'

'THE THREE SISTERS' (*)

9. 1 CHEKHOV

Letters, 'The Oxford Chekhov', trans. and ed.
R. Hingley, Oxford University Press, vol. 3,
1964, pp. 305-6, 313-14

Am I writing a new play? It is nibbling at the bait, but I haven't
started writing, I don't feel like it and I must wait till the warm
weather anyway.
(Letter to V.I. Nemirovich-Danchenko, 10 March 1900.)

I'm writing a play, I've already written a lot, but I can't judge it
till I'm in Moscow. Perhaps what I'm producing isn't a play, but
boring Crimean rubbish. It's called 'Three Sisters' (as you already
know) and I've done a part for you in it, that of second master at a
high school, the husband of one of the sisters. You will wear a
schoolmaster's regulation frock-coat and have a medal on a ribbon
round your neck. If the play turns out no good for this season I'll
alter it next season.
(Letter to A.L. Vishnevsky, 5 Aug. 1900.)

Can you believe it - I've written a play. As it won't be put on
now, but only next season, I haven't made a fair copy of it. Let it
lie around for a bit. Writing 'Three Sisters' was terribly hard.
There are three heroines after all, and each one has to be cut
according to her own pattern. And all three are general's daughters! The action takes place in a provincial town such as Perm in
an army (artillery) milieu.
(Letter to Maxim Gorky, 16 Oct. 1900.)

I've absolutely got to be present at rehearsals, I've got to!
Four responsible female parts, four educated young women, I can't
leave them to Stanislavsky, with all my respect for his talent and
understanding. I must at least look in on rehearsals.
(Letter to O.L. Knipper, 15 Sept. 1900.)

Do describe at least one rehearsal of 'Three Sisters' for me.
Doesn't anything need adding or taking away? Are you yourself
acting well, darling? But do watch out. Don't look sad in any of
the acts. You can look angry, that's all right, but not sad.
People who have been unhappy for a long time, and grown used to it,
don't get beyond whistling and are often wrapped up in their
thoughts. So mind you look thoughtful fairly often on the stage
during the conversations. Do you understand?
(Letter to O.L. Knipper, 2 Jan. 1901. Olga Knipper took the part
of Masha in 'Three Sisters'.)

You write that Natasha, making her rounds of the house at night in
Act Three, puts out the lights and looks for burglars under the
furniture. But it seems better to me for her to cross the stage
in a straight line without looking at anybody or anything, like
Lady Macbeth, with a candle. It's quicker and more frightening
that way.
(Letter to K.S. Stanislavsky, 2 Jan. 1901.)

Here are the answers to your questions:
   1. Irina doesn't know that Tuzenbakh is going off to fight a
duel, but she guesses that some awkward incident occurred on the
previous day, an incident which may have important consequences,
and bad ones at that. But when a woman guesses something she
always says, 'I knew it, I knew it.'
   2. Chebutykin sings only the words, 'Be so good as to accept
one of these dates.' These words come from an operetta which was
once performed at the Hermitage Theatre. I don't remember what
it was called .... Chebutykin mustn't sing anything else, otherwise his exit will take too long. [...]
(Letter to I.A. Tikhomirov, 14 Jan. 1901.)

Of course you can come in wearing a service-dress jacket in Act
Three, that's quite all right. But why do you come into the
drawing-room wearing a fur coat in Act Two? Why? Perhaps it does
come off all right actually. Have it your own way.
(Letter to A.L. Vishnevsky, 17 Jan. 1901. Vishnevsky took the part
of Vershinin in 'Three Sisters'.)

Of course Act Three must be conducted quietly on the stage to
convey the feeling that people are tired and want to go to bed.
What's all the noise about? The points at which the bells are to
be rung off stage are shown.

(Letter to O.L. Knipper, 17 Jan. 1901. She had written to Chekhov
on 11 Jan. 1901, saying that Stanislavsky, in a rehearsal of Act
Three, had 'created a terrible hullabaloo on the stage with everyone running in all directions and getting excited'.)

Well, how's 'Three Sisters' getting on? Judging by your letters
you're all talking outrageous rubbish. 'Noise in Act Three' -
but why noise? The noise is only in the distance - off stage, a
vague, muffled noise - while everyone here on stage is tired and
almost asleep. If you spoil Act Three you'll ruin the play and I
shall be hissed off the stage in my old age ... Vershinin pro-
nounces his 'Ti tum ti tum ti' as a question, and you appear to
answer it. And you think this is such an interesting trick that you
bring out your 'tum tum tum' as if it amuses you ... You bring out
your 'tum tum tum' and give a laugh, but not a loud one, just a
little one. And while you're about it you don't want to look as
you do in 'Uncle Vanya' [Olga Knipper took the part of Sonya in
'Uncle Vanya']. You should look younger and more lively.
Remember, you're fond of laughing and easily get angry. Anyway, I
put my trust in you, darling, you're a good actress.
     I said at the time that it would be awkward to carry Tuzenbakh's
body past on your stage, but Stanislavsky insisted he couldn't do
without the body. I wrote to him that the body wasn't to be
carried past. I don't know whether he got my letter.
(Letter to O.L. Knipper, 20 Jan. 1901.)

Darling, Masha's repentance in Act Three isn't repentance at all,
it's no more than a frank talk. Act it with feeling, but not des-
perately. Don't shout, put in some smiles, even if only a few,
and in general act it so that people feel the tiredness of the
night. And make them feel you're cleverer than your sisters - or
at least that you think yourself cleverer. About your 'tum tum
tum', do as you like. You're a clever girl.
(Letter to O.L. Knipper, 21 Jan. 1901.)

I've heard from you that you're leading Irina round by the arm in
Act Three. Why is that? Is that consistent with your mood? You
mustn't leave the sofa. Don't you think Irina can get about on
her own?
(Letter to O.L. Knipper, 24 Jan, 1901.)

NOTE

* 'The Three Sisters' was first performed at the Moscow Art Theatre
  on 31 January 1901.

9. 2   M.N. STROYEVA

'The Three Sisters' at the M[oscow] A[rt] T[heatre],
trans. E.R. Hapgood, 'Tulane Drama Review', 9 (1),
1964-5, pp. 42-3, 48-51, 53-4

'The Three Sisters' was the first play Chekhov wrote especially
for the Art Theatre; actually, on order from it. After a preliminary discussion, Nemirovich-Danchenko [co-founder and co-
director of the MAT] went abroad, so that the rehearsals were conducted by Stanislavski alone. His production plan (now in the MAT
archives) clearly includes rehearsal changes, since Stanislavski
finished it on January 8, 1901, and the first full run-through
took place at the end of December, 1900.
    What strikes one on examining it is Stanislavski's handling of
the play as an integral unit, as a completely developed harmonious symphonic work. [...] In 'The Three Sisters' all elements
were logically integrated, woven into the very texture of the
production, and closely bound up with the director's central concern - to reveal the ruling idea of the play, which could be
defined as man's inner struggle against the power of triviality.
This conflict between character and environment had been tried
on earlier occasions by Stanislavski, but it had never emerged so
sharply. [...] In 'The Three Sisters' this living background
becomes fully consonant with the author's thought; active,
aggressive, a much more dangerous force. It seems to corrode
people's lives, it gradually traps them in its toils, it invades
the most intimate sides of their lives, it clings to them whenever they move. With cold indifference and scorn, it dulls their
inner desires and dreams. But a Chekhov character, a person of
lively, sensitive, delicate feelings, richly gifted, will not
remain static. In this play inner activity no longer requires an
external solution, however strongly it exists and seeks its
objective. The objective in this play is to find the true path to
happiness through a free, rewarding life of work.
    The clash between two hostile forces provides the dramatic core
for the entire production-play. This clash begins in the second
act. The first act, as in all Chekhov plays, is bright: a happy
prelude to 'a party, springtime, gaiety, birds singing, sunshine...
The branches with their buds just turning green look in at the
window, only just opened now after the winter. Irina is preparing
food for the birds, you can hear them chirping outside, beyond the
bay window ... In a mood of springtime, Andrei offstage is playing
some melodious sonata on his violin.' Thus the first act in
Stanislavski's production plan begins. There are lots of flowers
on the stage, you hear music, loud laughter, happy exclamations.
Any wistfulness is quickly interrupted; a smile chases all tears
away. Stanislavski put in whole scenes of laughter, amusing
banter, unexpected outbursts of gaiety, in order to underscore
the atmosphere of a buoyant love of life. Dreams of going to
Moscow easily still any nostalgic memories of the past. The
struggle between the two motifs and the quick victory of a springtime hope for the future provide the basis for the opening scenes.

But, as in 'The Seagull' and 'Uncle Vanya,' the trivialities
of life take over in the second act and engulf the leading characters. Later, in the third act, these two elements clash and
result in an explosion which completely annihilates every hope of
a real existence corresponding to their dreams. All that remains
to them is a most unselfish faith in a better future for humanity.
[...]
    In the third act the clash of hostile forces is heightened.
The whole atmosphere becomes highly charged. Stanislavski states
it expressly:

Wherever possible in this act the tempo should be nervous.
Pauses must not be overdone. The crosses, all movement, should
be nervous and quick. Now it is no longer a question of a
gnawing mouse, the squeaking sounds of a music box, or the
distant sounds of drunken revellers which create the 'mood.'
All during the act one hears with increasing frequency the
insistent sound of a fire alarm ... the engines roar by the
house carrying the firemen, there is a red glow from the windows
which falls in streaks across the floor.

In this moment of confusion and disturbance the forces of
triviality take the offensive. An embattled Natasha defends her
rights as the all-powerful lady of the house. In the second act
she was still able to handle Andrei or Irina 'with tenderness,'
indeed 'almost with affection.' Now in the scene with Anfisa she
speaks 'quietly but with great emphasis and boldness and dismisses
her with a single gesture.' Later, with Olga, she begins to speak
again, 'quietly but firmly, and when Olga makes the slightest move
she becomes increasingly irritated. She finally winds up with a
squeaky hysterical shriek. She squeaks with tears in her voice.'
Then, having established herself in this manner as the head of the
household, Natasha stalks across the whole room with a candle, not
looking at anyone, and angrily slams the door. It should be
pointed out that this was very close to the author's intent.
Chekhov wrote to Stanislavski, 'It is better if Natasha crosses
the stage in a straight line, without looking at anybody or anything, with a candle in her hand, à la Lady Macbeth - this would be
shorter and more awe-inspiring.' Originally, as Stanislavski had
written Chekhov, the plan was to have 'Natasha go through the house
at night, putting out lights and looking for burglars under the
furniture.'
    In these circumstances, the feeling of frustration in the lives
of Chekhov's leading women works up to the point of unbearable suffering. Irina groans with yearning, shakes her head, throws herself restlessly around, rolls on the bed, sobs, 'I can't, I can't
bear any more!... I can't, I can't.' She hasn't the strength to
tear herself away and, as if she were appealing to others to do
this for her, to help her, 'she almost screams "throw me out, throw
me out, I can't bear any more!" After this she goes off into real
hysterics (behind a screen) in rising crescendo...' But 'not out
of control, for Heaven's sake,' Stanislavski added.
    The third act consists of the sisters making an intensified
effort to find a way out through action. Masha, the strongest and

most daring, would seem to have found her solution and is
determined to break with the cheerless triviality of her life.
This is how Stanislavski staged her confession to her two sisters.

> Masha stands up quickly, she is excited, she has made her
> decision, she is nervously wrought up, she nervously stretches
> out her arms, she gets down on her knees, as does Olga, by the
> head of Irina's bed; she puts one arm around Irina, the other
> around Olga. She speaks in a low voice ('I love this man...
> I love Vershinin') as she draws their two heads closer to her
> own. The heads of the three sisters are close to one another...
> Masha looks up at the ceiling dreamily and with a glow on her
> face, recalls her whole romance...

After Olga's words, 'Do stop. I'm not listening to you anyhow,' Masha 'gets up with disappointment, brushes off her knees,
then goes over lightly to Olga; her tone is desperate, she has
decided to throw discretion to the winds ....'
Stanislavski points out that Olga, at heart, understands and
sympathizes with Masha (which is something Chekhov does not bring
out in this scene). 'Olga caresses her, the sinner, as she does
innocent Irina. Olga kisses Masha tenderly, pats her.' Stanislavski finds it important to show that their common aspirations
unite the sisters. In this regard we have his interesting note:
'Masha goes out of her way to comfort Irina although this is not
part of her character.'
The shared hopes of the three sisters, all struggling to find
a way out of their impasse, are especially clear in the scene
where Masha is going out: 'As Masha leaves she is nervous and
upset; she hugs Olga, and speaks as she moves towards the door.
At the door, Olga, in a tender, motherly way, kisses her. She
really understands Masha, and realizes deep down that she would do
the same thing in her place. Now she no longer criticizes her but
pities her. Therefore she kisses her tenderly as a mother would.'
Then, to underline the importance of this moment as a turning
point in Masha's destiny, the fire engines are heard again in the
street. 'They rumble past the house, there is a big racket, bells
ring, the empty water barrels they carry resound, two voices yell
at one another against the background of all this noise.'
The fourth act brings the death blow to all their hopes; they
must surrender all dreams of possible happiness. 'There is no
happiness for us; it cannot, it will not be ... We must work, and
happiness - that will be for our far-off descendants.' That is
the leitmotif of the last act. To make a contrast with the first
act, which was laid in spring, Stanislavski gives these directions:
'The mood is autumnal. It is cool; they all wear coats - light
overcoats. All during the act yellow leaves drift down to fall
here and there. As the curtain rises there is the sound of bells
ringing at a nearby church (after mass has been said for the
departing troops).'
There is a lot of movement to and fro by people of all sorts,
a yardman, an orderly, a cook, a maid, etc., seeing the military
off. Baggage is being hauled away, the garden gate is slammed and
slammed. Each one of the leading characters is immersed in his own

sorrow, his grief at the parting. Tusenbach 'keeps looking about anxiously; he frequently glances at his watch, he keeps clearing his throat nervously. Irina notices the state he is in and anxiously watches him.' He knows that the duel is unavoidable, and he foresees the tragic outcome for himself. Yet in saying goodbye to Irina he tries to suppress his own grief and makes every effort to appear light-hearted. This is how Stanislavski builds up the scene of the farewells:

The music comes closer ... Tusenbach caresses Irina, smooths her hair, wraps her shawl more snugly around her, kisses every finger on her hand. Irina concentrates completely on Tusen-bach. She never takes her eyes off him .... He pats her on the head. She clings closely to him ... Tusenbach says: 'I feel so happy.' He is much more spirited, livelier ... Then, 'Now I must go; it's time.' He quickly kisses her hand, goes to the garden gate, and takes hold of the latch to open it. Irina rushes after him with an anxious look, grabs his arm and holds him back. Tusenbach forces himself to smile. Irina embraces him and lays her head on his shoulder. Tusenbach looks wistfully in the direction of the garden.

Masha is in the same state of unhappy premonition. 'Some cranes fly by. Masha hurriedly stands up. She is distraught, she bursts into tears... The music recedes into the distance. Masha wipes her forehead, gives a deep sigh, shakes her head... She looks at her watch, she is very nervous, and sunk in thought.'
Meanwhile, as the atmosphere of restlessness and sadness outside the house gets heavier and heavier, inside a life quite alien to that of the suffering people in the garden goes on in its own spe-cial way. Natasha and Protopopov, now inseparable, hold sway. Echoes of this life are carried out from time to time into the garden, in noisy, indifferent dissonances. In order entirely to shut out what is going on in the garden, Natasha 'yanks' a curtain over the balcony and inside one hears loud laughter, 'especially the deep bass laughter of Protopopov.'
Out on the stage there is the gentle lyricism of sadness, punc-tured now and again by the heartless gaiety coming from within the house, 'voices, the tinkling of a musical top, the sound of a large ball being bounced on the floor, the noise of a wooden ball rolling across the floor. Now and then a burst of loud laughter (noticeably the bass voice of Protopopov).' Stanislavski, wishing to show that this atmosphere intruded into the garden, notes: 'At one point a ball bounces out through the balcony; the nurse comes out to pick it up in the garden and carry it back indoors.'
But when the grief, the human suffering, reaches its climax, Stanislavski removes all traces of triviality from the stage:

Up to the point of the farewell scene (between Masha and Vershinin) the sounds of playing with toys and balls have not interfered with the action on the stage; but now they die away to nothing...
Masha, distraught, comes rapidly along the garden path.
Vershinin says: 'I have come to say good-bye.' Masha replies

'Good-bye!' and throws herself into Vershinin's arms and sobs.
He can scarcely hold back his tears. Olga wants to take hold
of Masha but Irina advises her not to interfere, to let her
cry herself out.

The surmounting of the sorrow at the end of this play is the
most important task of all for a director. He sees the 'affirma-
tive thought of the author' as Chekhov's characters, even in
times of deepest personal grief, find the strength to raise themselves to the level of dreams about the future happiness of humanity. Stanislavski directed that Olga's final words be spoken 'as
buoyantly as possible.'
Stanislavski's production plan for 'The Three Sisters' shows
how profoundly he entered into the lives of the Chekhov characters.
Here one senses his fusion with the playwright; his composition is
based concretely on Chekhov's creative intentions.
He saw in Chekhov's plays a confrontation of two mutually hostile forces set among the so-called 'intelligentsia' of those
times. The social implication of this confrontation is that
although the forces of bourgeois triviality triumph, the moral
victory goes to the anti-bourgeois characters; in this case the
three sisters who inwardly free themselves from the power of the
narrow confines of their existence. At the same time, in his production plan, Stanislavski clearly emphasized an affirmation of
life in the beginning of the play - the dreams of Chekhov's
leading characters and their resistance to the horrors of reality.
This is what lent dramatic dynamism to the production. The
aspirations of the sisters, Vershinin, and Tusenbach to free themselves from the tyranny of ordinary life, their efforts to extricate themselves from the rule of such as Protopopov and Natasha,
provide the pivotal point of the whole play as Stanislavski saw
it.
It is safe to say that in working on his plan he used practical
and concrete means to realize his concept of a 'through-line of
action.' It enabled him to carry out a 'flow of life' as Chekhov
did: not just a concatenation of accidental daily episodes and
details piled on each other, but an illumination of life itself as
it develops and moves, in which apparently unrelated words and
accidentally noticed objects all serve to forward the author's
thoughts. [...]
But even while revealing the playwright's intentions, Stanislavski did not hesitate at times to ignore some of Chekhov's own
stage directions. He was so absorbed in keeping the central idea
in high relief that he was ready to suppress other ideas which he
felt were purely subsidiary. In order to underline the breaking
down, the growing shallowness of the sisters' lives he deliberately
'demoted' them in 'rank.' Nothing in their home suggests that they
are the daughters of a general. On the contrary, the house is
'most ordinary, with cheap furnishings.' (Simov recalls that
Stanislavski asked him to design the house as if they were the
daughters of a captain.)
Stanislavski made every effort to envelop the main characters in
a stuffy, oppressive atmosphere, planning it down to the last
little detail so that one would sense at once that to continue such

an existence would be unthinkable - thus he made their conflict
with reality inevitable. Yet this conflict could only become the
active pivot-point of the play if the people involved reacted with
sufficient force against it.

According to Stanislavski, the right solution occurred because
of something 'unexpected' that happened at one of the rehearsals,
and it was only then that 'the Chekhov characters came to life.
... It turned out that they were not dragging around their burden
of sorrow but were really looking for gaiety, laughter, animation;
they want to live and not just vegetate. I sensed the truth in
this attitude, it encouraged me, and I intuitively realized then
how I must proceed.'

It is typical that the production only got into full swing when
its super-objective was pinpointed and set forth by the director
in the phrase quoted above: 'they want to live and not just vegetate.' Only an active, vital super-objective like this could have
helped the actors 'live' on the stage and not just 'act,' for true
living in the theatre depends on finding true action. [...]

9. 3   ROBERT BRUSTEIN

Anton Chekhov, 'The Theatre of Revolt', Methuen,
1965, pp. 162-7

[...] Masha - dressed in black to illustrate her depression - is
perpetually bored; Irina is perpetually tired; and Olga suffers
from perpetual headaches. As for Andrey, their gifted brother, he
trails his life along with no apparent aim, followed by the senile
Ferrapont, as by an ignominious Nemesis. In this lifeless atmosphere, they are drying up, their culture falling from them like
shreds of dead skin - each, in turn, will ask, 'Where has it all
gone?' For whatever might have made them seem unusual in Moscow
is here merely a superfluous layer - useless, unnecessary, and
gradually being forgotten. Andrey, carefully trained for a distinguished university career, holds a position in which his education is meaningless. Masha,once an accomplished pianist, now 'has
forgotten' how to play - just as Tchebutykin has 'forgotten' his
medical training - just as the entire family is forgetting the
accomplishments of their hopeful youth. Thus, the Prozorovs
alternate between hysteria and despair, their hopes disintegrating
in an environment where everything is reduced to zero:

IRINA (sobbing): Where? Where has it all gone? Where is it?
Oh, my God, my God! I have forgotten everything, everything ...
everything is in a tangle in my mind... I don't remember the
Italian for window or ceiling .... I am forgetting everything;
every day I forget something more and life is slipping away and
will never come back, we shall never, never go to Moscow ...
I see that we shan't go ...

Life is slipping by, and time, like a cormorant, is devouring hopes,
illusions, expectations, consuming their minds, souls, and bodies

in its tedious-rapid progress towards death. (1)

While their culture is being forgotten, however, the Prozorovs
do try to preserve a pocket of civilization in this dreary waste-
land; and their house is open to limited forms of intellectual
discussion and artistic activity. Generally, the discussions at
the Prozorovs' reflect the banality of the surrounding area [...]
but occasionally, genuine ideas seem to come out of these soirées.
Attending the discussions are the Prozorovs' cultural allies, the
military officers stationed in town. Chekhov, according to Stanislavsky, looked on the military as 'the bearers of a cultural
mission, since, coming into the farthest corners of the provinces, they brought with them new demands on life, knowledge, art,
happiness, and joy.' Masha suggests Chekhov's attitudes when she
observes the difference between the crude townspeople and the more
refined soldiers: 'among civilians generally there are so many
rude, ill-mannered, badly-brought up people,' but 'in our town the
most decent, honourable, and well-bred people are all in the army.
Her attraction to Colonel Vershinin is partially explained by his
superior refinement, for he is associated in her mind with the old
Muscovite charm and glamor. In part, he probably reminds her of
her father (also identified with culture), for he lived on the
same street, was an officer in her father's brigade, and has now
taken command of her father's old battery. Attracted to educated
men (she married Kuligin because she mistakenly thought him 'the
cleverest of men'), Masha unquestionably finds a suitable intellectual companion in Vershinin; even their courtship reveals their
cultural affinities - he hums a tune to which she hums a reply.
Magarshack calls this 'the most original love declaration in the
whole history of the stage' - actually, Congreve's Mirabel and
Millamant employ much the same device, when he completes a Waller
verse which she begins - but in both cases, the couples signify
their instinctual rapport, and their superior sophistication to
other suitors.

While Masha tries to find expression through an extramarital
affair which is doomed to failure, Irina tries to discover a substitute commitment in her work. In this, her spiritual partner,
though she doesn't love him, is Tusenbach, because he too seeks
salvation in work, finally, in a Tolstoyan gesture, resigning his
commission for a job in a brickyard. Irina's faith in the dignity
of labor, however, is gradually destroyed by depressing jobs in a
telegraph office and on the town council - in this district, work
can have no essential meaning or purpose. In the last act, Irina
looks forward to 'a new life' as a schoolteacher; but we have
Olga's enervating academic career as evidence that this 'new life'
will be just as unfulfilling as the old. And when Tusenbach is
killed in a duel with Solyony (*his* despoiler), even the minor con-
solations of a loveless marriage are denied her.

Everything, in fact, fails the family in 'The Three Sisters.'
And as their culture fades and their lives grow grayer, the forces
of darkness and illiteracy move in like carrion crows, ready to
pick the last bones. There is some doubt, however, whether this
condition is permanent. And the question the play finally asks is
whether the defeat of the Prozorovs has any ultimate meaning; will
their suffering eventually influence their surroundings in any

positive way? The question is never resolved in the play, but it is endlessly debated by Vershinin and Tusenbach, whose opinions contrast as sharply as their characters. Vershinin - an extremely unhappy soul - holds to optimistic theories, while Tusenbach - inexplicably merry - is more profoundly pessimistic. This conflict, though usually couched in general terms, is secretly connected with the fate of the Prozorovs. When Masha, for example, declares, 'We know a great deal that is unnecessary,' Vershinin takes the opportunity to expound his views:

> What next?... I don't think there can be a town so dull and dismal that intelligent and educated people are unnecessary in it. Let us suppose that of the hundred thousand people living in the town, which is, of course, uncultured and behind the times, there are only three of your sort. It goes without saying that you cannot conquer the mass of darkness round you; little by little as you go on living, you will be lost in the crowd. Life will get the better of you, but still you will not disappear without a trace. After you there may appear perhaps six like you, then twelve and so on until such as you form a majority. In two or three hundred years life on earth will be unimaginably beautiful, marvelous.

Vershinin, in short - anticipating the eventual transformation of the surrounding area by people like the Prozorovs - believes in the progressive march of civilization towards perfection. And this perfection will be based on the future interrelationship of the benighted mass and the cultured elite ('You know, if work were united with culture, and culture with work') - a synthesis of beauty and utility.

Tusenbach, on the other hand, is more skeptical. Seeing no special providence in the fall of a sparrow or the flight of migratory cranes, he doubts the ability of anyone to influence anything:

> Not only in two or three hundred years but in a million years life will be just the same; it does not change, it remains stationary, following its own laws which we have nothing to do with or which, anyway, we shall never find out.

Vershinin's view awakens hope that there is some ultimate meaning to life; Tusenbach's leads to stoicism and tragic resignation. It is the recurrent conflict between the progressive and the static interpretation of history, and its outcome is as insoluble as life itself.

In the last act, in fact, both views are recapitulated without being reconciled. The military is leaving the town - a sad departure, because it signifies not only the end of Masha's affair with Vershinin, but also the disintegration of the last cultural rampart. Tusenbach anticipates that 'dreadful boredom' will descend upon the town, and Andrey notes (reminding us of Natasha's symbolic role), 'It's as though someone put an extinguisher over it.' The end of the Prozorov way of life has almost come. Masha has turned obsessive and hysterical; Olga is installed in a position she loathes; Andrey, likened to an expensive bell that has fallen and smashed, has become hag-ridden and mediocre. Only Irina preserves some hope, but even these hopes are soon to be dashed. The entire family is finally facing the truth: 'Nothing turns out as we would have it' - the dream of Moscow will never be realized, the mass of darkness has overwhelmed them. In the requiem which concludes the play, the three sisters meditate on the future, just as, in the beginning of the play, they reflected on the past, while Andrey pushes the pram, Kuligin bustles, and Tchebutykin hums softly to himself.

Their affirmations, showing the strong influence of Vershinin's view of life, are inexplicably hopeful and expectant. Masha expresses her determination to endure; Irina has faith that a 'time will come when everyone will know what all this is for'; and Olga affirms that 'our sufferings will pass into joy for those who live after us, happiness and peace will be established on earth, and they will remember kindly and bless those who have lived before.' The gay band music played by the military evokes in the three sisters the will to live. But the music slowly fades away. Will hope fade away as well? Olga's anxious questioning of life ('If we only knew - if we only knew!') is - as if to suggest this - antiphonally answered by Tchebutykin's muttered denials ('It doesn't matter, it doesn't matter!'), the skepticism of Tusenbach reduced to its most nihilistic form. And on this double note - the dialectic of hope and despair in a situation of defeat - Chekhov's darkest play draws to its close.

NOTE

1 Chekhov heightens this effect by using a technique which Samuel
   Beckett will later imitate: he makes time pass while giving
   the impression that time is standing still. The action of the
   play covers three and a half years; yet, each act seems to
   follow the other as if no time had elapsed at all. There is
   another interesting parallel between Chekhov and Beckett, for
   Chekhov once planned a play with similarities to 'Waiting for
   Godot.' As Simmons describes this unwritten drama, 'During the
   first three acts the characters discuss the life of the hero
   and await his coming with great expectation. But in the last
   act they receive a telegram announcing the hero's death.'

'THE CHERRY ORCHARD' (*)

9. 4 CHEKHOV

   Letters, 'The Oxford Chekhov', trans. and ed.
   R. Hingley, Oxford University Press, vol. 3,
   1964, pp. 317-21, 325-31

The next play I write will definitely be funny, very funny - at

least in intention.
(Letter to O.L. Knipper, 7 March 1901.)

There are moments when an overwhelming desire comes over me to
write a four-act farce or comedy for the Art Theatre. And I shall
write one if nothing prevents me, only I shan't deliver it to the
theatre before the end of 1903.
(Letter to O.L. Knipper, 22 April 1901.)

The central part in this play is that of an old woman [Mrs.
Ranevsky], to the author's great regret!
(Letter to V.F. Komissarzhevskaya, 27 Jan. 1903.)

I'm counting on getting down to the play after 20 February and I
shall finish it by 20 March. It's already completed in my head.
It's called 'The Cherry Orchard', it has four acts and in Act One
cherry trees can be seen in bloom through the windows, the whole
orchard a mass of white. And ladies in white dresses.
(Letter to K.S. Stanislavsky, 5 Feb. 1903.)

Your part is a complete fool of a girl. Do you want to play a
silly girl [Varya]? A kind-hearted simpleton.
(Letter to O.L. Knipper, 22 Feb. 1903.)

If the play doesn't work out the way I've planned it, you must
punch my head. There's a comic part [Lopakhin] for Stanislavsky,
and one for you too.
(Letter to O.L. Knipper, 5 and 6 March 1903.)

There will be a 'Cherry Orchard' and I shall try to have as few
characters as possible, that makes it more intimate.
(Letter to O.L. Knipper, 21 March 1903.)

Will you [the Moscow Art Theatre] have an actress for the part of
the elderly lady in 'The Cherry Orchard'? If not there won't
even be any play, I won't even write it.
(Letter to O.L. Knipper, 11 April 1903.)

Now, as regards my ... play 'The Cherry Orchard', everything's
fine so far. I'm getting on with the work bit by bit. Even if I
am a bit late with it, it won't matter all that much. I've reduced
the décor side of the play to the minimum, no special sets will be
needed and no special displays of ingenuity required.
    In Act Two of my play I've substituted an old chapel and a well
for the river. It's more peaceful that way. Only in Act Two you
must give me some proper green fields and a road and a sense of

distance unusual on the stage.
(Letter to V.I. Nemirovich-Danchenko, 22 Aug. 1903.)

It hasn't turned out as a drama, but as a comedy, in places even
a farce, and I'm afraid I may get into hot water with Vladimir
Ivanovich [Nemirovich-Danchenko].   Konstantin Sergeyevich [Stanis-
lavsky] has a big part.   There aren't many parts altogether.
(Letter to M.P. Alekseyeva [Lilina], 15 Sept. 1903.)

I can look at my manuscript without being angry now, I'm writing
already, and when I've finished I'll send you a telegram at once.
The last act will be gay.   Actually the whole play is gay and
frivolous.
(Letter to O.L. Knipper, 21 Sept. 1903.)

Act Four of my play will be thin in content compared with the other
acts, but effective.   The end of your part seems not bad to me.
In general don't be down-hearted. Everything's fine.
   My regards to Vishnevsky, and tell him to stock up with gentle-
ness and elegance for a part [Gayev] in my play.
(Letter to O.L. Knipper, 23 Sept. 1903.)

Oh, if only you could take the part of the governess in my play!
It's the best part.   I don't like the others.
(Letter to O.L. Knipper, 29 Sept. 1903.)

My play is moving, and I'm finishing copying Act Three today and
starting Act Four.   Act Three is the least boring, but the second
act is as boring and as monotonous as a cobweb.
   Who, oh who, will play my governess?
(Letter to O.L. Knipper, 8 Oct. 1903.)

The play's finished now, finally finished, and tomorrow evening,
or at the latest on the morning of the 14th, will be sent to Moscow.
At the same time I'll send you one or two comments.   If any alterations are needed I think they'll be very small ones.   The worst
thing about the play is that I didn't write it at a sitting, but
spent a long, long time over it, so it's bound to seem a bit spun
out.   Anyway, we'll see what happens.
(Letter to O.L. Knipper, 12 Oct. 1903.)

You will play Lyuba Ranevsky since there's nobody else to.   She's
not dressed luxuriously, but with great taste.   She's intelligent,
very kind and absent-minded.   She's nice to everybody and always
has a smile on her face.
   Anya absolutely must be played by a young actress ....
   Gayev is for Vishnevsky.   Ask Vishnevsky to listen to people

playing billiards and write down as many billiard terms as possible. I don't play billiards, or rather I did play at one time
and have forgotten all about it now, and everything about it in
the play is haphazard. I'll settle the thing with Vishnevsky
later on and make the necessary insertions....
    It's an old manor house. At one time people lived there in
great style and this must be conveyed by the set. There is an
atmosphere of riches and comfort.
    Varya's a bit crude and a bit stupid, but very kind-hearted.
(Letter to O.L. Knipper, 14 Oct. 1903.)

The thing that frightened me most was the sluggishness of Act Two
and a certain unfinished quality about the student Trofimov.
You see, Trofimov is in exile off and on and gets chucked out of
the university every so often, and how is one to depict that kind
of thing?
(Letter to O.L. Knipper, 19 Oct. 1903.)

I'd very much like to look in on rehearsals. I'm afraid Anya
might be a bit weepy (for some reason you find her similar to
Irina) and I'm afraid of her being played by an actress who isn't
young. Anya doesn't cry once in my text, she nowhere talks in a
weepy tone of voice. She does have tears in her eyes in Act Two,
but the mood is gay and lively. What's this in your telegram
about the play being full of people crying? Where are they?
Varya's the only one, but that's because Varya's a cry-baby by
nature, and her tears shouldn't depress the audience. You'll
often find the stage-direction 'through tears' in my text, but
that only shows the mood of the characters and not their tears.
There isn't a cemetery in Act Two.
(Letter to V.I. Nemirovich-Danchenko, 23 Oct. 1903.)

No, I never wanted to make Mrs. Ranevsky a person who has calmed
down. Nothing less than death can calm a woman like that. But
perhaps I don't understand what you mean. It's not hard to play
Ranevsky. It's only necessary to strike the right note from the
very beginning. It's necessary to invent a smile and a way of
smiling, and it's necessary to know how to dress. Anyway, you'll
manage all that with a little good will and good health.
(Letter to O.L. Knipper, 25 Oct. 1903.)

Stanislavsky will make a most excellent and original Gayev, but in
that case who's to play Lopakhin? After all, the part of Lopakhin
is the central one. If it doesn't come off the whole play will be
a flop. Lopakhin mustn't be played by anyone rowdy, and he
doesn't inevitably have to be a [typical] merchant. He's a
gentle person.
(Letter to O.L. Knipper, 30 Oct. 1903.)

When I wrote the part of Lopakhin I thought of it as your part.   If
you don't like the look of it for some reason, then take Gayev.
True, Lopakhin is a merchant, but he's a decent person in the full
sense of the words and his bearing must be that of a completely
dignified and intelligent man.   There must be nothing petty about
him, no tricks, and my idea was that you'd make a brilliant
success of this part, which is the central one in the play.   If
you take Gayev, give Lopakhin to Vishnevsky.   He won't make an
artistic Lopakhin, but at least he won't be a petty one.   Luzhsky
would be only a cold foreigner in this part.   Leonidov would make
a typical profiteering peasant of him.   When choosing an actor for
this part it must not be forgotten that Lopakhin was loved by
Varya, a serious and religious girl.   She wouldn't love some
wretched money-grubbing peasant.
(Letter to K.S. Stanislavsky, 30 Oct. 1903.)

I don't know why Mariya Petrovna [Lilina] is so keen on playing
Anya.   After all it's a short part and not a very interesting one.
My idea is that Varya suits her much better.   Nemirovich writes
that she's afraid of the resemblance between Varya and Sonya in
'Uncle Vanya'. But what resemblance is there?   Varya's a nun, a
silly girl.
(Letter to O.L. Knipper, 1 Nov. 1903.)

Anya can be played by anyone you like, a completely unknown
actress even, as long as she's young and looks like a little girl
and talks in a young, ringing voice.   This isn't one of the important parts.
    Varya is a more serious part - that is, if Mariya Petrovna
[Lilina] should take it.   Without M.P. this part will turn out
flat and crude, and it will be necessary to revise it and tone it
down.   Mariya Petrovna is unable to repeat herself, firstly
because she's a talented person, and secondly because Varya does
not resemble Sonya and Natasha.   She's a figure in a black dress,
a nun, a silly girl, a cry-baby, etc. etc.
    Gayev and Lopakhin - let Konstantin Sergeyevich [Stanislavsky]
choose between these parts and try them out.   If he should pick
Lopakhin and succeed in this role the play would succeed.   You see,
if Lopakhin's colourless and is played by a colourless actor both
the part and the play will fail....
    Charlotte is an important part. ... This is the part for Miss
Knipper. (1) ...
    The stationmaster who declaims The Sinful Woman in Act Three
should be an actor with a bass voice.
    Charlotte talks good - not broken - Russian.   Only she occasio-
nally mixes up hard and soft consonants at the end of a word and
confuses adjectives of the masculine and feminine gender.   Pishchik
is a Russian, an old man crippled with gout, old age and good
living.   He is stout and is dressed in a peasant's sleeveless
coat ... with heelless high boots.   Lopakhin has a white waistcoat
and brown boots, he waves his arms about as he walks, takes long
strides and meditates while walking about - walking in a straight

line. His hair isn't short and so he often throws back his head.
He absent-mindedly combs his beard from back to front - i.e. from
his neck in the direction of his mouth. Trofimov's quite clear,
I think. Varya wears a black dress with a broad belt.

I spent three years preparing to write 'The Cherry Orchard' and
for three years I've been telling you to engage an actress for the
part of Lyuba Ranevsky. So don't complain if you now find yourselves playing a game of patience which just won't come out.
(Letter to V.T. Nemirovich-Danchenko, 2 Nov. 1903.)

The house in the play has two stories and is large. After all
there is a mention in Act Three of a staircase going downstairs.

The house must be large and solid. Whether it's made of wood...
or stone, that doesn't matter. It's very old and large. Summer
holiday-makers don't rent that kind of house. That kind of house
is usually pulled down and the material is used to build summer
cottages. The furniture is old-fashioned, of good style and
solid. The furniture and fittings haven't been affected by finan-
cial ruin and debts.

When people buy a house of this kind they argue as follows:
it's cheaper and easier to build a smaller new one than to repair
this old one.
(Letter to K.S. Stanislavsky, 5 Nov. 1903.)

Tell her [Muratova] to be funny in the part of Charlotte, that's
the main thing. I doubt whether Lilina will succeed with Anya,
she'll just be an old-fashioned girl with a squeaky voice and no
more.
(Letter to O.L. Knipper, 8 Nov. 1903.)

Of course you can use the same set for Acts Three and Four, the one
with a hall and staircase. In general please don't stint yourself
with the scenery - I defer to you. In your theatre I'm always
stunned and usually sit with my mouth wide open. There's nothing
more to be said about this. Whatever you do will be splendid, a
hundred times better than anything I could think of.

Dunyasha and Yepikhodov stand in the presence of Lopakhin, they
don't sit down. After all, Lopakhin is very much at his ease,
behaves like a squire and calls the servants 'thou', while they
call him 'you'.
(Letter to K.S. Stanislavsky, 10 Nov. 1903.)

I've received the plan of Act One. The house will have two
stories, which means that the garden-room also has two stories.
But you know, there won't be much sunlight in the little patio
formed by this garden-room, and cherries wouldn't grow there.
(Letter to O.L. Knipper, 20 Nov. 1903.)

Haymaking usually takes place between 20 and 25 June, at which time

I think the corncrake no longer cries, and frogs also are silent
at this time of year. Only the golden oriole sings then. There
isn't a cemetery. There *was* one a long time ago. Two or three
gravestones lying around any old how, that's all that's left. The
bridge is a very good idea. If you can show a train without any
noise, without a single sound, then carry on. I haven't anything
against a single set for Acts Three and Four as long as the
entrances and exits are convenient in Act Four.
(Letter to K.S. Stanislavsky, 23 Nov. 1903.)

Konstantin Sergeyevich [Stanislavsky] wants to bring on a train in
Act Two, but I think he must be restrained. He also wants frogs
and corncrakes.
(Letter to O.L. Knipper, 23 Nov. 1903.)

I'm deeply convinced that my 'Cherry Orchard' doesn't suit you at
all. The central female part in this play is that of an old woman
bound up with the past, who has nothing to do with the present, and
the other parts, at least the women's, are rather petty and crude
and not interesting for you.
(Letter to V.F. Komissarzhevskaya, 6 Jan. 1904.)

My play was put on yesterday, so I'm not feeling too good. I want
to slip off somewhere and I'll probably go to France by February,
or at least to the Crimea.
(Letter to I.L. Leontyev, 18 Jan. 1904.)

If you arrive at carnival time, that's fine. Only as far as I can
see, it will be carnival time at least before our actors come to
themselves and start playing 'The Cherry Orchard' less confusedly and
flamboyantly than now.
(Letter to F.D. Batyushkov, 19 Jan. 1904.)

Lulu and K.L. [relatives of O.L. Knipper] saw 'The Cherry Orchard'
in March. Both of them say that Stanislavsky [as Gayev] plays
repulsively in Act Four and drags things out most painfully. This
is really dreadful! An act which ought to last for a maximum of
twelve minutes - you're dragging it out for forty. The only thing
I can say is that Stanislavsky has ruined my play. Oh, well, the
less said about him the better.
(Letter to O.L. Knipper, 29 March 1904.)

Why do they so obstinately call my play a 'drama' in play-bills and
newspaper advertisements? What Nemirovich and Stanislavsky see in
my play definitely isn't what I wrote and I'm ready to swear anything you like that neither of them has read through my play carefully once. I'm sorry to say so, but I assure you I'm right.
(Letter to O.L. Knipper, 10 April 1904.)

NOTES

1 Olga Knipper in fact took the part of Mrs. Ranevsky.
* 'The Cherry Orchard' was first performed at the MAT on 17 January 1904.

9. 5 VSEVOLOD MEYERHOLD

> 'Meyerhold on Theatre', trans. E. Braun, Methuen,
> 1969, pp. 28-9

Time is a very precious element on the stage. If a scene visualized by the author as incidental lasts longer than necessary, it casts a burden on to the next scene which the author may well intend as most significant. Thus the spectator, having spent too long looking at something he should quickly forget, is tired out before the important scene. The director has placed it in a distracting frame. One recalls how the overall harmony was disturbed in the Moscow Art interpretation of Act Three of 'The Cherry Orchard'. The author intended the act's leitmotiv to be Ranevskaya's premonition of an approaching storm (the sale of the cherry orchard). Everybody else is behaving as though stupefied: they are dancing happily to the monotonous tinkling of the Jewish band, whirling round as if in the vortex of a nightmare, in a tedious modern dance devoid of enthusiasm, passion, grace, even lasciviousness. They do not realize that the ground on which they are dancing is subsiding under their feet. Ranevskaya alone foresees the disaster; she rushes back and forth, then briefly halts the revolving wheel, the nightmare dance of the puppet show. In her anguish, she urges the people to sin, only not to be !namby-pambies'; through sin man can attain grace, but through mediocrity he attains nothing.
The following harmony is established in the act: on the one hand, the lamentations of Ranevskaya with her presentiment of approaching disaster (fate in the new mystical drama of Chekhov); on the other hand, the puppet show (not for nothing does Chekhov make Charlotte dance amongst the 'philistines' in a costume familiar in the puppet theatre - a black tail-coat and check trousers). Translated into musical terms, this is one movement of the symphony. It contains the basic elegiac melody with alternating moods in pianissimo, outbursts in forte (the suffering of Ranevskaya), and the dissonant accompaniment of the monotonous cacophony of the distant band and the dance of the living corpses (the philistines). This is the musical harmony of the act, and the conjuring scene is only one of the harsh sounds which together comprise the dissonant tune of the stupid dance. Hence it should blend with the dancing and appear only for a moment before merging with it once more. On the other hand, the dance should be heard constantly as a muffled accompaniment, but only in the background. (1)
The director at the Art Theatre has shown how the harmony of the act can be destroyed. With various bits and pieces of equipment, he makes an entire scene of the conjuring, so that it is long and

complicated.   The spectator concentrates his attention on it for
so long that he loses the act's leitmotiv.   When the act ends the
memory retains the background melody, but the leitmotiv is lost.

In 'The Cherry Orchard', as in the plays of Maeterlinck, there
is a hero, unseen on the stage, but whose presence is felt every
time the curtain falls.   When the curtain falls at the Moscow Art
Theatre one senses no such presence; one retains only an impression
of 'types'.   For Chekhov, the characters of 'The Cherry Orchard'
are the means and not the end.   But in the Art Theatre the characters have become the end and the lyrical-mystical aspect of the
play remains unrevealed.

Whereas in Chekhov the director loses sight of the whole by
concentrating on its parts, because Chekhov's impressionistically
treated images happen to lend themselves to portrayal as clearly
defined figures (or *types*), Ibsen is considered by the naturalistic
director to require *explanation* because he is too obscure for the
public.

NOTES

1   Similar instances of dissonant notes emerging fleetingly from
the background and encroaching on the act's leitmotiv are:
the station-master reading poetry; Yepikhodov breaking his
billiard cue; Trofimov falling downstairs.   And note how
closely and subtly Chekhov interweaves the leitmotiv and the
accompaniment:

> ANYA (*agitatedly*):   And just now someone said that the cherry
> orchard was sold today.
> RANEVSKAYA: Sold to whom?
> ANYA: He didn't say who; he's gone now.
> (*Dances with Trofimov.*)   [Meyerhold's note.]

*   Meyerhold was an actor and experimental director with the MAT.

9. 6   FRANCIS FERGUSSON

> The Plot of 'The Cherry Orchard', 'The Idea of a
> Theater', Princeton University Press, Princeton,
> N.J., 1949, pp. 161-5

'The Cherry Orchard' is often accused of having no plot whatever,
and it is true that the story gives little indication of the play's
content or meaning; nothing happens, as the Broadway reviewers so
often point out.   Nor does it have a thesis, though many attempts
have been made to attribute a thesis to it, to make it into a
Marxian tract, or into a nostalgic defense of the old regime.   The
play does not have much of a plot in either of these accepted
meanings of the word, for it is not addressed to the rationalizing
mind but to the poetic and histrionic sensibility.   It is an imitation of an action in the strictest sense, and it is plotted

according to the first meaning of this word which I have distinguished in other contexts: the incidents are selected and arranged
to define an action in a certain mode; a complete action, with a
beginning, middle, and end in time. Its freedom from the mechanical order of the thesis or the intrigue is the sign of the perfection of Chekhov's realistic art. And its apparently casual incidents are actually composed with most elaborate and conscious
skill to reveal the underlying life, and the natural, objective
form of the play as a whole. [...]
    'The Cherry Orchard' is a drama 'of pathetic motivation,' a
theater-poem of the suffering of change; and this mode of action
and awareness is much closer to the skeptical basis of modern
realism, and to the histrionic basis of all realism. Direct
perception before predication is always true, says Aristotle; and
the extraordinary feat of Chekhov is to predicate nothing. This
he achieves by means of his plot: he selects only those incidents,
those moments in his characters' lives, between their rationalized
efforts, when they sense their situation and destiny most directly.
So he contrives to show the action of the play as a whole - the
unsuccessful attempt to cling to the Cherry Orchard - in many
diverse reflectors and without propounding any thesis about it.
    The slight narrative thread which ties these incidents and
characters together for the inquiring mind, is quickly recounted.
The family that owns the old estate named after its famous orchard -
Lyubov, her brother Gaev, and her daughters Varya and Anya - is all
but bankrupt, and the question is how to prevent the bailiffs from
selling the estate to pay their debts. Lopahin, whose family were
formerly serfs on the estate, is now rapidly growing rich as a
businessman, and he offers a very sensible plan: chop down the
orchard, divide the property into small lots, and sell them off to
make a residential suburb for the growing industrial town nearby.
Thus the cash value of the estate could be not only preserved, but
increased. But this would not save what Lyubov and her brother
find valuable in the old estate; they cannot consent to the destruction of the orchard. But they cannot find, or earn, or borrow
the money to pay their debts either; and in due course the estate
is sold at auction to Lopahin himself, who will make a very good
thing of it. His workmen are hacking at the old trees before the
family is out of the house.
    The play may be briefly described as a realistic ensemble
pathos: the characters all suffer the passing of the estate in
different ways, thus adumbrating this change at a deeper and more
generally significant level than that of any individual's experience. The action which they all share by analogy, and which
informs the suffering of the destined change of the Cherry Orchard,
is 'to save the Cherry Orchard': that is, each character sees some
value in it - economic, sentimental, social, cultural - which he
wishes to keep. By means of his plot, Chekhov always focuses
attention on the general action: his crowded stage, full of the
characters I have mentioned as well as half a dozen hangers-on, is
like an implicit discussion of the fatality which concerns them
all; but Chekhov does not believe in their ideas, and the interplay he shows among his *dramatis personae* is not so much the play
of thought as the alternation of his characters' perceptions of

their situation, as the moods shift and the time for decision
comes and goes.

Though the action which Chekhov chooses to show on-stage is
'pathetic,' i.e., suffering and perception, it is complete: the
Cherry Orchard is constituted before our eyes, and then dissolved.
The first act is a prologue: it is the occasion of Lyubov's
return from Paris to try to resume her old life. Through her eyes
and those of her daughter Anya, as well as from the complementary
perspectives of Lopahin and Trofimov, we see the estate as it were
in the round, in its many possible meanings. The second act
corresponds to the agon; it is in this act that we become aware
of the conflicting values of all the characters, and of the
efforts they make (off-stage) to save each one *his* Orchard. The
third act corresponds to the pathos and peripety of the traditional tragic form. The occasion is a rather hysterical party
which Lyubov gives while her estate is being sold at auction in
the nearby town; it ends with Lopahin's announcement, in pride and
the bitterness of guilt, that he was the purchaser. The last act
is the epiphany: we see the action, now completed, in a new and
ironic light. The occasion is the departure of the family: the
windows are boarded up, the furniture piled in the corners, and
the bags packed. All the characters feel, and the audience sees in
a thousand ways, that the wish to save the Orchard has amounted in
fact to destroying it; the gathering of its denizens to separation;
the homecoming to departure. What this 'means' we are not told.
But the action is completed, and the poem of the suffering of change
concludes in a new and final perception, and a rich chord of feeling.

The structure of each act is based upon a more or less ceremonious social occasion. In his use of the social ceremony - arrivals,
departures, anniversaries, parties - Chekhov is akin to James. His
purpose is the same: to focus attention on an action which all
share by analogy, instead of upon the reasoned purpose of any individual, as Ibsen does in his drama of ethical motivation. Chekhov
uses the social occasion also to reveal the individual at moments
when he is least enclosed in his private rationalization and most
open to disinterested insights. The Chekhovian ensembles may
appear superficially to be mere pointless stalemates - too like
family gatherings and arbitrary meetings which we know off-stage.
So they are. But in his miraculous arrangement the very discomfort
of many presences is made to reveal fundamental aspects of the
human situation.

That Chekhov's art of plotting is extremely conscious and deliberate is clear the moment one considers the distinction between
the stories of his characters as we learn about them, and the
moments of their lives which he chose to show directly on-stage.
Lopahin, for example, is a man of action like one of the new capitalists in Gorki's plays. Chekhov knew all about him, and could
have shown us an exciting episode from his career if he had not
chosen to see him only when he was forced to pause and pathetically
sense his own motives in a wider context which qualifies their
importance. Lyubov has been dragged about Europe for years by her
ne'er-do-well lover, and her life might have yielded several sure-
fire erotic intrigues like those of the commercial theater. But

Chekhov, like all the great artists of modern times, rejected these standard motivations as both stale and false. The actress Arkadina, in 'The Seagull,' remarks, as she closes a novel of Maupassant's, 'Well, among the French that may be, but here with us there's nothing of the kind, we've no set program.' In the context the irony of her remark is deep: she is herself a purest product of the commercial theater, and at that very time she is engaged in a love affair of the kind she objects to in Maupassant. But Chekhov, with his subtle art of plotting, has caught her in a situation, and at a brief moment of clarity and pause, when the falsity of her career is clear to all, even herself.

9. 7 RAYMOND WILLIAMS.

Anton Chekhov, 'Drama from Ibsen to Brecht',
Chatto & Windus, 1968, pp. 106-10

[...] But in 'The Three Sisters' and 'The Cherry Orchard' some-thing new has happened: it is not the liberating individual against the complacent group; it is that the desire for libera-tion has passed into the group as a whole, but at the same time has become hopeless, inward-looking - in effect a defeat before the struggle has even begun. Chekhov, that is to say, is not writing about a generation of liberal struggle against false social forms, but about a generation whose whole energy is con-sumed in the very process of becoming conscious of their own inadequacy and impotence. The dramatic conventions of liberal struggle had been clear: the isolation of the individual; his contrast with his group; and then an action which took this for-ward - not to the point of change, which Ibsen could not see happening, but to the point where the effort and the resistance, the vocation and the debt, reached deadlock: the hero died still climbing and struggling, but with the odds against him. As we have seen, this deadlock was never merely external: the limiting consciousness of the false society - 'we are all ghosts ... all of us so wretchedly afraid of the light' - was seen, by Ibsen, as inevitably entering the consciousness of the man who was struggling: the deadlock with a false society was re-enacted as a deadlock within the self. The methods of Ibsen's last plays, particularly, are related to this internal deadlock.
    It was from this point that Chekhov began. He attempted the same action, and made it end in suicide. But he came to see this as 'theatrical': a significant description of one of those crucial moments when a structure of feeling is changing and when the con-ventions appropriate to it come suddenly to seem empty. As Chekhov explores his world, he finds not deadlock - the active struggle in which no outcome is possible - but stalemate - the collective recognition, as it were before the struggle, that this is so. Virtually everyone wants change; virtually no-one believes it is possible. It is the sensibility of a generation which sits up all night talking about the need for revolution, and is then too tired next morning to do anything at all, even about its own

immediate problems.

This world, this new structure of feeling, is very powerfully created in 'The Three Sisters' and in 'The Cherry Orchard'. In 'The Three Sisters' it is the longing to make sense of life, to have a sense of a future, in a stagnant and boring military-provincial society. In 'The Cherry Orchard' it is an attempt to come to terms with the past: to live without owning the orchard and its servants. In neither situation is any real success possible: what happens is not to change the situation, but to reveal it. The counter-movement, against what would be simple fantasy (the desire to be in Moscow, although they would be the same people there) or simple nostalgia (the desire to have the orchard and yet to be free to go away), is an emphasis on redemption, effort, work. Characteristically, these cannot materialize as events; they can only be spoken about:

> They will forget our faces, voices, and even how many there were of us, but our sufferings will turn into joy for those who will live after us ... Your orchard frightens me. When I walk through it in the evening or at night, the rugged bark on the trees glows with a dim light, and the cherry-trees seem to see all that happened a hundred and two hundred years ago in painful and oppressive dreams. Well, we have fallen at least two hundred years behind the times. We have achieved nothing at all as yet; we have not made up our minds how we stand with the past; we only philosophise, complain of boredom, or drink vodka. It is so plain that before we can live in the present, we must first redeem the past, and have done with it; and it is only by suffering that we can redeem it, only by strenuous unremitting toil.

Characteristically, this last speech is by Trophimov, who does practically no work. This does not mean that he is wrong, or that what he says can be disregarded: it is the dominant emotion of the play. But there is this precise paradox, in Trophimov and in the others, between what can be said and what can be done; what is believed and what is lived.

Inevitably, such a man, such a situation, such a generation can seem comic; it is easy to laugh at them and at what Chekhov calls their 'neurotic whining'. At the same time, to get even the strength to see what is wrong, to sit up talking to try to get it clear, can be, in such a time, a major effort. In its inadequacy and yet its persistence it is heroism of a kind, an ambivalent kind. It is then this feeling - this structure of feeling - that Chekhov sets himself to dramatize.

The consequences in method are important. First, there will be no isolated, contrasting characters; the crucial emotion is that of a group. Second, there will, so far as possible, be no action: things will happen, but as it were from outside: what happens within the group is mainly gesture and muddle. Third, the contradictory character, of the group and its feelings, has to be conveyed in the tone: a kind of nobility, and a kind of farce, have to co-exist. (This is not, by the way, a cue for the usual question: are we supposed to laugh or cry at such people and such

situations? That is a servile question: we have to decide our
response for ourselves. The point is, always, that the characters
and situations can be seen, are written to be seen, in both ways;
to decide on one part of the response or the other is to miss what
is being said.)

As we come to see that this is what Chekhov is doing, we are
faced with very difficult critical problems. He is attempting to
dramatize a stagnant group, in which consciousness has turned
inward and become, if not wholly inarticulate, at least unconnect-
ing. He is attempting to dramatize a social consequence - a
common loss - in private and self-regarding feeling. It is, inevitably, a very difficult balance, a very difficult method, to
achieve.

Now certainly, Chekhov's representation of living action is
impressive. The structure is more finely and more delicately constructed than that of any of his contemporaries. The same method
achieves, in his fiction, very valuable results. But the method,
I would say, is ultimately fictional. In the bare, economical,
and inescapably explicit framework of drama the finest structure of
incident and phrase, left to itself, appears crude. The convention
of general description, which in the novel is essentially a whole
structure of feeling, is very difficult to achieve, in this kind of
play. And then the miniatures are left suspended; there is a
sense, as in Ibsen's 'The Wild Duck', of disintegration, which
springs directly from this absence. A gap must be filled, and to
the rescue, as before, comes the unifying pressure of a device of
atmosphere. It is a poor compromise. The characters, which in
fiction are more than their separated selves, now dissociate, outline themselves, by the conditions of dramatic presentation. Deli-
neation degenerates to slogan and catchphrase, to the mumbled 'and
all the rest of it' with which old Sorin ends his every speech in
'The Seagull'. For of such is a 'character' built. The just comment is Strindberg's, in the Preface to 'Lady Julie':

> A character on the stage came to signify a gentleman who was
> fixed and finished; nothing was required, but some bodily
> defect - a club-foot, a wooden leg, a red nose; or the charac-
> ter in question was made to repeat some such phrase as 'That's
> capital', 'Barkis is willin'', or the like.

Nothing is more surprising, in the genuine detail of experience
which Chekhov so finely achieves, than the appearance - the repeated appearance - of that kind of fixed, external device of personality. Moreoever, that separable 'personality' is the more
contradictory in that what Chekhov is essentially expressing is a
common condition. It is this that is missed or weakened when personality declines to an idiosyncrasy or a 'human vignette'.

On the other hand, Chekhov attempted to develop a new kind of
dialogue which, paradoxically, would express disintegration without weakening the sense of a common condition. Such dialogue is
very hard to read and to play, and it is, I think, only intermit-
tently successful. But where it does succeed, something very original and in its own way powerful has come into modern drama. An
unfamiliar rhythm is developed, in which what is being said,

essentially, is not said by any one of the characters, but, as it
were inadvertently, by the group. This is not easy to illustrate,
since the printed convention, separating and assigning the speeches,
usually breaks it up. The major example, I think, is the second
act of 'The Cherry Orchard', which as a theme for voices, a condition and an atmosphere created by hesitation, implication,
unconnected confession, is more complete and powerful than anything else Chekhov wrote. A briefer example, from 'The Three
Sisters', may allow the method to be seen more clearly (I omit the
names of the speakers so that the form of a connected dialogue -
connected, paradoxically, to show disconnection - can be followed):

> We do not seen to understand each other. How can I convince
> you? Yes, laugh. Not only after two or three centuries, but
> in a million years, life will still be as it was; life does not
> change, it remains for ever, following its own laws which do
> not concern us, or which, at any rate, you will never find out.
> Migrant birds, cranes for example, fly and fly, and whatever
> thoughts, high or low, enter their heads, they will still fly
> and not know why or where. They fly and will continue to fly,
> whatever philosophers come to life among them; they may philo-
> sophize as much as they like, only they will fly...
>   Still, is there a meaning?
>   A meaning? Now the snow is falling. What meaning?
>   It seems to me that a man must have faith, or must search for
> a faith, or his life will be empty, empty. To live and not to
> know why the cranes fly, why babies are born, why there are
> stars in the sky. Either you must know why you live, or every-
> thing is trivial, not worth a straw.
>   Still, I am sorry that my youth has gone.
>   Gogol says: life in this world is a dull matter, my masters.
>   And I say it's difficult to argue with you, my masters.
> Hang it all.
>   Balzac was married at Berdichev. That's worth making a note
> of.Balzac was married at Berdichev.
>   Balzac was married at Berdichev.
>   The die is cast. I've handed in my resignation.

As we listen to this, it is obvious that what is being expressed
is not a dealing between persons, or a series of self-definitions;
it is a common, inadvertent mood - questioning, desiring, defeated.
To the degree that we separate the speeches out, and see them as
revealing this or that particular character, the continuing rhythm,
at once tentative and self-conscious, superficially miscellaneous
and yet deeply preoccupied, is quickly lost. And of course, in
performance, such continuity, such timing, is very difficult to
sustain, if each actor sees himself as acting a separate part. It
is the final paradox, in Chekhov's work, that the local identifying
features, of the members of his dramatic group, are truly superficial, yet are the constant cues. What comes through or can come
through is a very different voice - the human voice within and
beyond the immediate negotiation and self-presentation. But within
his conventions, and this is usually accentuated in performance,
this human voice is intermittent and inadvertent; an unusual

silence has to be imposed, if it is ever to be properly heard.

SHAW:
'MAJOR BARBARA' AND 'SAINT JOAN'

'MAJOR BARBARA' (*)

10. 1 SHAW

Letters, 'Collected Letters 1898-1910', ed.
Dan H. Laurence, Max Reinhardt, 1972,
pp. 542-3, 565-6, 580

Dear Calvert
Can you play the trombone? If not, I beg you to acquire a smatter-
ing of the art during your holidays. I am getting on with the new
play scrap by scrap; and the part of the millionaire cannon founder
is becoming more and more formidable. Broadbent and Keegan rolled
into one, with Mephistopheles thrown in; that is what it is like.
[...] Irving and Tree will fade into third class when Calvert takes
the stage as Andrew Undershaft. It will be TREMENJOUS, simply.
But there is a great scene at the end of the second act where he
buys up the Salvation Army, and has to take part in a march to a
big meeting. Barker will play the tamborine. You will have a
trombone - or a bombardon if you prefer that instrument - and it
would add greatly to the effect if you could play it prettily.
Besides, if you took to music you could give up those confounded
cigars and save your voice and your memory [...] for this immense
part. It is very long, speeches longer than Keegan's, and dozens
of them, and infinite nuances of execution. Undershaft is diaboli-
cally subtle, gentle, self-possessed, powerful, stupendous, as well
as amusing and interesting. There are the makings of ten Hamlets
and six Othellos in his mere leavings. Learning it will half kill
you; but you can retire next day as pre-eminent and unapproachable.
[...]
    But the trombone is the urgent matter of the moment. By the
way, trombone players never get cholera nor consumption - never
die, in fact, until extreme old age makes them incapable of working
the slide.
(Letter to Louis Calvert, 23 July 1905.)

Dear Murray

[...] I want to get Cusins beyond the point of wanting power.   I
shall use your passage to bring out the point that Undershaft is a
fly on the wheel; but Cusins would not make the mistake of imagining that he could be anything else.   The fascination that draws
him is the fascination of reality, or rather - for it is hardly a
fascination - the impossibility of refusing to put his hand to
Undershaft's plough, which is at all events doing something, when
the alternative is to hold aloof in a superior attitude and beat
the air with words.   To use your metaphor of getting his hand on
the lever, his choice lies, not between going with Undershaft or
not going with him, but between standing on the footplate at work,
and merely sitting in a first class carriage reading Ruskin &
explaining what a low dog the driver is and how steam is ruining
the country.

I am writing the whole scene over again.   The moisture which
serves for air in Ireland spoiled it hopelessly.   I will send the
new version to you when it is in shape.

I have taken rather special care to make Cusins the reverse in
every point of the theatrical strong man.   I want him to go on his
quality wholly, and not to make the smallest show of physical
robustness or brute determination.   His selection by Undershaft
should be a puzzle to people who believe in the strong-silent-
still-waters-run-deep hero of melodrama.   The very name Adolphus
Cusins is selected to that end.

As to the triumph of Undershaft, that is inevitable because I
am in the mind that Undershaft is in the right, and that Barbara
and Adolphus, with a great deal of his natural insight and cleverness, are very young, very romantic, very academic, very ignorant
of the world.   I think it would be unnatural if they were able to
cope with him.   Cusins averts discomfiture & scores off him by wit
& humorous dexterity; but the facts are too much for him; and his
strength lies in the fact that he, like Barbara, refuses the
Impossibilist position (which their circumstances make particularly
easy for them) even when the alternative is the most sensationally
anti-moral department of commerce.   The moral is drawn by Lomax
'There is a certain amount of tosh about this notion of wickedness.

I have been writing this letter in scraps for three days -
impossible to write letters here.   I shall be back in London on
Friday at latest.

Handsome of me not to make you a Rhodes scholar, by the way.
(Letter to Gilbert Murray, 7 October 1905.)

Dear Miss Russell

I made a few notes today which I may as well give you.

When Bill says 'If you want to bring a charge agen me, bring
it,' look puzzled, as Barbara doesnt know what on earth he means.
Then, when he says 'My name's Bill Walker' you are enlightened, as
you think he means charging him for hitting Jenny.

When Undershaft coughs and you say 'It's all right, papa: we
havnt forgotten you,' dont laugh.   Say it in a businesslike way,
and it will be more effective.

When Bill comes out with his plan of paying Jenny, Barbara should

have a sort of impulse towards him, as it is really his second
attempt to right himself - a sign of conscience on his part. And
the smile at the earl's granddaughter should come through this
feeling - not a smile of pure dry fun, but a smile on the surface
of an emotion.

'Nonsense! of course its funny' might be a little more peremptory. There are one or two points, like the 'Nonsense! she must
do as she's told' (about Rummy) in which Barbara, with all her
sweetness, shews that she is her mother's daughter, and that it
comes very natural to her to order people about. There is a
curious touch of aristocratic pride at the very end, where she
says she does not want to die in God's debt, and will forgive
him 'as becomes a woman of her rank' for all the starvation &
mischief he is responsible for. Barbara has great courage,
great pride & a high temper at the back of her religious genius;
and you need not hesitate to let them flash through at moments if
any of the passages catch you that way. [...]
(Letter to Annie Russell, 20 November 1905.)

NOTE

*   'Major Barbara' was first performed at the Court Theatre on
    28 November 1905 with Louis Calvert as Andrew Undershaft and
    Annie Russell as Major Barbara.

10. 2 SHAW

    Letter to Theresa Helburn at the Theatre Guild,
    New York, L. Langner, 'G.B.S. and the Lunatic',
    Atheneum Publishers, New York, 1963, pp. 109-10

I do not suppose there is much danger of Winifred Lenihan making
Barbara a low-spirited person with large eyes, looking like a
picture on the cover of The Maiden's Prayer, though that is the
traditional stage view of a religious part.

Bear in mind that Lady Britomart has a most impo. ant part, and
requires a first-rate robust comedian and grande dame to play it;
for the clue to a great deal of Barbara is that she is her mother's
daughter, and that she bullies and bustles the Salvation Army
about just as Lady Britomart bullies and bustles her family at
home. Barbara is full of life and vigor, and unconsciously very
imperious.

Cusins is easy for any clever actor who has never seen the
original (Professor Gilbert Murray). The next best model is
perhaps Harold Lloyd.

Do not let Mr. Waram make the mistake of making up like a thug
as Bill Walker. In appearance he is just an ordinary workman
excited by drink and a sense of injury, not in the least like a
murderer in a nightmare or a melodrama. He should be clean and
good-looking enough to make the scene in which Barbara breaks down
his brutality - which is a sort of very moving love scene - look

natural, which it will not if Bill is disgusting physically and
sanitorily.
    The most effective dress for Lady Britomart is a Queen Mary or
Queen Alexandra dress, long and purposely a generation out of date.
(10 November 1928.)

10. 3 SHAW

        To Audiences at 'Major Barbara', (*) 'Shaw on
        Theatre', ed. E.J. West, Hill & Wang Dramabook,
        New York, 1959, pp. 118-21

Major Barbara is the third of a group of three plays of exceptional weight and magnitude on which the reputation of the author
as a serious dramatist was first established, and still mainly
rests. The first of the three, completed in 1903, the author's
forty-seventh year, was Man and Superman, which has never been
performed in its prodigious entirety in America, nor in England
until the present year. The second, John Bull's Other Island,
followed in 1904, and was an immediate success. The third of the
series was Major Barbara, which arrived in 1905. It made demands
on the audience but the demands were conceded. The audience left
the theatre exhausted, but felt the better for it and came again.
The second act, the Salvation Army act, was a play in itself.
Regarded in that way, it may be said to be the most successful of
all the author's plays.
    The possibility of using the wooing of a man's soul for his
salvation as a substitute for the hackneyed wooing of a handsome
young gentleman for the sake of marrying him had occurred to
Bernard Shaw many years before, when, in the course of his cam-
paigns for socialism, he had often found himself on Sunday morn-
ings addressing a Socialist meeting in the open air in London
or in the provinces while the Salvation Army was at work on the
same ground. He had frequently, at the conclusion of his own
meeting, joined the crowd round the Salvation lasses and watched
their work and studied their methods sympathetically. Many of
them sang, with great effect, songs in which the drama of salvation was presented in the form of a series of scenes between a
brutal and drunken husband and a saved wife, with a thrilling
happy ending in which the audience, having been persuaded by the
unconscious art of the singer to expect with horror a murderous
attack on the woman as her husband's steps were heard on the
stairs, were relieved and delighted to hear that when the villain
entered the room and all seemed lost, his face was lighted with
the light of Heaven; for he too had been saved. Bernard Shaw was
not at that time a playwright; but such scenes were not lost on
him; the future dramatist was collecting his material everywhere.
    Many years afterwards when he had acquired a considerable repu-
tation as a critic of music, Bernard Shaw saw in a daily paper a
silly remark describing some horrible noise as being almost as bad
as a Salvation Army band. He immediately wrote to the paper pointing out that the Salvation Army bands were mostly good, and that

some of them were of very conspicuous excellence. This compliment
from an unexpected quarter made quite a commotion at the Army's
headquarters in London. The general quoted it again and again in
public, and the author was invited to attend one of the musical
festivals of the Army. He did so and wrote an elaborate critical
report on the bands, besides declaring that the performance of
the Dead March from Handel's Saul at the great meeting at the
Albert Hall in commemoration of Mrs Booth by the combined bands
of the Army, headed by the International Staff Band, was incom-
parably the finest he had ever heard, and the only one which
showed any understanding of the magnificent triumphal character
of the closing section.

Shaw took advantage of the relations thus established to ask
the Army staff why they did not develop the dramatic side of their
ritual by performing plays. He even offered to write a short play
as a model of what might be done. The leaders of the Army,
though interested and not themselves hostile to the proposal,
could not venture to offend the deep prejudices against the theatre
that still form part of English evangelism. They could only say
rather doubtfully that if the author of a play could guarantee
that everything in it had actually happened, that 'it was all
true,' it might be possible to reconcile the stricter Salvationists to it. Shaw put forward the old defence made by Bunyan
that parables were allowable; but he was met with the assurance
that the Salvationists believed the parables to be records of facts
as well as vehicles of instruction.

Finally, Mrs Bramwell Booth told the author frankly that a
subscription would be more useful to the social work of the Army
than a model play; and so the matter dropped. But it bore fruit
in Major Barbara; and during its run the spectacle was seen for
the first time of a box filled with Salvation Army officials in
uniform, sitting in a theatre and witnessing a play. Their testimony was useful. Some of the critics, in an inept attempt to
be piously shocked, tried to present the play as a gibe at the
Army, on the ground that the Salvationists were represented as
being full of fun, and that they took money from the distiller.
The Army received this with the scorn it deserved, declaring that
Barbara's fun was perfectly correct and characteristic, and that
the only incident that seemed incredible to them was her refusal
to accept the money. Any good Salvationist, they said, would,
like the commissioner in the play, take money from the devil himself, and make so good use of it that he would perhaps be converted, as there is hope for everybody.

The play, however, raises larger issues than those of popular
Salvationism. Undershaft, with his terrible trade - so grimly
flourishing just now - and his doctrine that money comes first,
and that poverty is the worst of crimes and the only unbearable
crime, strikes the deepest note in the play as Barbara sounds the
highest. It was the allusions to Nietzsche which he provoked that
elicited from the author the well-known preface in which he pro-
tested against the habit of the English critics of referring every
trace of intellect in the English drama to Norwegian and German
writers when all the doctrines which so surprised them were to be
found in the literature of the English language. His reference

to Samuel Butler as the greatest English exponent of Undershaft's
doctrine of the importance of money was the beginning of the vogue
of that remarkable writer which has persisted and spread ever
since.

It is an open secret that the part of Adolphus Cusins, the very
unusual *jeune premier* of the play, owes its originality to the
fact that Mr Gilbert Murray, the Regius professor of Greek at
Oxford University, served the author as a very interesting model.
He quotes his own famous translations of Euripides. Undershaft is
perhaps the most exacting part that has fallen to the lot of an
actor since Shakespear's big parts; it belongs thoroughly to the
new drama in which a tragedy and comedy and even broad fun, are
so intimately bound up that it needs the greatest versatility and
flexibility on the part of the actor, and the most alert vigilance on the part of the audience, to avoid confusing them.

It is curious that ten years should have elapsed between the
production of Major Barbara in London and its first appearance on
the American stage. It has been the subject of many proposals,
but until today the artistic conditions have never seemed to the
author favorable enough to warrant him in venturing on an author-
ization. Miss Grace George's appearance in London has doubtless
had its weight in his decision. But Shaw has always said that for
plays of this class, the great question is whether the audience
will be a failure or a success.

NOTE

* Note circulated to the press prior to the 1915 and 1916 American
  production.

10. 4 SHAW

    Author's note, new Preface in programme for
    'Major Barbara', Wyndham's Theatre, 5 March 1929 (*)

In reviving a play 24 years old, I shall find myself, as usual, up
against that sanguine belief in progress which classes everything
unpleasant with old unhappy far-off things and battles long ago.
Quite recently a play of mine on the subject of marriage was criticized as out of date because it dealt with abuses that have long
since disappeared. As a matter of fact the only abuse which had
disappeared in the meantime was one which was not mentioned in the
play. Every proposal to remedy the others has been funked and
rebuffed. I therefore venture to offer our amateurs of progress
a hint or two as to how far the passage of time has affected the
actuality of Major Barbara.

First, the problem of the unemployed, with which the Salvation
Army is seen struggling in the play, grew to an unprecedented
magnitude in 1920; and as the unemployed now consist to a considerable extent of demobilized soldiers, and their successors with the
colours do not enjoy the confidence of the Government in the matter

of compelling them to starve, the old restraints upon indiscrimi-
nate outdoor relief under the Poor Law have been thrown to the
winds, bankrupting the Guardians in all the centres of unemployment, and sending up rates and taxes to a point at which Major
Barbara's grandfather's poverty on £7,000 a year has become titled
destitution on little more than half that pittance.

In consequence 'the bribe of bread' which so troubled Major
Barbara is now anticipated by a variety of so-called doles, rang-
ing from unemployment insurance benefit to outdoor relief to wives
and children, and even to ablebodied men under pretexts available
for easy going guardians (not, by the way, always Labor Guardians).
But there are still ablebodied men, out of benefit and without
wives or children, who are as destitute as Peter Shirley in the
play; and unfortunately the typical cases are not now those of
skilled men 'too old at 46,' but of young men who have never had
any industrial training. Having grown up since the great industrial debâcle of 1920, they have had their mouths stopped with
Poor Rates, Lord Mayors' Funds, and doles of one sort or another
until, if there were any commercial employment within their reach,
they would be unemployable for want of the habit and training of
steady work. Only in the case of the soldier is it recognised
that he must be kept in full health and training between his jobs.
For the civilian, we think it enough to throw the poor fellow a
good natured half-crown, and hurry away in the opposite direction
whilst he goes to the devil.

When the war came Undershaft and Lazarus did not do so well as
was expected of them, because Lazarus had obtained too much control; and after a frightful slaughter of our young men through
insufficient munitions the Government had to organize the business
in national factories, and to send public officials to teach Lazarus how to conduct as much of it as was left to him. But the
moment the war was over, Undershaft and Lazarus came back with all
their newspapers shouting that they had saved the country, and
that the national factories were sinks of corruption and incompetence. They then plunged into an orgy of over capitalization
followed by wholesale repudiation, which they called reconstruction
and stabilization; so that every blunder and every swindle on their
part left the public more and more impressed with their gigantic
grasp of business and finance, incidentally providing our playwrights with materials for much tragic farce.

Undershaft, however, survived the wreck. His policy of high
wages and ruthless scrapping of obsolete methods proved more lucra-
tive than sweating and doing what was done last time. His well-
paid employees became his best customers. He emerged in fiction
as Clissold and in fact as John Ford. And the spectacle of his
successes in making money gave great satisfaction to the huge
majority who have rather less chance of achieving it themselves
than of winning the Calcutta Sweep.

West Ham meanwhile is in the same old mess as when the play was
written, except that the rates have risen to such impossible
heights that the Government has had the brilliant idea of camouf-
laging them by adding them to the rents. The Salvation Army still
spends in a struggle with poverty the zeal that was meant for a
struggle with sin and the money that Undershaft and Bodger

subscribe for the reasons set forth in the play. And the author
is still of opinion that the best comedies for British audiences
are those which they themselves provide by trying to run an
international civilization on the precepts of our village Sunday
Schools and the outlook of our suburban nurseries.

NOTE

* Sybil Thorndike played Major Barbara.

10. 5 FRANCIS FERGUSSON

> On Shavian Theatricality: the Platform and the
> Drawing-Room, 'The Idea of a Theater', Princeton
> University Press, Princeton, N.J., 1949, pp. 179-81

Mr. Eric Bentley, in his very useful study 'George Bernard Shaw,'
has pointed out that Shaw's comedy in its beginnings is based upon
the same enlightened drawing room as Oscar Wilde's. 'Major Barbara' is an example of this early period in his development. Lady
Brit's drawing-room feels as stable and secure as the traditional
cosmos of the Greeks or Elizabethans, but it is as clear and small
as a photograph; the London version of the bourgeois world. And
the story of the play may be read as a typical sentimental parlor
comedy for the carriage-trade. Lady Brit is an absurd but likeable
pillar of society; her estranged husband, Undershaft, a fabulously
wealthy munitions-maker of great wisdom and kindliness; her daughter
Barbara a sincere but misguided major in the Salvation Army.
She is in love with Cousins, a professor of Greek, a character suggested by Professor Gilbert Murray. The main issues are between
Barbara and her father: the relative merits of the Salvation Army
and munitions-making as ways to be saved. Cousins disapproves both
of the Salvation Army and the Undershaft industry of destruction,
but at the end he marries Barbara and places his Greek-trained
intellect together with her revivalistic fervor in the service of
bigger and better bombs. Shaw apparently wants us to believe in
Barbara as a real human being in the round, instead of a caricature,
and to take her dramatic conversion to her father's business seriously. At any rate he rejoices, and bids us sentimentally rejoice,
at the end of his fable when the girl, the man, and the money are
at last brought together. The audience may go home (in spite of
the witty dialectics it has heard) in laughter, tears, and complacency, spiced, at most, with a touch of the shocking - for the
secure basis of their little world, the eternity of the drawing-
room, is never seriously questioned. Where, in all this, is the
Shavian quality?
  The play may be read as a thesis, a proof that munitions-making
is the way to be saved; and this is in fact one of the bases of the
many witty debates. It is a wonderfully farcical idea, but Shaw is
far from offering it as Brieux offers his theses. As he uses it,
it has depths of irony which Brieux never dreamed of: Shaw neither

believes nor disbelieves it; its relation to reality is never
digested - not its relation to the sentimental story that Shaw puts
with it. Its usefulness lies in its theatrical fertility: it is
a paradox which may be endlessly debated, but it is in no sense the
truth as Brieux thought he was proving the truth. The characters
are conceived on a similar basis of paradox - except Barbara, who,
as I have said is supposed to be real. But Lady Brit, Undershaft, and each of the minor characters clearly has his paradoxical platform. Lady Brit's is that she must have both the Undershaft money and the creed of the Church of England. The two are
logically incompatible; but granted this non-Euclidean postulate,
everything she does follows with unanswerable logic. And so for
Undershaft, who presents himself as wise, kind, and completely
dedicated to destruction. These platforms no doubt represent
clarifications or schematizations of real attitudes in contemporary society. In the play, the rationalized platforms, as they
are debated and developed, constitute the brisk mental life which
we enjoy; but the relation of this life of the mind - this farce
of rationalizing - to the human reality is no more defined than
that of the paradoxical thesis to truth. Thus the play is a
parlor-game, based upon the freedom of the mind to name and then
to rationalize anything, without ever deviating from the concept
to the thing - the British Empire and Original Sin as light and
portable as the blueprints of the social planners and human engi-
neers. Shaw the moralist invites us into this brisk exchange for
therapeutic reasons, as gymnasium-instructors instigate boxing
or softball: not to win, not to prove anything, but for the sake
of a certain decent fitness in the moral void. But Shaw the clown
sees his and our agility as a rather frightening farce.
   If one thinks over these elements - the sentimental story, the
farcical-profound paradoxical thesis, and the complacency of the
audience - one may get spiritual indigestion. But if one sees a
performance, one may understand how it all hangs together for
those quick two hours: it is because its basis in the upholstered
world of the carriage-trade is never violated. On this basis it
is acceptable as a string of jokes which touch nothing. And Shavian comedy of this period still flatters and delights our pros-
perous suburbs. But Shaw himself, as the world changed and the
London drawing-room appeared to be less than eternal, became
dissatisfied with it. [...]

10. 6 HERBERT BLAU (*)

        Counterforce 1: the Social Drama, 'The Impossible
        Theater', Macmillan, New York, 1964, pp. 211-12

Nevertheless, the play - taken seriously - was still troubling.
There were themes that seemed as true today as they were at the
turn of the century: though we may have somewhat less of it, the
crime of poverty; the establishment of religions on blood money;
the superiority of blood money to no money; the dominance of Undershaft and Lazarus in affairs of state. But as for the making of

war on war by making explosives, it seemed to some of us that the
limitation of the Life Force is that it could never free itself of
Victorian illusions, because gunpowder is not exactly strontium
90.

'Well,' says one of the characters, 'the more destructive war
becomes the sooner it will be abolished, eh?' If the play is just
short of being instantaneously modern, it is because the character who advances that theory is at first glance the most oafish.
But times change; yesterday's fool is tomorrow's oracle. Today
that same character, flourishing his computer, may be advising
the administration.

While we were rehearsing 'Major Barbara,' William H. Honan
published an article in 'The New Republic,' The Peaceful Use of
Terror, in which he lists a number of the nineteenth-century
scientists and inventors, headed by Alfred B. Nobel, who believed in that idea. 'Like Andrew Undershaft in Shaw's "Major
Barbara," Nobel was an "idealistic" munitions manufacturer. His
object was not to advance the art of war, but, on the contrary,
to abolish it, as if with a pedagogical *reductio ad absurdum*.
"On the day when two Army corps will be able to annihilate each
other in one second," he once told a friend, "all civilized
nations will recoil from war in horror and disband their forces."
And later, "I should like to be able to turn out a substance or a
machine of such horrible capacity for mass annihilation that
thereby wars would become altogether impossible."' Honan points
out, with no more argument than facing the evidence of history,
that 'man continues to hope, blindly and sublimely, that the
terror of his own destructiveness will repress his warlike nature.
It never has.'

Actually, the comparison of Nobel to Undershaft needs to be
qualified. The latter says he is an impenitent 'profiteer in
mutilation and murder,' though he might have put it thus bluntly
to provoke his family, to shake up Wilton Crescent. His motto,
however, is Blood and Fire. And he no more believes that the more
destructive war becomes the sooner it will be abolished than he
does in making excuses for his trade. He agrees with Mr. Honan,
and goes one step further: 'The more destructive war becomes,' he
says, 'the more fascinating we find it.' Which may be why we are
not appeased when. Shaw seems to urge us to convert Money and Gunpowder to the purposes of social revolution by marrying the daughter of the munitions king to a Greek scholar. We feel then that
he lived in a world of more limited terrors, where such Platonic
romances could be imagined with reason, and where one didn't shud-
der when he said, as Undershaft does, 'What can blow up people
can blow up society.' It's hard to keep the explosives straight.
Still, if one understands the spirit of Shaw's incendiarism, he
realizes there is no solution *in* the play; the characters' brain-
storms are left in tension by the drama, and the play's symbolic
marriage is in the same realm of zany hope as Giraudoux's Madwoman
saving the earth from rapine by pushing the capitalists into the
sewer.

NOTE

* Herbert Blau is a contemporary American director. With Jules
  Irving, he founded The Actor's Workshop in San Francisco and
  later directed for the Repertory Theater of Lincoln Center in
  New York.

10. 7 LEON HUGO

  1904-1912: Wot Price Salvation?, 'Bernard Shaw:
  Playwright and Preacher', Methuen, 1971, pp. 154-60

'The Bacchae' reflects two transcending characteristics of the
Dionysian cult, the first to do with morality, the second with
the emotions. Morality is the wrong word, but no other will do,
our range of concepts being as limited as they are; morality
really stops short of Dionysus, for this god knows no morality;
nor does he know immorality, or, for that matter, amorality and
unmorality. He was simply the pagan I AM, being neither pitiless
nor pitying, neither merciless nor merciful, neither full of hate
nor full of love. He is the deification of the natural cycle and
supremely true only to himself. It may be that some of the
greatness of Greek drama begins here, in the acknowledgement of a
divinity as inevitable as the rising sun, as miraculous as bursting leaves. It seems certain that Shaw was fired by these qualities, and by a third, the sheer determinism of the god's declaration of himself. Here, in what we may regard as the prime ethic
of nature, in this MUST and WILL BE of the manifestation, is the
key to an understanding of 'Major Barbara'.
     Undershaft's gospel is patently derived from this ethic. He
boldly flaunts his motto, UNASHAMED, in the eyes of horrified con-
ventionality, usurps the plaintive 'oughts' of timid liberalism
and reinstates the full-bodied 'shall' of Dionysus, turns his
machine-guns and cannons and aerial torpedoes on mankind to wipe
out poverty and slavery, dealing in and thriving on death so that
the world might be reborn to full life. He proudly quotes his predecessors, all of whom, not necessarily excluding the one who had
no literary skill, give evidence of a decided bent for the paradox of mystical utterance. This is the point: Undershaft is an
out-and-out mystic who has the power of life in his hands because
he has the power of death. The tension of opposites implicit here
is no resolution, and for this reason many people who know the
play are disturbed. But resolution is impossible: the lyre is
not a lyre if the tension is removed; the harmony of the quivering
strings resides precisely in opposite tendencies. The harmony of
the spheres, as Pythagoras postulated this, derives from the magical numbers of the taut bow. What is at variance agrees with
itself: creation strains against itself: life is all one.
     To which one may imagine the response that Shaw is taking the
Devil out of Hell and putting him back in Heaven. He is not, of
course. To him there is no Devil and hell shall be obliterated
when poverty is obliterated. If our further response should be

that an abolished Devil displays a hopeful rather than realistic
view of evil, Shaw's answer in the play is that hope - the hope
expressed by Barbara in the epiphany - when coupled with power can
be the only admissible religious reality.

But the quarrel goes on, and the most urgent protest, raised by
Barbara's cry 'My God: why hast thou forsaken me?' and teased to
anger by the glorification of Money and Gunpowder, is:'What about
Jesus?' Which Jesus? the play asks: the Jesus who on the one
hand condones and even makes shift to exalt the hideous face of
physical starvation and spiritual degradation and on the other
hand condones and even makes shift to accept Bodger's bribe for
salvation - the Jesus of doublethink and two faces, of deprivation for the many and privilege for the few: the Jesus of Crosstianity? Or the Jesus who condemns and would make every shift to
eradicate the crime of poverty and the crime of parasitic wealth,
the humanitarian Jesus, who so loves the world that he would destroy it to make his word manifest: the Jesus of Dionysian Christianity? Shaw repudiates the first Jesus; he makes this the very
price of salvation: he cleaves to the second Jesus, and makes
this the prize of salvation.

It is a kind of Augean cleansing of the soul that Barbara
endures and Shaw would have the world endure. Crosstianity must
be scrapped; a religion that fitted the facts must be introduced.
We may, if we wish, call this Christian, or Dionysian, or Chris-
tian-Dionysian, or whatever else in whatever combinations that
appeal. Religion, as Shaw saw it, as Cusins saw it, as Undershaft saw it, and as Barbara comes to see it, is not true by virtue of the name coupled to it:

> The business of the Salvation Army is to save, not to wrangle
> about the name of the pathfinder. Dionysus or another: what
> does it matter?

It does not matter one jot. What does matter is the universal of
religion, that which makes Moslem, Buddhist, Christian, and pagan,
brothers, uniting them in the family of humanity. That which Shaw
has attempted to realise by going back to the source of Western
(perhaps also Eastern) religious practice; by drawing an ethical
philosophy from it. By trying in Acts II and III, and in my view
succeeding thrillingly, to recreate the spirit of eternal religion - the excitement, the ecstasy of surrender to something
greater than one's self.

This brings us to the second transcending characteristic of 'The
Bacchae' - the emotion of religious worship. It must be understood
that this emotion has nothing to do with the licentious extravagance we tend to associate with the word 'bacchanal'; it is purely
religious; purely devotional, even in its extreme form, when fervour gives way to ecstasy and this gives way to madness. Thus
Euripides depicts the Bacchae, whose frenzy is the glorification
of their god, no matter how outrageous it may seem to those who
have not been affected by his divinity. Human tragedy does follow
on the divine rage, desolation and horror fill the souls of those
on whom the god's hand falls. But over and against this is the
triumph of the god, his will done, and the heavens opening to

receive him.   How small in the scale of things - how tinpot - is
the human tragedy, how overwhelmingly vast is the power and the
mystery of the divine will.

The unspoken admission of religious practice is that words alone
cannot express such power and mystery, and so ritual and song come
spontaneously forth to augment the word.   This is the intoxicant of
worship, that which can so work on a person's spirit that he will
lose himself to the rhythms and notes, lose himself to the cosmic
I AM and be transfigured.

Dionysus was worshipped in the dithyramb, a song less of
praise than of identification with his being. A choral song, it
was initiated by one person (perhaps the one most under the influence of wine), who led others.   We transfer the pagan custom to
'Major Barbara' and Cusins immediately comes to mind.   With his
big bass drum he beats thunderous praise of salvation, for to
begin with he is not aligned with Dionysus; then abstract salvation becomes concrete as Money and Gunpowder; Bodger's money and
Undershaft's money saves the Salvation Army; cymbals clash, cor-
nets peal, the trombone blares, the drum booms; shouts of praise
and thanksgiving go upward; the march down Mile End Road begins,
and the brassy torrent of sound sweeps to a crescendo, clash,
peal, and boom, 'Glory, Halleluja!', 'Money and Gunpowder!', crowd
one on the other until the air seems a fierce clamour, and violent upheaval seems to shake the Army shelter.   Then stunned
silence, and Barbara's cry of desolation piercing the emotions.
The dithyramb is over.

Add to this thunderous assault the fine, hard thrust and parry
between Undershaft and Cusins and the tragi-comedy of the unregen-
erate Bill Walker, and we may willingly acknowledge the 'impulsive
power of an original work', which (in this, the second act, at
least) transforms ancient myth into reverberant modern drama.

I hesitate to say the same of the second part of Act III,
although the argument, if too long, has its own excitement.   Such
a speech as this will show the eloquence Shaw was capable of:

> Come, come, my daughter! dont make too much of your little
> tinpot tragedy.   What do we do here when we spend years of
> work and thought and thousands of pounds of solid cash on a
> new gun or an aerial battleship that turns out just a hairs-
> breadth wrong after all? Scrap it.   Scrap it without wasting
> another hour or another pound on it.   Well, you have made for
> yourself something that you call a morality or a religion or
> what not.   It doesnt fit the facts.   Well, scrap it.   Scrap it
> and get one that does fit.   That is what is wrong with the
> world at present.   It scraps its obsolete steam engines and
> dynamos; but it wont scrap its old prejudices and its old
> moralities and its old religions and its old political consti-
> tutions. Whats the result?   In machinery it does very well;
> but in morals and religion and politics it is working at a
> loss that brings it nearer bankruptcy every year.   Dont persist
> in that folly.   If your old religion broke down yesterday, get
> a newer and better one for tomorrow.

This is as blatantly doctrinaire as any party politician's speech,

let alone a dramatic character's speech.   One tends to wish that
it were not so baldly what it is, for example, that 'That is what
is wrong with the world at present' had been scoured out of the
first draft.   But Shaw would have been less Shaw (and Undershaft
less Undershaft) if this general diagnosis of the world's ills were
to have been diluted with more 'art' and cleaned of its didactic
grit, and so we must see what we can make of it as it stands.   We
detect the ghost of Shaw behind the speech, the ghost of a thousand
and more platforms and committee rooms and pamphlets.   T.S. Eliot
would not have approved and neither would many others who insist on
the extinguished personality of the creative artist.   We can have as
little expected Shaw to extinguish his personality as we can expect
Ireland to stop breeding revolutionists; besides, the ineffaceable
stamp of art, of painting and music, no less than of literature, is
the personality of the artist, or if not the person himself, the
person in his time always.

The ghost of Shaw may therefore be left to hover.   But perhaps
this is not the objection; perhaps it is not the ghost but what
the ghost is putting into the speaker's mouth that we object to:
with apparent justification, because Undershaft, for all his
splendid confidence, cannot be thought to be speaking whole
truths.   Three-quarter truths at most, which is also to say quarter falsehoods.   Is the ghost accordingly to be hailed before a
self-elected jury of pundits and given a fair trial before banishment?   This is what has happened to Shaw more often than bears
recounting, and yet the underlying fallacy burrows away unchecked.
This fallacy is that Undershaft's quarter falsehoods are Shaw's
whole truths and that whatever anybody else has to say in dispute
with Undershaft must be ignored as not having any ghostly authority.   Which is palpable nonsense, as a glance at the concluding
passages of the play - what, in tracing the Dionysian ritual, I
am calling the epiphany - will bear out.

With arguments such as that quoted above Undershaft slowly
wins Cusins to his side.   What, however, about Barbara?   During the
general conversation outside the high explosives shed she says very
little; by her withdrawal from the group and her silence she indicates a spirit yet undecided, yet uncommitted.   Then she and Cusins
are left alone and she opens her heart and soul to him.

It would seem that Dionysos-Undershaft has won unconditionally,
and yet this is not so.   Barbara is not the sort of girl who can be
won over unconditionally.   As Cusins and Undershaft say of her in
Act II:

CUSINS:... The power Barbara wields here - the power that
wields Barbara herself - is not Calvinism, not Presbyterianism,
not Methodism -
UNDERSHAFT: Not Greek Paganism either, eh?
CUSINS: I admit that, Barbara is quite original in her
religion.
UNDERSHAFT: (*triumphantly*) Aha! Barbara Undershaft would be.
Her inspiration comes from within herself.

There is in this girl a spirit of independence, a fervour - or even
a 'madness' - for salvation work, which not all the high explosives

in the world and not the most compelling arguments of her father
can wholly overthrow. In accepting the power of Money and Gunpowder, she accepts as well the four hundred years old tradition
of Capitalism; this will not go unchallenged, we feel, nor will
the exhortation to scrap the 'old religion' be carried out fully.
Dionysos-Undershaft may not know it, but in claiming this redoubt-
able daughter for his own he seems to me to have introduced a new
and not fully expected high explosive into the Salvation works
of Perivale St Andrew. New and yet as old as human aspiration, a
proud, free, fierce religion of life itself:

> BARBARA:... My father shall never throw it in my teeth again
> that my converts were bribed with bread. (*She is trans-*
> *figured*.) I have got rid of the bribe of bread. I have got
> rid of the bribe of heaven. Let God's work be done for its
> own sake: the work he had to create us to do because it
> cannot be done except by living men and women. When I die,
> let him be in my debt, not I in his; and let me forgive him as
> becomes a woman of my rank.
> CUSINS: Then the way of life lies through the factory of
> death?
> BARBARA: Yes, through the raising of hell to heaven and of
> man to God, through the unveiling of an eternal light in the
> Valley of the Shadow. (*Seizing him with both hands*) Oh, did
> you think my courage would never come back? did you believe
> that I was a deserter? that I, who have stood in the streets,
> and taken my people to my heart, and talked of the holiest and
> greatest things with them, could ever turn back and chatter
> foolishly to fashionable people about nothing in a drawing
> room? Never, never, never, never: Major Barbara will die
> with the colors....

'SAINT JOAN' (*)

10. 8 SHAW

> Letter, 'Bernard Shaw and Mrs. Patrick Campbell:
> Their Correspondence', ed. A. Dent, Gollancz, 1952,
> pp. 146-7

[...] Strangely enough I have never been in Orleans before, though
I have been all over the Joan of Arc country. How they canonize
her you may see from the previous postcard. I shall do a Joan
play some day, beginning with the sweeping up of the cinders and
orange peel *after* her martyrdom, and going on with Joan's arrival
in heaven. I should have God about to damn the English for their
share in her betrayal and Joan producing an end of burnt stick in
arrest of Judgment. 'What's that? Is it one of the faggots?'
says God. 'No', says Joan, 'it's what is left of the two sticks a
common English soldier tied together and gave me as I went to the
stake; for they wouldn't even give me a crucifix; and you cannot

damn the common people of England, represented by that soldier
because a poor cowardly riff raff of barons and bishops were too
futile to resist the devil.'
    That soldier is the only redeeming figure in the whole busi-
ness. English literature must be saved (by an Irishman, as
usual) from the disgrace of having nothing to show concerning
Joan except the piffling libel in Henry VI, which reminds me
that one of my scenes will be Voltaire and Shakespear running
down bye streets in heaven to avoid meeting Joan. Would you like
to play Joan and come in on horseback in armour and fight innumerable supers? [...]
(8 September 1913)

NOTE

* Shaw wrote 'Saint Joan' in 1923.

10. 9 SHAW

        Letters to the Theatre Guild, (*) New York,
        L. Langner, 'G.B.S. and the Lunatic',
        Atheneum Publishers, New York, 1963, pp. 58,
        63, 69, 74-5, 76-7

'Saint Joan' is finished except for revising and inserting stage
business. It's a star play for one woman and about twenty men.
Sybil Thorndike is to play it in London. [...]
    The scenes in 'Joan' can all be reduced to extreme simplicity.
A single pillar of the Gordon Craig type will make the cathedral.
All the Loire needs is a horizon and a few of Simonson's lanterns.
The trial scene is as easy as the cathedral. The others present
no difficulty. There should be an interval at the end of the
Loire scene and one (very short) after the trial scene, and even
that makes an interval too many: the act divisions should be
utterly disregarded.
(1923)

I read the play to Sybil Thorndike from the second set of proofs;
and the dialogue occupied exactly three hours and three minutes.
Since then I have made another and more drastic revision which has,
I think, got the last bits of dead wood out of the play, and have
certainly saved the odd three minutes. I think therefore it should
be possible to begin at 8 and finish at 11:30. The English edition
of 'Heartbreak House', uniform with the proofs just sent you, contains 110 pages, including only two specifications of scenery.
'Joan' contains seven different scenes. Compare the number of
pages and you will see that your estimate of four hours is far
over the mark.
    Simonson must not make the scenery fantastic. It may be very
simple; but it must suggest perfectly natural scenery. Joan was an

extremely real person; and the scenery should be keyed to her
reality. [...]
(3 December 1923)

I have had your cables including the one you dictated to poor
Winifred. You ought to be ashamed of yourselves for getting a
young actress into trouble with an author like that. Anyhow *I*
am ashamed of you - thoroughly. Your nerves seem to have reached
the Los Angeles level. You get such a magnificent press (considering) that it is extensively reproduced in London; and yet
you run screaming to me to say that Messrs. Broun, Corbin & Co.
want the play cut, and that you will be ruined if you don't obey.
When I urged you to have some consideration for the public in
'Methuselah' you insisted on the horror of two plays in a night,
sending around buckets of coffee and finishing at two in the
morning. Now that you can play in 3½ hours and begin at 7:30 if
you like, you want to cut the play and to tell the public that I
have cut it, and that you are beaten and that it is now quite
like the 'Garden of Allah' and 'Chu Chin Chou'. And then you ask
me to trust your judgment on the ground that you don't trust mine!
If Shubert treated me like this I would never speak to him
again. [...]
(3 January 1924)

The pictures have arrived. [...] On the whole there is nothing to
complain of, which is a pity, as I complain so well. However
lots of things are wrong; so here goes.
      In Act I the Steward should be much older than Baudricourt; and
both Baudricourt and Poulengy should be in half armor and be obviously soldiers and not merchants. This is important, as it
strikes the note of France in war time. As it is, Poulengy's coat
should not be belted. Baudricourt should be smart, a *beau sabreur*.
The Steward should not be a zany, but a respectable elderly man
whom nobody nowadays would dream of assaulting. Otherwise B's
handling of him becomes mere knockabout farce.
      In the second act Joan's hair should be bobbed; and she should
be dressed as a soldier, quite definitely masculine in contrast to
her girlish appearance in the first act. And at the end of the
act she should be in front of all the rest, in command of the
stage in the good old fashioned way from the point of view of the
audience, and not beautifully composed in the middle of the picture with all the other people turning their backs to the spectators. Why don't you carry out my directions and get my effects
instead of working for pictorial effects? As to the Dauphin I
believe his wig is wrong. His portrait shows that his hair was
completely concealed by the fashion of the time, giving him a
curiously starved and bald appearance that would be very effective
on the stage.
      The Bishop looks about right for the Inquisitor and the Inqui-
sitor for the Bishop. My effect of a very mild and silvery Inquisitor and a rather stern Bishop has been missed as far as the
make-up is concerned. The altar and candles in the middle of the

cathedral scene are feebly stagy, and do not give the effect of a
corner of a gigantic cathedral as my notion of one big pillar
would. And it leads to that up-stage effect, with a very feminine
operatic-looking Joan in the centre, which I wanted to avoid. The
drag toward the conventional is very evident; and is the last word
in operatic artificiality (an angry woman tears a thing downward
and throws it to the floor); but still, it is all very pretty in
the American way, and might have been worse. I am going to see
Charles Ricketts' plans and sketches for the London production
this afternoon; and it will be interesting to see what he makes
of them. I must break off here, but you cannot complain of the
shortness of my letter.
(1 February 1924)

[...] The play has repeated its American success here: it is
going like mad; and everyone, to my disgust, assures me it is the
best play I have ever written. Sybil Thorndike's acting and
Charles Ricketts' stage pictures and costumes have carried everything before them. I am convinced that our production knocks the
American one into a cocked hat. Why don't you come over and see
it?
     The press notices here were just like the American ones: play
too long: cut out the epilogue; magnificent play only needing
the blue pencil to be a success, etc., etc.
     Cardinal Hayes's medal [presented to Winifred Lenihan for her
performance] was a Godsend, as a press correspondent named Thomas
had just written to the French papers to say that I had [made a
laughing-stock of] Joan. The medal brained him and left him for
dead. [...]
(28 May 1924)

NOTE

*   Produced by the Theatre Guild, 'Saint Joan' was first performed
    at the Garrick Theatre in New York City on 28 December 1923 with
    Winifred Lenihan as Joan. The first production in England was
    at the New Theatre on 26 March 1924 with Sybil Thorndike as Joan.

10. 10   LUIGI PIRANDELLO

          Pirandello Distills Shaw, 'New York Times'
          (Magazine Section), 13 January 1924, pp. 1, 14

In fact, as we look carefully and deeply at this work of Shaw,
taken as a whole, we cannot help detecting in it that curious half-
humorous melancholy which is peculiar to the disillusioned idealist. Shaw has always had too keen a sense of reality not to be
aware of the conflict between it and his social and moral ideals.
The various phases of reality, as they were yesterday, as they are
today, as they will be tomorrow, come forward in the persons who

represent them before the ideal phantom of Joan (now a Saint without her knowing it). Each of these type persons justifies his
own manner of being, and confesses the sin of which he was guilty,
but in such a way as to show that he is unable really to mend his
ways - so true is it that each is today as he was yesterday, and
will be tomorrow as he is today. Joan listens to them all, but
she is not angry. She has for them just a tolerant pity. She can
only pray that the world may some time be made beautiful enough to
be a worthy abode for the saints!

   This new tolerance and pity rise from the most secret depths of
poetry that exist in Shaw. Whenever, instead of tolerating,
instead of pitying, he loses his temper at the shock of reality
against his ideals, and then, for fear of betraying his anger -
which would be bad mannered - begins to harass himself and his
hearers with the dazzling brilliancy of his paradoxes, Shaw, the
artist properly speaking, suffers more or less seriously - he
falls to the level of the jeu d'esprit which is amusing in itself,
though it irremediably spoils the work of art. I may cite in
point a passage in the second act of 'Saint Joan,' where the Arch-
bishop expatiates on the differences between fraud and miracles.
'Frauds deceive,' says he. 'An event which creates faith does not
deceive, therefore it is not a fraud but a miracle.' Such word
play is for amusement only. A work that would do something more
than amuse must always respect the deeper demands of art, and so
respecting these, the witticism is no longer a witticism but true
art.

   In none of Shaw's work that I can think of have considerations
of art been so thoroughly respected as in 'Saint Joan.' The four
acts of this drama begin, as they must begin, with Joan's request
for soldiers of Robert de Baudricourt to use in driving the
English from 'the sweet land of France.' And they end, as they
must end, with the trial and execution of Joan. Shaw calls this
play a chronicle. In fact, the drama is built up episode by episode, moment by moment, some of them rigorously particular and
free from generality - truly in the style of the chroniclers -
though usually they tend to be what I call deliberate 'construc-
tiveness.' The hens have not been laying, when suddenly they begin
to lay. The wind has long been blowing from the east, and suddenly
it begins blowing from the west. Two miracles! Then there are
other simple, naive things, such as the recognition of the 'blood
royal' in the third act, which likewise seems to be a miracle.

   But these moments are interspersed with other moments of irony
and satire, of which either the Church or the English are the victims. However, this attempt to present the chronicle inside what
is really history does not seem to me quite as happy as it was in
'Caesar and Cleopatra.' In 'Saint Joan,' history, or rather character historically conceived, weighs a bit too heavily on the
living fluid objectivity of the chronicle, and the events in the
play somehow lose that sense of the unexpected which is the breath
of true life. We know in advance where we are going to come out.
The characters, whether historical or typical, do not quite free
themselves from the fixity that history has forced upon them and
from the significant role they are to play in history.

   Joan herself, who is presented to us as a fresh creature of the

open fields, full of burning faith and self-confidence, remains
that way from the beginning to the end of the play; and she makes
a little too obvious her intention not to be reciting a historical
role and to remain that dear, frank, innocent, inspired child
that she is. Yes, Joan, as she really was in her own little
individual history, must have been much as Shaw imagined her. But
he seems to look on her once and for all, so to speak, quite
without regard for the various situations in which she will meet
life in the course of the story.

And she is kept thus simple and unilinear by the author just to
bring her airy, refreshing ingenuousness into contrast with the
artificial, sophisticated - or, as I say, 'deliberate' or 'constructed' - complexity of her accusers. There is, in other words,
something mechanical, fore-ordained, fixed, about her character.
Much more free and unobstructed in his natural impulses, much more
independent of any deliberate restraints, and accordingly much more
'living' (from my point of view) is the Chaplain, de Stogumber, the
truly admirable creation in this drama, and a personage on which
Shaw has surely expended a great deal of affectionate effort.

At a certain moment Joan's faith in her 'voices' is shaken. And
this charming little creature, hitherto steadfastly confident in
the divine inspiration which has many times saved her from death in
battle, is suddenly filled with terror at the torment awaiting her.
She says she is ready to sign the recantation of all that she has
said and done. And she does sign it. But then, on learning from
her judges that the sentence of death is only to be changed into a
sentence of life imprisonment, she seizes the document in a sudden
burst of emotion and tears it to pieces. 'Death is far better than
this!' she cries. She could never live without the free air of the
fields, the beauty of the green meadows, the warm light of the sun.
And she falls fainting into the arms of the executioners, who drag
her off to the stake.

At this moment Shaw carries his protagonists to a summit of
noble poetry with which any other author would be content; and we
may be sure that any other author would have lowered the curtain on
this scene. But Shaw cannot resist the pressure and the inspiration of the life he well knows must be surging in such circumstances in his other character - the Chaplain. He rushes on toward a
second climax of not less noble poetry, depicting with magnificent
elan the mad remorse, the hopeless penitence of Stogumber, thus
adding to our first crisis of exquisite anguish another not less
potent and overwhelming.

Rarely has George Bernard Shaw attained higher altitudes of
poetic emotion than here. There is a truly great poet in Shaw;
but this combative Anglo-Irishman is often willing to forget that
he is a poet, so interested is he in being a citizen of his country,
or a man of the twentieth century society, with a number of respectable ideas to defend, a number of sermons to preach, a number of
antagonists to rout from the intellectual battlefield. But here,
in 'Saint Joan,' the poet comes into his own again, with only a
subordinate role left, as a demanded compensation, to irony and
satire. To be sure, 'Saint Joan' has all the savor and all the
attractiveness of Shaw's witty polemical dialogue. But for all of
these keen and cutting thrusts to left and right in Shaw's usual

style of propaganda, 'Saint Joan' is a work of poetry from beginning to end.

   This play represents in marvellous fashion what, among so many
elements of negation, is the positive element, indeed the fundamental underpinning, in the character, thought and art of this
great writer - an outspoken Puritanism, which brooks no go-
betweens and no mediations between man and God; a vigorous and
independent vital energy, that frees itself restlessly and with
joyous scorn from all the stupid and burdensome shackles of
habit, routine and tradition, to conquer for itself a natural law
more consonant with the poet's own being, and therefore more
rational and more sound. Joan, in fact, cries to her judges:
'If the Church orders me to declare that all that I have done and
said, that all the visions and revelations I have had were not
from God, then that is impossible, I will not declare it for
anything in the world. What God made me do I will never go back
on; and what He has commanded, or shall command, I will not fail to
do, in spite of any man alive. That is what I mean by impossible.
And in case the Church should bid me to do anything contrary to
the command I have from God, I will not consent to it, no matter
what it may be.'

   Joan, at bottom, quite without knowing it, and still declaring
herself a faithful daughter of the Church, is a Puritan, like Shaw
himself - affirming her own life impulse, her unshakable, her even
tyrannical will to live, by accepting death itself. Joan, like
Shaw, cannot exist without a life that is free and fruitful.
When she tears up her recantation in the face of her deaf and
blind accusers, she exemplifies the basic germ of Shaw's art,
which is the germ also of his spiritual life.

10. 11 SHAW

     'Saint Joan', 'Listener', 3 June 1931, p. 947

The trial is very curious. It is not so much the trial of judges
who are speaking from the height of their position to a culprit.
The whole thing became something like a parliamentary argument, of
which she very often got the best, or the better. Now I cannot
elaborate that because my time has drawn to an end. I want only
to tell you this: that although the burning of Joan was an inexcu-
sable thing, because it was a uselessly cruel thing, the question
arises whether she was not a dangerous woman.

   Now, that question arises with almost every person of distinguished or extraordinary ability. Let us take an example from our
own times. After the late War the late Marshal Foch was asked by
somebody, 'How would Napoleon have fought this war?' Foch
answered, 'Oh! he would have fought it magnificently, superbly.
But', he said, 'what on earth should we have done with him afterwards?' Now, that question arose in Joan's case. I want to bring
it close to the present day. It is arising today in the case of a
very extraordinary man, a man whose name is Leon Trotsky. Leon
Trotsky's military exploits will probably rank with those of the

greatest commanders in future history. The history of Trotsky's
train - the railway train in which for a couple of years he practically lived while he threw back the whole forces of Europe, at a
time when the condition of his country seemed desperate - that
was a military exploit which we are too close to appreciate, but
there is no doubt whatever as to what history will say about him;
it will rank him along with the greatest commanders. But he is
just in the position of Napoleon: when the question arose what
was to be done with him afterwards, his own country, Russia,
banished him. They banished him to a place at first very much
like St. Helena, which we put Napoleon into, because we believed
it would kill him, and it did kill him. Trotsky was put in a very
unpleasant place. He is now in Turkey, under happier circumstances. But the question arises there. We are all very much
afraid of him; we dare not allow him to come to England, not so
much because we are afraid of him making war here, but because his
own country is so afraid of him that we feel that any hospitality
that we extended to him would be almost interpreted as an attack on
the Russian Government. You may think of Trotsky as being a sort
of male Saint Joan, in his day, who has not been burnt. You may
connect him, again, as I say, with Napoleon. You will have to
think it all out for yourself because I have no time here to-night
to go into it. I have already exceeded my time.

I will just give you one more thing to think about. If you
want to have an example from your own time, if you want to find
what women can feel when they suddenly find the whole power of
society marshalled against them and they have to fight it, as it
were, then read a very interesting book which has just appeared by
Miss Sylvia Pankhurst ['The Suffragette Movement', Longmans, 1931]
describing what women did in the early part of this century in
order to get the parliamentary vote. Miss Sylvia Pankhurst, like
so many other women in that movement, was tortured. In fact,
except for burning, she suffered actual physical torture which
Joan was spared. Other women suffered in that way with her. She
describes from her own experience what those women felt, and how
they did it. They were none of them exactly like Saint Joan, but
I believe every one of them did regard herself as, in a measure,
repeating the experiences of Saint Joan. Saint Joan inspired that
movement, that curious movement, which I think is within the
recollection of most of you. Think of it in that way. If you
read Miss Pankhurst, you will understand a great deal more about
the psychology of Joan, and her position at the trial, than you
will by reading the historical accounts, which are very dry.

Now, I say one thing finally. Joan was killed by the Inquisition. The Inquisition, you think, is dead. The Inquisition is
not dead. Whenever you have a form of government which cannot
deal with spiritual affairs, sooner or later you will have the
Inquisition. In England it was said there was no Inquisition.
That was not true. It was called by another name - it was called
'Star Chamber'; but you always will have a spiritual tribunal of
some kind, and unless it is an organised and recognised thing, with
a body of law behind it, it will become a secret thing, and a very
terrible thing; it will have all the worst qualities of the Inquisition without that subjection to a body of law which the

Inquisition finally had. And when in modern times you fall
behindhand with your political institutions, as we are doing, and
try to get on with a parliamentary institution which is entirely
unfitted to modern needs, you get dictatorships, as you have got
in Hungary, and in Italy, and - I need not go through the whole
list - as you may have at any moment, almost in any country,
because, as Signor Mussolini has so well said, there is a vacant
throne in almost every country in Europe; and when you get your
dictatorship you may take it from me that you will with the
greatest certainty get a secret tribunal, dealing with sedition,
with political heresy, exactly like the Inquisition.

NOTE

* Transcript of a talk broadcast by Shaw for the BBC on the 500th
  anniversary of the burning of Joan.

10. 12 MARGERY MORGAN

> 'Saint Joan', 'The Shavian Playground', Methuen,
> 1972, pp. 250-6

Cauchon's last words in the Epilogue, 'mortal eyes cannot distinguish the saint from the heretic', express the moral of the play.
From his Archimedean point, equidistant from the historical past
and the twentieth century, Shaw poses the question of whether
Joan was wrong, whether her private judgement brought good or evil
to the world. The difficulty has presented itself to the heroine
herself at her trial in subjective terms: 'What other judgement
can I judge by but my own?' Only a dialectical or dramatic mode
can contain the dangerousness of that truth. It will not solve
the problem to see the churchmen giving an entirely spurious
authority to their private judgements by identifying them with the
institution of the Church, for Joan surpasses them in identifying
hers with the will of God and the messages of the saints.
  She is, of course, innocent in the sense that the Inquisitor
recognizes, innocent through her uncorrupted instincts: she is not
self-seeking; she has a natural friendliness to all; her intentions
are good. Yet de Stogumber could be speaking for her in his words,
'I did not know what I was doing.' Such childish innocence is
dangerous in a world of power. The play was completed and performed in 1923 when the historical process Shaw (through Warwick
and Cauchon) represents Joan as initiating had reached its evolutionary climax. Cauchon's prophecies must then have had the ring
of topical comment:

> ... the Catholic Church knows only one realm, and that is the
> realm of Christ's kingdom. Divide that kingdom into nations,
> and you dethrone Christ. Dethrone Christ, and who will stand
> between our throats and the sword? The world will perish in
> a welter of war.

This is not simply the voice of the medieval Church; the intellectual attitude which saw the high medieval period as the end of
a cycle of faith and civilization giving way to the barbarism of
the modern world was currently respectable just before and after
the First World War. Yeats looked back to the beginning of the
Christian cycle itself for a parallel to the contemporary
situation:

> Odour of blood when Christ was slain
> Made all Platonic tolerance vain
> And vain all Doric discipline;

and his anticipations were symbolized in the 'rough beast' of the
Second Coming. As for Joan, Shaw's new Christ of the fifteenth
century, she stands to Cauchon as a figure of similar dark
prognostication:

> It will be a world of blood, of fury, of devastation, of each
> man striving for his own hand: in the end a world wrecked
> back into barbarism.

An interpretation of Joan as innocent fool is carried to some
extent by the pantomime conventions introduced into the play and
reasserted in the Epilogue, after lapsing in the trial scene.
The theatrical unreality of pantomime also serves to keep her in
focus as an enigma challenging the mind, never quite a tragic
heroine or a victim whose boldness is finally pathetic. The first
scene, with its blustering baron and hens that won't lay, the
nicknames, Polly and Jack and Dick the Archer, which the peasant
lass impertinently applies to Baudricourt's men, the comic abuse
('The worst, most incompetent, drivelling snivelling jibbering
jabbering idiot of a steward in France'), the cool high-
handedness of the girl with her feudal lord ('I have arranged it
all: you have only to give the order') establish the relation to
Christmas pantomime quite firmly, before the final absurd
'miracle' - 'The hens are laying like mad, sir. Five dozen eggs!'
- sets its seal on the style. Appropriately, Bluebeard himself
takes the stage in the second scene, though admittedly it is Bluebeard closer to actuality and remoter from fairy-tale than usual,
in a poise that the whole scene reflects. Joan appears here in
the usual masculine garb of the Principal Boy for the first time,
and the extent to which Shaw's characterization of her is a
refinement on the type of Jack or Dick (who grows up to play
Widow Twankey) is the more evident: her self-confidence, her
humour, her easy friendliness with all ranks, her brave attitudes
and her bossiness are rooted in the convention; and the language
she speaks ('Coom, Bluebeard! Thou canst not fool me. Where be
Dauphin?') is native to no other area. The Dauphin's clowning
supplies her with congenial company. For a moment their shared
response to the appearance and manners of the Duchess de la
Trémouille can delude us into seeing this only other female role
in the play as another female impersonation - an Ugly Sister,
perhaps:

> THE DUCHESS (*coldly*): Will you allow me to pass, please?
> JOAN (*hastily rising, and standing back*): Beg pardon, maam,
> I am sure.
> *The Duchess passes on. Joan stares after her; then whispers*
> *to the Dauphin.*
> JOAN: Be that Queen?
> CHARLES: No. She thinks she is.
> JOAN (*again staring after the Duchess*): Oo-oo-ooh! (*Her awe-*
> *struck amazement at the figure cut by the magnificently*
> *dressed lady is not wholly complimentary.*)

The epithet for la Trémouille himself follows pat, with no shift
of style: 'Who be old Gruff-and-Grum?'
   Though he never ceases to cut capers, the Dauphin merely *plays*
the fool, while being as astute as any character in the drama.
Even in Scene ii, his shrewdness penetrates further into the
complexities of an off-stage world than pantomime can usually
allow:

> I can tell you that one good treaty is worth ten good fights.
> These fighting fellows lose all on the treaties that they gain
> on the fights....

His coolly pragmatic viewpoint undercuts Joan's ecstasies even in
the Epilogue: 'You people with your heads in the sky spend all
your time trying to turn the world upside down.' History played
into Shaw's hands by letting the dogs of comedy, Charles and
Dunois (who also views Joan soberly and never sees her other than
life-size - as Hotchkiss proposes taking Mrs George for granted),
survive and prosper through the period of the Epilogue. It also
conveniently debarred Charles from the trial scene and the preparations for it, when the sense of make-believe had to be suspended for the intensity of crisis to be complete, and the
impression of Joan as a real human being required a playing-down
of the stage type. Yet these scenes substitute another clown for
the Dauphin: the Chaplain to Warwick, de Stogumber, whose absurdity modulates readily into pathos.
   Though politically they are on opposite sides, there is a
perceptible similarity between de Stogumber and Joan. Both are
innocents, country folk and patriots, out of their depth among
men of subtler, more sophisticated mind. But the Chaplain is a
representative of the common man, and Joan of the extraordinary,
'original' human being; the fault he exposes is lack of imaginative understanding, whereas she plays into her judges' hands
through the power of her imagination, the fact that she thinks in
images. Apart from this, his commonplace ignorance, prejudice and
self-righteousness, the narrow bigotry of his nationalism and
anti-Catholicism, caricature the attitudes of her more heroic
personality at the same time as they make him a figure of the
crude English philistinism which was Shaw's perpetual Aunt Sally.
By balancing the two simpletons in his design, Shaw effectively
throws into relief the questionableness of the principles Joan
represents. 'Sancta simplicitas!' is the blessing Cauchon confers
upon de Stogumber's folly and the cruelty it embraces. Her friend,

the Dauphin, is less able to contain his impatience with Joan's
self-justified fanaticism, the awkward and obstinate aspect of
original genius:

> It always comes back to the same thing. She is right; and
> everyone else is wrong.

Charles and Dunois do more than the other characters in the
play to keep Joan a natural size and unfalsified by glamour. (It
may be worth remarking that, in general type, Charles is a more
stylized version of the Shavian Caesar and Dunois a less flam-
boyant, more mature Appollodorus.) Dunois, in particular, responds to her with a liking that never disturbs his judgement, or
his sense of professional superiority. He has no doubt about how
much of the credit is due to Joan, how much to himself, and no
doubt that, when she is captured, he can do without her:

> Yes: I shall drive them out ... I have learnt my lesson,
> and taken their measure ... I have beaten them before; and
> I shall beat them again.

His freedom from infatuation enables him to foretell her fate on
reasonable grounds,and there is a Cromwellian balance that she
notably lacks in his hard, practical sense, untainted by any
superstition:

> I tell you as a soldier that God is no man's daily drudge,
> and no maid's either ... once on your feet you must fight
> with all your might and all your craft.

He is as brutal as Undershaft in his verdict on mere idealism:

> ... some day she will go ahead when she has only ten men to
> do the work of a hundred. And then she will find that God
> is on the side of the big battalions.

Under so clear and realistic a gaze, Joan's complaint that 'the
world is too wicked for me' sounds less like pride of spiritual
perfection than a sigh of naïve despair that the world is not
simple.

In the Epilogue, the *revenante* Joan can be allowed a more
sophisticated understanding of things. Her raillery of Cauchon
(who is the tragic figure of the Epilogue) - 'Still dreaming of
justice, Peter? See what justice came to with me!' - is not so
much glibly satiric of the ways of the public world as lucidly
perceptive of the truth to which this play, with its trial scene,
testifies as absolutely as 'The Doctor's Dilemma' did in its
lighter vein: that justice, if it is more than a game, is an
ideal which it is not desirable to have translated into actual
terms. The dramatic verdict of 'Saint Joan,' too, goes against
justice in favour of irony: the ability to perceive and weigh all
the issues and, if choice is compelled, to preserve a knowledge of
its provisional and limited validity. Such irony recognizes what
is admirable in the heroic nature, but won't follow it to hell.

So Charles adds his share to the 'Te Deum':

> The unpretending praise thee, because thou hast taken upon
> thyself the heroic burdens that are too heavy for them.

Yet it is part of the expansive ironic vision that it should
know its own weakness: its very lack of the direct simplicity,
the absolute commitment, which is the virtue of the saint and,
apart from which, the cynical Warwicks possess the world. For
all Shaw's conscious ingenuity in structuring the play, 'Saint
Joan' has often been found less than satisfactory by critics,
mechanical, facile, or puerile in its incidental effects; yet
the central character transcends the play as an imaginative
creation. Whereas the writing of the play was not a protracted
business, (1) the figure of Joan had long been growing in the
dramatist's consciousness as an image of his profoundest dream.
Actresses who either overplay the erotic attractiveness of
Joan, or suppress it altogether, fail in the role. For Shaw's
view fluctuates and, though it is faint and subtle and shouldn't
protrude on consciousness at all, the feminine erotic quality
faintly colours the figure. (It may be worth comparing Shakespeare's Viola who, like Joan, appears in woman's clothing only
briefly at the beginning of the play - and was, of course, a
more thoroughly androgynous figure in Shakespeare's theatre than
in the theatre of Shaw's day.) The kind of appeal this has for
audiences and readers recalls the appeal of Dick Dudgeon, in
'The Devil's Disciple', where Shaw utilized the glamour of one
type of romatic hero as a vehicle for the serious revision of
values. Joan's charm depends on her equal rejection of the
Victorian womanly ideal and the identity of fashionable, elegant
woman-of-the-world type, or *femme fatale* as it appears to others
than men-of-the-world, as Victorian popular instinct had rejected
them in its cult of the Principal Boy, more vulgar, even sexually
more vital and less insipid that the romantic heroine of pantomime. Joan contains too much that is redolent of the popular
stage and indicative of the sturdy peasant for the neurotic
associations of the New Woman to corrode her image, though play
and Preface accept the likelihood that the historical soldier-
girl's mission was fired to some extent by abnormal sexuality.
The relevance of the Court's questions about her male attire
is endorsed by Joan's own reference to the breach-of-promise
case ('I never promised him. I am a soldier: I do not want to be
thought of as a woman. I will not dress as a woman'), by her
assertion that she has only a soldier's responsiveness to children
and, with strongest emphasis from the inventive dramatist himself,
by her summing up in the Epilogue, that if she *had* been a man, 'I
should not have bothered you all so much then.' Shaw was not
intent on a realistic psychological study and, in fact, gives
shifting impressions even of Joan's sexual nature that tend away
from realism. If she appears sometimes asexual, still Baudricourt is able to suspect, at the start of the play, that Bertrand
de Poulengy has a sexual interest in her and, though she is 'no
beauty', she is deliberately associated with Dunois, 'the brave
Dunois, the handsome Dunois, the wonderful invincible Dunois, the

darling of all the ladies, the beautiful bastard', who is cut out
to be the romantic lead and lends her something of his own more
conventional charm.   In his company she appears unmistakably the
most feminine creature in the play's sexual spectrum, perhaps
something of a daughter-figure; though even here Shaw manages a
sleight-of-hand with the lyrical scene on the banks of the Loire:
there is a slight but definite touch of the troubadour about
Dunois, as the blue flash of the kingfisher conspires to suggest
that the coming of Joan to him, despite the disguise of her
armour and bobbed hair and country bourgeois manner, has some
quality of a visitation by the Virgin to her knight.   'Mary in
the blue snood, kingfisher color' is very weak poetry, and the
whole scene verges perilously on whimsy, so that only its brevity
in the playing can save it; but the conception is evident, and the
kingfisher as a traditional symbol of Christ (as it is used by
G.M. Hopkins) becomes an attribute of the androgynous Shavian
saint.[...]
   Certainly Joan is a figure of the exploring spirit, single and
free, not nurse, protector and conserver of life.   Shaw associates her with the air ('head in the sky'), with flight ('Are you
afraid I will fly away?'), with freedom on the hills, in the light
and the wind.   The similarity between Joan's impulse towards such
freedom and Barbara Undershaft's cry for the wings of a dove is
significant: both are ideal figures, as well as idealists who
need to work in partnership with practical men and in conditions
of practical necessity.   Joan's final cry marks her as an impossibilist, a utopian:

   O God that madest this beautiful earth, when will it be ready
   to receive Thy saints?   How long, O Lord, how long?

It is a formal, rhetorical close, the last flourish of the work of
art; but it also marks the dramatist's release from the strain of
maintaining throughout the play a necessary intellectual poise,
committed in no direction, not even to irony.   [...]

NOTE

1   A sign of careless haste in the writing of the play is the
    occurrence at least three times in the text of the same
    rational explanation of the French failure in warfare before
    Joan's coming and success after: Joan herself makes the neces-
    sary criticism in the first scene; Dunois explains the matter
    to her in the fifth, only to have her explain it back to him
    a few moments later.

PIRANDELLO:
'SIX CHARACTERS
IN SEARCH OF AN AUTHOR'

11. 1 PIRANDELLO

Preface (1925), trans. E. Bentley, 'Naked Masks:
Five Plays by Luigi Pirandello', Dutton, New York,
1957, pp. 366-75

[...] 'Why not,' I said to myself, 'present this highly strange fact
of an author who refuses to let some of his characters live though
they have been born in his fantasy, and the fact that these
characters, having by now life in their veins, do not resign
themselves to remaining excluded from the world of art? They are
detached from me; live on their own; have acquired voice and
movement; have by themselves - in this struggle for existence
that they have had to wage with me - become dramatic characters,
characters that can move and talk on their own initiative; already
see themselves as such; have learned to defend themselves against
me; will even know how to defend themselves against others. And
so let them go where dramatic characters do go to have life: on a
stage. And let us see what will happen.'
    That's what I did. And, naturally, the result was what it had
to be: a mixture of tragic and comic, fantastic and realistic, in
a humorous situation that was quite new and infinitely complex, a
drama which is conveyed by means of the characters, who carry it
within them and suffer it, a drama, breathing, speaking, self-
propelled, which seeks at all costs to find the means of its own
presentation; and the comedy of the vain attempt at an improvised
realization of the drama on stage. First, the surprise of the poor
actors in a theatrical company rehearsing a play by day on a bare
stage (no scenery, no flats). Surprise and incredulity at the
sight of the six characters announcing themselves as such in search
of an author. Then, immediately afterwards, through that sudden
fainting fit of the Mother veiled in black, their instinctive
interest in the drama of which they catch a glimpse in her and in
the other members of the strange family, an obscure, ambiguous
drama, coming about so unexpectedly on a stage that is empty and
unprepared to receive it. And gradually the growth of this

interest to the bursting forth of the contrasting passions of
Father, of Step-Daughter, of Son, of that poor Mother, passions
seeking, as I said, to overwhelm each other with a tragic,
lacerating fury.

And here is the universal meaning at first vainly sought in
the six characters, now that, going on stage of their own accord,
they succeed in finding it within themselves in the excitement of
the desperate struggle which each wages against the other and all
wage against the Manager and the actors, who do not understand
them.

Without wanting to, without knowing it, in the strife of their
bedevilled souls, each of them, defending himself against the
accusations of the others, expresses as his own living passion and
torment the passion and torment which for so many years have been
the pangs of my spirit: the deceit of mutual understanding
irremediably founded on the empty abstraction of the words, the
multiple personality of everyone corresponding to the possibilities of being to be found in each of us, and finally the inherent
tragic conflict between life (which is always moving and changing)
and form (which fixes it, immutable).

Two above all among the six characters, the Father and the
Step-Daughter, speak of that outrageous unalterable fixity of
their form in which he and she see their essential nature expressed
permanently and immutably, a nature that for one means punishment
and for the other revenge; and they defend it against the facti-
tious affectations and unaware volatility of the actors, and they
try to impose it on the vulgar Manager who would like to change it
and adapt it to the so-called exigencies of the theatre.

If the six characters don't all seem to exist on the same
plane, it is not because some are figures of first rank and others
of the second, that is, some are main characters and others minor
ones - the elementary perspective necessary to all scenic or narrative art - nor is it that any are not completely created - for
their purpose. They are all six at the same point of artistic
realization and on the same level of reality, which is the fantastic level of the whole play. Except that the Father, the Step-
Daughter, and also the Son are realized as mind; the Mother as
nature; the Boy as a presence watching and performing a gesture
and the Baby unaware of it all. This fact creates among them a
perspective of a new sort. Unconsciously I had had the impression that some of them needed to be fully realized (artistically
speaking), others less so, and others merely sketched in as
elements in a narrative or presentational sequence: the most
alive, the most completely created, are the Father and the Step-
Daughter who naturally stand out more and lead the way, dragging
themselves along beside the almost dead weight of the others -
first, the Son, holding back; second, the Mother, like a victim
resigned to her fate, between the two children who have hardly any
substance beyond their appearance and who need to be led by the
hand.

And actually! actually they had each to appear in that stage of
creation which they had attained in the author's fantasy at the
moment when he wished to drive them away.

If I now think about these things, about having intuited that

[handwritten marginal note:] The various beings of the Step-daughter vengeful yet vulnerable damaged + damaging

necessity, having unconsciously found the way to resolve it by
means of a new perspective, and about the way in which I actually
obtained it, they seem like miracles. The fact is that the play
was really conceived in one of those spontaneous illuminations of
the fantasy when by a miracle all the elements of the mind answer
to each other's call and work in divine accord. No human brain,
working 'in the cold,' however stirred up it might be, could ever
have succeeded in penetrating far enough, could ever have been in
a position to satisfy all the exigencies of the play's form.
Therefore the reasons which I will give to clarify the values of
the play must not be thought of as intentions that I conceived
beforehand when I prepared myself for the job and which I now
undertake to defend, but only as discoveries which I have been
able to make afterwards in tranquillity.

I wanted to present six characters seeking an author. Their
play does not manage to get presented - precisely because the
author whom they seek is missing. Instead is presented the comedy
of their vain attempt with all that it contains of tragedy by
virtue of the fact that the six characters have been rejected.

But can one present a character while rejecting him? Obviously,
to present him one needs, on the contrary, to receive him into
one's fantasy before one can express him. And I have actually
accepted and realized the six characters: I have, however,
accepted and realized them as rejected: in search of *another*
author.

What have I rejected of them? Not themselves, obviously, but
their drama, which doubtless is what interests them above all but
which did not interest me - for the reasons already indicated.

And what is it, for a character - his drama?

Every creature of fantasy and art, in order to exist, must have
his drama, that is, a drama in which he may be a character and for
which he *is* a character. This drama is the character's *raison
d'être,* his vital function, necessary for his existence.

In these six, then, I have accepted the 'being' without the
reason for being. I have taken the organism and entrusted to it,
not its own proper function, but another more complex function
into which its own function entered, if at all, only as a datum.
A terrible and desperate situation especially for the two - Father
and Step-Daughter - who more than the others crave life and more
than the others feel themselves to be characters, that is, absolutely need a drama and therefore their own drama - the only one
which they can envisage for themselves yet which meantime they
see rejected: an 'impossible' situation from which they feel they
must escape at whatever cost; it is a matter of life and death.
True, I have given them another *raison d'être,* another function:
precisely that 'impossible' situation, the drama of being in
search of an author and rejected. But that this should be a *raison
d'être,* that it should have become their real function, that it
should be necessary, that it should suffice, they can hardly suppose; for they have a life of their own. If someone were to tell
them, they wouldn't believe him. It is not possible to believe
that the sole reason for our living should lie in a torment that
seems to us unjust and inexplicable.

I cannot imagine, therefore, why the charge was brought against

me that the character of the Father was not what it should have
been because it stepped out of its quality and position as a
character and invaded at times the author's province and took it
over. I who understand those who don't quite understand me see
that the charge derives from the fact that the character expresses
and makes his own a torment of spirit which is recognized as mine.
Which is entirely natural and of absolutely no significance.
Aside from the fact that this torment of spirit in the character
of the Father derives from causes, and is suffered and lived for
reasons, that have nothing to do with the drama of my personal
experience, a fact which alone removes all substance from the
criticism, I want to make it clear that the inherent torment of
my spirit is one thing, a torment which I can legitimately - provided that it be organic - reflect in a character, and that the
activity of my spirit as revealed in the realized work, the activity that succeeds in forming a drama out of the six characters in
search of an author is another thing. If the Father participated
in this latter activity, if he competed in forming the drama of
the six characters without an author, then and only then would it
by all means be justified to say that he was at times the author
himself and therefore not the man he should be. But the Father
suffers and does not create his existence as a character in search
of an author. He suffers it as an inexplicable fatality and as a
situation which he tries with all his powers to rebel against,
which he tries to remedy: hence it is that he is a character in
search of an author and nothing more, even if he expresses as his
own the torment of my spirit. If he, so to speak, assumed some of
the author's responsibilities, the fatality would be completely
explained. He would, that is to say, see himself accepted, if
only as a rejected character, accepted in the poet's heart of
hearts, and he would no longer have any reason to suffer the despair of not finding someone to construct and affirm his life as a
character. I mean that he would quite willingly accept the *raison
d'être* which the author gives him and without regrets would forgo
his own, throwing over the Manager and the actors to whom in fact
he runs as his only recourse.

    There is one character, that of the Mother, who on the other
hand does not care about being alive (considering being alive as
an end in itself). She hasn't the least suspicion that she is *not*
alive. It has never occurred to her to ask how and why and in
what manner she lives. In short, she is not aware of being a
character, inasmuch as she is never, even for a moment, detached
from her role. She doesn't know she has a role.

    This makes her perfectly organic. Indeed, her role of Mother
does not of itself, in its natural essence, embrace mental activity. And she does not exist as a mind. She lives in an endless
continuum of feeling, and therefore she cannot acquire awareness
of her life - that is, of her existence as a character. But with
all this, even she, in her own way and for her own ends, seeks an
author, and at a certain stage seems happy to have been brought
before the Manager. Because she hopes to take life from him, perhaps? No: because she hopes the Manager will have her present a
scene with the Son in which she would put so much of her own life.
But it is a scene which does not exist, which never has and never

could take place. So unaware is she of being a character, that
is, of the life that is possible to her, all fixed and determined, moment by moment, in every action, every phrase.

She appears on stage with the other characters but without
understanding what the others make her do. Obviously, she
imagines that the itch for life with which the husband and the
daughter are afflicted and for which she herself is to be found
on stage is no more than one of the usual incomprehensible extravagances of this man who is both tortured and torturer and -
horrible, most horrible - a new equivocal rebellion on the part
of that poor erring girl. The Mother is completely passive.
The events of her own life and the values they assume in her
eyes, her very character, are all things which are 'said' by the
others and which she only once contradicts, and that because the
maternal instinct rises up and rebels within her to make it clear
that she didn't at all wish to abandon either the son or the husband: the Son was taken from her and the husband forced her to
abandon him. She is only correcting data; she explains and knows
nothing.

In short, she is nature. Nature fixed in the figure of a
mother.

This character gave me a satisfaction of a new sort, not to be
ignored. Nearly all my critics, instead of defining her, after
their habit, as 'unhuman' - which seems to be the peculiar and
incorrigible characteristic of all my creatures without exception -
had the goodness to note 'with real pleasure' that at last a *very
human* figure had emerged from my fantasy. I explain this praise
to myself in the following way: since my poor Mother is entirely
limited to the natural attitude of a Mother with no possibility of
free mental activity, being, that is, little more than a lump of
flesh completely alive in all its functions - procreation, lacta-
tion, caring for and loving its young - without any need therefore
of exercising her brain, she realizes in her person the true and
complete 'human type.' That must be how it is, since in a human
organism nothing seems more superfluous than the mind.

But the critics have tried to get rid of the Mother with this
praise without bothering to penetrate the nucleus of poetic values
which the character in the play represents. A very human figure,
certainly, because mindless, that is, unaware of being what she is
or not caring to explain it to herself. But not knowing that she
is a character doesn't prevent her from being one. That is her
drama in my play. And the most living expression of it comes
spurting out in her cry to the Manager who wants her to think all
these things have happened already and therefore cannot now be a
reason for renewed lamentations: 'No, it's happening now, it's
happening always! My torture is not a pretence, signore! I am
alive and present, always, in every moment of my torture: it is
renewed, alive and present, always!' This she *feels,* without
being conscious of it, and feels it therefore as something inexplicable: but she feels it so terribly that she doesn't think it
can be something to explain either to herself or to others. She
feels it and that is that. She feels it as pain, and this pain is
immediate; she cries it out. Thus she reflects the growing fixity
of life in a form - the same thing, which in another way, tortures

the Father and the Step-Daughter. In them, mind. In her, nature.
The mind rebels and, as best it may, seeks an advantage; nature,
if not aroused by sensory stimuli, weeps.

Conflict between life-in-movement and form is the inexorable
condition not only of the mental but also of the physical order.
The life which in order to exist has become fixed in our corporeal
form little by little kills that form. The tears of a nature thus
fixed lament the irreparable, continuous aging of our bodies.
Hence, the tears of the Mother are passive and perpetual.
Revealed in three faces, made significant in three distinct and
simultaneous dramas, this inherent conflict finds in the play its
most complete expression. More: the Mother declares also the
particular value of artistic form - a form which does not delimit
or destroy its own life and which life does not consume - in her
cry to the Manager. If the Father and Step-Daughter began their
scene a hundred thousand times in succession, always at the
appointed moment, at the instant when the life of the work of art
must be expressed with that cry, it would always be heard,
unaltered and unalterable in its form, not as a mechanical repetition, not as a return determined by external necessities, but on
the contrary, alive every time and as new, suddenly born *thus
forever!* embalmed alive in its incorruptible form. Hence, always,
as we open the book, we shall find Francesca alive and confessing
to Dante her sweet sin, and if we turn to the passage a hundred
thousand times in succession, a hundred thousand times in succession Francesca will speak her words, never repeating them mecha-
nically, but saying them as though each time were the first time
with such living and sudden passion that Dante every time will
turn faint. All that lives, by the fact of living, has a form,
and by the same token must die - except the work of art which
lives forever in so far as it *is* form.

The birth of a creature of human fantasy, a birth which is a
step across the threshold between nothing and eternity, can also
happen suddenly, occasioned by some necessity. An imagined drama
needs a character who does or says a certain necessary thing;
accordingly this character is born and is precisely what he had
to be. In this way Madame Pace is born among the six characters
and seems a miracle, even a trick, realistically portrayed on the
stage. It is no trick. The birth is real. The new character is
alive not because she was alive already but because she is now
happily born as is required by the fact of her being a character
- she is obliged to be as she is. There is a break here, a sudden
change in the level of reality of the scene, because a character
can be born in this way only in the poet's fancy and not on the
boards of a stage. Without anyone's noticing it, I have all of
a sudden changed the scene: I have gathered it up again into my
own fantasy without removing it from the spectator's eyes. That
is, I have shown them, instead of the stage, my own fantasy in the
act of creating - my own fantasy in the form of this same stage.
The sudden and uncontrollable changing of a visual phenomenon from
one level of reality to another is a miracle comparable to those
of the saint who sets his own statue in motion: it is neither
wood nor stone at such a moment. But the miracle is not arbitrary. The stage - a stage which accepts the fantastic reality of

the six characters - is no fixed, immutable datum. Nothing in this
play exists as given and preconceived. Everything is in the
making, is in motion, is a sudden experiment: even the place in
which this unformed life, reaching after its own form, changes and
changes again contrives to shift position organically. The level
of reality changes. When I had the idea of bringing Madame Pace
to birth right there on the stage, I felt I could do it and I did
it. Had I noticed that this birth was unhinging and silently,
unnoticed, in a second, giving another shape, another reality to my
scene, I certainly wouldn't have brought it about. I would have
been afraid of the apparent lack of logic. And I would have committed an ill-omened assault on the beauty of my work. The fervor
of my mind saved me from doing so. For, despite appearances, with
their specious logic, this fantastic birth is sustained by a real
necessity in mysterious, organic relation with the whole life of
the work.

That someone now tells me it hasn't all the value it could have
because its expression is not constructed but chaotic, because it
smacks of romanticism, makes me smile.

I understand why this observation was made to me: because in
this work of mine the presentation of the drama in which the six
characters are involved appears tumultuous and never proceeds in
an orderly manner. There is no logical development, no concatenation of the events. Very true. Had I hunted it with a lamp I
couldn't have found a more disordered, crazy, arbitrary, complicated, in short, romantic way of presenting 'the drama in which
the six characters are involved.' Very true. But I have not presented that drama. I have presented another - and I won't undertake to say again what! - in which, among the many fine things
that everyone, according to his tastes, can find, there is a discreet satire on romantic procedures: in the six characters thus
excited to the point where they stifle themselves in the roles
which each of them plays in a certain drama while I present them
as characters in another play which they don't know and don't suspect the existence of, so that this inflammation of their passions
- which belongs to the realm of romantic procedures - is humor-
ously 'placed,' located in the void. And the drama of the six
characters presented not as it would have been organized by my
fantasy had it been accepted but in this way, as a rejected drama,
could not exist in the work except as a 'situation,' with some
little development, and could not come out except in indications,
stormily, disorderedly, in violent foreshortenings, in a chaotic
manner: continually interrupted, sidetracked, contradicted (by
one of its characters), denied, and (by two others) not even
seen.

There is a character indeed - he who denies the drama which
makes him a character, the Son - who draws all his importance and
value from being a character not of the comedy in the making -
which as such hardly appears - but from the presentation that I
made of it. In short, he is the only one who lives solely as 'a
character in search of an author' - inasmuch as the author he seeks
is not a dramatic author. Even this could not be otherwise. The
character's attitude is an organic product of my conception, and it
is logical that in the situation it should produce greater confusion

and disorder and another element of romantic contrast.

But I had precisely to *present* this organic and natural chaos.
And to present a chaos is not at all to present chaotically, that
is, romantically. That my presentation is the reverse of confused,
that it is quite simple, clear, and orderly, is proved by the
clarity which the intrigue, the characters, the fantastic and
realistic, dramatic and comic levels of the work have had for
every public in the world and by the way in which, for those
with more searching vision, the unusual values enclosed within it
come out.

Great is the confusion of tongues among men if criticisms thus
made find words for their expression. No less great than this confusion is the intimate law of order which, obeyed in all points,
makes this work of mine classical and typical and at its catastro-
phic close forbids the use of words. Though the audience eventually understands that one does not create life by artifice and
that the drama of the six characters cannot be presented without
an author to give them value with his spirit, the Manager remains
vulgarly anxious to know how the thing turned out, and the
'ending' is remembered by the Son in its sequence of actual moments,
but without any sense and therefore not needing a human voice for
its expression. It happens stupidly, uselessly, with the going-off
of a mechanical weapon on stage. It breaks up and disperses the
sterile experiment of the characters and the actors, which has
apparently been made without the assistance of the poet.

The poet, unknown to them, as if looking on at a distance during
the whole period of the experiment, was at the same time busy creating - with it and of it - his own play.

11. 2 ROBERT BRUSTEIN

Luigi Pirandello, 'The Theatre of Revolt',
Methuen, 1965, pp. 310-16

The relationships between the fictional characters and the living
actors become exceedingly complex; and the conflict of the play,
as Francis Fergusson has perceived, proceeds on several planes of
discourse. On the one hand, the characters create friction with
the theatre people who first disbelieve their story, then find it
too squalid for the stage, and finally travesty it in the act of
imitation. On the other hand, the characters struggle among
themselves, for they detest each other, and are bound together in
mutual hatred. As the drama of the characters is interrupted by
the comedy of the actors, and the two parallel conflicts begin to
grate, the tragi-comic alternations create an atmosphere of the
grotesque. The characters, furthermore, quarrel among themselves
over the details of their story. And the first act is almost entirely taken up with trying to determine the vague outlines of this
'historical' narrative.

For the author has only completed two scenes of the drama: one
in Madame Pace's dress shop, the other in the Father's garden.
The rest, conceived but never written down, is therefore open to

interpretation by the characters. In brief, the written scenes
are form (fixed and immutable), while the unwritten background
material is life (fluid and changing). Together, these elements
constitute the 'book,' both form and life, which are the constituents of the characters themselves, and can only be learned from
them. Here, in Pirandello's mind, is a statue that moves; his
fictional creations have developed an existence of their own.
Except for the Mother, who is unaware she is a 'character,' and
the Boy and the Child, both of whom are mute, the characters
possess a reflective life beyond the form their author gave them.
In typical Pirandellian manner, they both suffer and think about
their suffering; they both perform and see themselves performing,
as in a mirror. Immobilized in written roles, caught up in an
action which is 'renewed, alive, and present, always!' they are
also cursed with hindsight and, therefore, know exactly what form
their purgatory will take. [...]
  The second act is devoted to the scene in Madame Pace's dress
shop, which is performed by the characters involved, and then by
the actors who take their parts. For the actors, who 'play at
being serious,' the performance is a game, but for the characters,
who are in deadly earnest, it is a compulsion: their drama is
their lives. Thus, while the Father and the Stepdaughter want to
play the scene, the one to expunge his guilt and remorse, the other
to shame the Father, the Mother adamantly refuses to play it, in
order to protect their privacy and hide their disgrace. But none
of them really has a choice - the scene is already determined.
When the Manager puts together some makeshift scenery, and a sev-
enth character, Madame Pace, materializes, 'attracted by the very
articles of her trade' and whispering instructions to the Step-
daughter, the Father and the Stepdaughter thereupon proceed to
reenact the origin of their shame and torment.
  It is this scene which is altered, censored, and parodied by
the actors in a manner which reverberates with Pirandello's shrill
animus against the stage. The function of the actors, according
to the Father, is to lend their shapes 'to living beings more
alive than those who breathe and wear clothes: being less real
perhaps, but truer!' But although these 'living beings' cannot
breathe without the theatre, the theatre makes them even less real
than they are, and much less true. 'Truth up to a certain point,
but no further,' cries the Manager, when confronted with a scene
too violent and strong. He is concerned over the sensibilities of
the critics and the audience: the limitations of the theatre are
those of a society which will not face an unpleasant reality. The
vanity of the star performer, the expediency of the designer, the
commercial-mindedness of the director, the timidity of the spectator - all throw a vast shadow between the author's intention and
the theatre's execution, a shadow which lengthens in the artificiality of the theatrical occasion.
  Still, it is not just that the theatre scants its possibilities;
in a deeper sense, it is incapable of realizing the author's vision
or capturing the feel of reality. Madam Pace's whispers are
inaudible, because 'these aren't matters which can be shouted at
the top of one's voice' - private conversations are none of the
spectator's business. Similarly, the actor is unable to penetrate

the secret heart of a character, because it is as elusive as a
human being's identity. And dialogue is an added block to understanding:

> But don't you see that the whole trouble lies here. In words,
> words [cries the Father]. Each one of us has within him a
> whole world of things, each man of us his own special world.
> And how can we ever come to an understanding if I put in the
> words I utter the sense and value of things as I see them;
> while you who listen to me must inevitably translate them
> according to the conception of things each one of you has
> within himself. We think we understand each other, but we
> never do.

Like Henry IV, each man stands like a beggar before the locked door
of others, and words make the lock secure. Both unwilling and
unable to overcome this obstacle, the Manager transforms the sordid,
semi-incestuous happenings in the dress shop into a romantic and
sentimental love scene between the Leading Man and the Leading Lady.
And it is at this point that the Father understands how the author
came to abandon them - in a fit of disgust over the conventional
theatre.
    Still, if the second act embodies Pirandello's satire on the
stage, the third act embodies his conviction that theatrical art is
more 'real' than life. The Father has already accused the Manager
of trying to destroy 'in the name of a vulgar, commonplace sense of
truth, this reality which comes to birth attracted and formed by
the magic of the stage itself.' Now he proceeds to show how the
reality of the characters is not only deeper than that of actors,
but also deeper than that of living persons. As the Father tells
the skeptical Manager, a character in fiction knows who he is; he
possesses a 'life of his own'; his world is fixed - and for these
reasons, he is 'somebody.' But a human being - the Manager, for
example - 'may very well be "nobody."'

> Our reality doesn't change! It can't change! It can't be
> other than what it is, because it is fixed forever. It's
> terrible. Ours is an immutable reality which should make
> you shudder when you approach us if you are really conscious
> of the fact that your reality is a mere transitory and fleeting
> illusion, taking this form today and that tomorrow, according
> to your conditions, according to your will, your sentiments,
> which in turn are controlled by an intellect that shows them to
> you today in one manner and tomorrow ... who knows how? ...
> Illusions of reality represented in this fatuous comedy of life
> that never ends ...

The arguments are by now familiar and it is difficult not to share
some of the Manager's impatience with the Father's perpetual, and
rather windy, 'philosophizing.' But the cerebrations of the character have been carefully motivated, and it is the Father himself
who justifies them: 'For man never reasons so much or becomes so
introspective as when he suffers; since he is anxious to get at the
cause of his sufferings, to learn who produced them, and whether it

is just or unjust that he should have to bear them.' The Father's
sufferings have, Hamlet-like, intensified his introspective tendencies, just as the historical line of the play has intensified
its philosophical ramifications. The staple of the argument tends
towards verbosity, but it opens the play out of the theatre, and
into the theatre of existence itself. [...]

But the suicide has created pandemonium in the theatre. The Boy
is lying lifeless on the ground. Is he really dead, or is the
suicide merely pretence? 'Reality, sir, reality,' insists the
Father, as the actors carry the Boy's body off the stage. Bewil-
dered by this crosspatch of apparent realities and real appearances, the Manager can only throw up his hands in disgust, and on
this note of dissonance and irresolution, the curtain falls. The
ending of the play, however, suggests another reason why Pirandello
left the 'historical' action unfinished: it is too operatic to be
convincing. But by enclosing this action within the frame of the
theatre, he has created a probing philosophical drama about the
artifice of the stage, the artifice of art, and the artifice of
reality in generally suspenseful and exciting rhythms.

Pirandello's most original achievement in his experimental plays,
then, is the dramatization of the very act of creation. If he has
not made a statue that moves, he has made a statue which is the
living signature of the artist, being both his product and his
process. The concept of the face and the mask has become the basis
for a totally new relationship between the artist and his work.
Thus, Pirandello completes that process of Romantic internalizing
begun by Ibsen and Strindberg. Ibsen, for all his idealization of
personality, still believed in an external reality available to all,
and so did Chekhov, Brecht, and Shaw. Strindberg had more doubts
about this reality, but believed it could be partially perceived by
the inspired poet and seer. For Pirandello, however, objective
reality has become virtually inaccessible, and all one can be sure
of is the illusion-making faculty of the subjective mind. After
Pirandello, no dramatist has been able to write with quite the same
certainty as before. In Pirandello's plays, the messianic impulse
spends itself, before it even fully develops, in doubts, uncertain-
ties, and confusions.

BRECHT: 'MOTHER COURAGE' AND 'GALILEO'

'MOTHER COURAGE'

12. 1 BRECHT

> The Curtains, 'Poems 1913-1956', ed. J. Willett
> and R. Manheim, Eyre Methuen, 1976, p.425

On the big curtain paint the cantankerous
Peace dove of my brother Picasso. Behind it
Stretch the wire rope and hang
My lightly fluttering half curtains
Which cross like two waves of foam to make
The working woman handing out pamphlets
And the recanting Galileo both disappear.
Following the change of plays they can be
Of rough linen or of silk
Or of white leather or of red, and so on.
Only don't make them too dark, for on them
You must project the titles of the following
Incidents, for the sake of tension and that
The right thing may be expected. And please make
My curtain half-height, don't block the stage off.
Leaning back, let the spectator
Notice the busy preparations being so
Ingeniously made for him, a tin moon is
Seen swinging down, a shingle roof
Is carried in; don't show him too much
But show something. And let him observe
That this is not magic but
Work, my friends.

12. 2   BRECHT

Weigel's Props, 'Poems 1913-1956',ed. J. Willett
and R. Manheim, Eyre Methuen, 1976, pp. 427-8

Just as the millet farmer picks out for his trial plot
The heaviest seeds and the poet
The exact words for his verse so
She selects the objects to accompany
Her characters across the stage. The pewter spoon
Which Courage sticks
In the lapel of her Mongolian jacket, the party card
For warm-hearted Vlasova and the fishing net
For the other, Spanish mother or the bronze bowl
For dust-gathering Antigone. Impossible to confuse
The split bag which the working woman carries
For her son's leaflets, with the moneybag
Of the keen tradeswoman. Each item
In her stock is hand picked: straps and belts
Pewter boxes and ammunition pouches; hand picked too
The chicken and the stick which at the end
The old woman twists through the draw-rope
The Basque woman's board on which she bakes her bread
And the Greek woman's board of shame, strapped to her back
With holes for her hands to stick through, the Russian's
Jar of lard, so small in the policeman's hand; all
Selected for age, function and beauty
By the eyes of the knowing
The hands of the bread-baking, net-weaving
Soup-cooking connoisseur
Of reality.

12. 3   BRECHT

Notes to 'Mother Courage and her Children',
trans. E. Bentley and H. Schmidt, 'Encore',
12 (3), 1965, pp. 5-10, 18, 22, 26-7, 29, 42, 47-50

MODELS

If life goes on in our ruined cities after the war, it is a different life. It is the life of different or at least of differently composed groups. And it is inhibited and guided by the new
environment whose new aspect is the state of destruction. Where
the great piles of rubble lie, there too are the priceless sub-
structures, all the canals and the network of gas and electricity.
Even the undamaged large building is affected by the half-destroyed
one and by the rubble in the midst of which it stands, and may
even be an obstacle to new planning. Provisional structures must
be erected, and there is the danger that they might become permanent. Art reflects all this; ways of thinking are part and parcel

of ways of life. As far as the theatre is concerned, we throw our
Models into the gap. They will immediately be resisted by the
defenders of the Old, of routine that pretends to be experience,
and of convention that pretends to be free creative genius. And
the Models will be misused by those who accept them and have not
learned how to handle them. Intended to make things easier, they
are not easy to handle. Moreover, they are not made to exclude
thought, but to inspire thought; they are not made to replace
artistic creativity, but to compel it.

As a beginning, one need only imagine that the information concerning certain events given in the text - in this case the adventures and losses of Mother Courage - had been amended somewhat,
that one has found out, in addition, that the woman was sitting
next to her dumb daughter when they brought before her her dead
son, etc. These are points of information, let us say, that a
painter may obtain for his presentation of a historic event by
questioning eye-witnesses. Thereafter he may still change this or
that, as it may for some reason appear advisable. Before having
reached a very high level of inspired and imaginative copying - or
making - of Models, one should not copy too much. The 'mask' of
the cook, the costume of Courage and the like, need not be imitated. One should not squeeze the last ounce from the Model. [...]

When studying the following remarks, consisting of a number of
thoughts and ideas conceived while rehearsing a play, one should -
when faced with certain solutions to problems - recognise primarily the problems.

MUSIC

Paul Dessau's music for 'Mother Courage' does not enter the ear
smoothly; as in the matter of stage design, there remained something for the audience to do: the spectator's ear had to unite
voice and melody. Art is no land of Cockaigne. In order to switch
to music, to redirect the spectator's attention to music, we
lowered a music emblem from the flies, consisting of a trumpet,
a drum, a flag, and lighted spherical lamps, whenever a song
occurred that did not come directly out of the action, or, if it
did, remained outside it. A delicate and playful thing, lovely
to look at, even though seedy and torn in the 9th scene. To some,
it was a mere knick-knack, and unrealistic. However, one should
not be too severe with the playful element in theatre - as long as
it does not run riot. Moreover, it was not simply unrealistic, in
that it lifted music out of the real action; it served us to make
visible the change to a different aesthetic realm, that of music;
the impression one gained thereby was not the erroneous one that
the songs 'grew out of the action', but the correct one, that they
were inserted there. Whoever is against this effect resists the
episodic, the 'inorganic', the method of montage, mainly because he
can't bear to have illusion destroyed. He should not protest
against the music emblem but rather against the way the musical
pieces are arranged within the structure of the play, as inserts.

The musicians sat in a box near the stage - a position which
made their presentations small concerts. Independent contributions

at appropriate places in the play. The box was connected to the
back-stage so that the musicians could go back in case there were
signals to be sounded or music occurred within the action.

We began with the overture to set the stage for the confusion
of wartime, somewhat thinly - there were but four musicians - but
not without a certain festivity.

STAGE DESIGN

For the production of the Berlin Deutsches Theater described here,
we used the famous design that Teo Otto had made for the Zurich
Schauspielhaus during the War. In that design there were, within
a permanent frame, consisting of large screens, materials of 17th
century war camps: tent cloth, wooden beams held together by ropes,
etc. Buildings such as the parsonage and the farmhouse, set up
three-dimensionally, realistic in architectural style and materials, were merely suggested in an artistic manner, showing only as
much as was serviceable for the play. Colour projections appeared
on the cyclorama, and a revolving stage was used for all wagon
movements. We (at the Deutsches Theater) changed the size and
position of the screens, and used them in the camp scenes only,
so that camp scenes and road scenes were clearly distinguished
from one another. The Berlin stage designer created the buildings
(2, 4, 5, 9, 10, 11) freely on his own, at the same time observing
the principle. We did without the background projections of the
Zurich production and hung signs with the names of the different
countries, in black letters, across the scenes. We used even,
uncoloured light, and in the greatest possible quantity. Thereby
we removed the last vestige of that 'atmosphere' which makes
events slightly romantic. We kept almost everything else, down to
the smallest detail very often, (chopping block, fireplace, etc.),
and especially the excellent placing of the covered wagon. This
last point is significant, since a good deal of the grouping and
the sequence of events was predetermined that way.

Surprisingly little is lost by renouncing the complete freedom
of 'artistic creativity'. No matter what, one must start somewhere, and with something; why should it not be something that had
been thought through before? One regains one's freedom, no doubt,
by the spirit of contradiction that stirs here and there inside one.

REALISTIC THEATRE AND ILLUSION

In 1826, Goethe wrote about the 'Imperfections of the English
Theatre Stage' of Shakespeare. He said: 'There is no sign of that
demand for naturalism to which we have become accustomed, gradually,
through improvements of stage mechanics, of the art of perspective,
and of the costumes.' He asks: 'Who would accept anything like
this at the present time? Under such circumstances, Shakespeare's
plays were, at the most, highly interesting fairy tales, but told
by several people who, for a greater effect, had masked themselves
characteristically, moved back and forth according to necessity,
entered and exited, but left it to the spectator to imagine, at his

liberty, a paradise and palaces on the desolate stage.'
Since this statement was made, the mechanics of our theatre
have been improved for a hundred years, and the 'demand for
naturalness' has led to such an illusionism that we moderns may
be quite willing to accept a Shakespeare on a desolate stage
rather than one who neither demands nor generates imagination.
In Goethe's day, the attempt to improve stage mechanics to
create illusion was not an alarming matter since it was so imperfect, so much in the 'infancy of the beginning', that the theatre
as such always remained a reality, and imagination as well as
invention could still turn nature into art. The stages were still
theatrical exhibits in which the stage designer created the places
of action artistically and poetically.
The theatre of bourgeois classicism was at that fortunate mid-
point in the development toward the naturalistic-illusionistic
where mechanics could produce enough illusionistic elements to
present several natural things more perfectly, but not yet so many
that the audience was led to believe that they were no longer in
the theatre. It was the time of the happy medium where art did
not yet consist of destroying the impression that what one saw was
a matter of art. Lighting effects, without the electric bulb, were
primitive. Whenever a deficiency in taste thought a sunset necessary, imperfect mechanics stood in the way of complete bewitchment.
The authentic costumes of the court theatre of Meiningen were a
somewhat later accomplishment. They were always splendid, if not
always beautiful, and they were, after all, counterbalanced by
unnatural rhetoric. In short, theatre was still theatre wherever
it failed in the business of deception. Today, the re-establishment
of theatre as theatre is a prerequisite of the realistic presentation of human relationships. If illusion as to locality is
increased beyond a certain point, and if the style of acting is so
'magnetic' that the impression given is that one is witnessing a
momentary, 'authentic' event, everything appears so natural that
one can no longer apply one's judgment, imagination, and response:
one subordinates oneself, one simply sympathises, one is victimised
by this naturalness. The illusion of the theatre must be only partial, so that it can always be recognised as an illusion. Reality,
in all its perfection, must be changed through the fact of artistic
presentation, so that it may be recognised and treated as changeable. And this is the basis of our present demand for realism: we
wish to change the nature of our human relationships.

ILLUSIONISTIC ELEMENTS?

The completely empty stage with cyclorama (in the Prelude, in the
7th and the last scene) creates no doubt the illusion of a flat
landscape and a sky. This effect is in order, since a poetic
stirring in the soul of the spectator is necessary for producing
this illusion. It is produced easily enough, in that the actors,
merely through their acting, can create at the beginning an open
landscape that offers itself to the enterprising spirit of the
small business family, and, in the end, an immense desert confront-
ing the exhausted seeker of fortune. It is to be hoped that the

formal impression will be blended with the substantive one, that
the spectator may participate in the initial nothingness, from
which everything originates, by seeing at first the empty stage,
soon to be populated. On this *tabula rasa* of a stage, as he knows,
the actors have acquainted themselves with the events of the
chronicle, rehearsing and working for weeks, trying out this and
that, by enacting the chronicle, by judging it. Now the action
starts, and the wagon of Courage rolls onto the stage. If there is
a beautiful approximateness in great matters, there is none in
small things. Carefully worked-out details of costumes and props
are important for a realistic presentation; for in these matters
the imagination of the spectator can add nothing. The tools for
working and eating must be prepared with loving care. Naturally,
the costumes must not look as if they came straight from a costume
pageant; they have to show individual characteristics, as well as
class characteristics. They should be worn longer or shorter,
made of cheap or expensive material, cared for or not cared for,
etc. [...]

WHAT SHOULD ABOVE ALL BE SHOWN IN A PRODUCTION OF 'MOTHER COURAGE AND HER CHILDREN'

That the big deals in a war are not made by the little people.
That war is a continuation of business by other means, making
human virtues fatal, even to the virtuous. That no sacrifice is
too great for combating war.

PRELUDE

The Long Road into War

[...] The presentation of the long road the woman takes to get to
the war seemed to us to be a sufficient indication of her active
and voluntary participation in war. Many discussions with spectators, and many reviews showed, however, that Courage was considered
by many simply as the representative of the 'small people' who were
'drawn into war', 'couldn't do anything about it', 'are helplessly
at the mercy of accidents of war', etc. A deeply-rooted habit
makes the spectator of a play pick out only the more emotional
statements of the characters, and overlook everything else.
Matters of business are accepted with a sense of boredom, like descriptions of nature in novels. The 'atmosphere of business' is
simply the air one breathes and which one need not expressly mention. In discussions, the war appeared again and again as a timeless abstract matter, no matter how much we tried to present it as
the sum of the business enterprises of all.

SECOND SCENE

Giehse's Mother Courage

In the Munich production, which followed the Berlin Model, Therese
Giehse showed how a great actress can use the arrangement and
theatrical material of a Model performance to build a unique and
unmistakable figure. Giehse had created the role of Courage during
the War in Zurich. Now she invented beautiful modifications which
also can enrich the model. In one scene she held the guilder she
got by exploiting the triumph of her son, in her raised fist, and
so performed a small triumphal march. In another one Eilif,
stumbling into the kitchen, greeted her with a barbaric roar -
obviously in the style of the Fierling family. She responded with
an ill-humoured variation of the same roar. The box on the ear
has thus been prepared. (Weigel, on the other hand, had played
joy at seeing him again, and then, suddenly remembering Eilif's
carelessness, she slapped him.)

THIRD SCENE

An Important Point

Courage's never diminishing readiness to work is important. She
is hardly ever seen not doing some kind of work. It is this effi-
ciency that makes Courage's failure so moving.

The Colonel

The colonel whom the camp whore drags along so that he buys her the
wagon of Courage, is a hard part to play, since he is a purely
negative figure. He only has to show at what price the camp whore
buys her rise; that's how gruesome he must be. Georg Peter Pilz
drew the age of the colonel in a subtle fashion by making him display a fervent passion which he couldn't for a single moment live
up to. His lust erupted, as it were, on cue, and the senile fellow
seemed to forget his surroundings. Immediately thereafter he forgot
his lust and stared absent-mindedly into space. The actor achieved
a bold effect with a cane. In his passionate moments, he pressed
it against the ground so hard that it bent, and then he straight-
ened it up immediately, thereby indicating a luridly aggressive
impotence in an irresistibly comic fashion. Such things are kept
within the framework of good taste only by considerable elegance in
performance.

FOURTH SCENE

Courage's State of Mind at the Beginning of the Scene

During the first rehearsals, Weigel opened this scene in an attitude of dejection. This was not correct. Courage learns by

teaching. She teaches and learns the Capitulation. The scene
requires indignation at the beginning, and dejection in the end.

Courage's Wickedness

Courage's wickedness is in no scene greater than here, where she
teaches the young man to capitulate before the mighty in order to
be able to do so herself. And yet Weigel's face shows a certain
light of wisdom, even nobility, in this scene; and this is as it
should be. We are faced not so much by her wickedness as by that
of her class, and she rises above it a little, at least, by showing an understanding of such weakness, and even anger at it.

Giehse in the Role of Courage

Giehse gave an aggressive turn to the song of the Great Capitulation
by including the audience in the last refrain - she was appearing
in the 'City of the Nazi Movement' and of re-armament (Munich).
    For the end of this scene, in Munich, she gave up the ending
she used in Zurich, i.e., speaking the words 'I don't want to complain' in a military stance, at attention: Courage walked with
lowered head along the footlights, past the scrivener, thus stress-
ing her defeat.

If This Scene Were to be Played Without Alienation

Such a scene is socially disastrous if the actress playing Courage
invites the audience, through a hypnotic acting style, to feel
empathy. The audience will merely strengthen their own inclination
to resign and capitulate, and, moreover, will enjoy the pleasure of
looking down upon their own foibles. They will not manage to feel
the beauty and attraction of a social problem.

FIFTH SCENE

In What Sense the Scene Depends on Pantomime

The effect of the scene on the battle field depends on the minute
pantomime of the actress playing Kattrin in showing her rising anger
over her mother's inhumanity. Angelika Hurwicz ran to and fro between the injured peasants and her mother like an excited mother hen.
Before beginning to argue with her mother in gestures, she did not
suppress the lustful curiosity of infantile people amid lurid
events. She carried the infant from the house like a thief, at the
end of the scene, then bounced him up and down, with her arms
raised, as if to make him laugh. If her mother has got the fur
coat - she has got the infant as booty.

Kattrin

In the scene on the battle field, Dumb Kattrin threatens to kill
her mother because she refuses linen to the wounded peasants. It
is necessary to represent Kattrin as an intelligent person from
the beginning. (Her affliction might mislead actresses to represent her as dimwitted.) At the beginning, she is light and gay,
of perfectly balanced mind. Hurwicz even gave her a kind of awkward charm in her conversation with her brother in the third scene.
To be sure, her linguistic affliction affects her body, and yet it
is war that breaks her, not her affliction. Speaking technically:
war must find something in her that can be broken.

One misses everything if one portrays her love for children as
a dull, animalistic feeling. Saving the city of Halle is an
intelligent act. How else could it become clear, as it must, that
in this instance the most helpless one is ready to help?

ELEVENTH SCENE

The Dramatic Scene

The drum scene excited the audience in a special manner. This was
sometimes explained by the fact that this is the most dramatic
scene of the play, and that the audience preferred the dramatic to
the epic. Actually, epic theatre is able to present much more than
agitated events, clashes, complots, mental tortures, etc., but it
is also able to represent these. Spectators may identify themselves with dumb Kattrin in this scene; they may project their
personality into this creature; and may happily feel that such
forces are present in them, too. They will, however, not have been
able to project in this manner throughout every bit of the play;
hardly, e.g. in the first scenes.

Alienation

If one wants to keep the scene free from wild excitement on the
stage - excitement that spells destruction to whatever is remarkable in the scene - one must carry out certain 'alienations'
especially carefully.

E.g., the conversation of the farm people about the surprise
attack is in danger of being simply sympathised with, if it is part
of a general turmoil. It would not show how they justify their
doing nothing and assure each other of the necessity of doing
nothing - so that the only 'action' possible is prayer.

Therefore the actors were told, during rehearsals, to add after
their lines 'said the man', 'said the woman'. As follows:
'"The watchman will give warning," said the woman.'
'"They must have killed the watchman," said the man.'
'"If only there were more of us," said the woman.'
'"But being that we are alone with that cripple," said the man.'
'"There is nothing we can do, is there?" said the woman.'
'"Nothing," said the man,' etc.

TWELFTH SCENE

The Peasant

The attitude of the peasants toward Courage is hostile. She got
them into great difficulties, and they will be saddled with her if
she does not catch up with the regiments. Besides, she is to
blame for the accident herself, in their opinion. And moreover the
canteen woman is not part of the resident population, and now, in
time of war, she belongs to the fleecers, cut-throats, and maraud-
ers in the wake of the armies. When they condole with her by shak-
ing her hand, they merely follow custom.

The Bow

During this entire scene, Weigel, as Courage, showed an almost
animal indifference. All the more beautiful was the deep bow that
she made when the body was carried away.

The Lullaby

The lullaby must be sung without sentimentality and without the
desire to arouse sentimentality. Otherwise, its significance does
not get across. The thought that is the basis of this song is a
murderous one: the child of this mother was supposed to be better
off than other children of other mothers. Through a slight stress
on the 'you', Weigel revealed the treacherous hope of Courage to
get her child, and perhaps only hers, through the war alive. The
child to whom the most common things were denied was promised the
uncommon.

Paying for the Funeral

Even when paying for the funeral, Weigel gave another hint at the
character of Courage. She fished a few coins from her leather
purse, put one back, and gave the rest to the peasant. The over-
powering impression she gave of having been destroyed was not in
the least diminished by this.

Discoveries of the Realists

Wherein lies the effectiveness of Weigel's gesture when she mecha-
nically puts one coin back into her purse, after having fished her
money out, as she hands the farmer the funeral money for dead
Kattrin? She shows that this tradeswoman, in all her grief, does
not completely forget to count, since money is so hard to come by.
And she shows this as a discovery about human nature that is shaped
by certain conditions. This little feature has the power and the
suddenness of a discovery. The art of the realists consists of
digging out the truth from under the rubble of the evident, of

connecting the particular with the general, of pinning down the
unique within the larger process.

Mother Courage Learns Nothing

In the last scene, Weigel's Courage seemed a woman of eighty. And
she comprehends nothing. She reacts only to statements that are
connected with war, such as that one must not remain behind. She
overhears the crude reproach of the peasants that Kattrin's death
was her fault.
   Courage's inability to learn from the unproductiveness of war
was a prophecy in the year 1938 when the play was written. At the
Berlin production in 1948 the desire was voiced that Courage should
at least come to a realisation in the play.
   To make it possible for the spectator to get something out of
this realistic play, i.e., to make the spectator learn a lesson,
theatres have to arrive at an acting style that does not seek an
identification of the spectator with the protagonist.
   Judging on the basis of reports of spectators and newspaper
reviews, the Zurich world premiere, e.g. - although artistically on
a high level - presented only the image of war as a natural catastrophe and as an inevitable fate, and thereby it underscored to
the middle-class spectator in the orchestra his own indestructi-
bility, his ability to survive. But even to the likewise middle-
class Courage, the decision, 'Join in or don't join in' was always
left open in the play. The production, it seems, must have presented Courage's business dealings, profiteering, willingness to take
risks, as quite natural, 'eternally human' behaviour, so that she
had no other choice. Today, it is true, the man of the middle
class can no longer stay out of war, as Courage could have. To him,
a production of the play can probably teach nothing but a real
hatred of war, and a certain insight into the fact that the big
deals of which war consists are not made by the little people. In
that sense, the play is more of a lesson than reality is, because
here in the play the situation of war is more of an experimental
situation, made for the sake of insights. I.e., the spectator
attains the attitude of a student - as long as the acting style is
correct. The part of the audience that belongs to the proletariat,
i.e. the class that actually can struggle against and overcome war,
should be given insight into the connection between business and
war (again provided the acting style is correct): the proletariat
as a class can do away with war by doing away with capitalism. Of
course, as far as the proletarian part of the audience is concerned,
one must also take into consideration the fact that this class is
busy drawing its own conclusions - inside as well as outside the
theatre.

12. 4   ERIC BENTLEY

'Mother Courage', 'Theatre of War', Eyre Methuen,
1972, pp. 165-71

The role of Mother Courage is hard to play and is always being
miscast. Why? 'Because middle-aged actresses are such ladies and
lack earthiness.' But who has succeeded in the role? Outstand-
ingly, Helene Weigel. Is she very earthy, is she notably proletarian? On the contrary - there is nothing proletarian about her
except her opinions. Then what is it those other ladies lack that
Helene Weigel has? Among other things, I would suggest an appreciation of the role, an understanding of what is in it, and above all
the ability to portray contradictions. For whenever anyone says,
'Mother Courage is essentially X,' it is equally reasonable for
someone to retort: 'Mother Courage is essentially the opposite of
X.'
   Mother Courage is essentially courageous. That is well known,
isn't it? Tennessee Williams has written of the final moment of
Brecht's play as one of the inspiring moments in all theatre -
inspiring because of the woman's indomitability. On she marches
with her wagon after all that has happened, a symbol of the way
humanity itself goes on its way after all that has happened, *if* it
can find the courage. And after all we don't have to wait for the
final scene to learn that we have to deal with a woman of considerable toughness and resilience. This is not the first time she has
shown that she can pick up the pieces and continue. One might
even find courage in the very first scene where we learn that she
has not been content to cower in some corner of Bamberg but has
boldly come to meet the war. A trouble maker, we might say on
first meeting the lady, but the reverse of a coward.
   Yet it is impossible to continue on this tack for long without
requiring an: *On the other hand.* Beginning with the reason why she
is nicknamed 'Courage' in the first place.

   They call me Mother Courage because I was afraid I'd be ruined,
   so I drove through the bombardment of Riga like a madwoman with
   fifty loaves of bread in my cart. They were going moldy, what
   else could I do?

Did those who gave her the name intend a joke against an obvious
coward? Or did they think she was driven by heroic valor when in
fact she was impelled by sheer necessity? Either way her act is
utterly devoid of the moral quality imputed. Whether in cowardice
or in down-to-earth realism, her stance is Falstaffian. What is
courage? A word.
   Somewhere hovering over this play is the image of a pre-eminently
courageous mother who courageously tries to hold on to her young.
More than one actress, offering herself for the role, has seen this
image and nothing else. Yet valor is conspicuously absent at those
times when Mother Courage (however unwittingly) seals the fate of
her children. At moments when, in heroic melodrama, the protagonist would be riding to the rescue, come hell or high water, Mother
Courage is in the back room concluding a little deal. For her, it

is emphatically not 'a time for greatness.' *She is essentially cowardly.*

A basic contradiction, then, which the actress in the role must play both sides of, or the play will become the flat and simple thing which not a few journalistic commentators have declared it to be. An actress may be said to be beginning to play Mother Courage when she is putting both courage and cowardice into the role with equal conviction and equal effect. She is still only beginning to play it, though; for, as she proceeds with her inter- pretation, she will find that, in this play, courage and cowardice are not inherent and invariable qualities but by-products.

Of what? We can hunt for the answer by looking further into particular sequences of action. It is not really from cowardice that Mother Courage is in the back room concluding a little deal when her children are claimed by the war. It is from preoccupation with 'business.' Although 'Mother Courage' is spoken of as a war play, it is actually a business play, in the sense that the inci- dents in it, one and all, are business transactions - from the deal with the belt in Scene One, through the deal with the capon in Scene Two, the deal with the wagon in Scene Three, the deals with bullets and shirts in Scene Five, through to the economical funeral arrangements of the final scene. And since these trans- actions (except for the last) are what Courage supports her child- ren by, they are 'necessary.' Those who condemn her have to face the question: What alternative had she? Of what use would it have been to save the life of Swiss Cheese if she lacked the wherewithal to *keep* him alive? The severe judge will answer that she could take a chance on this, provided she does save his life. But this is exactly Mother Courage's own position. She is fully prepared to take the chance if she has to. It is in determining whether she has to that her boy's life slips through her fingers: life or death is a matter of timing.

To say that Swiss Cheese is a victim of circumstances, not of Courage's character, will not, however, be of much use to the act- ress interpreting this character. If cowardice is *less* important here than at first appears, what is *more* important? Surely it is a failure in understanding, rather than in virtue. Let me elaborate.

Though only one of Brecht's completed plays is about anyone that a university would recognize as a philosopher, several of his plays present what one might call philosophers in disguise, such as Schweyk, the philosopher of a pub in Prague, and Azdak, the philo- sopher of a Georgian village. To my mind, *Mother Courage is above all a philosopher,* defining the philosopher along Socratic lines as a person who likes to talk all the time and explain everything to everybody. (A simple trait in itself, one would think, yet there have been actresses and directors who wish to have all Courage's speeches shortened into mere remarks. Your philosopher never makes remarks; he always speechifies; hence such abridgment enforces a radical misinterpretation of character.) I do not mean at all that Courage is an idle or armchair philosopher whose teachings make no contact with life. On the contrary, her ideas are nothing if not a scheme of life by which, she hopes, her family is to do pretty well in a world which is doing pretty badly.

Here one sees the danger of thinking of Mother Courage as the

average person.   Rather, she resembles the thoughtfully ambitious
modern mother of the lower-middle or better-paid working class
who wants her children to win scholarships and end up in the
Labour Cabinet.   (Minister of Education: Kattrin. Chancellor of
the Exchequer: Swiss Cheese. Minister of War: Eilif.) Has it
escaped attention that if one of her children turns out a cut-
throat, this is blamed on circumstances ('Otherwise, I'd have
starved, smarty'), while *the other two are outright heroes?* Anyone who considers this an average family takes a far higher view
of the average than is implicit in the works of Bertolt Brecht.
    What is the philosophy of this philosopher? Reduced to a single
proposition, it is that if you concede defeat on the larger issue,
you can achieve some nice victories in smaller ways. The larger
issue is whether the world can be changed. It can't. But brandy
is still drunk, and can be sold. One can survive, and one can help
one's children to survive by teaching each to make appropriate use
of the qualities God gave him. The proposition I have just mentioned will apply to this upbringing. A child endowed with a particular talent or virtue should not pursue it to its logical end:
defeat on such projects should be conceded at the outset. The
child should cunningly exploit his characteristic talent for its
incidental uses along the way. In this fashion the unselfishness
of a Swiss Cheese or a Kattrin can be harnessed to selfishness.
The result, if the philosophy works,is that while the world may
shoot itself to blazes, the little Courage family, one and all,
will live out its days in moderate wealth and moderate happiness.
The scheme is not utopian. Just the opposite: the hope is to make
optimism rational by reducing human demands to size.
    The main reason it doesn't work is that the little world which
Mother Courage's wisdom tries to regulate is dependent upon the big
world which she has given up as a bad job. Small business is part
of the big war which is part of the big business of ownership of
all the means of production and distribution. No more than the
small businessman can live in a separate economic system from the
big can the small philosopher live in a separate philosophic system
from the big. 'Mother Courage,' one can conclude, exposes the
perennial illusions of the petit bourgeois scheme of things. This
has of course often been done before in modern literature. But
usually only the idealism has been exposed. Mother Courage, on the
other hand, could claim to be a cynic. She has the theatre audience
laughing most of the time on the score of this cynicism - by which
she deflates illusions. Cynicism is nothing, after all, if not
'realistic.' What a cynical remark lays bare *has* to be the truth.
Brecht makes the truth of his play the more poignant through the
fact that the cynicism in it ultimately favors illusion. Mother
Courage had gone to all lengths to trim her sails to the wind but
even then the ship wouldn't move. So there is irony within irony
(as, in Brecht's work, there usually is). Courage's cynicism can
cut down the windy moralizing of the Chaplain easily enough, but
only to be itself cut down by a world that cannot be comprehended
even by this drastically skeptical kind of thinking.
    What alternative did Mother Courage have? The only alternatives
shown in the play are, on the one hand, the total brutalization of
men like the Swedish Commander (and, for that matter, her own son

Eilif) and, on the other hand, the martyrdom achieved by Swiss
Cheese and Kattrin. Presumably, to the degree that the playwright
criticizes her, he is pushing her toward the second alternative.
Yet, not only would such a destiny be completely out of character,
within the terms of the play itself it is not shown to be really
preferable. Rather, the fruitlessness of both deaths is underlined. Why add a third?

Given her character, Mother Courage had no alternative to what
she thought - or, for that matter, to the various 'bad' things she
did. In this case, can she be condemned? Logically, obviously
not; but was Brecht logical? The printed editions of the play
indicate that he made changes in his script to render Mother
Courage less sympathetic. In other words, after having made her
thoroughly sympathetic in his first version, Brecht later wanted
her less so. One can see the sense of the changes in polemical
terms: he did not wish to seem to condone behavior which is to
be deplored. But to make this point, is it necessary to make
Mother Courage a less good person? Personally I would think not,
and I should like to see 'Courage' played sometime in the Urtext
of 1940 and without the later 'improvements.' But one should not
minimize the complexity of the problem. Like many other playwrights, Brecht wanted to show a kind of inevitability combined
with a degree of free will, and if it doesn't matter whether
Courage is less good or more, because she is trapped by circumstances, then the play is fatalistic. I tend to think it is fatalistic as far as the movement of history is concerned, and that
the element of hope in it springs only from Brecht's rendering of
human character. Brecht himself is not satisfied with this and
made changes in the hope of suggesting that things might have been
different had Mother Courage acted otherwise. (What would she
have done? Established socialism in seventeenth-century Germany?
One must not ask.)

Brecht has stressed, in his Notes, that Mother Courage never
sees the light, never realizes what has happened, is incapable of
learning. As usual, Brecht's opinions, as stated in outside comments, are more doctrinaire than those to be found embodied in the
plays. It may be true that Mother Courage never sees that 'small
business' is a hopeless case, though to prove even this Brecht had
to manufacture the evidence by inserting, later, the line at the
end: 'I must get back into business.' She does see through her
own philosophy of education. The Song of Solomon in Scene Nine
concedes that the program announced in Scene One has failed. The
manipulation of the virtues has not worked: 'a man is better off
without.' The song is perhaps more symbolic, as well as more schematic, than most Brechtians wish Brecht to be, for there is a verse
about each of her children under the form of famous men (Eilif is
Caesar, Swiss Cheese is Socrates, Kattrin is Saint Martin), but
more important is that this is the Song of Solomon (from 'The
Threepenny Opera') and that Solomon is Courage herself:

King Solomon was very wise
So what's his history?
He came to view this world with scorn
Yes, he came to regret he ever had been born

Declaring: all is vanity.
King Solomon was very wise
But long before the day was out
The consequence was clear, alas:
It was his wisdom brought him to this pass.
A man is better off without.

I have heard the question asked whether this conclusion was not
already reached in the Song of the Great Capitulation in Scene
Four. Both songs are songs of defeat (Brecht's great subject) but
of two different defeats. The second is defeat total and final:
Courage has staked everything on wisdom, and wisdom has ruined
her and her family. The first is the setback of 'capitulation,'
that is of disenchantment. When Yvette was only seventeen she was
in love, and love was heaven. Soon afterward she had learned to
'fraternize behind the trees'; she had capitulated. It is perhaps
hard to imagine Courage as a younger and different person from the
woman we meet in the play, but in the Song of the Great Capitulation
we are definitely invited to imagine her as a young woman who
thought she could storm the heavens, whose faith seemed able to move
mountains.
    Scene Four is one of several in this play which one can regard
as the whole play in miniature. For Brecht is not finished when he
has set forth the character of Mother Courage as one who has passed
from youthful idealism to cynical realism. For many a playwright,
that would no doubt be that, but Courage's exchange with the angry
young soldier leads to other things. We discover that Mother
Courage is not a happy Machiavellian, boasting of her realism as an
achievement. We find that she is deeply ashamed. And in finding
this, we discover in Courage the mother of those two roaring idealists (not to say again: martyrs) Swiss Cheese and Kattrin. 'Kiss
my arse,' says the soldier, and why? His bad language had not
hitherto been directed at her. But she has been kind to him only
to be cruel. If she has not broken his spirit, she has done something equally galling: she has made clear to him how easily his
spirit can be broken. When you convert a man to the philosophy of
You Can't Win, you can hardly expect to earn his gratitude at the
same time.
    In the way Courage puts matters to the soldier we see how close
she came to being a truly wise woman. We also discover in this
scene that, despite the confident tone of her cynical lingo,
Courage is not really sure of herself and her little philosophy.
She teaches the soldier that it is futile to protest, but she apparently does not know this herself until she reminds herself of it,
for she has come here precisely to protest. Here we learn to
recognize in Courage not only contradiction but conflict. She
knows what she has thought. She is not sure what to think.
    And this is communicated by Brecht in a very bold - or, if you
prefer, just poetic - manner. For while Courage does not give herself to despair until the end (and not even then for those who can
take at face value her: 'I must get back into business'), she had
correctly foreseen the end from the beginning: the despair she
gives herself to had been there from the moment of capitulation.
At times it would strike her between the eyes: she is very

responsive and, for example, has worked out the Marxist interpretation of religion for herself. Scene Two contains a song she had
taught Eilif as a boy: it accurately predicts the manner of his
death. In Scene One she predicts doom for the whole family in her
elaborate pantomime of fortunetelling. It could be said that
everything is there from the start, for the first thing Mother
Courage does is to try and sell things by announcing an early
death for her prospective customers. The famous Song of Mother
Courage is the most extraordinary parody of the kind of song any
real *vivandière* might try to attract customers with. Mother
Courage's Come and buy! is nothing other than: Come and die! In
that respect, her fortunetelling is on the level, and her wisdom
is valid.

Scene Four, I have been saying, is one of several in this play
which one can regard as the whole play in miniature. The main
purpose of the play, for Brecht, was, I think, to generate anger
over what it shows. Yet Brecht realizes how pointless angry plays
have been - and angry speeches outside the drama. It is said that
Clifford Odets's 'Waiting for Lefty' made millionaires angry for
as long as it took them to get from their seats to where their
chauffeurs tactfully waited for them at the end of the block. Such
is the anger of the social drama in general.

There is the anger of a sudden fit, which boils up and over and
is gone. And there is the anger which informs the work of long
years of change. *Why* can't the world be changed? For Mother
Courage, it is not from any inherent unchangeability in the world.
It is because our wish to change it is not strong enough. Nor is
this weakness innate. It is simply that our objection to the present world isn't as strong as it once was. What is outrageous does
not outrage us as it once did. Today, it only arouses the 'short
rage' of Brecht's soldier - and of Courage herself - not the long
one that is required. Because we - they - have capitulated.

Capitulation is not just an idea but a feeling, an agony in
fact, and is located not just in the scene of the Great Capitulation but in the whole play of 'Mother Courage.' Everything that
happens is related to it, above all the things that are furthest
away from it, namely, the deaths of Swiss Cheese and Kattrin. And
if these children are what their mother made them, then their refusal to capitulate stems from her, is her own youth, her own original
nature.

The ultimate achievement of an actress playing this role would
be that she made us sense to what an extent Courage's children are
truly hers.

'GALILEO'

12. 5   BRECHT

A Short Organum for the Theatre (paragraph 63),
'Brecht on Theatre', trans. J. Willett, Eyre
Methuen, 1964, pp. 198-200

Let us get down to the problem of gestic content by running through
the opening scenes of a fairly modern play, my own 'Life of
Galileo.' Since we wish at the same time to find out what light
the different utterances cast on one another we will assume that
it is not our first introduction to the play. It begins with the
man of forty-six having his morning wash, broken by occasional
browsing in books and by a lesson on the solar system for Andrea
Sarti, a small boy. To play this, surely you have got to know
that we shall be ending with the man of seventy-eight having his
supper, just after he has said good-bye for ever to the same
pupil? He is then more terribly altered than this passage of time
could possibly have brought about. He wolfs his food with unres-
trained greed, no other idea in his head; he has rid himself of
his educational mission in shameful circumstances, as though it
were a burden: he, who once drank his morning milk without a care,
greedy to teach the boy. But does he really drink it without care?
Isn't the pleasure of drinking and washing one with the pleasure
which he takes in the new ideas? Don't forget: he thinks out of
self-indulgence.... Is that good or bad? I would advise you to
represent it as good, since on this point you will find nothing in
the whole play to harm society, and more especially because you
yourself are, I hope, a gallant child of the scientific age. But
take careful note: many horrible things will happen in this connection. The fact that the man who here acclaims the new age will
be forced at the end to beg this age to disown him as contemptible,
even to dispossess him; all this will be relevant. As for the
lesson, you may like to decide whether the man's heart is so full
that his mouth is overflowing, so that he has to talk to anybody
about it, even a child, or whether the child has first to draw the
knowledge out of him, by knowing him and showing interest. Again,
there may be two of them who cannot restrain themselves, the one
from asking, the other from giving the answer: a bond of this sort
would be interesting, for one day it is going to be rudely snapped.
Of course you will want the demonstration of the earth's rotation
round the sun to be conducted quickly, since it is given for nothing, and now the wealthy unknown pupil appears, lending the
scholar's time a monetary value. He shows no interest, but he has
to be served; Galileo lacks resources, and so he will stand between
the wealthy pupil and the intelligent one, and sigh as he makes his
choice. There is little that he can teach his new student, so he
learns from him instead; he hears of the telescope which has been
invented in Holland: in his own way he gets something out of the
disturbance of his morning's work. The Rector of the university
arrives. Galileo's application for an increase in salary has been

turned down; the university is reluctant to pay so much for the
theories of physics as for those of theology; it wishes him, who
after all is operating on a generally-accepted low level of
scholarship, to produce something useful here and now. You will
see from the way in which he offers his thesis that he is used to
being refused and corrected. The Rector reminds him that the
Republic guarantees freedom of research even if she doesn't pay;
he replies that he cannot make much of this freedom if he lacks
the leisure which good payment permits. Here you should not find
his impatience too peremptory, or his poverty will not be given
due weight. For shortly after that you find him having ideas
which need some explanation: the prophet of a new age of scientific truth considers how he can swindle some money out of the
Republic by offering her the telescope as his own invention. All
he sees in the new invention, you will be surprised to hear, is
a few scudi, and he examines it simply with a view to annexing it
himself. But if you move on to the second scene you will find
that while he is selling the invention to the Venetian Signoria
with a speech that disgraces him by its falsehoods he has already
almost forgotten the money, because he has realized that the
instrument has not only military but astronomical significance.
The article which he has been blackmailed - let us call it that -
into producing proves to have great qualities for the very
research which he had to break off in order to produce it. If
during the ceremony, as he complacently accepts the undeserved
honours paid him, he outlines to his learned friend the marvellous
discoveries in view - don't overlook the theatrical way in which
he does this - you will find in him a far more profound excitement
than the thought of monetary gain called forth. Perhaps, looked
at in this way, his charlatanry does not mean much, but it still
shows how determined this man is to take the easy course, and to
apply his reason in a base as well as a noble manner. A more significant test awaits him, and does not every capitulation bring the
next one nearer?

12. 6   ERNST SCHUMACHER

    The Dialectics of 'Galileo', trans. J. Neugroschel,
    'Drama Review', 12 (2), winter 1968, pp. 124, 128-32

In the early fifties, Brecht wanted to change from 'epic' theatre
to 'dialectical' theatre. The latter was to keep the 'narrative
element' of the former, but had a distinct aim: '...*deliberately*
to develop features - dialectical vestiges - from earlier forms of
theatre and make them enjoyable' ('Schriften zum Theatre,' vol. 7.
p. 316). 'Developmental laws' were to be worked out by means of
'the dialectic of the classical writers of socialism, so that we
could perceive and enjoy the alterability of the world.' To this
end, it would be necessary to make perceptible the 'imperceptible
contradictions' in all things, people, processes. Alienation
techniques were to be used to depict the 'contradictions and
development of human co-existence,' and to make dialectic 'a source

of learning and enjoyment.' [...]

A form of dialectic also determines 'Galileo''s characterization: it is manifested as a relation in each person between the
individual and the typical. As Brecht wrote ('SzT,' 7, p. 34):

> If a character is historicized and responds in accordance to
> his period but would respond otherwise in different periods,
> isn't that character *Everyman?* A person acts according to
> his time and his class; if he had lived at a different time,
> or for a shorter time, or on the rough side of life, his reply
> would invariably be different. But shouldn't we ask whether
> there are further characteristics in his reponse? Where is he
> himself, the living man, who cannot be mistaken for another,
> who is not quite the same as people similar to him? Obviously,
> he too must be visible - and will be so if this contradiction
> is incorporated in his portrayal. The historicizing portrait
> must keep some lines from sketches showing traces of other
> movements, other characteristics, within the completed figure.
> One might imagine a man making a speech in a valley, occasion-
> ally changing his opinions or making contradictory statements,
> simply so the echo can confront one sentence with another.

Brecht's Galileo has essentially the (if not *the* essential)
features of the historical figure, but includes characteristics
which the author considered typical of modern-day scientists, as
well as 'projections' from the behavior of 'ideal' scientists.
These are determined by contradictions in society and in the individual: Galileo combines patience and impatience, courage and
cowardice, pride and servility, sobriety and enthusiasm, acumen
and narrowmindedness, affability and tactlessness, gentle humor and
acerbic irony, sensuality and asceticism, commitment and cynicism,
democratic ways and kowtowing to the nobles, love of truth and
betrayal of truth.

Not all these traits are developed in the same way or to the
same degree. Some are contradictory, some are complementary. Some
seem negative but have a positive meaning. Impatience is shown by
those who are no longer willing to put up with something; tactlessness can be a way of clarifying things; denial of truth can result
from a love of truth. The contradictory is not necessarily anta-
gonistic. None of these characteristics have value per se - they
derive their significance from the 'supreme jurisdiction' of the
basic gesture, which comes from that gesture's significance for
society. Not all personal qualities can be judged within a specific situation - they must be viewed in terms of the totality and
the end. In ['The Creation of a Role'], Brecht speaks of a 'type
of play' that 'in its details reasonably depends on a knowledge of
the whole' ('SzT,' 7, p. 53). We can get at the 'specific weight'
only by adding up every detail that carries weight. As the kalei-
descope turns, the various fragments of the stage character
finally fall into shape. Our pleasure in this picture would be
incomplete if the figure did not have historical and social relevance for past, present, and future; but this enjoyment would still
lack something without the idiosyncrasies which make a character
the 'property' of an audience and of society.

Galileo's behavior reproduces -in counterpoint, as it were -
the dialectical growth of the other characters. The enthusiasm of
the adult Galileo is repeated in the boy Andrea's passionate adhe-
rence to the new cause. Galileo's genius is reflected in the
young initiate's intellectual maturation. Andrea's character,
however, is an alternative to Galileo's, rather than simply alternating with it. Through following his master, he demonstrates
consequences. Although much younger than Galileo, he seems older.
Led along, he seems led astray. The result of his devotion: the
prototype of a scientist prone to any recantation, denial, refusal,
obedience - to whom Galileo's behavior seems natural, rather than
dubious, as long as it is a contribution to science. Andrea is not
only willing to learn but becomes learnèd as well. Yet while
everyone else in 'Galileo' should be seen and judged in terms of
the end of the play, Andrea is to be judged in terms of his future.
So he has at once the rosy bloom of youth and the grayness of old
age: intellectual irresponsibility towards mankind. We see corrupt innocence, ruined hope, unfulfilled promise. 'Welcome to the
gutter, fellow scientist and traitor!' echoes terrifyingly within
us. At the end, Andrea adds another line, but we know even this
isn't the end of the stanza, whose cynical meaning is clear. 'We
are actually only at the beginning,' he says reassuringly at the
close of the play. For better *and* for worse. Galileo sees himself
as a dead tree, but Andrea, the 'green wood,' is not free of rot.
We can no more follow Andrea, who has once been led astray, unconditionally than we can follow Galileo: instead, we must find better
ways of our own.

Virginia is a further example. This character is based on, but
quite different from, a historical model. Her primary function is
to demonstrate that the conflict between a new science and an old
faith, or - speaking more generally - between social progress and
reaction, penetrates the personal and family sphere. Galileo must
exist for the whole world, not just for his daughter. He has to
ferret out and develop intelligence everywhere; only his daughter's
mind is an exception. He accepts the responsibility of being her
father and provider but not her intellectual parent. From the
beginning, he entrusts her to the Church. Instead of letting her
look through the telescope he brushes her aside, saying it is not
a toy. His daughter enters the Church to return as a totally different person. Science was her pass into society: Galileo let
her circulate as one of his works. She promptly ran into the arms
of the Cardinal Inquisitor: the weapon reversed. The unaroused
intellect aroused; the misunderstood daughter understood; the girl
who was asked nothing asked a great deal. The useless daughter
from a good home becomes a useful daughter to the Church.

She still believes that she will marry, and she believes it for
eight years, but at the crucial moment she remains for Galileo what
she was: a person of secondary importance. Once, she was to be
married off as quickly as possible, but now she's left in the
lurch. The maiden becomes an old maid. And then she becomes, in
effect, a nun. Her only objection to her father's captivity is
that she can't be his sole custodian. She is both housekeeper and
spiritual advisor to him, supplementing his physical diet with a
spiritual one, countering fleshly desires with food for the soul.

To the dictates of the two new sciences, she opposes the commands of the old faith, parrying Galileo's logic with theo-logic. She wards off his penitence with the reiteration of charges. She confronts the malice of his ambiguities with the unequivocalness of malicious kindness. She replies to his irony with patience and indulgence. She was once a means to an end for him, and now the situation is reversed. The powerful man is now in her power. The cold that science once brought into their relationship is outdone by the coldness of Christian life.

Never having taught Virginia knowledge, or even tried to teach her, Galileo now cannot be wise. He can only be sly, but his slyness won't save him from damnation and is useless against her condemnation. His hell is terrible not because he has thrown away his own intellectual gift but because he hasn't developed his daughter's - and her own rigidity shows that her life is merely the survival of a destroyed existence.

Ludovico's characterization is also dialectical, although he functions primarily as a type. If he is an individual, then it is only despite, not because of, his class. Virginia could have been a different person, but not he. His presence is determined by what he represents, his diction by his class idiocy, his individuality by the rigidity of his caste. Although a man of the world, he is unable to cross the boundaries of his world. He has an expanded horizon - seen from a tower on his estate. When science is accepted by both Court and Church, the scientist's daughter is desirable and eligible for marriage. But the anti-Copernican decree warns him against hasty consequences. It is the father and not the daughter who must endure a period of probation; the daughter need not swear that she is pure, but the future father-in-law must promise to put an end to his impure research. The phases of Venus may have nothing to do with the daughter's behind, but they are intimately connected with the father's appearance. Ludovico may be a scientific layman and a blockhead, but he knows as much as Galileo about the connection between heaven and earth and heaven on earth, and while the Little Monk thinks about the internal agitations of the peasants, Ludovico thinks about the external ones. He has had too much experience with the dynamics of social forces not to realize that the proof of astral motion can be political dynamite. He knows he is right - because Galileo grows nasty while Ludovico sticks to the point, remaining discreet and arguing well. When Galileo, losing his temper, goes so far as to threaten to write his works in the Florentine vernacular so that the masses can read them, Ludovico is convinced that this man will always remain a 'slave to his passions.' Marrying Galileo's daughter could easily jeopardize one's family and social position, so he breaks the engagement.

But although Ludovico in this sense embodies forethought, Galileo incarnates afterthought. And that makes all the difference. Galileo may speculate correctly, but Ludovico calculates correctly. Galileo can act cold but not remain cold. Ludovico, however, can be cool, and turn icy. He is able to remain objective, while Galileo is an object lesson, a cause. Ludovico's profile is sharply hewn because it is so impersonal. Galileo carries out functions, but Ludovico is functionalized: a proper manor-lord.

The iron-founder Vanni resembles Ludovico in the way his characterization is placed within a sharply defined social role. Vanni's part in the play is extremely important; without him the Galileo 'case' would not be understandable in the way Brecht wished it to be, i.e., as an act of treason against society. But this functionalizes Vanni's role, like Ludovico's. Vanni represents the bourgeoisie of those times. Despite the great respect he, as a layman, has for the scientist, he considers himself on the same level because he is struggling for the same goal: liberation from dependence on feudal power and narrowmindedness. He assumes that Galileo can distinguish between friend and foe, and identifies himself as Galileo's friend. He joins the struggle as an economic force that the Grand Duke must take into consideration, for Florence is wedged between the Papal State and the northern Italian city states; she cannot survive without the latter. Galileo's fate hangs in the balance - then he goes over to the Princes and Popes. Vanni has no choice but to leave, regretful but upright, just as he entered. Galileo, who believed he would somehow be able to get out of it as an individual, continues his bootlicking; yet, despite all his writhing and wriggling, he finds no way out.

Of all the characters representing the Church, the Little Monk is the most dialectical: not only a priest but an astronomer. He sees with his own two eyes that Galileo's teachings are right, yet he dare not see this because it is contrary to the Supreme Truth he has been taught. He cannot acknowledge the new knowledge because the consequences will be terrible for the simple people whose misery he is acquainted with and who - in his opinion - so as to endure their misery, need faith in a divine providence underlying the social order. His confusion is great because the contradiction is great. The Little Monk believes that the decree necessarily contains a higher wisdom, but the things he has viewed on heaven and earth, on the moon and in the Campagna, have been so convincing that he cannot take the decree for granted, as do other believers. His passionate craving to unravel the truth from all contradictions is irresistible: it drives him to attempt Galileo's 'conversion,' and yet forces him to listen to the scientist's arguments, although they not only tear away the scar tissue that religion has spread over the wound in his soul, but enlarge and deepen the injury. The Little Monk confirms Galileo's faith in the gentle power of reason. His actions show that in the long run it will do rulers no good to regimentize thought, influence the minds of their subjects, or enroll as party members the very people they oppress. The chasm between ideology and reality will deepen and widen. Appealed to, called upon, awoken, the 'Little Monks' will bring about the victory of reason. Yet at the end of the play he has abandoned research and rests in peace in the church.

Similarly dialectical characterizations can be easily demonstrated for all the figures in the play, and in their language. The dialogue is marked by vivid imagery: the 'prosaic,' the penetration of new ideology and new 'objective' relations on the basis of new conditions of production, is transposed into metaphor. The parabolic diction of the Bible is used verbatim in many ways, because of the very nature of the subject matter; but metaphors

create the specific nature of the language, and are used by each
character according to his social class and function. As for
dialectics, our main concern here, the dialogue is remarkably
antithetical, not only in a thesis-and-reply pattern which at
times becomes stichomythic, but within individual speeches and
lines. Opposing views are transcended and dissolved through
gnomic maxims, contradictions resolved by 'dictums' in which logic
and image form a graspable unity. In this constant creation and
transcendence of antitheses, a part is played by the association
of images and concepts, and occasionally by the evocative use of
alliteration. The syntax throughout, in coordinate and subordinate
clauses, is used to develop crucial contrasts.

For example: The curator describes the 'slavery under whose
whip science sighs in many places.' 'They've cut their whips out
of old leather folios. You don't have to know how the stone
falls, you have to know what Aristotle writes about it. Eyes are
only for reading. Why bother with new laws of falling bodies, if
only the laws of genuflection are important?' The Little Monk
explains the agony his parents would suffer if the new concept of
the universe turned out to be right: 'There will be no meaning
in their misery. Hunger will simply mean not having eaten, rather
than being a test of strength. Hard work will simply be bending
and lugging, and not be a virtue.' Galileo's reply to him emphasizes a whole series of contradictions: The Campagna peasants are
paying for the war fought in Spain and Germany by the mild Lord
Jesus' deputy - and why does the pope place the earth in the center
of the universe? 'So that Saint Peter's throne may stand at the
center of the earth!' He goes on:

> If your parents were prosperous and happy, they might develop
> the virtues of happiness and prosperity. Today the virtues of
> exhaustion are caused by the exhausted land. For that my new
> water pumps could work more wonder than their ridiculous super-
> human efforts. Be fruitful and multiply: for the fields are
> barren and war is decimating you! Should I lie to your people?

Finally Galileo sums up: 'I can see your people's divine patience,
but where is their divine wrath?'

This method of extracting truth from antitheses is also reflected in Galileo's entire approach to research. Thus, before starting to investigate sunspots, he says:

> My intention is not to prove that I was right but to find out
> *whether* I was right. 'Abandon hope all ye who enter - an
> observation.' Before assuming these phenomena are spots,
> which would suit us, let us first set about proving that they
> are not - fishtails .... In fact, we will approach this observ-
> ing of the sun with the firm determination to prove that the
> earth stands still, and only if hopelessly defeated in this
> pious undertaking can we allow ourselves to wonder if we may
> not have been right all the time: the earth revolves.

'Unhappy is the land that breeds no hero.' / 'Unhappy is the land
that needs a hero.' Galileo is trapped in a contradiction of

principles from which he cannot extricate himself. At his last
meeting with Andrea he says that he has taught knowledge by denying the truth - Brecht drew the truth from contradictions, through
the play's murderous analysis. Galileo's 'final words' signify
initial knowledge: 'Scientists cannot remain scientists if they
deny themselves to the masses; the powers of nature cannot be
fully developed if mankind does not know how to develop its own
powers; machines, meant to bring relief to man, may merely bring
new hardships; progress may merely progress away from humanity.'

12. 7 RAYMOND WILLIAMS

Bertolt Brecht, 'Drama from Ibsen to Brecht',
Chatto & Windus, 1968, pp. 284-90

We cannot say, with any certainty, why Brecht did not embody his
major dramatic conflicts in a contemporary action. His distancing,
there, produces effective scenes, but not a whole action, and the
technique of distancing may itself be connected with this. It
seems to me at least possible that the full dramatic action was too
painful to see in contemporary terms: not that he drew back from
dramatizing brutality and betrayal - those painful scenes were,
paradoxically, the easiest to realize; but that the claims of
immediate satisfaction, not as argument but as experience, were at
once undeniable and insupportable, in the realities of contemporary
struggle. What could be seen as the claims of immediate life, in
historical situations, translated too quickly, in a structured contemporary world, into evasion. Brecht could, in this view, only
release his full dramatic action, giving all its impulses a full
creative weight, by this particular kind of distancing: an action
away from immediate issues and names.
    The point is very complicated, for this kind of historical dis-
tancing is so normal in dramatic art, is indeed so much more common than the realization of contemporary action, that in any case
but that of Brecht no particular notice would need to be taken.
It is just the paradox of a contemporary urgency and a profound
distancing that irresistibly holds the attention. And it must be
made clear, also, that Brecht does not, by his historical distancing, express what can be called a 'creative truth' as opposed to
what is often called his 'doctrinaire truth'. On the contrary,
the actions of 'Mother Courage' and of 'Galileo' are at the heart
of Brecht: not only integrating the creative impulse and the political beliefs, but also, by this fact, enabling a major dramatic
achievement, the triumphs of his particular form.
    Complex seeing, in 'Mother Courage' and 'Galileo', is not an
attitude to the action, or a battery of separable techniques and
effects; it *is* the action, in a profound way. We obscure this when,
for example, in a convenient brevity, we shorten the title of
'Mother Courage and her Children' to 'Mother Courage', the separable
figure. But then it is just in the fact that she can be separated,
that in one (and her own) way of seeing the action she can be isolated, and is isolated, as a heroically persistent figure, that the

complexity of the action reveals itself. She has to persist, and
she has to be isolated, so that the full action can be shown.
What has to be created, as communicable experience and not merely
as an argument, is just her hard lively opportunism (it is the
recognizable voice of Peachum or Azdak), until it engages; until
it not only seems but is a way to live. And then the depth of the
drama is not what is said about this, by some device of exposition
or commentary; it is in the rest of the action, in what *other*
things happen. The point is then not (as in so much discussion of
the play) whether Mother Courage, as a person, is meant to be
admired as heroically persistent, or despised as wickedly opportu-
nist. That separable moral judgement is precisely what the play
confounds. For not an attitude but an experience drives through
the action: what else can be done, here, in this war across Europe? The formal submission to an uncontrollable power; the preservation of life by going on with the system, dragging the cart
after the armies: these not only seem but are inevitable; they
have to convince, as experience, before the full dramatic shock
can come: that life isn't preserved; that a family, before our
eyes, is destroyed; that the cart is dragged on, but the dead are
multiplying. It is not the abstract question, 'are they good
people?', or 'what should they have done?' It is, inescapably, at
once 'what are they doing?' and 'what is this doing to them?' It
is in this way that a complex seeing is integrated in the action
itself:

> CHAPLAIN: Mother Courage. I see how you got your name.
> MOTHER COURAGE: The poor need courage. They're lost, that's
> why. That they even get up in the morning is something, in
> *their* plight. Or that they plough a field, in wartime. Even
> their bringing children into the world shows they have courage,
> for they have no prospects. They have to hang each other one
> by one and slaughter each other in the lump, so if they want
> to look each other in the face once in a while, well, it takes
> courage.

It certainly takes courage: not the isolable moral quality, but
this character, this action. Past the justifications, the excuses,
the 'bad luck', the inevitabilities, it takes this action - of a
mother destroying her family with the aim of preserving life - to
see what is happening; to be able to bear to see it. If she were
not so strong and persistent, there would be no life at all; and
at the same time, because she is strong and persistent, in a destructive society, she destroys the life that she has herself
created. This deep and complex image, in a character and in an
action, is Brecht's central structure of feeling, directly dramatized. It is by looking this action, this character, in the face,
that we see what we are doing: the essential contradiction; the
destructive acquiescence in the name of life; the persistent
vitality in a continuing destruction. The desperate urgency, of
the real preservation of life, is articulated only in the drum-
ming of the dumb girl, to waken and save the city: a defiance
that gets her killed, but that is as inevitable as her mother going
on with the cart. It is to that experience, of a crushed revolt,

as well as to the other experience, of a desperate acquiescence,
that the soldiers sing, in the same essential action:

> And though you may not long survive
> Get out of bed and look alive.

The vitality and the danger are inseparable; the reality and the
pretence, until the action is played through, are indistinguish-
able. The conflict is pushed through, seen from every side, until
it connects with our own conflict.

The dramatic action of 'Mother Courage and Her Children' is
Brecht's major achievement. The achievement of 'The Life of
Galileo' is different: a dramatic consciousness. Thematically,
the connection is clear: Galileo, under pressure, renounces what
he knows to be the truth; gains two things - the physical continuity and satisfaction he must have, and also the time to write the
'Discorsi'; and loses the connection of his truth, his science,
with the needs - the physical continuities and satisfactions - of
the majority of men. In saving his life he has destroyed a connected life: in saving his science he has altered it. The dramatic method is not historical reconstruction: Galileo, and the
action surrounding him, are specifically created so that we can
see, in a proper complexity, the complexity of the real choices.
Galileo stripped to the waist, explaining the rotation of the
earth with an apple, is the claim of immediate life, in the most
direct way: physical satisfaction and understanding. It is there,
undeniable, except that a corrupt system denies it. Once again, as
in 'Mother Courage and Her Children', we are then 'torn in two':
except that this is only ever a metaphor - the tearing happens,
between the body and the mind, the satisfaction and the truth, but
both are still in one person, one need, one consciousness. What is
then especially brilliant is that the intolerable tension is overcome, as it must be in life, by a specific distortion: a partial
validity extended until it is a false but effective consciousness.
Galileo had asked:

> Could we deny ourselves to the crowd and still remain scientists?

The answer, of course, is yes: but scientists of a different kind.
In the beginning there was a connection between the truth about the
solar system and the truth about the social system: a falsehood in
one had been used to maintain an oppression in the other; Galileo,
in challenging one, is challenging both:

> The most solemn truths are being tapped on the shoulder; what
> was never doubted is now in doubt. And because of that a great
> wind has arisen, lifting even the gold-embroidered coat-tails
> of princes and prelates, so that the fat legs and thin legs
> underneath are seen; legs like our legs.

It is this connection that Galileo betrays, taking science out of
the street and into the service either of a court or of a private
study. The images of this resolution are powerfully created in
their own terms: Galileo the survivor, going on with his work in

his exiled intelligence; the manuscript of the 'Discorsi' crossing
the border to freedom. But they are not simple images; they are
seen, in the action, in complex ways. The vitality of the earth
and the apple, in the first scene, are the smearing fat of the
goose in the fourteenth. In the last scene, when the manuscript
crosses the border, it is hidden in a coach, and the boys playing
at the frontier - the boys who would have been Galileo's audience
- are talking of devils and witches. Both things happen: a way
of continuing science, and a way of detaching it from ordinary
life. And the solution is in the service of Galileo's ordinary
life: the goose and the opportunity to work, both of which he
had every right to. A complex consciousness, in which not only
this but also that must be said, is then brilliantly created.

Brecht's important dramatic conventions can be briefly summarized.
He is able to use with a new freedom, at many points in his work,
conventions of exposition and commentary which belong to a contemporary consciousness, rather than to an imitation of older forms.
Again, with a new freedom, he is able to range, in language, from
a vigorous naturalism, through the formalities of argument, to the
intensity of song. In learning to present characters, rather than
assuming and developing their existence, he found ways of combining
an intense physical presence, backed up with all the vigour of an
intensely physical imagery, with the possibility of detachment, of
suspension, allowing the presence to be examined and looked at, yet
without abstraction. And what, in his major work, holds these conventions together, is a form so simple, at first sight, that we
can easily overlook its originality. To see the open action of
'Mother Courage' or 'Galileo' - the sequence of scenes which are
'for themselves', sharp and isolated, yet connect in a pattern that
defines the action - is to see what can appear an unstudied form:
a mere series: a setting-down of scenes. But what has gone, from
the ordinary shape of most modern plays, is more noticeable, as
we look closer. What has gone is a form that encloses the characters, in fixed places and at fixed times. The shape of separable,
enclosed acts, with fixed beginnings and climaxes, has been
replaced by this open sequence of scenes, which is not only technically flexible and mobile, undominated by fixed scene and persistent situations, but is basically a movement corresponding to a flow
of action - a process rather than a product. The form is not, of
course, an innovation by Brecht; it derives, essentially, from the
Elizabethan drama and especially from Shakespeare; through Büchner
and others. But it is a form which corresponds exactly to the realization of process - an isolation, a contrast but then a connection
of scenes - which is the determining dramatic experience. Put one
way, Brecht's drama is that of isolated and separated individuals,
and of their connections, in that capacity, with a total historical
process. He is hardly interested at all in intermediate relationships, in that whole complex of experience, at once personal and
social, between the poles of the separated individual and the
totally realized society. His dramatic form, isolating and dialectic, serves this structure of feeling exactly; it is his precise
development of an expressionist mode, and the dimension of social
realism is absent in his work, both in substance and in any

continuing contemporary experience, because the structure is of
that kind. Put another way, Brecht's expressionism is unusually
open, is a development of possibilities and even at times a transformation of effective conventions, because he took up the position of explaining rather then exposing: an overall critical-
objective position, rather than the intensity of special pleading
on behalf of an isolated figure. Retaining the characteristic poles
of expressionism - the isolated suffering individual and the totality of the world in which he suffers - he reversed the normal positive and negative references. The previously overwhelming positive
reference - the isolated individual - becomes negative: is seen
not subjectively, as in conventional expressionism, but object-
ively, as a characteristic even symptomatic figure. The positive
reference, the source of values and explanation, is at the other
pole: the totality, the historical process. The strength of his
form is that it permits this kind of clarification: at once
clipped, bitter, distant, and yet, in its assumption of a common
complicity, a common weakness, connecting and humane in very general ways: a human need and satisfaction ironically known and
recalled. Because the polar relationship is still there and decisive, the drama is retrospective, in a deep sense: the intolerable isolation is a fact, and when we see men producing themselves
and their situations it is this, essentially, that they produce;
that is seen as inevitable and yet is rejected. The dramatic form
is not oriented to growth: the experiences of transforming relationship and of social change are not included, and the tone and
the conventions follow from this: men are shown why they are
isolated, why they defeat themselves, why they smell of defeat and
its few isolated, complicit virtues. It is a major originality,
not because it enters a new world, but because it values an old
world differently: the world created directly, in drama, by Ibsen
and Strindberg and Chekhov - a world of defeat, frustration, isolation; a world rationalized by Pirandello and the absurdists to
a total condition, an inherent insignificance and loss of values;
a world purged now, by Brecht, of pity and acceptance - held at
arm's length, criticized, explained. On to an alienated world,
that had been dramatized mainly from the inside, Brecht turned an
alienated consciousness: meeting a negative with a negative;
intransigent, detached, open. It is this connection between a
structure of feeling and conventions that we must end by emphasi-
zing: the Brechtian mode, in any serious sense, belongs to that
consciousness; its particular methods, without the consciousness,
are merely fashionable techniques. What comes through, as always,
when the consciousness and the conventions are deeply connected,
is the power of a major writer: a way of seeing that permanently
alters dramatic possibilities. Looking back from Brecht, we see
the drama of the last hundred years differently: see its consciousness and its methods from the outside, in a fully critical
light. We do not, because of that, at all lessen our respect: the
power of the masters is what it was. But the power of this different master is conclusive. With this last shift, a particular
dramatic world - that of the individual against society - is now
wholly seen. Without the substance created by others, Brecht's
critical epilogue - his dramatic negative - could not have been

written. But now that it has been written, in two or three great
plays and in a wider achievement of a powerful and unforgettable
dramatic consciousness, we have to struggle to enter, as Brecht
himself insisted, a new kind of world.

BECKETT: 'WAITING FOR GODOT'

13. 1   JACK MacGOWRAN (*)

MacGowran on Beckett, Interview with Richard
Toscan, 'Theatre Quarterly', 3 (11), 1973,
pp. 16-17

[...] I have always felt, you know, that his plays are not so complicated as people would like to think - that there is an underlying simplicity.

What do you mean by simplicity?

I find that with all great writers, people complicate what they
have written by looking for more than what they have said - reading
in symbols that were never meant. I usually find that they simply
meant what they said. For instance, with a passage in Beckett
that might be interpreted in several different ways, I would dis-
card, in the beginning anyway, the obvious interpretations, and I'd
find a different way. When I started working with Beckett, he
said, 'No, no, the first one is the right one' - the simple one.
Actually he means what he is saying. There's no symbolic quality
necessarily, though people can read symbols into the plays if they
want to.
     What Beckett has done is taken man's situation and mankind's
misfortune to the n'th degree and made men survive in conditions
which normally would lead any man to commit suicide - where death
would be a welcome relief. There is a kind of lust for death and
yet a zest for life - a strange paradox that runs through much of
his work.
     What makes him unhappy, too, at times, is the fact that he feels
man's life is too short for the things he wants to accomplish, with
an intellect like his. Hence Pozzo's line, 'They give birth astride
of a grave, the light gleams an instant, then it's night once
more.' Life is so short a span in which to do all the things man
wants to do, that survival becomes the first necessary - because
as long as he's alive, man will be able to do something. In 'How

It Is', one of his latest novels, man is reduced to an animal
state, crawling through the mud; he is constantly seeking touch
with a fellow human being somewhere, simply so he can be in contact. But it's a struggle to live, to survive without giving up,
and not dying. This is the struggle Beckett puts all his characters into. For instance, Winnie in 'Happy Days' is in a very
unhappy position, being buried up to her waist in sand, but she
makes light of her plight. There's nothing Winnie could say she
was happy about and yet it's both a funny and a sad play. There's
a Browning pistol, if you notice, near her. She's only got to
pick that up and shoot herself yet she never touches it. She considers surviving as part of the day. Even when she's buried up to
the neck in the following act, it doesn't matter - she'll still
survive. [...]

*Does he begin by explaining to you the point of the play and the
effect he's trying to get?*

Yes, he does, but only when you are doing his work. For the casual
person who asks him questions, he just doesn't feel he can answer
them, because they're not going to be involved in his work -
they're only curious - but when it concerns doing his work he will
open up completely about it. He's often been questioned about
'Waiting for Godot'. Because Godot begins with g-o-d, people have
got the idea that he's referring to God. But he categorically
states that that is not the point at all, that it doesn't mean
God at all. The whole play's about waiting.

But waiting for something?

Waiting for something, whatever it may be, whatever personal thing
a person's waiting for - if they have the patience to survive and
wait for it, it may happen. He writes about human distress, not
human despair. Because Estragon and Vladimir live on a kind of
hope that, if it doesn't come tomorrow, it'll come the next day or
the next day. There is the same idea in the novel 'The Unnamable'
when he says, 'I can't go on, you must go on, I'll go on.'

*When you played Lucky, what sections of 'Godot' did you discuss
with Beckett?*

The rhythm of Lucky's speech. That speech has always been a problem to most actors. Because I had access to Beckett - I got from
him what it means and also the rhythms of the speech, which are
terribly important. Every time I've seen 'Godot', Lucky's speech
has been a jumble - you couldn't make anything out, it's delivered
so quickly. But this needn't be the case. When Beckett was trying
to explain the rhythms to me, he said, 'I can't explain what a
rhythm is except that it's iambic pentameter or trochaic; outside
that they are just specific rhythms of my own.' And I said, 'Well,
the only way we can do it is if I hear them.' So he recorded
Lucky's speech for me on a tape recorder and I listened to that
many, many times. That is how I got the rhythm of the speech, and
from those rhythms I could actually hear what was being said. It's

really one long sentence that ends with the conclusion that man
'wastes and pines wastes and pines.'

In the early part of the play when Vladimir makes biblical refer-
ences, how did you handle that?   What is Beckett's attitude
toward that?

There's a sentence from St. Augustine which reads, 'Do not despair; one of the thieves was saved. Do not presume; one of the
thieves was damned.' Beckett said that is the key to the whole
play, the shape of what he needed. Vladimir questions the fact
that only one of the gospels refers to the thieves. Estragon, who
says he's forgotten all he's read about the Bible - he remembers
the maps and the blue sea, but nothing else - has read it all and
thrown it all aside as a lot of nonsense. He says, 'People are
bloody ignorant apes.' Whereas poor Vladimir tries to puzzle out
why only one of the four refers to the thieves and the others make
no reference to them at all, to Estragon it doesn't matter.
    I think sometimes the roles are reversed. I think Estragon is
the one who has read and known everything and thrown it away and
become completely cynical. Vladimir, who appears to be the
brighter of the two, is in fact the half-schooled one, madly trying
to find out answers and pestering Estragon the whole time. Otherwise, Estragon couldn't quote Shelley as he does and misquote him
deliberately: 'Pale for weariness of climbing the heavens and
gazing at the likes of us.' This gives you the impression that
Estragon has read everything and dismissed it.

When you were developing the role of Vladimir, did you find it
necessary to talk with Beckett about the difference between the two?

Yes, and he said to me, 'Treat it as a movable force meeting an
immovable object' (Vladimir being the movable force and Estragon
being the immovable object). But, he said, 'They are interdependent; one needs the other.' Estragon has so many nightmares, he
must have someone to talk to. And Vladimir could not bear to be
alone, because he cannot find any answers to the questions he is
seeking. He hopes Estragon will provide the answers. Also, part
of Vladimir is very much concerned about the plight of mankind.
After Pozzo and Lucky fall down and Pozzo keeps shouting for help,
suddenly Vladimir says that they are the only ones who can lend
assistance: 'Let us make the most of it before it is too late.'

When you played Lucky, what was your approach to the scene in the
second act when Pozzo and Lucky return, one dumb and one blind?
Again, did you talk to Beckett about it?

No, I didn't find I had to talk to him very much about that. In
the first act Lucky is an extremely damaged person mentally -
hence his speech disintegrates because his mind is disintegrating.
Pozzo says, 'I am bringing him to the fair, where I hope to get a
good price for him.' They arrive back in the second act when
Pozzo hasn't been able to get rid of Lucky because he's blind and
he needs the halter to hold onto. But there can be no communication

because Lucky has gone dumb and cannot answer; he has said all he
has to say and can say no more.   But they remain interdependent.

*Did you envisage the play as taking place in the present time or
as though it were in the future?*

I just saw them as two men isolated in an area where people
weren't about.   I didn't play it in any futuristic sense;   I
played it as happening in the present time.

NOTE

*   Jack MacGowran acted in most of Beckett's plays, collaborating
    closely with Beckett himself.   He played Lucky in a production
    of 'Waiting for Godot' at the Royal Court Theatre in 1964-5
    with Nicol Williamson as Vladimir.

13. 2   SEAN O'CASEY

   Not Waiting for Godot, 'Encore', Easter, 1956,
   p. 7 (reprinted in 'Blasts and Benedictions',
   ed. R. Ayling, Macmillan, 1967, pp. 51-2)

[...] Beckett?   I have nothing to do with Beckett.   He isn't in
me; nor am I in him.   I am not waiting for Godot to bring me life;
I am out after life myself, even at the age I've reached.   What
have any of you to do with Godot?   There is more life than Godot
can give in the life of the least of us.   That Beckett is a clever
writer, and that he has written a rotting and remarkable play,
there is no doubt; but his philosophy isn't my philosophy, for
within him there is no hazard of hope; no desire for it; nothing
in it but a lust for despair, and a crying of woe, not in a wil-
derness, but in a garden.
   The earth isn't either a grave-yard or a roaring camp - save
in a war, when it is both; but today war is a *non est,* for with the
new nuclear explosive power, all are within range of death; the
rich and the poor, the ones who go out to fight, the ones who
remain at home; the Catholic pope and the Catholic peasant share
its shivers, and so aren't ready to nod the head in favour of
strife.   And there is life and energy even in decay (not Beckett's,
but nature's), for dead leaves turn to loam, and dry bones to
phosphates.
   What witnesses does this Beckett call?   A dowdy and a doleful
few: Camus, Kafka, Orwell, Graham Greene, Huxley, with T.S. Eliot
a wan follower, cross on breast and hands clenched in an obscure
prayer.   And what witness have we?   A cloud of them: Copernicus,
Newton, Beethoven, Angelo, Shelley, Whitman, Balzac, Faraday,
Titian, and, yes, by God, and Shakespeare, too, with ten thousand
others close up to the greatest!

13. 3 MARTIN ESSLIN

Samuel Beckett: the Search for the Self, 'The
Theatre of the Absurd', Eyre & Spottiswoode,
1962, pp. 33-46

'Waiting for Godot' does not tell a story; it explores a static
situation. 'Nothing happens, nobody comes, nobody goes, it's
awful.' On a country road, by a tree, two old tramps, Vladimir
and Estragon, are waiting. That is the opening situation at the
beginning of act I. At the end of act I they are informed that
Mr Godot, with whom they believe they have an appointment, cannot
come, but that he will surely come tomorrow. Act II repeats precisely the same pattern. The same boy arrives and delivers the
same message. Act I ends: (1)

    ESTRAGON: Well, shall we go?
    VLADIMIR: Yes, let's go.
    (*They do not move.*)

Act II ends with the same lines of dialogue, but spoken by the
same characters in reversed order.
    The sequence of events and the dialogue in each act are dif-
ferent. Each time the two tramps encounter another pair of
characters, Pozzo and Lucky, master and slave, under differing
circumstances; in each act Vladimir and Estragon attempt suicide
and fail, for differing reasons; but these variations merely
serve to emphasize the essential sameness of the situation - *plus
ça change, plus c'est la même chose*.
    Vladimir and Estragon - who call each other Didi and Gogo,
although Vladimir is addressed by the boy messenger as Mr Albert,
and Estragon, when asked his name, replies without hesitation,
Catullus - are clearly derived from the pairs of cross-talk comedians of music halls. Their dialogue has the peculiar repetitive
quality of the cross-talk comedians' patter.

    ESTRAGON: So long as one knows.
    VLADIMIR: One can bide one's time.
    ESTRAGON: One knows what to expect.
    VLADIMIR: No further need to worry.

And the parallel to the music hall and the circus is even explicitly stated:

    VLADIMIR: Charming evening we're having.
    ESTRAGON: Unforgettable.
    VLADIMIR: And it's not over.
    ESTRAGON: Apparently not.
    VLADIMIR: It's only the beginning.
    ESTRAGON: It's awful.
    VLADIMIR: It's worse than being at the theatre.
    ESTRAGON: The circus.
    VLADIMIR: The music hall.
    ESTRAGON: The circus.

In accordance with the traditions of the music hall or the circus, there is an element of crudely physical humour: Estragon loses his trousers, there is a protracted gag involving three hats that are put on and off and handed on in a sequence of seem- ingly unending confusion, and there is an abundance of pratfalls - the writer of a penetrating thesis on Beckett, Niklaus Gessner, lists no fewer than forty-five stage directions indicating that one of the characters leaves the upright position, which symbol- izes the dignity of man.

As the members of a cross-talk act, Vladimir and Estragon have complementary personalities. Vladimir is the more practical of the two, and Estragon claims to have been a poet. In eating his carrot, Estragon finds that the more he eats of it the less he likes it, while Vladimir reacts the opposite way - he likes things as he gets used to them. Estragon is volatile, Vladimir persis- tent. Estragon dreams, Vladimir cannot stand hearing about dreams. Vladimir has stinking breath, Estragon has stinking feet. Vladi- mir remembers past events, Estragon tends to forget them as soon as they have happened. Estragon likes telling funny stories, Vladimir is upset by them. It is mainly Vladimir who voices the hope that Godot will come and that his coming will change their situation, while Estragon remains sceptical throughout and at times even forgets the name of Godot. It is Vladimir who conducts the conversation with the boy who is Godot's messenger and to whom the boy's messages are addressed. Estragon is the weaker of the two; he is beaten up by mysterious strangers every night. Vladimir at times acts as his protector, sings him to sleep with a lullaby, and covers him with his coat.   The opposition of their tempera- ments is the cause of endless bickering between them and often leads to the suggestion that they should part. Yet, being comple- mentary natures, they also are dependent on each other and have to stay together.

Pozzo and Lucky are equally complementary in their natures, but their relationship is on a more primitive level: Pozzo is the sadistic master, Lucky the submissive slave. In the first act, Pozzo is rich, powerful, and certain of himself; he represents worldly man in all his facile and shortsighted optimism and illusory feeling of power and permanence. Lucky not only carries his heavy luggage, and even the whip with which Pozzo beats him, he also dances and thinks for him, or did so in his prime. In fact, Lucky taught Pozzo all the higher values of life: 'beauty, grace, truth of the first water'. Pozzo and Lucky represent the relationship between body and mind, the material and the spiritual sides of man, with the intellect subordinate to the appetites of the body. Now that Lucky's powers are failing, Pozzo complains that they cause him untold suffering. He wants to get rid of Lucky and sell him at the fair. But in the second act, when they appear again, they are still tied together. Pozzo has gone blind, Lucky has become dumb. While Pozzo drives Lucky on a journey without an apparent goal, Vladimir has prevailed upon Estragon to wait for Godot. [...]

Yet whether Godot is meant to suggest the intervention of a supernatural agency, or whether he stands for a mythical human being whose arrival is expected to change the situation, or both of these possibilities combined, his exact nature is of secondary importance. The subject of the play is not Godot but waiting, the act of waiting as an essential and characteristic aspect of the human condition. Throughout our lives we always wait for something, and Godot simply represents the objective of our waiting - an event, a thing, a person, death. Moreover, it is in the act of waiting that we experience the flow of *time* in its purest, most evident form. If we are active, we tend to forget the passage of time, we *pass* the time, but if we are merely passively waiting, we are confronted with the action of time itself. As Beckett points out in his analysis of Proust, 'There is no escape from the hours and the days. Neither from tomorrow nor from yesterday because yesterday has deformed us, or been deformed by us... Yesterday is not a milestone that has been passed, but a daystone on the beaten track of the years, and irremediably part of us, within us, heavy and dangerous. We are not merely more weary because of yesterday, we are other, no longer what we were before the calamity of yesterday.' (2) The flow of time confronts us with the basic problem of being - the problem of the nature of the self, which, being subject to constant change in time, is in constant flux and therefore ever outside our grasp - 'personality, whose permanent reality can only be apprehended as a retrospective hypothesis. The individual is the seat of a constant process of decantation, sluggish, pale and monochrome, to the vessel containing the fluid of past time, agitated and multicoloured by the phenomena of its hours.' (3)

Being subject to this process of time flowing through us and changing us in doing so, we are, at no single moment in our lives, identical with ourselves. Hence 'we are disappointed at the nullity of what we are pleased to call attainment. But what is attainment? The identification of the subject with the object of his desire. The subject has died - and perhaps many times on the way.' (4) If Godot is the object of Vladimir's and Estragon's desire, he seems naturally ever beyond their reach. It is significant that the boy who acts as go-between fails to recognize the pair from day to day. The French version explicitly states that the boy who appears in the second act is the same boy as the one in the first act, yet the boy denies that he has even seen the two tramps before and insists that this is the first time he has acted as Godot's messenger. As the boy leaves, Vladimir tries to impress it upon him: 'You're sure you saw me, eh, you won't come and tell me tomorrow that you never saw me before?' The boy does not reply, and we know that he will again fail to recognize them. Can we ever be sure that the human beings we meet are the same today as they were yesterday? When Pozzo and Lucky first appear, neither Vladimir nor Estragon seems to recognize them; Estragon even takes Pozzo for Godot. But after they have gone, Vladimir comments that they have changed since their last appearance. Estragon insists that he didn't know them.

```
VLADIMIR:  Yes you do know them.
ESTRAGON:  No I don't know them.
VLADIMIR:  We know them, I tell you.  You forget everything.
```

(*Pause.   To himself.*) Unless they're not the same ...
ESTRAGON: Why didn't they recognize us, then?
VLADIMIR: That means nothing.   I too pretended not to recog-
nize them.   And then nobody ever recognizes us.

In the second act, when Pozzo and Lucky reappear, cruelly
deformed by the action of time, Vladimir and Estragon again have
their doubts whether they are the same people they met on the
previous day.   Nor does Pozzo remember them: 'I don't remember
having met anyone yesterday.   But tomorrow I won't remember having
met anyone today.'
Waiting is to experience the action of time, which is constant
change.   And yet, as nothing real ever happens, that change is in
itself an illusion.   The ceaseless activity of time is self-
defeating, purposeless, and therefore null and void.   The more
things change, the more they are the same.   That is the terrible
stability of the world.   'The tears of the world are a constant
quantity.   For each one who begins to weep, somewhere else another
stops.'   One day is like another, and when we die, we might never
have existed.   As Pozzo exclaims in his great final outburst:

Have you not done tormenting me with your accursed time?....
One day, is that not enough for you, one day like any other he
went dumb, one day I went blind, one day we'll go deaf, one day
we were born, one day we'll die, the same day, the same
second ... They give birth astride of a grave, the light gleams
an instant, then it's night once more.

And Vladimir, shortly afterwards, agrees: 'Astride of a grave
and a difficult birth.   Down in the hole, lingeringly, the
gravedigger puts on the forceps.'
Still Vladimir and Estragon live in hope: they wait for Godot,
whose coming will bring the flow of time to a stop.   'Tonight perhaps we shall sleep in his place, in the warmth, dry, our bellies
full, on the straw.   It is worth waiting for that, is it not?' (5)
This passage, omitted in the English version, clearly suggests the
peace, the rest from waiting, the sense of having arrived in a
haven, that Godot represents to the two tramps.   They are hoping
to be saved from the evanescence and instability of the illusion
of time, and to find peace and permanence outside it.   Then they
will no longer be tramps, homeless wanderers, but will have arrived
home.
Vladimir and Estragon wait for Godot although their appointment
with him is by no means certain.   Estragon does not remember it at
all.   Vladimir is not quite sure what they asked Godot to do for
them.   It was 'nothing very definite...a kind of prayer ... a
vague supplication'.   And what had Godot promised them?   'That
he'd see...that he would think it over...'
When Beckett is asked about the theme of 'Waiting for Godot',
he sometimes refers to a passage in the writings of St Augustine:
'There is a wonderful sentence in Augustine.   I wish I could remember the Latin.   It is even finer in Latin than in English.   "Do not
despair: one of the thieves was saved.   Do not presume: one of
the thieves was damned."'   And Beckett sometimes adds, 'I am

interested in the shape of ideas even if I do not believe in them.
... That sentence has a wonderful shape. It is the shape that
matters.'

The theme of the two thieves on the cross, the theme of the
uncertainty of the hope of salvation and the fortuitousness of
the bestowal of grace, does indeed pervade the whole play.
Vladimir states it right at the beginning: 'One of the thieves
was saved .... It's a reasonable percentage.' Later he enlarges
on the subject: 'Two thieves....One is supposed to have been
saved and the other ... damned....And yet how is it that of the
four evangelists only one speaks of a thief being saved? The
four of them were there or thereabouts, and only one speaks of a
thief being saved....Of the other three two don't mention any
thieves at all and the third says that both of them abused him.'
There is a fifty-fifty chance, but as only one out of four witnesses reports it, the odds are considerably reduced. But, as
Vladimir points out; it is a curious fact that everybody seems
to believe that one witness: 'It is the only version they know.'
Estragon, whose attitude has been one of scepticism throughout,
merely comments, 'People are bloody ignorant apes.'

It is the shape of the idea that fascinated Beckett. Out of
all the malefactors, out of all the millions and millions of
criminals that have been executed in the course of history, two,
only two, had the chance of receiving absolution in the hour of
their death in so uniquely effective a manner. One happened to
make a hostile remark; he was damned. One happened to contra-
dict that hostile remark; he was saved. How easily could the
roles have been reversed. These, after all, were not well-
considered judgements, but chance exclamations uttered at a
moment of supreme suffering and stress. As Pozzo says about
Lucky, 'Remark that I might easily have been in his shoes and he
in mine. If chance had not willed it otherwise. To each one his
due.' And then our shoes might fit us one day and not the next:
Estragon's boots torment him in the first act; in act II they fit
him miraculously.

Godot himself is unpredictable in bestowing kindness and
punishment. The boy who is his messenger minds the goats, and
Godot treats him well. But the boy's brother, who minds the sheep,
is beaten by Godot. 'And why doesn't he beat you?' asks Vladimir.
I don't know, sir', the boy replies, using the words of the *apache*
who had stabbed Beckett. The parallel to Cain and Abel is evident: there too the Lord's grace fell on one rather than on the
other without any rational explanation - only that Godot beats
the minder of the sheep and cherishes the minder of the goats.
Here Godot also acts contrary to the Son of Man at the Last Judgement: 'And he shall set the sheep on his right hand, but the
goats on the left.' But if Godot's kindness is bestowed fortui-
tously, his coming is not a source of pure joy; it can also mean
damnation. When Estragon, in the second act, believes Godot to be
approaching, his first thought is, 'I'm accursed.' And as Vladimir
triumphantly exclaims, 'It's Godot! At last! Let's go and meet
him,' Estragon runs away, shouting. 'I'm in hell!'

The fortuitous bestowal of grace, which passes human understanding, divides mankind into those that will be saved and those that

will be damned. When, in act II Pozzo and Lucky return, and the
two tramps try to identify them, Estragon calls out, 'Abel!
Abel!' Pozzo immediately responds. But when Estragon calls out,
'Cain! Cain!' Pozzo responds again. 'He's all mankind.' concludes
Estragon.

There is even a suggestion that Pozzo's activity is concerned
with his frantic attempt to draw that fifty-fifty chance of salvation upon himself. In the first act, Pozzo is on his way to
sell Lucky 'at the fair'. The French version, however, specifies that it is the Market of the Holy Saviour to which he is
taking Lucky. Is Pozzo trying to sell Lucky to redeem himself?
Is he trying to divert the fifty-fifty chance of redemption from
Lucky (in whose shoes he might easily have been himself) to
Pozzo? He certainly complains that Lucky is causing him great
pain, that he is killing him with his mere presence - perhaps
because his mere presence reminds Pozzo that it might be Lucky
who will be redeemed. When Lucky gives his famous demonstration
of his thinking, what is the thin thread of sense that seems to
underlie the opening passage of his wild, schizophrenic 'word
salad'? Again, it seems to be concerned with the fortuitousness
of salvation: 'Given the existence...of a personal God...outside
time without extension who from the heights of divine apathia
divine athambia divine aphasia loves us dearly with some exceptions for reasons unknown...and suffers ... with those who for
reasons unknown are plunged in torment....' Here again we have
the personal God, with his divine apathy, his speechlessness
(aphasia), and his lack of the capacity for terror or amazement
(athambia), who loves us dearly - with some exceptions, who will
be plunged into the torments of hell. In other words, God, who
does not communicate with us, cannot feel for us, and condemns
us for reasons unknown.

When Pozzo and Lucky reappear the next day, Pozzo blind and
Lucky dumb, no more is heard of the fair. Pozzo has failed to
sell Lucky; his blindness in thinking that he could thus influence
the action of grace has been made evident in concrete physical
form.

That 'Waiting for Godot' is concerned with the hope of salvation
through the workings of grace seems clearly established both from
Beckett's own evidence and from the text itself. Does this,
however, mean that it is a Christian, or even that it is a religious, play? There have been a number of very ingenious interpretations in this sense. Vladimir's and Estragon's waiting is
explained as signifying their steadfast faith and hope, while Vladimir's kindness to his friend, and the two tramps' mutual inter-
dependence, are seen as symbols of Christian charity. But these
religious interpretations seem to overlook a number of essential
features of the play - its constant stress on the uncertainty of
the appointment with Godot, Godot's unreliability and irration-
ality, and the repeated demonstration of the futility of the hopes
pinned on him. The act of waiting for Godot is shown as essentially
absurd. Admittedly it might be a case of ['Believing because it
is absurd'], yet it might even more forcibly be taken as a demonstration of the proposition ['It is absurd to believe.']

There is one feature in the play that leads one to assume there

is a better solution to the tramps' predicament, which they themselves both consider preferable to waiting for Godot - that is,
suicide. 'We should have thought of it when the world was young,
in the nineties....Hand in hand from the top of the Eiffel Tower,
among the first. We were respectable in those days. Now it's
too late. They wouldn't even let us up.' Suicide remains their
favourite solution, unattainable owing to their own incompetence
and their lack of the practical tools to achieve it. It is precisely their disappointment at their failure to succeed in their
attempts at suicide that Vladimir and Estragon rationalize by
waiting, or pretending to wait, for Godot. 'I'm curious to hear
what he has to offer. Then we'll take it or leave it.' Estragon,
far less convinced of Godot's promises than Vladimir, is anxious
to reassure himself that they are not tied to Godot.

ESTRAGON: I'm asking you if we are tied.
VLADIMIR: Tied?
ESTRAGON: Ti-ed.
VLADIMIR: How do you mean tied?
ESTRAGON: Down.
VLADIMIR: But to whom. By whom?
ESTRAGON: To your man.
VLADIMIR: To Godot? Tied to Godot? What an idea! No
question of it. (*Pause.*) For the moment.

When, later, Vladimir falls into some sort of complacency about
their waiting - 'We have kept our appointment ... we are not
saints - but we have kept our appointment. How many people can
boast as much?' Estragon immediately punctures it by retorting,
'Billions.' And Vladimir is quite ready to admit that they are
waiting only from irrational habit. 'What's certain is that the
hours are long ... and constrain us to beguile them with proceedings ... which may at first sight seem reasonable until they
become a habit. You may say it is to prevent our reason from
foundering. No doubt. But has it not long been straying in the
night without end of the abyssal depths?'
     In support of the Christian interpretation, it might be argued
that Vladimir and Estragon, who are waiting for Godot, are shown
as clearly superior to Pozzo and Lucky, who have no appointment,
no objective, and are wholly egocentric, wholly wrapped up in
their sadomasochistic relationship. Is it not their faith that
puts the two tramps on to a higher plane?
     It is evident that, in fact, Pozzo is naïvely overconfident
and self-centred. 'Do I look like a man that can be made to
suffer?' he boasts. Even when he gives a soulful and melancholy
description of the sunset and the sudden falling of the night, we
know he does not believe the night will ever fall on him - he is
merely giving a performance; he is not concerned with the meaning
of what he recites, but only with its effect on the audience.
Hence he is taken completely unawares when night does fall on him
and he goes blind. Likewise Lucky, in accepting Pozzo as his
master and in teaching him his ideas, seems to have been naïvely
convinced of the power of reason, beauty, and truth. Estragon
and Vladimir *are* clearly superior to both Pozzo and Lucky - not

because they pin their faith on Godot but because they are less
naïve. They do not believe in action, wealth, or reason. They
are aware that all we do in this life is as nothing when seen
against the senseless action of time, which is in itself an illusion. They are aware that suicide would be the best solution.
They are thus superior to Pozzo and Lucky because they are less
self-centred and have fewer illusions. In fact, as a Jungian
psychologist, Eva Metman, has pointed out in a remarkable study of
Beckett's plays, 'Godot's function seems to be to keep his depen-
dents unconscious.' (6) In this view, the hope, the habit of
hoping, that Godot might come after all is the last illusion
keeps Vladimir and Estragon from facing the human condition and
themselves in the harsh light of fully conscious awareness. As
Dr Metman observes, it is at the very moment, toward the end of
the play, when Vladimir is about to realize he has been dreaming,
and must wake up and face the world as it is, that Godot's messenger arrives, rekindles his hopes, and plunges him back into the
passivity of illusion.

For a brief moment, Vladimir is aware of the full horror of
the human condition: 'The air is full of our cries....But habit is
a great deadener.' He looks at Estragon, who is asleep, and
reflects, 'At me too someone is looking, of me too someone is
saying, he is sleeping, he knows nothing, let him sleep on...
I can't go on!' The routine of waiting for Godot stands for habit,
which prevents us from reaching the painful but fruitful awareness
of the full reality of being.

Again we find Beckett's own commentary on this aspect of 'Waiting for Godot' in his essay on Proust: 'Habit is the ballast that
chains the dog to his vomit. Breathing is habit. Life is habit.
Or rather life is a succession of habits, since the individual is
a succession of individuals....Habit then is the generic term for
the countless treaties concluded between the countless subjects
that constitute the individual and their countless correlative
objects. The periods of transition that separate consecutive
adaptations ... represent the perilous zones in the life of the
individual, dangerous, precarious, painful, mysterious, and fertile, when for a moment the *boredom of living* is replaced by the
suffering of being.' (7) 'The suffering of being: that is the free
play of every faculty. Because the pernicious devotion of habit
paralyses our attention, drugs those handmaidens of perception
whose cooperation is not absolutely essential.' (8)

Vladimir's and Estragon's pastimes are, as they repeatedly
indicate, designed to stop them from thinking. 'We're in no
danger of thinking any more....Thinking is not the worst....What
is terrible is to have thought.'

Vladimir and Estragon talk incessantly. Why? They hint at it
in what is probably the most lyrical, the most perfectly phrased
passage of the play:

    VLADIMIR: You are right, we're inexhaustible.
    ESTRAGON: It's so we won't think.
    VLADIMIR: We have that excuse.
    ESTRAGON: It's so we won't hear.
    VLADIMIR: We have our reasons.

```
ESTRAGON:   All the dead voices.
VLADIMIR:   They make a noise like wings.
ESTRAGON:   Like leaves.
VLADIMIR:   Like sand.
ESTRAGON:   Like leaves.
(Silence.)
VLADIMIR:  ·They all speak together.
ESTRAGON:   Each one to itself
(Silence.)
VLADIMIR:   Rather they whisper.
ESTRAGON:   They rustle.
VLADIMIR:   They murmur.
ESTRAGON:   They rustle.
(Silence.)
VLADIMIR:   What do they say?
ESTRAGON:   They talk about their lives.
VLADIMIR:   To have lived is not enough for them.
ESTRAGON:   They have to talk about it.
VLADIMIR:   To be dead is not enough for them.
ESTRAGON:   It is not sufficient.
(Silence.)
VLADIMIR:   They make a noise like feathers.
ESTRAGON:   Like leaves.
VLADIMIR:   Like ashes.
ESTRAGON:   Like leaves
(Long silence.)
```

This passage, in which the cross-talk of Irish music-hall
comedians is miraculously transmuted into poetry, contains the key
to much of Beckett's work.   Surely these rustling, murmuring
voices of the past are the voices we hear in the three novels of
his trilogy; they are the voices that explore the mysteries of
being and the self to the limits of anguish and suffering.   Vladimir and Estragon are trying to escape hearing them.   The long
silence that follows their evocation is broken by Vladimir, 'in
anguish', with the cry 'Say anything at all!' after which the two
relapse into their wait for Godot.

The hope of salvation may be merely an evasion of the suffering
and anguish that spring from facing the reality of the human condition.   There is here a truly astonishing parallel between the
Existentialist philosophy of Jean-Paul Sartre and the creative
intuition of Beckett, who has never consciously expressed Existentialist views.   If, for Beckett as for Sartre, man has the duty
of facing the human condition as a recognition that at the root
of our being there is nothingness, liberty, and the need of constantly creating ourselves in a succession of choices, then Godot
might well become an image of what Sartre calls 'bad faith' -
'The first act of bad faith consists in evading what one cannot
evade, in evading what one is.' (9)

While these parallels may be illuminating, we must not go too
far in trying to identify Beckett's vision with any school of
philosophy.   It is the peculiar richness of a play like 'Waiting
for Godot' that it opens vistas on so many different perspectives.
It is open to philosophical, religious, and psychological

interpretations, yet above all it is a poem on time, evanescence,
and the mysteriousness of existence, the paradox of change and
stability, necessity and absurdity. [...]

NOTES

1 All quotations from 'Waiting for Godot', Faber, 1959.
2 'Proust', Grove Press, N.Y., n.d., pp. 2-3.
3 ibid., pp. 4-5.
4 ibid., p. 13.
5 Beckett, 'En Attendant Godot', Editions de Minuit, Paris,
   1952, p. 30.
6 Eva Metman, Reflections on Samuel Beckett's plays, 'Journal
   of Analytic Psychology', London, January 1960, p. 51.
7 'Proust', p. 8.
8 ibid., p. 9.
9 Jean-Paul Sartre, 'L'Etre et le néant', Gallimard, Paris, 1943,
   p. 111.

13. 4   ALAIN ROBBE-GRILLET (*)

        Samuel Beckett, or 'Presence' in the Theatre, trans.
        B. Bray, 'Twentieth Century Views: Samuel Beckett',
        ed. M. Esslin, Prentice-Hall, Englewood Cliffs, N.J.,
        1965, pp. 110-13

There had of course been previous attempts to dispense with bourgeois theatrical conventions regarding action. But 'Godot' marks
a sort of culmination. No one had ever taken so great a risk
before. For what this play is dealing with is the essential,
without any beating about the bush, and the means employed to deal
with it had never been so pared down, nor the margin for mis-
understanding so narrow. We must turn back a little in order
to assess this risk and this austerity.
    It seemed reasonable to suppose until recently that if an artis-
tic medium like the novel, for example, could free itself from many
of its traditional rules and adjuncts, the theatre at least had to
be more careful. A play, in fact, can only come into its real
existence by entering into an understanding with some sort of
public. It was supposed, therefore, that that public must be
wooed, presented with unusual characters, kept interested by intri-
guing situations, caught up in the meshes of a plot, or jolted out
of itself by a perpetual verbal inventiveness related either to
poetry or, on occasion, to mere frenzy.
    What does 'Waiting for Godot' offer? To say nothing happens in
it is an understatement. Besides, the absence of plot or intrigue
of any kind had been met with before. But here *less than nothing*
happens. It is as if we were watching a sort of regression beyond
nothing. As always in Beckett, that little we are given to begin
with, and which we thought so meager at the time, soon decays under
our very eyes - disintegrates like Pozzo, who comes back bereft of

sight, dragged by a Lucky bereft of speech; like the carrot, which
as if in mockery has dwindled by the second act into a radish.
    'This is becoming really insignificant,' says one of the prin-
cipals at that point. 'Not enough,' replies the other. His
answer is followed by a long silence.
    We can see from this one exchange alone how far we have come
from the verbal outpourings mentioned above. From beginning to
end the dialogue is dying, agonizing, at the end of its tether.
It stands always on those frontiers of dissolution inhabited by
all Beckett's 'heroes,' of whom one can sometimes hardly say for
certain that they have not already crossed them. In the midst of
the silences, the repetitions, the ready-made phrases ('One is
what one is ... The essential doesn't change.'), one or the other
of the two tramps suggests something to pass the time - making
conversation, 'repenting,' hanging themselves, telling stories,
insulting one another, playing at 'Pozzo and Lucky.' But each
time the attempt founders: after a few uncertain exchanges they
peter out, give up, admit failure.
    As for the plot, that is summed up in four words, which recur
over and over again like a refrain: 'We're waiting for Godot.'
But it is a senseless and wearisome refrain: no one is interested in this waiting: as such it has no theatrical value. It
represents neither hope nor longing nor even despair. It is
merely an excuse.
    In all this disintegration there is a peak, or rather, the
opposite - a lowest depth, a nadir. Lucky and Pozzo, now both
crippled, have fallen in a heap on top of one another in the
middle of the road and can't get up. After haggling about it for
some time Didi comes to their rescue, but he too stumbles and
falls. It is his turn to call for help. Gogo stretches out his
hand, and stumbles and falls likewise. Now there is no one left
standing upright. There is nothing on the stage but this seeth-
ing, groaning heap. from which the face of Didi emerges to pro-
nounce, almost with satisfaction, 'We are men.'
    We knew all about the theatre of ideas. It was a healthy
intellectual exercise which had its own public, even if it did
sometimes give situation and dramatic progression short shrift.
It was just a bit boring, but it made you 'think' right enough,
in the audience as well as on the stage. Thought, even when it
is subversive, is always in a sense comforting. Speech - fine
speech - is comforting too. It is impossible to estimate the
number of misunderstandings due to noble and harmonious discourse,
with its power to conceal either ideas or their absence.
    Here there can be no misunderstanding: both thought and elo-
quence are conspicuous by their absence, both figure in the text
only in the form of parody, as yet one more reversal, one more
corpse.
    Speech is that 'twilight' described by Pozzo - introduced as a
set piece with great clearings of the throat and crackings of the
whip, larded with choice expressions and dramatic gestures, but
ruined by sudden interruptions, vulgar exclamations, and grotesque
failures of inspiration: '(*Lyrical*) An hour ago (*he looks at his
watch, prosaic*) roughly (*lyrical*) after having poured forth ever
since (*he hesitates, prosaic*) say ten o'clock in the morning

(*lyrical*) tirelessly torrents of red and white light it began to
lose its effulgence, to grow pale ...,' down to the final twist,
snarled out gloomily after a silence, 'That's how it is on
this bitch of an earth.'

And thought? The two tramps have asked Pozzo a question, but
no one can remember what it is. All three take off their hats
simultaneously, press their hands to their foreheads and strain
to concentrate. Long silence. Suddenly Gogo cries 'Ah!' He's
got it. 'Why doesn't he put down his bags?'

He means Lucky. It's the question that was asked a few minutes
earlier. But in the meanwhile Lucky *has* put down the bags, and
everyone is quite satisfied when Didi argues: 'Since he has put
down the bags it is impossible that we should have asked why he
did not do so.' Logic itself. In this universe where time
stands still, the words 'before' and 'after' have no meaning. All
that counts is the present: the bags *are* down, and so it is as if
they always had been.

We have met such arguments before, in Lewis Carroll and Jarry.
Beckett goes even further: he shows us his expert thinker, Lucky.
At his master's command, 'Think, pig!' he begins:

> Given the existence as uttered forth in the public works of
> Puncher and Wattmann of a personal God quaquaquaqua with white
> beard quaquaquaqua outside time without extension Who from the
> heights of divine apathia divine athambia divine aphasia loves
> us dearly with some exceptions for reasons unknown but time
> will tell and suffers like the divine Miranda ...

and so on. To stop him the others have to knock him down and beat
and kick him, and finally - the only effective remedy - sieze his
hat. As one of the tramps says, 'Thinking is not the worst.'

The importance of such reflexions cannot be overstressed.
More than seven thousand years of analysis and metaphysics,
instead of making us modest, have tended instead to make us forget
the feebleness of our resources when it comes to what is essential.
It is as if the real importance of any question were to be
measured by our inability to apply our minds to it squarely,
except to scale it down.

This tendency, this dangerously contagious regression, is pointed out in all Beckett's work. Lucky and Pozzo, the two secondary
characters, disintegrate from one act to the next, like Murphy,
Molloy, Malone, and the rest. Carrots are reduced to radishes.
Didi even ends by losing the thread of the circular song about the
dog. And so with all the other elements in the play.

But the two tramps remain unchanged and unimpaired, and so we
are sure, this time, that they are not mere puppets whose role is
limited to masking the absence of the protagonist. It is not the
Godot they are supposed to be waiting for who has yet to be, but
they, Didi and Gogo.

We suddenly realize, as we look at them, the main function of
theatre, which is to show what the fact of *being there* consists in.
For this is what we have never seen on the stage before, or not
with the same clarity, not with so few concessions and so much
force. A character in a play usually does no more than *play a*

part, as all those about us do who are trying to shirk their own existence. But in Beckett's play it is as if the two tramps were on the stage without a part to play.

They are there; so they must explain themselves. But they do not seem to have the support of a prepared and carefully learned text. They must invent. They are free.

Of course their freedom is not put to any use. Just as there is nothing for them to recite, so there is nothing for them to invent, either, and their conversation, which has no continuous thread to sustain it, is reduced to absurd fragments: automatic exchanges, word-play, mock arguments all more or less abortive. They try everything, at random. The only thing they are not free to do is go away, cease to be there: they have to stay because they are waiting for Godot. They are there from beginning to end of the first act, and when the curtain comes down it falls, in spite of their announced departure, on two men still waiting. There they are again in the second act, which adds nothing new; and again, in spite of the announcement of their going, they are still on the stage when the curtain falls. They will be there again the next day, and the next, and the day after that - 'Tomorrow and tomorrow and tomorrow' - standing alone on the stage, superfluous, without future, without past, irremediably there.

NOTE

*   Alain Robbe-Grillet is the main spokesman and practitioner of
    the 'new novel' in France as well as a film director and critic.

REVIEWS

14. 1 'OEDIPUS REX', COVENT GARDEN, 1912

Obviously, what has faded out from the tragedy is what our fore-
fathers would have called its 'argument.' All the story, that is,
that happens before the play, its postulate, the story of
Oedipus's sin, is to a modern audience the story of a cock and a
bull. We cannot believe in it for a moment. Nor can we believe
in the present conduct of some of the people. What? Oedipus
has been married to Jocasta for years - for he has two little
girls entering upon their teens - and yet he has never till this
moment told her that story about the trouble at the cross-roads!
And Jocasta, for all those years, has never breathed a word to her
husband about the child exposed on Kithairon! The very foundation of the play, then, is to us incredible and absurd.

(A.B. Walkley, 'The Times', 16 January 1912)

14. 2 DODD'S AGUECHEEK IN 'TWELFTH NIGHT', DRURY LANE, 1785

Few now remember Dodd. What an Aguecheek the stage lost in him!
Lovegrove, who came nearest to the old actors, revived the character some few seasons ago, and made it sufficiently grotesque; but
Dodd was *it*, as it came out of nature's hands. It might be said
to remain *in puris naturalibus*. In expressing slowness of
apprehension this actor surpassed all others. You could see the
first dawn of an idea stealing slowly over his countenance,
climbing up by little and little, with a painful process, till it
cleared up at last to the fulness of a twilight conception - its
highest meridian. He seemed to keep back his intellect, as some
have had the power to retard their pulsation. The balloon takes
less time in filling, than it took to cover the expansion of his
broad moony face over all its quarters with expression. A glimmer
of understanding would appear in a corner of his eye, and for
lack of fuel go out again. A part of his forehead would catch
a little intelligence, and be a long time in communicating it to

the remainder.

(Charles Lamb, On Some of the Old Actors, 'The Essays of Elia',
Dent, 1906, p. 159)

14. 3 OLIVIER'S MALVOLIO IN 'TWELFTH NIGHT', STRATFORD-UPON-
       AVON, 1955

Thus there was nothing to frame, in a contrast of careless with
careful folly, Sir Laurence Olivier's low-toned and highly
original Malvolio. Still pointing the 'Twelfth Night' moral of
self-love humbled, this is no conventional sketch of a pompous
old fool gripped by *folie de grandeur*. Thick, crinkled hair of an
untrustworthy brown frames beady eyes, a needle-sharp nose almost
spears a pinched, rat-trap mouth; and when this youngish Malvolio
speaks it is in uneasily needling accents which grope with narrow
doggedness after correct vowel sounds as means to greatness. The
walk is quick and prissy, the demeanour efficient. The whole is
a cunning portrait of a man not without wit - observe his sardonic
backward glance at Olivia when she sends him after Viola with the
ring; and not without humanity - witness the surprising moment
when, falling preoccupied off a garden seat, he even goes so far as
to laugh at himself. This genuine amusement he hastens to catch in
a mirror; for he knows his weaknesses, and smiling is for him no
laughing matter.
    A wretched fellow, narrowly determined to get on in the world,
he is absurd, but not quite contemptible; above all, a man; when,
in the last scene of all, he bays his cry of revenge, something
has happened to him, one feels, of the sort which must once have
happened to Iago.

(J.W. Lambert, 'Sunday Times', 24 April 1955)

14. 4 OLIVIER'S MACBETH, STRATFORD-UPON-AVON, 1955

Nobody has ever succeeded as Macbeth, and the reason is not far to
seek. Instead of growing as the play proceeds, the hero shrinks;
complex and many-levelled to begin with, he ends up a cornered
thug, lacking even a death-scene with which to regain lost stature.
Most Macbeths, mindful of this, touch off their big guns as soon as
possible, and have usually shot their bolt by the time the dagger
speech is out. The marvel of Sir Laurence Olivier's reading is
that it reverses this procedure, turns the play inside out, and
makes it (for the first time I can remember) a thing of mounting,
not waning, excitement. [...]
    He begins in a perilously low key, the reason for which is soon
revealed. This Macbeth is paralysed with guilt before the curtain
rises, having already killed Duncan time and again in his mind.
Far from recoiling and popping his eyes, he greets the air-drawn
dagger with sad familiarity; it is a fixture in the crooked furniture of his brain. Uxoriousness leads him to the act, which
unexpectedly purges him of remorse. Now the potrait swells; seeking

security, he is seized with fits of desperate bewilderment as the
prize is snatched out of reach. There was true agony in 'I had
else been perfect': Banquo's ghost was received with horrific
torment, as if Macbeth would shriek 'I've been robbed!', and the
phrase about the dead rising to 'push us from our stools' was
accompanied by a convulsive shoving gesture which few other
actors would have risked.

(Kenneth Tynan, 'The Observer', 12 June 1955)

14. 5 GUINNESS'S MACBETH, ENGLISH STAGE COMPANY, ROYAL COURT,
        1966

[...] This Macbeth is as Scottish as Olivier's Othello is African.
Without distorting it, Guinness pours the poetry into a soft Scots
rhythm, burring his r's, crooning his o's. Somehow he has even
found a Scottish glance and walk, a flatfooted, almost dainty
sword-dancer's tread. It cries out for a kilt. [...]
    From there Guinness constructs his Macbeth around the hint in
Caroline Spurgeon's study of the play's imagery. This, as
perfectly as we may hope to see it played, is the Macbeth too
small for the robes he snatches; the poor player who struts and
frets in a role too big for him. From his first entry, Guinness
gives him acute, anxious awareness of the impression he creates on
others.
    His insecurity breaks out before the murder. Steeling himself
to follow in Tarquin's steps, he imitates them awkwardly, like a
man acting to a mirror in an empty train compartment. But for his
wife's goading, he would collapse in hysteria - this paves the way
for the nervous vanity with which he plans Banquo's murder: he
will prove he can kill alone.
    Crowned, he reveals appallingly that he has been a royalty-
watcher. Those smirks, those stiff, gracious little gestures have
been studied, secretly practised. Carefully, he acts royal bon-
homie at the banquet: it shatters in gibbering terror at sight of
Banquo's ghost. In the exhausted quiet of his 'It will have
blood,' he reaches the heart of his characterisation. The penny-
ante gambler has gambled beyond his emotional means. Riding his
winning streak, he has trapped himself in a lifetime strain for
which he has already spent his energy. All he wants now is the
snap.
    But the witches give their edged promises, and he hugs them
with the desperate confidence of a bad conjuror. He waits for his
enemies with a senile, tipsy elation which terrifies his servants:
he himself has become 'patch,' a staring clown more whey-faced
than the messenger he abuses. To the last he thinks in terms of
an audience. He can bear death, but not to be found out.

(Ronald Bryden, 'The Observer', 23 October 1966)

14. 6 ANTIGONUS AND THE BEAR, 'THE WINTER'S TALE', OLD VIC, 1925

I know of no scene in any play that gives or communicates more
freshly and absolutely the sensation produced by sunshine after
rain than the scene in 'The Winter's Tale' where the Old Shepherd
finds his fairy gold. It is a real gem - and very well done in
the new revival at the Old Vic. I was, however, sorry that Mr.
Robert Atkins omitted the bear. 'Exit, pursued by a Beare', says
the First Folio stage direction at the close of Antigonus's monologue. As there was no bear to be seen, his last words - 'This
is the chase, I am gone for ever' - were unintelligible to anybody not already conversant with the play.[...] Antigonus, by the
way, seems to have been a man of great presence of mind. The
bear got him, and the Clown describes how, even as the brute was
busy on his shoulderbone, 'he cried to me for help, and said his
name was Antigonus, a nobleman.' In the teeth of a savage beast I,
too, would cry for help, but I should be too much put about to
think of adding, 'My name is Herbert Farjeon, a dramatic critic...'

(Herbert Farjeon, 'The Shakespearean Scene', Hutchinson, n.d.,
p. 77)

14. 7 'TARTUFFE', NATIONAL THEATRE COMPANY, OLD VIC, 1967

[...] Why should Orgon be taken in? Moliere has planted the clue
in the famous passage when Orgon punctuates Dorine's, the maid's,
tale of Tartuffe's gluttony with the repeated exclamation: 'Le
pauvre homme!' (The poor fellow!). Orgon feels guilty about his
own affluence and security. He sees Tartuffe's crudeness, his
bad manners, his shabbiness, his greed and covetousness; but these,
being the consequence of Tartuffe's social handicaps, merely
strengthen Orgon's guilt-feelings, his pity for the poor fellow,
who has been starved so long that he cannot be blamed for wanting
to eat his fill. That is why Orgon, in the end, gives all his
property to Tartuffe. [...]
    And this is the stroke of genius in Sir Tyrone Guthrie's con-
ception of the character of Tartuffe; instead of the old cliché of
the oily old Uriah Heep of a hypocrite, he has made Robert
Stephens into a young man with a country accent, dirty clothes
and an enormous chip on his shoulder. That is why all the other
members of the household can see through Tartuffe, why they are
never in doubt about his true character. [...] But Orgon, a man so
good and kind that he cannot even see such obvious abjectness
without feeling sorry for the man, and guilty about his own superior chances, cannot but want to give him all the advantages of
his wealth and happiness.
    [...] Sir John Gielgud [...] brings out precisely this decisive
quality in Orgon: kindness, indulgence towards other people's
vices, the blindness that springs from excessive charity - these
are the strokes with which he paints his masterly portrayal of the
perennial liberal who sacrifices to an abstract ideal of goodness

the very people who are in need of its concrete manifestation.
This is a high comedy performance in the great tradition. And in
the end it shades into truly tragic suffering.

(Martin Esslin, 'Plays and Players', January 1968)

14. 8   EDITH EVANS'S MILLAMANT, 'THE WAY OF THE WORLD', LYRIC
         THEATRE, HAMMERSMITH, 1924

[...] Her Millamant is impertinent without being pert, graceless
without being ill-graced. She has only two scenes, but what scenes
they are of unending subtlety and finesse! Never can that astonishing 'Ah! idle creature, get up when you will' have taken on greater
delicacy, nor 'I may by degrees *dwindle* into a wife' a more delicious mockery. '*Adieu*, my morning thoughts, agreeable wakings, indo-
lent slumbers, all ye *douceurs, ye sommeils du matin, adieu*' - all
this was breathed out as though it were early Ronsard or du Bellay.
And 'I nauseate walking', and 'Natural, easy Suckling!' bespoke the
very genius of humour. There is a pout of the lips, a jutting forward of the chin to greet the conceit, and a smile of happy deliverance when it is uttered, which defy the chronicler. This face, at
such moments, is like a city in illumination, and when it is withdrawn leaves a glow behind. One fault I find, and one only. Millamant's first entry bears out Mirabell's announcement: 'Here she
comes, i'faith, full sail, with her fan spread and her streamers
out.' The actress made her appearance somewhat lapwing fashion, a
trifle too close to the ground. It is possible, too, that Mrs.
Abington gave the whole character a bigger sweep. Miss Evans conceived her as a rogue in porcelain, and kept her within that conception. [...]

(James Agate, 'Red Letter Nights', Cape, 1944, p. 34)

14. 9   MAX VON SYDOW'S GREGERS, 'THE WILD DUCK', ROYAL DRAMATIC
         THEATRE OF SWEDEN, ALDWYCH, 1973

[...] The pivot of the production, however, is Max von Sydow's
performance as Gregers Werle. Instead of playing him as the usual
impassioned, proselytising figure whom any sane man would have
turned out of the house in two minutes, he presents us with a shy,
gawky, repressed fellow blatantly nervous of any human contact.
He prowls warily round the edge of conversational groups watching
other people's reactions, makes his point about the moral stench in
Ekdal's household while staring fixedly at the table and (ironically) is at ease only when listening to Hedvig talking about the
wild duck. It's a superb performance in that it shows that Gregers's
destructive effect is out of all proportion to his harmless physical
presence and that idealism need not be equated with fanaticism. [...]

(Michael Billington, 'Guardian', 29 May 1973)

14. 10   'ROSMERSHOLM', VAUDEVILLE, 1891

[...] On February 23rd, 1891, Miss Florence Farr produced at the
Vaudeville a hitherto unattempted play - 'Rosmersholm' - and this
time the critics spoke out with·no uncertain note. Only one of
them wavered, the critic of the 'Daily Telegraph', who admitted
that 'Say what we will about Ibsen, he unquestionably possesses a
great power of fascination. Those who most detest his theories,
his doctrines, his very methods of art, confess to a strange
absorbing interest.' These startling admissions were very far
from finding an echo in the Press in general. If gall had been
poured forth on 'A Doll's House', 'Rosmersholm' was douched with
vitriol -

'A handful of disagreeable and somewhat enigmatical
personages....Ibsen is a local or provincial dramatist.' -
'Times'.
'Impossible people do wild things for no apparent reason...
Those portions of the play which are comprehensible are utterly
preposterous...Ibsen is neither dramatist, poet, philosopher,
moralist, teacher, reformer - nothing but a compiler of rather
disagreeable eccentricities.' - 'Standard'.
'The brain-sick extravagancies of the Norwegian playwright.'
- 'Daily News'.
'A dreary and dismal function was that undergone at the
Vaudeville on Monday afternoon.' - 'Sporting and Dramatic
News'.
'A singularly gloomy and ineffectual function was that
undergone at the Vaudeville on Monday afternoon.' - 'Observer'.
'Love, truth, religion, and self-respect have still some
hold upon us, and it is hardly likely that Ibsen's gloomy
ideas will be generally accepted.' - 'Morning Post'.
'The stuff that Ibsen strings together in the shape of plays
must nauseate any properly-constituted person.' - 'Mirror'.
'Ibsen's gruesome play...His repulsive drama...Greeted with
the silence of contempt when the curtain finally fell.' -
'People'.
'Studies in insanity best fitted for the lecture-room in
Bedlam ... At the fall of the curtain there was loud applause,
and but the faintest attempt at hissing.' - 'Stage'.
'The whole affair is provincial and quite contemptible.' -
'Saturday Review'.
'Mr. Ibsen does not call "Rosmersholm" a farce; but that is
because of his modesty...To judge it seriously either as litera-
ture or as drama is impossible.' - 'St. James's Gazette'.
'These Ibsen creatures are "neither men nor women, they are
ghouls," vile, unlovable, unnatural, morbid monsters, and it
were well indeed for society if all such went and drowned themselves at once.' - 'Gentlewoman'.
'To descant upon such morbid, impractiable rubbish would be
an insult to the understanding of every reader, except an
Ibsenite...If Herr Ibsen were well smothered in mud with his

two creations and with every copy of his plays, the world
would be all the better for it.' - 'Licensed Victuallers'
Gazette'.

Alas, poor Ibsen! It is well that he does not read English,
else who knows but the disesteem of the 'Licensed Victuallers'
Gazette' might drive him into his mausoleum in good earnest.

(William Archer, The Mausoleum of Ibsen, 'Fortnightly Review',
54, July-December 1893, pp. 79-80)

14. 11 'ROSMERSHOLM', ENGLISH STAGE COMPANY, ROYAL COURT,
        1959

The real struggle is not between opposed causes but between those
who are closest: Rosmer, Rebecca and the place itself. In the
Royal Court production, it is Rosmer who comes off best. A good
man may be hard to find, but he is even harder to act. Yet without the least wavering, Eric Porter managed to create the impression of a goodness that was neither innocence nor willed virtue
but a natural and contagious gentleness that had survived his
frozen marriage and was now relaxing in such tentative freedom as
it could find. He never once succumbed to the devils of priggish-
ness, didacticism or weakness. Considering the temptations, one
can't say better than that. In comparison, Dame Peggy Ashcroft
seemed much less convincing. [...] Dame Peggy gave a carefully
studied performance, but of a subdued, twilit Rebecca. She suffered and was remorseful; at the climax her gestures were pathetically helpless, like those of some captive; but she seemed to lack
altogether the girl's inner power and compulsion. In place of
tragic strength Dame Peggy substituted gentility. She moved, of
course, with great dignity, but her resolutely modulated voice
remained perilously close to the merely genteel. In the end, she
was destroyed not by the clash between her own guilt and the superstitions of Rosmersholm, with its white horses and trolls from the
unconscious; she seemed, instead, more a victim of social snob-
beries. But then, since the Rosmer family portraits appeared to
include those of Dostoevsky, Schubert, Laud and Katherine Parr, one
can't blame her.

(A. Alvarez, 'New Statesman', 28 November 1959, p. 746)

14. 12 'MISS JULIE', PLAY-ROOM SIX, 1927

I could see nothing in 'Miss Julie' but Strindberg's 'servant'
complex (see 'The Son of a Servant' passim), his morbid desire to
be kicked himself when loved, and the revolt of his masculine pride
against that 'complex', taking the form of detestation of the
object which satisfies it.
    One midsummer night; thus the outline of the story runs, Julie,

the only daughter of a Swedish count, bullies her father's footman into taking her to his bedroom; afterwards he has the opportunity of bullying her. They are both thoroughly frightened, and the solution which recommends itself is to lend her the razor, with which he was about to make himself respectable before carrying up his master's boots and coffee, in order that she may cut her throat. Strindberg's temperament has here stepped in and excluded all possibility of our feeling pity for the girl (he would never allow that) consequently the mood in which the fall of the curtain leaves one is: 'Well, well, she cut her throat and her father rang for his breakfast.'

This is hardly a 'catharsis'. It may have relieved Strindberg to send a high-born minx to an ugly death, but in me it inspired what is best described as a state of depressed equanimity. The dramatist's attitude towards the footman [...] is rather more difficult to determine. He is certainly innocent in all that pre- ceded their embraces. He behaved like a natural straightforward fellow and told her she was a fool not 'to keep her place', though her tumble from it in a way rejoiced him. [...] Julie's love of the bird, which she brought down in a cage as her sole luggage when they intended to elope together (I never quite grasped why this solution of their predicament was finally dropped) was, I fear, intended to exemplify the unfathomable falseness of feminine emotion.

There were, of course, vital and remarkable passages in the dialogue. The fact that when Julie falls, she falls, not to her servant's level but below it, was admirably brought out. The naturalness and integrity of his relations to the cook, Christine, who is his mistress, were made an excellent foil to the ugly muddle of his relations with his mistress in the other sense of the term. Of course, 'genius' was there, but - and this is my point - the very vehemence of the author's imagination served to throw into relief the disappointing emptiness and confusion of his conception behind the detail and the dialogue.

(Desmond MacCarthy, 'Drama', Putnam, 1940, pp. 180-2)

14. 13 'THE THREE SISTERS', FORTUNE, 1929

Tchehov is the dramatist of good-byes; good-byes to hopes and ambitions, good-byes between lovers. Yet out of this conception of life, which might be thought 'depressing', Tchehov makes a work of art which moves us and exalts us like a beautiful piece of music. It is not in a mood of depression one leaves the theatre after seeing 'The Three Sisters'. How true it is that a good play should be like a piece of music! For our reason it must have the logical coherence of fact, but for our emotions the sinuous unanalysable appeal of music. In and out, in and out, the theme of hope for the race and the theme of personal despair are interwoven one with the other. Each character is like a dif- ferent instrument which leads and gives way alternately, sometimes playing alone, sometimes with others, the theme of the miseries

of cultivated exiles, or the deeper one of the longing of youth;
the dreamy, once gay Irena, the sober and steady Olga, the passionate Masha, half ashamed of her greedy clutch on happiness -
vulgarizing herself, she knows, but not caring for that. And
what queer harsh notes proceed from that black pit of egotistic
megalomania and ferocious diffidence, Solyony! Solyony thought
himself a romantic Lermontov; nowadays he would pride himself
on being a ruthless superman of the underworld. *Plus ça change,
plus c'est la même chose.*

(Desmond MacCarthy, 'Drama', Putnam, 1940, pp. 121-2)

14. 14 'SAINT JOAN', GARRICK, NEW YORK, 1923

Unluckily it is the part of Joan that Shaw himself is least able
to write. You can see clearly what he intends to do for her. But
she remains talked rather than created. The intention behind the
part and the historical tradition manage to make this Joan more or
less acceptable; but the actual writing of her falls a long way
short of imagination or magnetism and certainly far from poetry,
humble or sublime as the instant may demand. Indeed if you
depend strictly on her speeches and reactions Shaw's Joan is far
from being either a great or a lovely or even a scourging spirit,
though she has the honesty and quick wits and lively obstinacy
and courage of her creator himself.
    Miss Lenihan's performance of Joan by comparison with most of
the actors available for the part, is good and certainly close
to the role as Shaw actually writes it ... Miss Lenihan, as she
plays this peasant girl with her heavenly voices and her power
over men, exhibits determination rather than the force of vision,
which is to be approached only with passionate effacement. Her
Joan has character rather than inspiration and confidence rather
than light. The quality of her Joan is direct enough but not
pure; it is not enough untouched with things outside it. For
most of the scenes Miss Lenihan and Bernard Shaw hurt each other
by evincing the same limitations for the creation of such a part.
What they do need is more of a contagious and beautiful fanaticism
and destroying flame. They need to know more of what arises out
of the wonder and solitude of the soul; to know how to be less
assertive and more luminous; and finally to know better what it
costs a fine spirit to be strong.

(Stark Young, 'New Republic', 16 January 1924, pp. 205-6)

14. 15 WEIGEL'S MOTHER COURAGE, DEUTSCHES-THEATER, EAST BERLIN,
        1949

[...] As the tireless old protagonist, dragging her canteen wagon
across the battlefields of the Thirty Years' War, Helene Weigel
played in a manner that shrank utterly from flamboyance; her

performance was graphic yet casual, like a shrug. At two carefully selected moments she was piercingly and unforgettably
moving - first in the soundless cry that doubles her up when her
son is executed, and again when, to avoid incriminating herself,
she must pretend not to recognize his body. She walks over to
the stretcher, wearing a feigned, frozen smile that does not
budge from her lips until she has surveyed the corpse, shaken her
head, and returned to her seat on the other side of the stage.
Then she turns to the audience, and we see for an instant the
drained, stone face of absolute grief. These moments apart, the
production achieved a new kind of theatrical beauty, cool and
meaningful, by deliberately avoiding climaxes of individual
emotion. [...]

(Kenneth Tynan, 'Curtains', Longmans Green, 1961, p. 467)

14. 16   LAUGHTON'S AND QUAYLE'S GALILEO

[...] as Galileo, Charles Laughton brought far more to the role
than Anthony Quayle ever will. First, he could effortlessly
portray a self-indulgent guzzler; second, he was able to seem an
intellectual, and even a genius. The *combination* of physical
grossness with intellectual finesse was theatrical in itself and
of the essence of Brecht's drama. In regard to playing the intellectual, this too should be said. It is not done by playing
intellect itself. It is done by making the characteristic
attitudes of the intellectual live - emotionally. For instance,
Laughton would always bristle when he talked with bureaucrats or
businessmen: his Galileo was allergic to them. Conversely, when
talking to his students he made it clear how much he got from
their admiration of him: the classroom was his element. Mr.
Quayle, on the other hand, treats everyone else on stage as a
stranger, and even likes to have them at a distance so he can
address them as a public meeting. [...] Mr. Quayle is convincing
neither as the guzzler nor as the thinker. For the first he
substitutes extravert heartiness; for the second, schoolmasterish-
ness. In the final scene he consents to play emotion, but it is
the comparatively uninteresting emotion of self-pity that comes
through. He sobs. This time his isolation from the others is to
the point. But self-pity is only self-pity. [...]

(Eric Bentley, 'What is Theatre?', Methuen, 1969, p. 444)

14. 17   'WAITING FOR GODOT', ARTS, 1955

[...] 'Waiting for Godot' frankly jettisons everything by which
we recognise theatre. It arrives at the custom-house, as it were,
with no luggage, no passport, and nothing to declare; yet it gets
through, as might a pilgrim from Mars. It does this, I believe,
by appealing to a definition of drama much more fundamental than

any in the books. A play, it asserts and proves, is basically a means of spending two hours in the dark without being bored.

(Kenneth Tynan, 'Curtains', Longmans Green, 1961, p. 101)